Principles of
Retail Management

Rosemary Varley

and

Mohammed Rafiq

palgrave
macmillan

First published 2004 by
PALGRAVE MACMILLAN
Houndmills, Basingstoke, Hampshire RG21 6XS and
175 Fifth Avenue, New York, N.Y. 10010
Companies and representatives throughout the world

PALGRAVE MACMILLAN is the global academic imprint of the Palgrave
Macmillan division of St. Martin's Press, LLC and of Palgrave Macmillan Ltd.
Macmillan® is a registered trademark in the United States, United Kingdom
and other countries. Palgrave is a registered trademark in the European
Union and other countries.

ISBN 10: 0–333–79297–1
ISBN 13: 978-0-333-797-1

This book is printed on paper suitable for recycling and made from fully
managed and sustained forest sources. Logging, pulping and manufacturing processes are
expected to conform to the environmental regulations of the country of origin.

A catalogue record for this book is available from the British Library.

Printed and bound in Great Britain by CPI Antony Rowe, Chippenham and Eastbourne

Contents

part three
Retail Marketing Management

part four
Retail Challenges

List of Figures, Tables and Vignettes

● **Figures**

● Tables

⬤ Vignettes

Acknowledgements

We would like to extend our thanks to the editorial team at Palgrave Macmillan for their support, and to the anonymous reviewers for their valuable commentary.

ROSEMARY VARLEY
MOHAMMED RAFIQ

Introduction

The retailers of the twenty-first century require a very special kind of manager. The challenges for the leaders of retail businesses have moved from being operational in focus to being of a more strategic nature. It is no longer enough to ensure that the shelves are full and people are available to take money from customers. A retail manager now has to be totally in touch with the customer base, have an understanding of their reasons for shopping, and then be adept at organizing an outlet to provide maximum value in that shopping experience. At the same time, the retail manager needs to ensure that their designated outlet is gaining the best returns on investment put into it, and they are also responsible for reflecting the values of the organization that they represent. Retailers are now brands; maintaining that brand integrity at the customer interface is the remit of the modern retail manager.

This textbook aims to reflect the diverse nature of retail management. It gives students of retailing an understanding of the various aspects of management that they could be faced with and provides a wealth of background knowledge that will prepare them for a career in the retail world.

The book is divided into four parts. The first part introduces the retail industry and explores its characteristics and the organizations that make up its structure. It examines the business environment in which the retailer operates, focusing on competition within the industry and the complexities of the modern consumer.

Part 2 is concerned with how a retail organization operates. It looks at how retailers formulate strategies, how they plan for the future, and how the organization of the retail business supports the implementation of those strategic plans. This section also examines how logistics and technology help retailers to achieve their strategic aims.

Retailers are increasingly marketing-oriented and customer-focused businesses, and so the third part of the book is devoted to retail marketing management. The various aspects that are incorporated into a retail brand are explored within this section including the location of an outlet, the designed environment within the outlet, the product assortment and brands offered, the use of promotions and customer communication and the level of price and service. Whether or not a retail manager has any direct input into a retailer's marketing strategy depends on their specific role within the organization; however, they all need to be fully conversant with the various retail marketing techniques and the implications associated with using them.

The final part of the book examines some specific challenges that are faced by retail managers in a modern retail industry. Retailers have to be prepared to operate in an international market, and to adapt to the new challenges that the Internet has thrown at the industry, as well as having an understanding of their legal and ethical obligations as large social organizations.

part one

The Retail Industry and its Environment

chapter one

An Introduction to Retailing

Learning objectives

- To understand the meaning of the term retailing.
- To understand the relationship between the retailer and the consumer, in terms of the distribution of goods.
- To understand the contribution that the retail industry makes within a society.
- To examine the structure of the retail industry and the recent trends within it, in order to appreciate the relationship between retailers and the economy within which they operate.
- To appreciate the diversity of the retail industry.

Introduction

Retailing is the activity of selling goods and services to final consumers for their own personal use. It is concerned with getting goods in their finished state into the hands of customers who are prepared to pay for the pleasure of eating, wearing or experiencing particular product items. Retailing is all about the distribution of goods and services because retailers play a key role in the journey that products make from a manufacturer, grower or service-provider to the person who consumes. Retailing is also one of the key elements of a marketing strategy; it facilitates the targeting process, making sure that a product reaches particular groups of consumers. It is important in a marketing strategy because it is concerned with matching the arena in which a product is purchased to the benefits and characteristics of the product itself and its price. Retailers provide a collection of service benefits to their customers such as being located in convenient places, editing product ranges according to shopping tasks, and selling goods in quantities that match personal consumption levels. Ensuring that this process runs smoothly presents a host of managerial challenges. Retailing is therefore a deceptively simple management process – yet fascinatingly complex in its detail.

● Retailing Defined

The word retailing has its origins in the French verb *retailler*, which means to cut up, and refers to one of the fundamental retailing activities which is to buy in larger quantities and sell on in smaller quantities. For example, a convenience store would buy tins of beans in units of two-dozen boxes, but sell in single-tin units. However, a retailer is not the only type of business entity to 'break bulk'. A wholesaler also buys in larger quantities and sells on to their customers in smaller quantities. It is the type of customer, rather than the activity, that distinguishes a retailer from other distributive traders; that distinction being that a retailer sells to final consumers, unlike a wholesaler who sells on to a retailer or other business organization. Baker (1998) defines a retailer as 'any establishment engaged in selling merchandise for personal or household consumption and rendering services incidental to the sale of such goods'.

There are, however, many businesses that carry out retailing activity that are not in themselves classified as retailers, for example a factory may engage in retailing activity by selling 'seconds'-quality goods in the shop attached to its manufacturing premises. In the UK a retailer is only classified as such for government reporting if the business gains over half of its income from selling to the final consumer.

The term retailing applies not only to the selling of tangible products like loaves of bread or pairs of shoes, but also to the selling of service products. Companies who provide meals out, haircuts and aromatherapy sessions are all essentially retailers, as they sell to the final consumer, and yet customers do not take goods away from these retailers in a carrier bag. The consumption of the service product coincides with the retailing activity itself.

● The Retailer within the Distribution Channel

From a traditional marketing viewpoint, the retailer is one of a number of possible organizations through which goods produced by manufacturers flow on their way to their consumer destiny. These organizations perform various roles by being a member of a distribution channel. For example, a chocolate producer like Cadbury's will use a number of distribution channels for its confectionery, which involve members such as agents, wholesalers, supermarkets, convenience stores, petrol stations, vending machine operators and so on. Channel members, or marketing intermediaries as they are sometimes referred to, take on activities that a manufacturer does not have the resources to perform, such as displaying the product alongside related or alternative items in a location that is convenient for the consumer to access for shopping. Figure 1.1 shows a number of alternative distribution channels that a chocolate confectionary producer might choose to use.

Intermediaries facilitate the distribution process by providing points at which deliveries of merchandise are altered in their physical state (for example being broken down into smaller quantities, or being repackaged) and are made available to customers in convenient or cost-effective locations. Figure

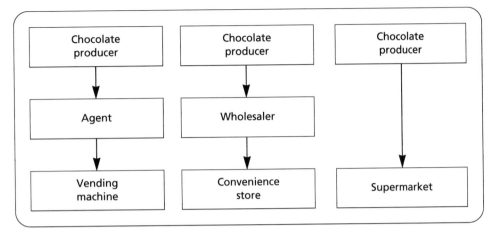

Figure 1.1   Alternative distribution channels for a chocolate confectionary producer

1.2 illustrates how marketing intermediaries (or 'middlemen') make the distribution of goods from producer to consumer more efficient.

Over time, and particularly since the laws that allowed manufacturers to set prices (RPM – resale price maintenance) were abolished in the mid-1960s, retailers in the UK have become more dominant in the distribution channel. Their passive distributor status has been transformed into a more aggressive one, using price as a competitive weapon, introducing ranges of own-branded goods and developing shopping environments that engender loyalty to an outlet rather than loyalty to a product. This shift in power from the manufacturer to the retailer has been further enhanced by information technology that has enabled retailers to gain a greater understanding of their customers' purchasing patterns and preferences (Howe, 1998; Harris and Ogbonna, 2001).

The Vertical Marketing system

Although Figure 1.1 illustrates the traditional distribution channels that are used in many instances to get products to consumers, there are a large number of marketing approaches that do not fit neatly into this model. Levi Strauss, for example, have a large network of shops through which only their own merchandise is sold. Their retailing activities are, in a marketing sense, of equal importance to their manufacturing activities (irrespective of the financial contributions of each activity), and the two facets of the business are highly integrated. In order to reflect this type of situation, the notion of a vertical marketing system was developed (Walters, 1979) as shown in Figure 1.3.

The vertical marketing system usefully depicts a more realistic view of the retail industry in developed economies. Many large multiple retailers like J. Sainsbury, Tesco and Wal-Mart are actively involved in marketing functions

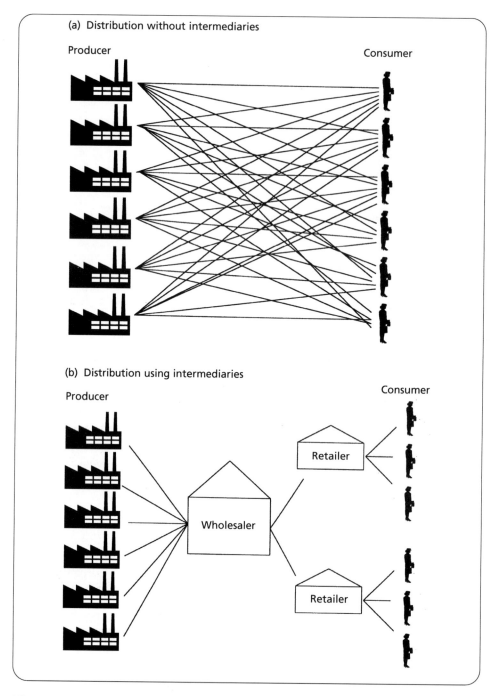

Figure 1.2 The efficiency of the marketing intermediary

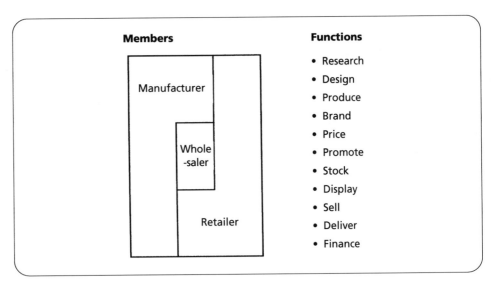

Figure 1.3   The vertical marketing system

that were at one time left to producers, such as product development, branding and advertising. Conversely, many producers are involved in retailing activities, either by running retail outlets dedicated to their own merchandise or by performing functions that at one time were the preserve of the retailer, such as allocating shelf space.

One of the results of the adoption of the vertical marketing system is the demise of the wholesaler within the distribution channel. Vertically-integrated manufacturers do not need to rely on wholesaling activities when they have their own network of retail outlets to distribute their products (see Vignette 1.1), and vertically-integrated retailers gain the benefit of cutting out the wholesaler's profit margin when they go directly to the producer. The contracting wholesale industry is one of the many structural changes that make the survival of the small, independent shopkeeper increasingly tenuous. Even though the demise of the wholesaler is inevitable, as retailers place orders directly with producers, the function that the wholesaler performs is still required in order to move products from a widespread (often global) supply base to a national or even international network of outlets in an efficient way. The large retailers have therefore developed a dedicated infrastructure of warehouses, distribution centres and transportation fleets in order to replace the network of independent intermediaries.

The Consumer-led Approach to Retailing

Although the vertical marketing system adequately models the way in which distribution as a marketing function has developed, it makes the assumption that marketing activity is shared between the channel members and that the final result is offered to the customer. This underplays the extent to which

Vignette 1.1

Thorntons

Thorntons, the UK's only dedicated high-street retailer of confectionery, was founded in 1911 by Joseph Thornton, who was a commercial traveller engaged in selling confectionery. From the outset the company devised its own recipes and manufactured and retailed the product, a pattern of vertical integration through ownership that has been maintained throughout the company's development. In 1997–98, Thorntons had a turnover of £133 million, employing 2,100 staff serving their network of 344 shops and 1,750 in manufacturing. In 1996 Thorntons appointed a new chief executive with a retail background, recognizing the need for an emphasis on retail development within the company's strategy. At the same time the company decided to retain their in-house manufacturing of the core product (chocolates) whilst introducing outside suppliers for peripheral ranges such as solid chocolate bars and ice cream. The retail–led strategy adopted in 1996 included shop development, with a programme of enlargement and relocation to high-volume locations, such as shopping centres.

Thorntons primarily compete in the boxed chocolate market where their 'Continental' brand has a 6 per cent share. As a gift Thornton's chocolates compete with a wide range of products, such as toiletries, lingerie, flowers and wine provided by other retailers, but as a retailer dedicated to specialist confectionery, the company has no large competitors in the UK, although to an extent the supermarkets, Boots, Marks and Spencer (to whom Thorntons is a supplier), BhS and Woolworths, offer competing products.

The products and services provided through Thorntons' shops are developed to achieve differentiation. Product quality is based on unique product recipes and the use of high-quality materials (the company's Champagne Truffle contains Moet et Chandon!). The retail outlets offer the opportunity for self-selection of an assortment of chocolates and the personalization of products (for example through messages written in icing on the company's two million Easter eggs sold each year). The design and layout of the shops were developed by an in-house team, with the use of an outside consultant. The appearance of the shops is changed as often as every two weeks, with the changes developed and evaluated in the company's two mock shops, prior to their high-street introduction. The company's in-house delivery fleet serves the outlets through a 48-hour order delivery cycle. Although Thorntons have considered outsourcing their physical distribution, the in-house service was retained due to considerations that included the fragility of some of the products, the difficulties of access to city-centre sites and issues concerning night delivery and shop security.

Thorntons described itself recently as a market-led, retail-driven business, however it is also substantially committed to the in-house manufacture of its products. While the equipment for the company's manufacturing is generally available, the company has over time developed knowledge and routines that are particular to the organization and provide the required product characteristics. Packaging is an important part of the product, for the appearance and to maintain the product in good condition, and so is designed in-house. In contrast, the basic liquid chocolate is supplied by a larger manufacturer who is able to achieve larger economies of scale in what is capital-intensive commodity processing.

Thorntons' ownership of retail outlets provides market access and higher margins than those that could be achieved by selling through other retailers, such as grocery chains. Their strategy of vertical integration provides a number of differentiating factors, helping to distance competition and limit the possibilities for other companies entering a part of the confectionery market that Thorntons has helped to develop, while their increasing coverage of prime locations adds to the barriers to entry. The company also gains benefit from the integration of activities and is able to access customer feedback to assist the processes of product and service innovation. The in-house manufacturing can be seen as determined by the characteristics of the product and the unique aspects of its associated technology (chocolate enrobing). The specific nature of the manufacturing technology greatly reduces the opportunity for outsourcing from a competitive supply market and self-manufacture avoids the risk of dependence on outside suppliers.

Source: Based on a case study by David Jennings originally published in the *International Journal of Retail and Distribution Management*, vol. 29, no. 4, pp. 176–87.

retailers and producers have become customer-focused, or perhaps in some instances customer-driven. The customer is not just the end result (they buy or they do not); the consumer is now an integrated member of the marketing channel. To determine how the customer buys, when they buy, what product combinations are purchased, and how they respond to promotional offers, are the type of challenges that members of distribution channels are all looking to meet, and increasingly they are pooling their resources to do so. Information technology enables marketing organizations to build up a wealth of data about customers that can then be used to gear up distribution channels that bring maximum choice and satisfaction to the consumer, but at the same time utilize the marketing channels members' resources in the most efficient way. This approach to retail distribution is called efficient consumer response (ECR) (Figure 1.4); it puts the consumer at the centre of all marketing activity and aligns all distribution channel members (or in

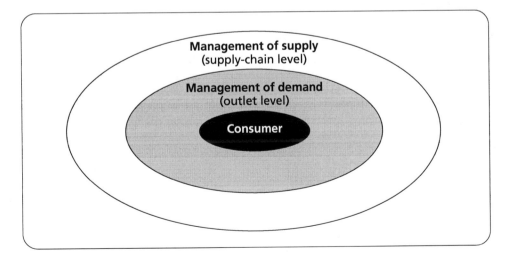

Figure 1.4 Efficient consumer response

modern terminology, supply-chain members) around the challenge of maximum customer satisfaction (Fernie and Sparks, 1998).

Alignment within the distribution channel relies on co-operation and collaboration between members. Manufacturers therefore cannot take the view that retailers are simply intermediaries to distribute products, they have to accept them as powerful sellers, or agents for a group of consumers defined by, for example, an ability to purchase or a geographical location. It is in the producer's interest to develop a relationship with these 'consumer agents' that is one of an ally rather than an adversary, in order to maximize sales opportunities with the final consumer.

The Retail Industry – its Contribution to the Economy

Moving away from the role of retailing in the marketing activity of an individual producer, retailing activity can also be viewed as a significant contributor to the economy in general. In the last two decades of the twentieth century, the UK and many other developed nations have seen their economies change from being manufacturing-led to being service-led, in terms of wealth creation, employment and investment. Around one-third of consumer expenditure takes place through retail outlets (Verdict, 2001), and the retail industry employs one in nine workers (BRC, British Retail Consortium, 2001).

The retail price index is a frequently referred to economic indicator. It is a measure that is based on a 'basket' of products across all retail sectors and compares prices over time in order to reveal the changes in the cost to households of typical purchase needs (Hart, 1996). In recent years the retail price index in the UK has been relatively stable, indicating stability in the economy. When the retail price index starts to rise, a government might introduce an interest rate rise to curb inflation, and if the price index looks like it might fall, an interest rate cut could help to prevent stagnation in the economy.

A Global Viewpoint

Retailing is increasingly a global business. A more structured retail industry with more multiple retailers (those with more than one outlet) is a sign that an economy is developing, as organizations specialize and gain economies of scale. Additionally, when disposable incomes rise, retailers play an active part in distributing increasingly discretionary goods to centres of population. Emerging markets are a real (although highly complex) opportunity for experienced retailers, especially if they are faced with high levels of retail provision and therefore competition in their traditional markets.

As the artificial barriers to trade, such as import duty and quota restrictions, are removed from the global economy, many retailers will view the world as their marketplace and make sourcing and outlet operation decisions on a set of criteria that are relevant across the globe. In the UK some of the strongest recent entrants to the retail market are non-domestic players, such as Wal-Mart, IKEA, Toys Я Us and Zara, and some UK-based retailers are having

Table 1.1 Selected retail occupations

Store-based occupations	Central-office-based occupations	Combined central office/store-based
Store manager	Buyer	Retail operations manager
Department supervisor	Merchandiser	Visual merchandiser
Sales associate	Distribution manager	Store development manager
Checkout operator	Human resource manager	
	Financial analyst	
	Product technologist	
	Public relations officer	
	Marketing manager	

considerable success on a global basis, such as Tesco and B&Q. However, long distances, political and cultural complexities are huge challenges to retailers, which can only be overcome by the strongest contenders. International retailing activities have often stemmed from retailers seeing opportunities for formats that are underrepresented in new markets, such as the entry by the 'hard discount' supermarket operators (Aldi, Netto, Lidl) into the UK in the early 1990s. An extensive discussion of international retailing can be found in Chapter 16.

Employment in the Retail Sector

The retail sector provides a great diversity in the 2.5 million jobs (BRC, 2001) that it provides to the UK workforce. Table 1.1 offers a selection of position titles that are frequently found within large retail organizations.

Although the wide variety of employment opportunities in retailing allows for a diverse application of skills and knowledge, the retail industry in the UK has traditionally found it hard to attract the best young people, and so in recent years new initiatives have been launched in order to build stronger relationships between education and retailing. Collaborations between bodies such as the British Institute of Retailing (BIR), the Distributive National Training Organization (DNTO) and the Department for Education and Employment (DfEE) aim to provide the education and skills base for a world-class retailing sector (DTI, 2000) and a basis for individual development in a challenging business sector.

A Retailer's Position in Society

As well as making a significant contribution to the economy, the retailer has always had a very important place in our personal and social life. From a very early age we are introduced to shopping environments, and they become familiar and comfortable places in which to spend time. As we get older we use shops as reference points when learning about the world and its opportunities.

We see some shops as places we like to be and others as places we 'wouldn't be seen dead in', whilst others might be intimidating or places that we aspire to shop in one day. Retailers therefore play an important part in our own development and the way we formulate ideas about ourselves. Emery (2001) suggests that shops have five distinctive roles in addition to the earlier identified function as breaker of bulk:

- *Advertising and promotion*. Shops introduce us to new products and remind us of old ones. Without shops, we would have to rely on other, often less suitable, media to discover what is on offer.
- Shops *provide advice and guidance*. Many shop staff are experts in their products and routinely provide relatively unbiased advice and guidance on what best meets each consumer's specific requirements.
- Shops *negotiate and form contracts*. Shops take the risk in what they sell, and in what they may value for part-exchange, thereby relieving those further back in the supply chain of many problems of quality, suitability, valuation and legality. For example, the shopkeeper decides whether the alcohol purchaser is over 18 or not.
- Shops *take or arrange for payment and accept risk of default*. Someone has to arrange for the secure transfer of funds, including funding any bridging period, and to judge which payment instrument provides the appropriate certainty of completion.
- Shops *handle warranty claims and after-sales facilities*. Shops provide the local points of responsibility when anything goes wrong and an entry point into repair and maintenance functions.

Retailers also provide an arena for us to carry our social activities. We may go shopping with a group of friends for clothes, or with a partner for home furnishings, or with the family for a day out combined with a visit to the cinema. Alternatively we may go shopping alone, in the hope that we can talk to a product expert about a specialist purchase that we are interested in making. Commercially viable small shops have traditionally provided goods and services to local consumers, provided an outlet for local produce, provided local job opportunities and acted as the central hub of a community. In the future, they may need to develop their businesses to fulfil the needs of a 'modern society' by providing services such as prepared food and drinks, web ordering and delivery, social information provision and internet access (DTI, 2000).

Many retailers state that an important aspect of their business is that of contributing to society. Tesco, for example, may feel that by bringing high quality and a huge diversity of products from around the globe, in a clean and standardized shopping environment, they are making a valuable contribution to society and, being market leaders in the grocery sector (in 2003), many consumers clearly agree. However, Farmer's Markets offer customers a different set of values as Vignette 1.2 shows. Retailers also make contributions to society in other ways. For example, Body Shop were leaders in the field when it came to what many women would feel to be 'enlightened' attitudes towards flexible working arrangements for parents; and B&Q have led the way in providing work to older employees. Retailers contribute to national and local

> ### Vignette 1.2
>
> ## Tesco vs the farmers' market
>
> Tesco is the largest retailer in the UK. In 2001 Tesco's share of the UK food market was 15.6 per cent generated by its portfolio of 678 stores. The retailer trades in 10 countries worldwide including the Republic of Ireland, France, Hungary, Czech Republic, Thailand and Korea. A Tesco superstore stocks around 40,000 food products, with a further offering in clothing and non-food lines. Own-branded products are an important part of the offer, accounting for around half of the total sales, and 2,000 new product introductions each year.
>
> In contrast to this massive retailing force, Farmers' Markets are a relatively new phenomenon on the UK retail landscape, providing the opportunity for small producers to gain direct access to local customers. The interaction between specialist and local producers and customers who value the unique and diverse range of high-quality produce is a highly sociable, almost fanatical gathering. The vast majority of stallholders at farmers' markets are smaller family food producers, usually from within 40 miles of the market. Customers can therefore feel confident about the source of the product, and that they are helping producers in the local community to survive. They can also gain first-hand knowledge about the product and the way it can be prepared. The annual turnover of farmers' markets in the UK was estimated to be £65 million in 2000 (compared with Tesco's annual sales of around £25 billion. However, with numbers of markets rising from single figures to over 200 in two years, it is a retail format that is gaining rapid acceptance, and a dedicated following of 'foodie' customers.
>
> *Source:* Tesco's website and http://www.farmersmarkets.net.

charities, sponsor sporting events, teams and individuals and support educational initiatives, thereby building on the close association with the consumer in the community.

● Retail Industry Structure and Trends

A mature retail market, such as the UK or the USA, is characterized by a number of factors that make it more or less attractive to new entrants. A number of these factors will be considered as the basis for a discussion on the structure of the retail industry.

High provision and market saturation

Where a retail market has a high level of retail provision there are a great number of choices of retail outlet from which consumers can choose to make their personal purchases. Retail provision is generally considered to be the number of shops available per capita, within a measured geographic area. However, as the use of non-store retail outlets such as mail order or electronic retailers has grown, measuring retail provision in this way does not give a completely accurate picture. Nevertheless, in most product sectors retail provision in the UK is generally considered to be high, with a large choice of outlet for the goods the consumer intends to purchase. In fact in many geographical areas the retail markets might appear to be close to saturation. In 2001 it was estimated that for every UK shopper, almost two square metres of retail space was provided (CB Hillier Parker, 2001).

In a situation where high provision and saturation looms, markets tend to become highly competitive. Industry players are competing for market share and will use a host of price and non-price orientated methods to attract customers to their outlet. In essence they all attempt to add value to the shopping process for the customer, and some of the ways in which retailers can add value over their competitors are listed below:

- Offer prices that are at a level that is, overall, lower than competitors.
- Offer really good bargains for specific products.
- Offer a superior level of customer service.
- Offer a more convenient shopping format.
- Offer an interesting, congenial or exciting shopping environment.
- Offer a more relevant range of products.
- Allow customers more flexibility in the way they shop.

Competition within a retail market, in theory, should promote new ideas and innovative approaches to retailing, as competitors strive for better ways to capture the spend of consumers. However, there is a force within a mature market that can work against innovation, which is the result of organizations' success in the past, and that is the extent of concentration within the market.

Concentration

A market that is characterized by high levels of concentration is one where a small number of competitors share a very large percentage of the sales within a market. Although monopoly and oligopoly markets are highly concentrated, these types of markets are rarely found in their pure form in the retail industry. The most concentrated industry sector in the UK is the grocery sector, where seven companies have a combined market share of 75 per cent (Nielsen, 2001). The clothing sector is overall less concentrated, but is dominated by large organizations such as Marks and Spencer, and NEXT, see Table 3.2 in Chapter 3). Davis (2001) anticipates that by 2010, the UK retail industry may be dominated by three leading food retailers and two leading department store companies.

Whilst industry concentration brings certain advantages to the consumer, such as expertise and economies of scale resulting in lower prices, it can also bring potential disadvantages including the erosion of market share of smaller retail organizations, the danger of price fixing between industry leaders, and the tendency for retailers to lack innovation.

Demise of the independent retailer

As large multiple retailers become more dominant in the industry, the small independent specialists are forced out of the market as they are unable to compete with the prices and assortments that the larger stores can offer. In particular many independent retailers in small market towns and rural villages have closed when superstores have opened nearby. This has negative implications not only for the less mobile members of society who may rely on local shops for everyday goods and services, but it can also mean the loss of the central hub of a local community.

Price cartels

If there are only a small number of competitors in a market, there is a risk that these companies might enter into informal arrangements with each other to keep prices artificially high. Severe price competition is not in the interest of the industry players' ability to generate high levels of profits, and so they may agree that they will not undercut each other in order to promote a price war, which would result in everybody having to cut their profit margins.

Lack of innovation

Another problem with a concentrated and saturated retail market is that there is a lack of opportunity for new retailers to enter into the market. Shops are often run on leases of a number of years, or they may actually be freehold properties. This reduces the need to make highly productive use of the space, and there is a danger of complacency and the acceptance of lower than ideal standards of trading. Newer and more exciting retailers are therefore unable to obtain good locations in order to give their businesses an encouraging start. Many high streets in the UK have had the same collection of retailers for many years. Some of these could be criticized as being stale and lacking in innovation, yet by occupying the prime space they survive because customers have little alternative. Some of these well-established retailers have been given a real shock when new competition has finally broken into a retail centre or redevelopment programmes have generated new location alternatives. In particular, the clothing sector dominated by the likes of Marks and Spencer, BhS and the Arcadia Group have tended to monopolize UK high streets. New entrants have had to fight their corner in secondary locations (a strategy employed by New Look in the early stages of development) or by taking sites in new shopping-centre developments. In June 2001 it was reported that having successfully broken into the UK market via the regional shopping centre-route, Spanish fashion retailer Zara was targeting prime city-centre locations in order to speed up awareness and acceptance of their retail brand (*Retail Week*, 2001).

The Diversity of Retailing

Retailing is a diverse industry; successful retail businesses can range from the one-person specialist to the multinational thousand-plus outlet retailer. Even in concentrated sectors such as the grocery sector, dominated by huge and powerful organizations, an enthusiastic retail entrepreneur has been there to exploit a gap when opportunities for new businesses have arisen (see

Vignette 1.3

Julian Graves

The first Julian Graves store opened in 1993. The product range comprises over 600 lines of dried fruit, nuts, herbs, spices and sweets. The shop targets middle-aged and elderly people, predominantly female customers, who gain a sense of nostalgia when browsing through the product range. This includes basic cooking ingredients, a product category that has been 'squeezed' by supermarket retailers in recent years, as well as gourmet items, such as porcini mushrooms, that might be considered a marginal item by most supermarket operators.

The store environment is clearly laid out with pine-wood fixtures that complements the 'natural' feel of the products. The goods are displayed in transparent packaging so that the colours and textures of the products themselves contribute to the aesthetics of the store. To reinforce the browsing and leisure shopping appeal of the store, the company prefers to operate in seaside and tourist towns, as well as prosperous market towns.

Julian Graves is a vertically integrated company; sourcing, packaging and distribution is all carried out in-house. In 2001 the company ran 93 outlets, including 14 factory outlets that sell misshapen products and short-dated, stock and in March of that year Julian Graves was named 'Rising Star of the Year' at the *Retail Week* Awards.

Source: Based on 'Julian Graves Cracks the Market', L. Morrell, *Retail Week*, 25 May 2001.

Vignette 1.3). The awareness of the importance of retailing to smaller communities and the emergence of consumer support for new initiatives like Farmers' Markets and community-owned shops will help smaller retail organizations resist the onslaught of the larger mass market retail operators (see Vignette 1.2).

● Adoption of New Technology

Over the years retailers have been fast to adopt new technologies that have allowed them to cut costs and improve customer service. The use of scanning technology is one example, and the more recent adoption of e-commerce in both retailer-to-consumer (B2C) and retailer-to-supply chain (B2B) is high on the agenda for many retail chief executive officers. Disintermediation is a term that describes the bypassing of traditional intermediaries in a distribution channel (such as the retailer) to enable producers to sell directly to individual consumers. The use of direct interactive marketing and internet-based retailers are threatening the domain of the traditional retailer, and in the meantime most large retailers are quickly adopting web-enabled multichannel strategies.

Whilst intermediaries may be removed from the distribution channels, their functions still need to be performed and it is the lack of infrastructure behind the website that has been the downfall of many internet retailers rather than any lack of ability to attract consumer interest. As we become familiar, competent and finally institutionalized internet users, the convenience benefits that online shopping can bring will be integrated into the modern lifestyle and wider and mobile access to the Internet will encourage its use at various stages in the shopping process at mass-market level. In the not too distance future, retailing services may manage a customer's personal inventory by monitoring products as they enter and leave consumer storage space (for example the refrigerator) using barcode readers and internet connection. For many, however, shopping in the real world retains a sense of excitement and fun, and provides a change of scene and a diversion when so many working hours are spent in front of a computer screen. The impact of the internet on retailing is considered in depth in Chapter 17.

Summary

Retailing is a vast and fast industry. It provides a diversity of size and character of business rarely encountered in other industry sectors. Retailers not only contribute to the general economy, but they are also part of the fabric of society itself. In this chapter, the increasingly dominant role that the retailer plays in the distribution of products to consumers has been explored, along with the resulting evolution in the general structure of the industry. The modern retail industry provides a challenging arena for dedicated and multi-skilled managers, providing both financial and personal rewards that are only limited by an individual's ambition. This introductory chapter has set the scene for further in-depth study of retailing, beginning with an overview of the various retail formats that constitute the industry in the proceeding chapter.

Questions

1 Explain how a retailer, as a marketing intermediary, makes the distribution of goods from a producer to a consumer more efficient.
2 Retailing is not just an economic activity, but also one of significant social meaning. Discuss.
3 Explain what is meant by a vertical marketing system. Referring to Vignette 1.1 on Thorntons, identify the advantages and drawbacks of using vertically-integrated marketing channels. Can you think of any other retailers who have successfully used vertical integration?
4 To what extent do you think that multi-outlet retailers have become too powerful? What are the negative aspects of a highly concentrated retail industry?
5 Look through some retail trade journals and find out the types of positions that retail companies are recruiting for. How do these titles compare to those given in Table 1.1?
6 Choose three retail sectors (such as grocery, clothing and DIY) and compare the levels of concentration within these sectors.

References and Further Reading

Baker, M. J. (1998) *Macmillan Dictionary of Marketing and Advertising*, 3rd edn, (Basingstoke: Palgrave Macmillan).

BRC (2001) 'British Retail Corporation', in Verdict (2001).

CB Hillier Parker (2001) *Shopping Centre Master List*, May.

Clarke, I. (2000) 'Retail Power, Competition and Local Consumer Choice in the UK Grocery Sector', *European Journal of Marketing*, vol. 34, no. 7/8.

Davies, K. (1998) 'Applying Evolutionary Models to the Retail Sector', *International Review of Retail, Distribution and Consumer Research*, vol. 8, no. 2, pp. 165–81.

Davis, R. (2000) '*Personal Perspectives on 2010*', in DTI (2000), *op. cit.*

Dawson, J. (2000) 'Viewpoint: Retailer Power, Manufacturer Power, Competition and some Questions of Economic Analysis', *International Journal of Retail and Distribution Management*, vol. 28, no. 1.

DTI (2000) *The Retail Revolution*, Retail and Consumer Services Panel, Department for Trade and Industry, UK.

Emery, D. (2000) '*Personal Perspectives on 2010*', in DTI (2000), *op. cit.*

Fernie, J. and Sparks, L. (1998) *Logistics and Retail Management: Insights into Current Practice and Trends from Leading Experts* (London: Kogan Page).

Guy, C. M. (1994) 'Grocery Store Saturation: Has It Arrived Yet?', *International Journal of Retail and Distribution Management*, vol. 22, no. 1, pp. 3–11.

Harris, L. C. and Ogbonna, E. (2001) 'Competitive Advantage in the UK Food Retailing Sector: Past, Present and Future', *Journal of Retailing and Consumer Studies*, vol. 8, no. 3, pp. 157–73.

Hart, N. A. (1996) *The CIM Marketing Dictionary*, 5th edn (Oxford: Butterworth Heinemann).

Howe, W. S. (1998) 'Vertical Market Relations in the UK Grocery Trade: Analysis and Government Policy', *International Journal of Retail and Distribution Management*, vol. 26, no. 6, pp. 212–24.

Jennings, D. (2001) 'Thorntons: The Vertically Integrated Retailer, Questioning the Strategy', *International Journal of Retail and Distribution Management*, vol. 29, no. 4, pp. 176–87.

Morrell, L. (2001) 'Julian Graves Cracks the Market', *Retail Week*, 25 May.

Neilson (2001) *Retail Pocket Book*, 2001, NTC Publications, Henley-on-Thames.

Retail Week (2001), Editorial, 8 June.

Verdict (2001) '*How Britain Shops*', Verdict, London.

Walters, D. (1979) 'Manufacturer/Retailer Relationships', *European Journal of Marketing*, vol. 13, no. 7, pp. 179–222.

Useful websites

http://www.foresight.gov.uk

http://www.marketspace.org.uk

http://www.tesco.com/fastfacts, 27 August 2001.

http://www.farmersmarket.com, 29 August 2001.

chapter two

Retail Organizations and Formats

Introduction

Retail organizations come in a whole variety of shapes and sizes. Having defined the process of retailing in the preceding chapter, the aim of this chapter is to present the diversity of the retail industry in terms of the variety of outlets used for the retailing activity. Retail outlets can be quite different in terms of the ownership of the retail business itself, the characteristics of the premises used (the format) and the orientation of the product range. Some types of retailing have been with us for over a century, while new kinds of retail outlets emerge and develop, offering the consumer a constantly evolving choice of shopping arena which embraces an enormously wide range of businesses. Many large retail organizations have branched off into alternative approaches to ownership, format and product orientation as part of their growth and development, and so an understanding of the scope of each of these facets of the retailer is a starting point for becoming familiar with the retail industry as a whole.

In spite of the current growth in home-based shopping methods, shop-based retailing is still the predominant section of the retail industry and so this chapter, which is essentially a discussion of all types of retailers, will start by considering all the different store-based retail types. It will attempt to provide definitions, descriptions and examples of a variety of store formats, including department stores, variety stores, supermarkets, warehouse stores and specialist stores. It will then discuss print-based retail offerings including mail-order catalogues and direct mail. The discussion will then move on to retailing methods that are based on technological applications. The concluding part of the chapter will consider the evolution of the retail industry as a whole.

● Retail Ownership

One way of making a distinction between different types of retailers is by looking at the organization in terms of ownership and control. Most retail organizations can be placed into one of four categories, the independent retailer, the small multiple retailer, the large multiple retailer, and the retail conglomerate.

The independent retailer

An independent retailer is a small-scale retail organization owned and managed by private individuals, with less than 10 branch stores. Many independents are sole traders, or family-run businesses operating out of a single site. The store may offer a specialized product range, such as a butcher or a greengrocer, or a wide variety of product items as in a village store. They can be located almost anywhere; from single sites to shopping centres, and while the majority of independent retailers operate out of physically small stores, there are still a number of independent department stores operating in the UK. Jenners, for example, is a multi-million pound department store business in Edinburgh, which is run by the descendents of James Kennedy who managed the business in 1881 (http://www.Jenners.com, 2003).

Independent retailers are often run by entrepreneurs who prefer to work for themselves and would feel stifled in a large corporation. However, small independent retailers are vulnerable in adverse trading conditions because they do not have the financial support of a large organization. At one time independent retailers accounted for the greatest section of retailers operating in any market sector in the UK, however many have found it impossible to survive the continuous competitive onslaught of multiple retail growth. Defensive strategies, such as reoriented product ranges or niche marketing have been the key to survival for many; covering product and markets that the large, dominant retailers are unable to serve.

The multiple retailer

Most 'high-street' retailers fall into the category of the multiple retailer, which is the term applied to retail organizations that have a central operational headquarters and a collection of branch stores under common ownership. Most, although by no means all, multiple retailers are public limited companies (plcs) and are therefore owned by a collection of shareholders to whom the directors of the companies are responsible. Private multiple retailers are sometimes family-owned and run businesses, and allow for a greater degree of personal operational control than in a publicly owned business. The size of the business will be related to the number of branch stores and the size of those stores. A small multiple retailer is one which runs between 10 and 50 stores, after which is termed a large retailer. Table 2.1 compares the number of outlets of leading multiple retailers in the UK.

The multiple retailer is a term that can only really be applied to store-based retailers, or to the store side of the business, and therefore this term may lose its meaning in the future as more retailers become multi-format organizations. Nevertheless, the multiple retailer has been the success story of UK retailing in the later part of the twentieth century, resulting in a concentrated industry dominated by large and powerful corporate entities. Another term that is often used for a multiple retailer is a 'chain store'.

Voluntary retail groups

One way in which independent retailers have been able to fight against the might of the multiple retailer is by becoming a member of a voluntary retail group. Such groups operate in a variety of ways, but the main objective is to gain some of the buying power advantages of multiple retailers by collating orders from a number of independent retailers and negotiating with suppliers through a central buying organization. Members pay a subscription that may

Table 2.1   Number of outlets of leading UK multiple retailers

Tesco	639
J. Sainsbury	706
ASDA	233
Marks and Spencer	476
Boots	2113
Dixons	987
WH Smith	668
HMV	323
Signet	606
Debenhams	94

Source: *The Retail Rankings*, 2000.

also cover the provision of additional retail services such as marketing and training. Some voluntary groups have a strong brand identity brought about by the requirement of members to trade under a common fascia and to stock a range of own-label products. The so-called 'symbol' groups, such as Spar, Londis, Costcutter and Mace, are all examples of voluntary retail chains. Other examples are Intersport, Toymaster and Merchant Vintners (Nielsen, 2001).

The retail conglomerate

As retailers become increasingly powerful corporations, there has been a growing amount of financial organizational activity in terms of mergers, takeovers, alliances and joint ventures. In many cases companies have been amalgamated under one retail brand, but in others separate brands or fascias have been retained with the holding company trading as a separate identity, giving rise to the retail conglomerate. Examples of these huge retail entities are given in Table 2.2.

A recent high-profile retail acquisition in the UK was the Wal-Mart–ASDA takeover in 1999. A key strategic decision will be whether Wal-Mart should retain the ASDA brand indefinitely and exclusively in the UK, and the extent to which the UK customer should be introduced to the Wal-Mart retail brand.

Franchising in retailing

Franchises are operated on the basis of an agreement between two separate business organizations. One (the franchiser) provides a product and/or a retail

Table 2.2 Retail conglomerates

Holding company	Trading companies
Dixons Group	UK: Dixons, PC World, Currys, The Link International: Elkjop, PC City, Electroworld, UniEuro, Codic, Kotsovolos S.A.
Carrefour	Carrefour, Champion, Shopi, 8 à Huit, Proxi, Dia, Ed
Wal-Mart	Wal-Mart, ASDA, Sam's Club, Tire and Lube Express, Interspar, Wertkauf
Gap Inc.	Gap, Gapkids, Babygap, Banana Rebubic, Old Navy
Great Universal Stores Plc	GUS Home Shopping, Argos, Burberry
Pinault-Printempts-Redoute	Printempts, La Redoute, Pinault Bois & Mater, Conforma, Fnac, Gucci, Yves Saint Laurent, Alexander McQueen, Stella McCartney, Sergio Rossi, Bottega Veneta, Boucheron, Balenciaga, Rexel, Guilbert, CFAO

Source: Company websites, 2003.

format, whilst the other provides the means by which an outlet is run. The franchisee provides the human resources and the finance required for the premises, is responsible for the operations management of the outlet and pays a royalty to the central organization. The problem with this type of organization is that the issue of ownership and control is often the cause of disputes between franchiser and franchisee. However, it does provide a method by which retailers can expand a successful formula very fast without the need for high levels of investment, and it offers outlet managers more autonomy as they are essentially running their own business. Franchising was used extensively in the 1980s by retailers such as Body Shop and Tie Rack to expand both domestically and internationally, although both of these companies have bought back a number of their franchised outlets in order to facilitate modernization programmes. Franchising is successfully used in the running of multiple food retailers such as McDonald's, Pizza Hut and Costa Coffee.

Co-operative retailers

The beginnings of co-operative retailing in the UK can be traced back to 1844, when a group of men known as the 'Rochdale Pioneers' began a trade in grocery produce based on the 'new' principles of fair prices for reliable quality goods. A cooperative is managed on the basis that the customers of a business are also the owners of the business. Each customer is entitled to become a member of the co-operative society, thereby receiving the benefits of success via a dividend payout. Co-operative retailing in the UK reached its heyday between the world wars, when the co-operative movement accounted for 11 per cent of total retail sales and a quarter of the grocery trade (Olins, 1997), but the fragmented organizational structure has prevented timely reactions to changes in the retail environment, and the co-operative retail movement has literally been left behind in the face of strong competition. In some European countries, however, co-operative retailers emerge as leading players. In Switzerland, for example, the dominant retail concern, Migros, is run on the basis of a 12-region co-operative structure which includes hypermarkets, large and small supermarkets, and specialist stores in a number of non-food sectors (*Retail Intelligence*, 1999).

● Retail Formats

Many large retail organizations have grown using a particular retail format. Table 2.3 shows some of the largest UK retail businesses by turnover, together with the retail format that they have traditionally used and recent format developments.

The particular format used, to a certain extent, can be considered to be part of a successful strategy for that retailer, and by adopting a successful format and repeating it on a geographical spread, the retailer obtains economies of scale, efficiency and a strong identity. Therefore, an understanding of the

Table 2.3 Formats used by UK retailers

Retailer	Traditional format	New format(s)
Tesco	Supermarket	Forecourt, internet
M&S	Variety store	Mail order, internet, specialist outlets
Arcadia	Specialist stores	Mail order, internet
GUS	Agency catalogues	Specialist catalogues, catalogue showrooms, internet

different retail formats used is important for gaining an understanding of a successful retail strategy.

⬤ Store-based Formats

Even though stores are increasingly under threat from more recent retail format developments, they are still responsible for the major part of the retail trade, and so the different types of stores will be discussed before other types of retail format.

Department stores

Department stores are the oldest form of large store. The format emerged in the early nineteenth century as a way of offering a collection of personal and home furnishings goods under one roof to the increasingly discriminating and affluent Victorian middle-class customers (Markham, 1998). They are still a powerful presence in today's retailing landscape, providing the focus for shopping centres around the world. A department store is a multi-level store (at one time six or seven stories were common, but today there tend to be two or three levels) which is split up into clearly defined areas or departments according to product category. Many department stores offer width and depth in the product range so that almost every shopping need can be met, but other department stores concentrate on fewer categories and aim to offer a great choice within those categories. Table 2.4 contrasts a general approach to department store retailing as exemplified by the John Lewis Partnership, with a specialist approach taken by Harvey Nichols.

Department stores in principal cities around the world are not only retailers; they also act as tourist attractions and sources of entertainment. Table 2.5 lists some of the famous department stores around the world.

Department stores have recently been through something of a revival. In the 1980s many traditional stores found they were faced with stiff competition from increasingly sophisticated retail offerings from a growing list of specialist stores, particularly in fashion, their most important product classification. Many department stores were suffering from outdated shop-fits and ineffective operations and systems that gave an old-fashioned image. During the 1990s, leisure shopping and a fashion trend that favoured designer branded goods helped the department store sector back onto its feet, and

Table 2.4 John Lewis and Harvey Nichols: product range comparison

Merchandise characteristic	John Lewis	Harvey Nichols
Price level	Medium	Premium
Fashion orientation	Classic	Directional
Own-brand orientation	Medium to high in most departments	Low
Product quality	High	High
Product categories	Diverse	Fashion-orientated
Depth of brand choice within category	Medium	Very deep

Table 2.5 Department stores around the world

London	Harrods, Selfridges
Edinburgh	Jenners
Paris	Galeries Lafayette, Printemps
Madrid	El Corte Ingles
New York	Macys, Bloomingdales
Hong Kong	Wing-On

towards the end of the 1990s a number of department stores have undergone regional expansion.

Variety stores

Variety stores emerged as a store concept at the turn of the twentieth century, when Woolworths, an American store chain, opened their first store in the UK. It is the format traditionally used by Marks and Spencer and British Home Stores (BhS), and so is a tried and tested formula. Variety stores are so named because they offer a large variety of goods under one roof, including both food and non-food items. They are different to department stores in a number of ways as shown in Table 2.6.

In terms of describing large stores, the boundaries of definition are becoming increasingly blurred. Some variety stores like the larger Marks and Spencer stores are becoming very much like department stores, as increased space allows the width and depth of the product range to be expanded. In contrast, some department stores traded down as a survival strategy in the late 1980s and early 1990s, leading to the evolution of the 'discount department store'. This format combines the product and brand choice of the department store with the low price orientation of the variety store, with service level and store environment lying somewhere in between (see Vignette 2.1).

Table 2.6   Contrasting department stores and variety stores

Department stores	Variety stores
Product range	
Wide – many product categories including clothing, furniture and home furnishings and food; depth in the product range including an extensive choice of manufacturer and designer-branded goods	Wide – can include clothing, food, home furnishings and furniture; high proportion of own-branded products, not much choice in many product categories
Store environment	
Interior store design elements and displays used extensively to define departments and provide interest; multi-level; high service level	Basic, uncluttered, clearly laid out; usually over one or two floors; straightforward approach to product display; self-service
Prices	
Traditionally higher to reflect the service level	Medium to low, value driven

Specialist stores

Although some department stores might be considered specialist stores because of the restricted product range (for example Harvey Nichols) or the customer market that they target (for example Harrods), most specialist stores are smaller, in line with the size of the product range offered. The majority of stores found in shopping centres or central retail areas are specialist stores due to the distinguishing feature of one product area dominating the retail offer (see Table 2.7). However, a store that targets a narrowly defined customer market segment such as the Left Hand Shop in Soho, London, can also be described as a specialist store.

Again, examples of successful retailers that do not fit neatly into the defined terms can be found. Lilywhites is a large, multi-level store that specializes in sports goods, but has a store environment that is reminiscent of a department store. Planet Organic is a supermarket that only stocks organic foods, so this retailer crosses the boundary between a specialist store and a supermarket (see below).

Specialist retailers are not restricted to the selling of products; many speciality outlets offer service products to consumers. Examples include fast-food outlets, cafes and restaurants, banks and building societies, repair centres and dry cleaners, hair salons, nail bars and beauty salons. Boots, for example, has trialled specialist services such as chiropody, dental and personal health care, facials, manicures and hair removal in its larger outlets, to complement its already established service offer in the Boots Opticians chain.

Category killers

The term category killer, which originated in the USA, describes the large specialist retailer that is typically found in an out-of-town or edge-of-town retail park or site. The product range is geared to a restricted merchandise area, but the large size of store allows a very extensive selection within that

Vignette 2.1

T. J. Hughes

T. J. Hughes is a retailer that is difficult to classify. Essentially, the company is a discount retailer, offering permanently low prices coupled with an ongoing programme of promotional events that convey an impression of bargains and offers. This is supported by a heavy and constant barrage of local press advertising to entice the bargain hunting C1, C2 and D socioeconomic group family shoppers that make up the majority of the company's customer base.

The product range is more typical of a department store, carrying a comprehensive collection of women's clothing, accessories and lingerie, men's and children's wear, footwear, home furnishings, house wares, toys and electrical appliances. Well-known brands such as Calvin Klein, DNKY, Nike, Levis, Adidas, Playtex and Sloggi are a key feature in the product offer, supplemented by own-label core lines. The company does in fact have roots in department store retailing, having evolved out of the Liverpool-based department store group Owen-Owen. Many of its older outlets have been traditional department stores under previous guises, but the newer stores have a more open layout. The company has recently taken advantage of the demise of C&A in the UK, and has moved into ready furnished outlets. Although biased towards its traditional trading area in the northwest and midlands, T J Hughes are currently bringing their successful formula to a wider geographical base, including Eastbourne in the south of England, and Glasgow in Scotland.

T. J. Hughes aim to contain costs in order to support their price-led offers. They are therefore often located in off-prime city-centre sites and refurbished centres in secondary cities and towns. A high proportion of the goods on offer are bought on an opportunity basis from the 'grey' or parallel import market; the experience of the product managers within the company ensures that no substandard or counterfeit products are sold, and that the 'Quality Discount Department Store' position is maintained. In the latter half of the 1990s and into 2001, the financial performance of the company has been strong, indicating that the shopping public has warmly welcomed this hybrid retail formula.

Source: Mintel (*Discount Retailing*, 2001).

Table 2.7 Examples of specialist stores

Retailer	Sector	Target market
Evans	Clothing	Larger women
Partners	Stationery	Wide market
The Link	Personal communications	Wide market
Blacks	Sports and outdoor	Active and outdoor types

classification. Comet, PC World, Toys Я Us, IKEA, B&Q, Petsmart and Staples are all examples of this type of retailer. The stores are based on a one-level format and the economies of scale and inexpensive locations allow a value-driven price offer. Many of the stores offer goods that satisfy complex needs (for example a computer or a carpet), and therefore specialist help is usually available, but the service orientation is relatively low key allowing customers the opportunity to browse.

Convenience stores (C-stores)

As yet, no official definition of a convenience store has been established, although the following criteria generally apply to this format: self service, 1,000–3,000 sq ft selling area, parking facilities, open 7 days a week for long hours, a wide range of goods, but limited brand choice, including groceries, CTN (confectionary, tobacco and newspaper) products, toiletries, OTC (over-the-counter) medicines, alcohol and stationery. Other products and services that might be offered are take-away foods, DIY, toys, video hire, film processing and petrol (Nielsen, 2001).

Mintel (1997) make the distinction that small, local supermarkets which only open during normal shopping hours are not C-stores, but the term could include a local 'corner' shop, a petrol forecourt shop, a shop at a travel terminal, as well as a clearly defined convenience store on a major route out of a city (such as 7-Eleven or Co-op Late Shop). The convenience store concept has been the saviour of many small retail businesses who have seen their trade taken away by large grocery orientated multi-outlet retailers. By adapting to provide an emergency, impulse purchase and top-up service, many small retailers have found a living with a product range that is reoriented towards convenience.

Supermarkets, superstores and hypermarkets

Supermarkets, a store concept imported from the USA in the middle of the twentieth century, have been a highly successful retail format. The real advantage that the supermarket offered the customer was a self-service, and therefore a much faster method of shopping. Instead of requesting products over a counter, the supermarket allowed the customer to get involved with the product prior to purchase. The ability to peruse the product offering, try new products and impulse purchase, appealed to the increasingly affluent postwar customer. In addition, the space and labour-saving factors allowed retailers to offer a wider choice of product at lower prices. The supermarket was therefore quickly adopted as the principal method for acquiring 'everyday goods'. Supermarkets now dominate the retail industry; they have grown into superstores, offering more and more products, adapting to lifestyle changes to provide the most convenient method of shopping for the majority of household goods for the majority of households.

Supermarkets, superstores and hypermarkets can be considered in the same 'family' of retail format, in that the stores are self-service, usually on one level and laid out in a functional grid pattern of aisles and shelving. Supermarkets are the smaller variant, usually located in a town centre or neighbourhood location, with a product range that concentrates on food and household consumables. Superstores are 25,000 square feet (approximately 8,000 square metres) or more, are usually in an edge or out-of-town location, and they have an extended product range featuring product categories such as clothing, home furnishing and home entertainment goods (for example ASDA and Casino). A hypermarket is a huge retail outlet (over 50,000 square feet) in an out-of-town location, which offers an extensive range of products with the proportion of non-food items being greater than a superstore (a hypermarket is typically 60 per cent non-food). Carrefour for example, sell car tyres and bicycles in their hypermarkets in France and Spain.

Warehouse clubs

A warehouse club is a retail outlet that stocks a limited range of grocery and household products, some home-orientated goods and some clothing products (usually 3,000–4,000 product lines). The distinguishing feature of a warehouse club is that you have to become a member to shop there. Prices are low, and the store environment is extremely basic. Most warehouse clubs operate in a similar way to a cash and carry outlet in that the goods have to purchased in larger quantities, but some (for example Costco), allow customers to purchase smaller quantities of some lines.

Catalogue shops

The best-known examples of catalogue shops (sometimes referred to as catalogue showrooms) in the UK are Argos and Index. These are the store-based outlets for the product ranges of catalogue retailers Argos and Littlewoods. Very little product is displayed in the outlet in comparison to the range as a whole, but the catalogues are available for customers to browse through if they wish to. Having specified the product and made a payment, the customer waits for a short time while the product is retrieved from a stockroom attached to the 'showroom' or store front. If the customer wishes, they can arrange for the product to be delivered to their home. In today's era of flexible shopping methods, the catalogue shop is a cost-effective way of providing a 'high-street' outlet. The format, however, introduces some problems in terms of product interaction and display, because of the reliance on the catalogue for representation rather than 'real' products.

Discount stores

Defining a discount store is not an easy task, because the key characteristic is the price of the merchandise, which is subject to individual customer perceptions. However, there has been a growing interest in the 'discounter' approach to retailing, fueled by its popularity in the USA (Fernie, 1996). A discount store is a retailer that sells merchandise at a price level that is lower than 'typical high-street stores'. A discounter uses an everyday low pricing policy, where prices remain constantly low, rather than a high–low pricing policy (see Chapter 13) where prices only drop at promotion times. Discount stores are sometimes run on the basis of a product range geared by opportunistic buys by the retailer, or they have planned ranges, sold with an unusually low profit margin. Discount stores can be small, such as Poundstretcher, or they may be large departmental stores, like T. J. Hughes or T. K. Maxx, whilst some of the most well-known discounters are supermarkets, for example Aldi, Netto and Lidl. Discount stores can be extremely minimal in terms of store environment and service, but a synthesis of the discounter and the specialist chain store has emerged in the form of the *value retailer*, who combines carefully planned product ranges, good service and store layout with an everyday low pricing policy. Examples of emerging strong players who have adopted this type of format are New Look, Primark and Ethel Austin in the clothing sector.

Factory outlets

A close relative of the discount store is the factory outlet. Factory outlet retailers offer customers a range of seconds-quality and/or previous season's stock. It gives manufacturers and retailers an opportunity to sell off unwanted merchandise without damaging the image of the main product or retail brand, and allows accessibility to customers who might not normally be able to afford the brands, or who are motivated by bargains. Factory outlets may be single-site retailers, or they may be located on one of the growing number of factory outlet villages.

Charity shops

Charity shops are usually run on the basis of selling stock that has been donated, although some, for example Oxfam, also have a range of specifically sourced products. Charity shops are often located in the 'quieter' areas of major cities or towns, or in smaller town or local precincts. The charity retail sector has grown considerably over the last decade or so in the UK, with a more 'professional' approach to organization and outlet operation (Broadbridge and Parsons, 2002).

● Non-Store Formats

The opportunities for consumers to purchase products using a shopping method that does not include a store at all have increased dramatically in recent years. In particular, growth has been significant in direct mail retailing and internet retailing. The great opportunity is to offer the consumer a higher level of convenience in the shopping process, in that shopping can be done at home, or in the case of internet shopping, from the office or via a hand-held device. The main benefits and drawbacks of store and home shopping are summarized in Table 2.8.

Mail order

Mail order retailers rely on printed media as the basis for their format. Catalogues are sent to consumers who order from the catalogue either by telephone, by post or online. In agency mail order, the consumer is offered the chance to order on behalf of friends and family, and to obtain a commission on those sales, but increasingly catalogues are issued on a direct basis whereby customers simply order for themselves and their families. In the UK there are a small number of large players who dominate the catalogue retail sector (Great Universal Stores, Littlewoods, Grattans, Freemans, Empire Stores, and

Table 2.8   Store Shopping and home shopping comparison

Store shopping	Home shopping
Advantages	*Advantages*
• Goods can be touched, and tried out	• Can be performed at any time of day
• A leisure activity or diversion	• Comfort factor is great; no crowds or queues
• Store environments are interesting and stimulating, home may not be!	• Can provide social interaction, especially party plan or agency mail order
• A social activity, a day out; combined with eating out perhaps	• Increased privacy for personal purchases
	• Less physically demanding
Disadvantages	*Disadvantages*
• Can be crowded and time spent queuing	• Usually relies on representation rather than actual product
• Lack of privacy, for example in changing rooms	• No opportunity to get away from home/family
• Parking charges	• Unsatisfactory products have to be repackaged and posted
• Physically demanding	• Postage and packaging charges
	• Some formats do not allow interaction with sales personnel for additional information

N. Brown). The rest of the mail-order sector is made up of an increasingly wide variety of specialist retailers who issue smaller catalogues to consumers via the postal system, or as enclosures with other publications. Mail order also includes printed media-based advertisements that rely on consumer response for the transaction to be completed.

Direct selling

Direct selling is the term used to describe one-to-one proactive offers from producers to consumers, and may take the form of direct mailing (to individual consumers), telesales, and personal retailing. It would also include any approaches made to individual consumers via the internet. Direct mail is increasingly being used as part of a direct marketing strategy that builds on one-to-one relationships between goods and service sellers and their database-captured customers.

Personal retailing

Personal approaches are perhaps the oldest form of retailing, grounded in the activity of the 'peddlers' who traveled from house to house with their wares. Door-to-door selling is rarely seen nowadays, but more organized approaches to direct selling have emerged. The party-plan formula is one example of this type of retailing, used successfully by companies such as Bettaware, Vie and Ann Summers. Another example is pyramid selling, used famously by Amway cleaning products, where sellers not only earn commission on sales, but also on the people they persuade to join the organization.

● Technology-based Retailing

Like most aspects of life, retailing is heavily influenced by technological developments. The ways in which technology has changed retail operations are discussed later on in Chapter 8, but these are generally concerned with the improvement of the service that traditional retail formats can offer to the customer. The issue that is currently uppermost in every retailer's mind is the impact that technology is having on the shopping process itself. We are beginning to experience a fundamental change in the way in which we shop, and this change is being driven by technology.

Vending

The oldest form of technology-based retailing is vending. Vending machines first appeared in the USA in the 1880s selling gum to New York City travelers and have since grown increasingly sophisticated as technology has improved. In 1995, vending accounted for over £1 billion of retail sales (Trapp, 1995) with clothing items (hosiery and jeans) being added to the growing list of convenience products sold in this manner.

Telesales

Another well-established method of retailing that is based on the application of technology is telesales, where product offerings are made by a personal telephone call from a seller to a consumer. Regarded by many as intrusive, telesales has a further, serious disadvantage of not being able to provide any product representation, and therefore its usefulness in many product categories is extremely limited. However, the telephone is a common method of consumer response to non-store retail offerings and so with call centres playing an increasingly major part in many retail transactions, the telephone is an important part of both inward and outbound communications between customers and retailers.

TV shopping

The earliest form of shopping via the television was by means of information provider networks such as Ceefax. This method of retailing suffers from the same product-presentation drawback as telesales, but has been useful for services retailing (travel, entertainment, insurance) when the product is intangible, information-based and the price offer is variable. More recent TV shopping developments have used the three-dimensional visual representation abilities of a screen image to provide dynamism to print-based retail offerings, first in the form of videos, and soon after in the form of a shopping channel, QVC, which was launched in 1983. One of the difficulties of programmed retail offerings is the need to provide the consumer with the opportunity to skip through unwanted product categories, and so interactive screen-based retailing is the most likely retailing format to offer the potential customer everything that is necessary to emulate the 'usual shopping experience'. The conversion to digital TV and broadband internet services will greatly facilitate the adoption of interactive TV shopping.

Internet retailing

As a sophisticated and interactive medium, the internet accessed by personal computer is showing every sign of being accepted as a mainstream shopping mode by an increasingly computer-literate society. Using the internet to access information has been accepted as part of everyday life for many sectors of society, and in the process of shopping it has become very useful to customers as a way of accumulating information about retailers' product and service offerings in a relatively fast and convenient manner. As a way of accessing specialist retailers that might be geographically remote from consumers, the internet provides a channel of discovery for the consumer, and a way of providing home shopping services for a wider target market for the retailer. The internet is also an efficient home-shopping device, enabling time-poor or less mobile consumers to order and take delivery of routinely purchased items such as basic groceries and household items. In view of the marked and far-reaching impact of the internet on industry, a chapter dedicated to this aspect of retailing can be found in Part 4 of this book.

Irrespective of the way we access the e-retailer, whether it is via the PC, the mobile phone or the hand-held personal organiser, consumers increasingly expect retail organizations to be able to offer flexibility in terms of information gathering (to supplement pre-sale shopping), purchase transaction, and taking delivery of the product or service (post-sale activity). By using a number of different retail formats, retail business are better able to allow consumers this flexibility. Most large retailers in the UK now fall into the category of the 'multi-channel' retailer, which is a term used to describe the strategy of using more than one 'route' to consumer markets. Typically, the multi-channel retailer runs stores and has a transactional website (the so-called 'clicks-and-mortar', or 'clicks-and-bricks' approach), but other combinations might be stores/catalogue, stores/catalogue/website, stores/website/direct mail. Offering alternative ways to shop may encourage customers to remain loyal to a favoured retail brand as lifestyles change, but it can also present retailers with new operational and competitive challenges.

● Generalist and Specialist Retailers

Another way in which a retailer might be viewed, whether they use stores or any other format, is according to their degree of specialism. Many retailers, such as supermarkets, could be considered as generalists who supply a relatively wide range of products to satisfy a large number of consumer requirements. Other retailers, however, offer a range of products that satisfy a particular or narrowly defined consumer need, and could therefore be considered to be specialist retailers.

Specialist retailers, whether they are a clothing specialist such as River Island or a computer games specialist such as Game, only offer the consumer a limited number of product categories. However, the depth of product variation

34 ● The Retail Industry and its Environment

within those categories is great. A generalist retailer offers a large number of categories of merchandise, but little product variation or brand choice within each product type. A neighbourhood supermarket, for example, will have a product range which is wide enough to satisfy the majority of basic consumer needs, but does not have the space to offer the brand and product variation in terms of flavour, colour and size that a superstore can. Superstores, like department stores, offer both depth and width in their product range and so cannot be easily classified as generalists or specialists. A small number of retailers successfully trade with a narrow and shallow product assortment; travel kiosks illustrate this type of approach.

The product orientation of a retail outlet has traditionally been the basis upon which trade and industry statistics are reported, with the sectors listed in Table 2.9 being the most important in the UK.

The largest sector is the mixed retail (non-specialist) sector into which many of the largest retail organizations fall. This is because many of the more successful retail players have reached their dominant position by extending their product ranges into more and more categories. All of the following retailers are classified as non-specialist, and therefore could be seen to be taking a generalist approach to their product offerings: Marks and Spencer, Argos, Savacentre, Woolworths, W. H. Smith, BhS.

A difficulty with the generalist/specialist approach to retail classification is that some retailers specialize in part of their product range, but adopt a generalist approach to others. Boots, for example, specializes in pharmacy, healthcare and beauty products, but adopts a more generalist approach in household goods and stationery. Petrol forecourt retailers specialize in products for the motor vehicle, complemented by a range of general groceries.

Non-store retailers can also take a generalist or a specialist approach. For example, the GUS catalogue would be considered a generalist retailer, given the number of product categories covered, but Waggers would be considered as a specialist retail business because it offers a limited number of product categories to a specific customer group in a small catalogue format (see Vignette 2.2).

Table 2.9 UK retail industry by product sector

Grocers	Clothing	Sports goods/camping and leisure
Butchers	Footwear	Electrical and other durable goods
Greengrocers	Furniture and carpets	TV rental
Bakers	Household textiles and	Music and video
CTN (confectioner-tobacconist-	furnishings	Hardware and china
newsagent)	Chemists and drugstores	DIY
Offlicences	Jewellers	Booksellers and stationers
Mixed goods	Opticians	Toys
		Garden centres

Source: *The Retail Pocket Book* (Nielsen, 2001).

Vignette 2.2

Waggers

Waggers represents a high level of retail specialization in mail order. It is the catalogue outlet for Comfy Pet and People Products, a company based in Devon, UK. For the person looking for products for their pooch, who does not want to embark on a trip to town, Waggers provides an extensive range of coats, baskets, blankets, leads, toys and food, all targeted at the canine customer (or rather their owner!). The product range comprises around 100 items, including the Waggers Lightweight Waterproof Dog Coat, the Waggers Car Harness, the Terrier Tunnel pet bed, and the Safety Flashing Dog Collar.

Waggers is run by a team of dog enthusiasts, who launched a collection of robustly designed products to combat the inevitable hair and mud problems associated with dog ownership. The company also trades via a website, and is represented at dog-shows throughout the year.

Source: Waggers Mail Order Catalogue, 2002.

The Evolution of Retailing

Like the products that are sold within retailers, the formats used for retailing evolve over time. A retailing concept that appeared revolutionary when first introduced may become dated within a couple of decades, and so retail businesses must constantly evolve their own portfolio of retail formats to reflect the changing requirements and aspirations of the shopping public, whilst responding to constraints imposed by the political and legal framework in which they operate.

The ways in which retailers evolve have been the subject of academic debate for over half a century. Many of the academic references use the term 'retail institutions' to describe a type of retail outlet. However, it is easy to confuse the term retail institution with a large retail business (stores like Marks and Spencer are often referred to as institutions) and so the term format will continue to be used in this discussion. The evolutionary theories attempt to provide some predictive suggestions relating to the likely pattern of development of retailer types rather than specific retail companies.

Cyclical theories

Industry observers and retail academics have been captivated by the cyclical nature of retail change for some time. This has resulted in the proposition of three key theories of cyclical development.

The generalist-specialist tendency – the accordion theory

The Accordion Theory (Hollander, 1966) concerns itself with the tendency that the retail industry has to alternate between periods of growth in specialist retail formats offering narrow product assortments, followed by periods of

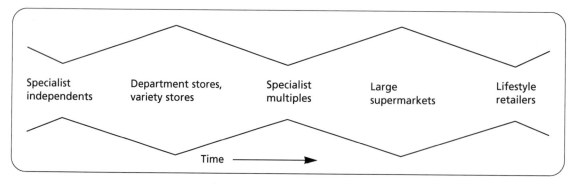

Figure 2.1 The accordion theory

growth in generalist retailing when a greater product variety is on offer within the format (Figure 2.1).

While many examples of retailers who have succeeded outside of this general pattern can be found, retailers may need to consider product range extension and specialization as part of a long-term strategic response to a changing competitive environment.

The retail life-cycle

Like products, retail formats seem to have a life-cycle that is influenced by fashion, technology and societal change, and that passes through introductory, growth, maturity and decline phases (Davidson *et al.*, 1976) (Figure 2.2).

The wheel of retailing

In many cases the decline in popularity of an established retail format is triggered by entry into the retail market by an innovative method of retailing. This type of evolutionary development is explored in the theory of the Wheel of Retailing (Brown, 1987), which suggests that traditional retailers are undermined by introduction of a new, low-cost approach to retailing, which subsequently trades up and finally becomes vulnerable itself to another retailing innovation (Figure 2.3).

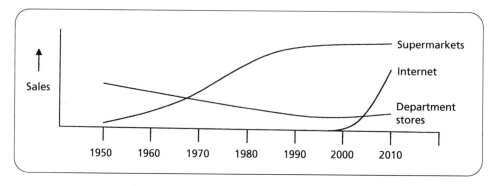

Figure 2.2 Retail life-cycles

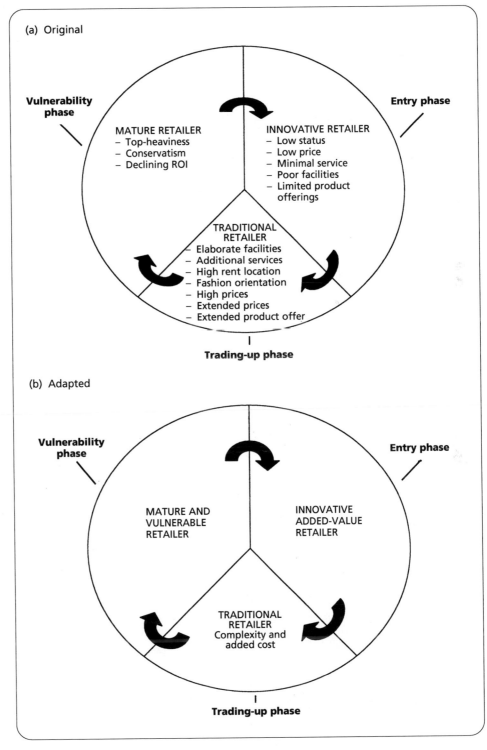

Figure 2.3 The wheel of retailing – original and adapted

While the wheel theory can be illustrated by the evolution of a number of types of retail organizations (institutions), such as department stores, supermarkets and factory outlets, it is increasingly difficult to apply because of the assumption that innovative retailers operate on a low-price, low-status minimalist basis. Recent innovations such as internet retailing and forecourt retailing offer added value to consumers in ways that are convenience, rather than price-driven. Nevertheless, the wheel concept should alert retail managers who depend on one particular retail format to the dangers of vulnerability in the face of indirect competition from innovative retailers.

Natural evolution theories

Moving away from cyclical theories, the basic notion of natural selection can be applied in a retail context to suggest that retail formats that are better adapted and continue to adapt to their environment will survive the longest (Levy and Weitz, 2001). The supermarket has proved to be a great success as a retail life form, adapted in size, product range orientation, internal design, and service augmentation to a variety of national and international habitats.

Success has also been achieved by cross-breeding retail format types. The dialectic process theory Gist (1968) suggests that positive characteristics are blended from two established formats (the thesis and antithesis) to produce a synthesis, which becomes a successful new format. The value retailer described earlier in this chapter could be considered to be a synthesis of the multiple specialist (the thesis) and the discount store (the antithesis of a specialist store).

Summary

The different approaches to classifying a retail business point to the complexity of the industry which includes many variations of store-based and non-store-based forms of retailing, different forms of ownership and varying degrees to which retailers offer specialization in their product ranges. No matter how powerful a retailer is on a national or international basis, undetected or ignored alternative formats may suddenly appear in the form of competition, which is the subject of the next chapter.

The retail industry is so diverse that conforming examples and exceptions to the rules can be found to present, support and counter arguments for established theories of retail industry change. From the perspective of retail management, the theoretical concepts should help retailers to be aware of their position in the changing retail landscape, so that they are able to view threats from emerging competitors as well as respond to opportunities in emerging markets. A continual review of their own organizational development will be necessary to ensure that any required adaptations are made in order to survive and prosper in a challenging retail environment.

Questions

1 Classify the following retail organizations by means of ownership, product orientation and retail format:
   Body Shop; SavaCentre; Selfridges; Racing Green; NEXT; PC World; Waterstones; Boots Opticians; BhS.
2 Compare and contrast shopping via stores and non-store shopping.
3 Using a retail conglomerate or large retail group of your choice, discuss the various retail formats used by the different retail subsidiaries within the group, and the reasons for the format variation.
4 Attempt to predict the retail life-cycle for a variety of retail formats over the NEXT 20 years. Use a diagram to illustrate your answer and justify your predictions.
5 Referring to the dialectic theory, describe a retailer who is operating a synthesis of previously established retail formats to compete effectively in a competitive retail environment.

References and Further Reading

Broadbridge, A. and Parsons, L. (2002) 'Retailing for Communities: Issues of Inclusion and Exclusion in the UK Charity Retail Sector', *Proceedings of the 2002 Annual Manchester Conference for Contemporary Issues in Retail Marketing*, Manchester Metropolitan University Business School, 13 September.

Brown, S. (1987) 'Institutional Change in Retailing: A Review and Synthesis', *European Journal of Marketing*, vol. 21(6), pp. 5–36.

Davidson, W. R., Bates, A. D. and Bass, S. J. (1976) 'The Retail Life-Cycle', *Harvard Business Review*, vol. 54(6), pp. 89–96.

Davies, K. (1998) 'Applying Evolutionary Models to the Retail Sector', *International Review of Retail, Distribution and Consumer Research*, vol. 8(2), pp. 165–80.

Fernie, S. (1996) 'The Future for Factory Outlet Centres in the UK: The Impact of Changes in Planning Policy Guidance on the Growth of a New Retail Format', *International Journal of Retail and Distribution Management*, vol. 24, no. 6, pp. 11–21.

Gist, R. R. (1968) cited in Brown (1987), *op. cit.*, *Retailing: Concepts and Decisions* (New York: Wiley).

Hollander, S.C. (1966) 'Notes on the Retail Accordion', *Journal of Retailing*, vol. 42 (Summer), pp. 29–40.

Keh, H. T. and Park, S.Y. (1998) 'An Expanded Perspective on Power in Distribution Channels: Strategies and Implications', *International Review of Retail Distribution and Consumer Research*, vol. 8, no. 1.

Levy, M. and Weitz, B. A. (2001) *Retailing Management*, 4th edn (New York: McGrawHill).

Markham, J. E. (1998) *Shopping on the Internet* (London: Palgrave Macmillan).

Mintel (1997) *Convenience Stores Retail Report*.

Mintel (2001) *Discount Retailing Report*.

Morganosky, M. A. (1997) 'Retail Market Structure Change: Implications for Retailers and Consumers', *International Journal of Retail and Distribution Management*, vol. 25, no. 8 pp. 269–74.

Olins, R. (1997) 'Co-op at the Crossroads', *The Sunday Times*, 11 November.

Nielsen (2001) *Retail Pocket Book 2001* (Henley-on-Thames, NTC Publications).

Retail Intelligence (1999) *Retail Sans Frontiers: The Internationalization of European Retailing* (London: Retail Intelligence).

Retail Intelligence (2000) *The Retail Rankings* (London: Retail Intelligence).

Trapp, R. (1995) 'Slot Machines that Pay Off', *Independent on Sunday*, 9 April.

Useful websites

http://www.jenners.com/about, 1 May 2003.

chapter three

Retailing and the Competitive Environment

Learning objectives

- To understand the nature and dynamics of retail competition.
- To explore the various ways in which retail competition can be measured.
- To distinguish between different types of retail competition.
- To provide a framework for analysing retail competition at industry level.
- To understand the nature and role of strategic groups in retail competition.
- To appreciate the role of competition regulation in retailing.

Introduction

The way a retail firm operates, the demand for its products, and the cost structures that it faces in the running of the business, are all affected by the competitive behaviour of other retailers in the sector. It is therefore crucial that retailers understand their competitors and the competitive situation facing them. Retailing is increasingly characterized by intense competition. Evidence of this is the withdrawal of the European retailer C&A from the British market at the beginning of 2001. It is also mirrored in the problems encountered by Marks and Spencer whose profits declined from a high of £1,116 million in 1998 to just £467 million in 2001, resulting in a major restructuring involving the closure of all its European stores, and the sale of its catalogue business and its US interests – Brooks Brothers and Kings Supermarkets. The new competition in fashion retailing has come from the emergence of new value-driven retailers such as Matalan and Primark, and the arrival of more fashionable retailers such as the Spanish fashion retailers Zara and Mango and the American chain Gap. The merger of Kwik Save and Somerfield in the grocery market resulted from squeezing of the two retailers by hard discounters such as Aldi and Netto at the bottom end of the market, and ASDA, Tesco and Sainsbury's at the other.

The reasons for the intense competition include slow market growth and the increasingly mature nature of many retail sectors. Other reasons include the emergence of new retailing formats such as the internet and changes in consumer expectations. Retailing competition has a number of unique features including intratype and intertype competition, the coexistence of large chains and small independents despite the increasing concentration, and the importance of local competition.

With increasing internationalization of retailers domestic competitors are not the only ones that retailers have to worry about. Whilst UK retailers are looking abroad for markets, foreign retailers have been entering UK markets. In the grocery market, the early 1990s saw the entry of European discounters Aldi, Netto and Lidl into the UK, and the end of the decade saw the entry of Wal-Mart via its acquisition of ASDA. Other significant entrants into the UK include IKEA and Toys R Us. All of these retailers have taken a significant percentage of market share in their respective markets. In fact, since their arrival IKEA and Toys R Us have become market leaders in their respective markets in the UK. The entry of foreign retailers leads to intensification of competition in the sectors that they enter.

The purpose of this chapter is to facilitate the analysis and understanding of the nature and dynamics of retail competition.

● Measures of Retail Competition

A frequently used measure of the degree of competitiveness of a market is the degree of concentration in the market. Retail concentration can be measured in a number of ways, but the one that is used most often is the percentage of the total market that is controlled by the largest four to five retailers in a particular sector. An alternative measure of concentration is the Hirschman-Herfindahl Index (HHI), which is the sum of the squares of the percentage market shares of all the competitors. The HHI ranges from approximately zero depicting perfect competition (large number of firms each with a miniscule market shares), to 10,000 indicating a monopoly situation. This measure has the advantage of giving more weight to retailers with the highest market share. However, it has the disadvantage of being a little more difficult to interpret. The trend in most of the developed countries is one of increasing concentration or dominance of the market by a small number of players.

The increase in concentration, in the main, is a result of organic growth by the multiples, that is, by the addition of extra branches rather than by mergers and acquisitions. This is particularly true of food retailing where rapid expansion of store numbers and size of stores in the 1980s and 1990s by the leading supermarket chains has led to a situation where the top five retailers have a market share of 65 to 70 per cent (Table 3.1). More recently, the relatively slow growth of retail markets has also helped to increase the degree of concentration. For instance, grocery sales in the UK grew by only 3.2 per cent in 2000, barely keeping up with the rate of inflation. One of the main reasons for the slow growth is the fact that retailing expenditure is declining as a proportion of total income. In the UK the proportion of expenditure on retailing declined from an estimated 40.4 per cent in 1984 to 35.6 per cent in 1999 (Nielsen, 2001). As a result, both intratype and intertype competition has intensified in the retailing sector.

A feature of retail concentration is that it tends to be much higher at the local than at national level. This has led to some discussion of local monopolies, that

Table 3.1 Multiple grocers' market share, 1992–2000

	Market share (%)								
	1992	1993	1994	1995	1996	1997	1998	1999	2000
[Market size	£69.2bn	£72.7bn	£76bn	£80.4bn	£85bn	£89bn	£93.3bn	£96.6bn	£97.9bn]
Tesco	10.1	10.4	11.4	13.4	14.2	14.8	15.2	15.6	15.8
Sainsbury's	11.9	12.1	12.3	12.2	12.2	12.4	12.2	11.8	11.7
ASDA	6.3	6.5	6.7	7.2	7.8	8.3	8.5	8.9	9.3
Safeway	7.3	7.5	7.6	7.3	7.6	7.6	7.6	7.4	7.5
Somerfield	4.3	4.3	4.4	4.2	4.0	3.8	6.9	6.2	5.7
Kwik Save	3.8	4.1	4.0	4.2	4.1	3.5	†	†	†
M&S	3.0	3.1	3.1	2.4	2.5	2.5	2.6	3.0	3.1
Wm Morison	1.7	1.9	2.2	3.0	3.1	3.0	2.9	2.9	2.9
Waitrose	1.7	1.6	1.6	1.7	1.8	1.8	1.8	1.9	2.0
Iceland	1.5	1.6	1.7	1.5	1.7	1.6	1.7	1.9	2.0
Total	51.6%	53.1%	55.0%	57.3%	58.9%	59.5%	59.5%	59.6%	60.0%
Co-ops	7.6	6.9	6.6	6.5	6.1	5.9	n.a.	n.a.	n.a.

†From 1998 Kwik Save figures included with Somerfield due to merger.
Source: Institute of Grocery Distribution (various years).

is local retailing being dominated by one or two retailers. The variation in local competition can lead to different levels of intensity of competition and hence retailers will tend to vary their competitive strategies depending on the local competition.

Whilst measures of retail concentration and market shares are good indicators of the intensity of competition, the data required for these measures are not always available. An alternative measure is the number of retail outlets of a particular type per thousand of population. The higher this ratio is, the higher the competitive intensity. When the ratio of stores to the population gets too high, the market is described as *overstored*. That is, the the size of the population is insufficient for all the stores to operate profitably, leading to intense competition as competing retailers try to improve their sales and profit performance. Conversely, if the ratio of stores to population is relatively small, the market is said be *understored*. In this situation there is unsatisfied demand and existing retailers will enjoy high profits. This leads to existing retailers expanding their operations and also attracts other retailers into the market. The above discussion assumes that all competing stores are of the same size. A more accurate measure is the total amount of retail space occupied by a particular type of retailer per thousand of population (or per head of population).

● Types of Competition

In retailing, measures of concentration are usually likely to understate the level of competition faced by retailers because such measures usually only

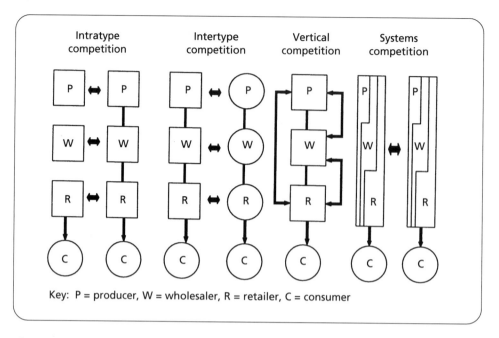

Figure 3.1 Types of retail competition

Source: Based on Lewison and Delozier (1986) *Retailing*, 2nd edn (Columbus, Ohio: Merrill Publishing Co.), p. 66.

include direct competitors; that is intratype competition. Intratype competition is direct competition between similar *types* of retail formats or trading styles (see Figure 3.1). The more similar the stores in terms of format, the more intense the competition. To reduce the impact of competition from similar retail formats, retailers must differentiate themselves from intratype competitors. However, retailers also face intertype competition.

Intertype competition is competition between different types of retail formats selling the same type of merchandise (Figure 3.1). For instance, music retailers such as HMV face competition not only from other specialists such as Virgin Megastore, but also from variety stores such as Woolworths and Boots, and supermarkets such as Tesco and ASDA. Hence, when developing competitive strategies, retailers have to take into account intertype competition as well as the direct competition from direct competitors.

Competition can also occur between different parts of the distribution channel. Vertical competition is competition between retailer and a producer, or a wholesaler selling products to the retailer's customers. For instance, if a retailer stocked a merchandise line that the producer was also offering through the internet, the retailer and the producer would be engaging in vertical competition.

Another type of competitive strategy in retailing is corporate systems competition. This is where the manufacturing, distribution and retailing are controlled by single-management. Examples include Thorntons (see Vignette 1.1 earlier), and IKEA. Corporate systems can be formed by either backward or forward integration. Forward integration occurs where a manufacturer sets

Vignette 3.1

ASDA Wal-Mart supercentres:
a new breed of competitor in the grocery market

ASDA Wal-Mart opened the UK's first 24-hour supercentre in Bristol in July 2000. The revamped and extended US-style store at Cribb's Causeway (close to the regional shopping centre, the Mall) is at around 93,000sq ft bigger than a football pitch. It has two entrances, 60 checkouts, 'price-checkers' on scooters and around 1,000 car-park spaces. The store includes an optician's, a pharmacy, a DIY centre, clothes (George collection, ladies, mens and childrenswear), photo processing, toys and electronics departments and sells 40,000 products from takeaway curry and 42 varieties of toilet roll to own-brand Posh and Becks prams. Around half the floor space in the store is dedicated to non-food merchandise.

ASDA Wal-Mart's aim is to be between 10–15 per cent cheaper in price than competitors on food and other items. When the Bristol store opened some bargain items were 60 per cent cheaper than rivals, For instance, RayBan sunglasses were selling for £29.99–£50 cheaper than at Boots and a child's quad bike was £16 less than at Toys R Us. Wal-Mart says its special prices, such as £349 for a widescreen Philips 28-inch television, were at a sharp discount compared to the competition

Given the range of merchandise sold in the supercentres, it is not simply its supermarket rivals such as Tesco and Sainsbury's that are going to face increased competitive pressure. The electrical superstore chain Curry's, which is located in the nearby Cribbs Causeway retail park, responded by issuing a direct challenge to Wal-Mart, saying it would undercut the store by at least £10 on electrical goods costing more than £200 in its shops around Bristol. Other stores likely to be under pressure in the area include Boots (located in the Cribbs Causewy Mall), as the supercentre has the biggest health and beauty section. ASDA also plans to be the biggest toy retailer in the UK, which is undoubted likely to have an impact on a number of stores including the nearby Toys R Us.

ASDA is accelerating its development of supercentres. Originally it planned to develop 10 by 2004/05, but by the end of 2002 13 were already trading including places such as Edinburgh, Livingston, Dagenham, Watford, Cardiff Bay and York, Havant (Hampshire) and Minworth in the West Midlands. Whilst the majority will be extensions of existing superstores, the largest to date, in Eastlands, Manchester, was a new build. It has 100,500 sq ft of sales space with a food/non-food split of 40%/60% compared to 70%/30% in an average ASDA superstore. The store is testing a number of new concepts, including the first supermarket Nail Bar and Health and Well-Being Centre. The Eastlands store is close to the ideal trading format for supercentres in the USA, except for the fact that average size of a supercentre there is between 150,000–220,000 sq ft. It is estimated that there is potential for at least 30 more supercentres in the UK.

Sources: Various, including Jim Pickard, 'Bristol Meets Wal-Mart's Greeters: The US Company is Bringing its Version of Superstore Shopping to Britain', *Financial Times*, 21 July 2000, p. 5: and Angelique Chrisafis, 'US Store Giant Puts Mammon on Wheels: ASDA Wal-Mart Opens First British Supercentre with Promise of Bargains but amid Fears for Small Retailers', *Guardian*, 25 July 2000, p. 6.

up its own distribution and retailing network, an example being Benetton which began as a manufacturer and then set up company-owned retail outlets as well as an international franchise network. Backward integration involves retailers becoming involved in the distribution and manufacturing of products.

However, major retailers attempt to achieve the same control without total ownership of the systems. For instance, Marks and Spencer is famous for its control over its suppliers; they and other large retailers are able to achieve this control because the suppliers may have few (if any) alternative customers, and may be solely concerned with retailer branded products. Another method of exercising control is by franchising parts of the system, for instance, the vast majority of car dealerships are operated as franchises by the major car manufacturers.

● A Framework for Analysing Competition

A useful model for analysing the forces driving competition is Porter's (1980) five forces model of competitive structure. According to Porter, the forces that drive competition within an industry are threats of potential entrants, the threat of substitute products or services, the bargaining power of suppliers, and the bargaining power of buyers (Figure 3.2). The different aspects of the model are discussed below.

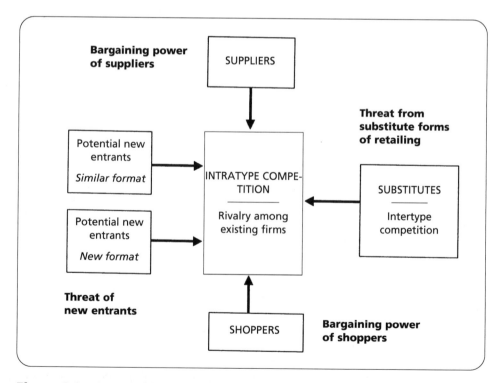

Figure 3.2 Forces driving retail competition

Source: Based on Porter (1980).

The threat of new entrants

A major force driving competition within retailing is the threat of potential new entrants into the industry. The degree to which potential entrants find a particular sector of retailing attractive to enter depends upon the level of profitability of the sector and the barriers to entry. Generally speaking, the higher the profitability of a retail sector, the more attractive it is to potential entrants. Similarly, the lower the barriers to entry, the greater the likelihood of new entrants.

Assuming that there are sufficiently high levels of profits within a retail sector, the threat of new competitors entering the industry depends on the height of entry barriers to the industry including capital requirements, economies of scale, access to customers, access to suppliers or distribution networks, the degree of differentiation, brand identity and store loyalty, and expected retaliation.

Capital requirements

The amount of capital required to enter into retailing is relatively small compared with other industries. For instance, the capital required to set up a bookshop is minimal compared with cost of entering capital-intensive car manufacturing or aircraft manufacturing industries. However, to be competitive against national retailers requires far more capital. This is because greater investment will be required in stock, stores, promotion, IT and other management systems.

Economies of scale

The ability to achieve a reduction in costs through efficient large-scale operations can prevent the entry of new competitors. In retailing, major scale economies can arise in the areas of buying, distribution and promotion.

Access to customers or availability of sites

In order to get access to customers, the main problem for new entrants is to find suitable sites/locations for their stores. New entrants will normally find that the best sites are already occupied by existing retailers. It also takes time for new retailers to acquire suitable sites and open new stores, which gives existing retailers plenty of time to formulate their competitive strategies to combat the threat posed by new entrants. New entrants wishing to open large stores find it particularly difficult to enter the market because of strict planning regulations.

Differentiation, brand identity and store loyalty

New entrants into an industry also have to overcome brand/store loyalty developed by existing retailers. New entrants may have little recognition in the market and will therefore require extensive promotional effort to inform potential customers about the retailer and to switch customers away from their existing stores. The cost to customers of switching to a new store may also make entry difficult for new entrants. However, the switching costs of customers are generally small and not a major obstacle to new entrants.

Access to suppliers/distribution networks

New retailers may find that they do not have access to some suppliers because the suppliers either lack the capacity or their relationship with existing retailers prevents them from supplying new entrants or on similar terms. The cost of building an efficient distribution network (warehousing facilities) also makes entry difficult for potential new competitors.

Expected retaliation

The strength of retaliation by existing retailers can put off potential new entrants. Such retaliation may be in the form of changes in pricing, advertising and promotions, merchandising, and service depending on the strength or perceived strength of the new entrant.

Figure 3.2 illustrates the fact that there are two types of potential entrant. One type uses a similar strategy and similar format to that already existing to enter a particular sector. For example, Wal-Mart's entry into the UK market via the acquisition of ASDA. Another type of entrant is one that uses a new type of retail format to enter the market. Examples include the Danish retailer Netto who entered the UK market using the hard discount format. New format entrants are potentially more difficult to deal with, as their basis of competition (or competitive advantage) is different from existing retailers. In the case of Netto (and other discounters), for example, it is able to offer prices 20–30 per cent lower than those of large supermarkets on a limited number of lines.

Bargaining power of suppliers

The dominance of the majority of the retail sectors by large retailers has transformed the power relations between retailers and suppliers. In the past, big brand manufacturers could virtually dictate to retailers the shelf price, product range, shelving and promotion of products within stores. However, the abolition of resale price maintenance in 1964 in the UK loosened the grip of suppliers on pricing. The development of own brands and the increase in size of retailers (and their resulting concentration) has further eroded the power of suppliers. An indication of the power of retailers is that large supermarkets can nowadays demand slotting allowances (or fees) from suppliers for stocking their merchandise in the stores. In the grocery sector, where concentration is the highest, concern over the buying power of retailers led to referral to the Monopolies and Mergers Commission in 1977 on retailers' abilities to obtain discounts and other special terms. The Commission eventually published its report in 1981 concluding that whilst the larger retailers had been able to obtain discounts and special terms equivalent to around 7 per cent of sales, that these practices were not against the public interest. The concern over retailer power has continued since and further reports have been published by the Commission, the most recent one in October 2000 (see Chapter 13).

The influence of suppliers on retailers depends on the relative size of the suppliers to the retailers. Some of the larger manufacturers such as Nestlé, Unilever, Procter and Gamble, and Pedigree Pet Foods, have market shares far in excess of retailers in their respective markets and are in a position to negotiate terms of trade. These suppliers derive their power from the strengths of their brands and the loyalty of customers to them.

Smaller retailers, on the other hand, are particularly vulnerable to pressure. They can be forced by suppliers to carry products they do not particularly want in return for the right to sell the products that they do want from the suppliers. Suppliers may also apply pressure on retailers to sell products within an acceptable price range. Franchisees are particularly prone to such pressures because of the contractual basis of the franchise relationship.

Bargaining power of shoppers

Shoppers as individuals have little impact on retailers' competitive strategies. The main reason for this is the fact that shoppers' purchases are normally small in comparison to the retailer's total sales. Shoppers are also relatively immobile and uninformed; immobile in the sense that they are not willing (or unable) to travel long distances to find the right products, and less informed than retailers about product prices, availability and quality, and so forth. However, the emergence of the internet has reduced the mobility and information barriers to some extent.

On the other hand, the relative smallness of shoppers' transactions means that the cost of switching from one retailer to another is also relatively small, hence retailers can find that shoppers are quick to switch when more competitive offers are available from another retailer. Retailers also have to be careful not to exploit their advantage in the market too much as they are likely to see their activities regulated and circumscribed by legislation and regulatory authorities. The Competition Commission reports are examples of regulatory authorities responding to consumer concerns.

Threat of substitutes

All retailers are likely to face some form of intertype competition. For instance, the majority of clothes sales are through clothes specialists and variety stores (such as NEXT, Marks and Spencer and others, see Table 3.2). However, clothes are also sold through department stores and mail order. The internet now also provides an alternative to virtually all forms of retailing.

Retailers can also face threats from outside of the retailing industry. For instance, eating out in restaurants competes directly with expenditure in grocery stores. The supermarkets have responded by providing increasing the quality and choice of convenience meals. Retail expenditure also competes with other forms of expenditure such as holidays and entertainment.

Table 3.2 Market shares for men's wear, 1996–2000 (%)

	1996	1997	1998	1999	2000
Specialists	62.7	62.2	61.4	61.3	61.7
M&S	13.6	14.0	13.7	12.5	11.4
Arcadia	7.6	7.3	7.4	7.3	6.8
NEXT	4.0	4.4	4.4	4.9	5.7
C&A†	2.4	2.3	2.2	2.0	2.4
Matalan	1.0	1.2	1.5	1.9	2.5
Moss Bros	2.1	2.3	2.4	2.4	2.4
BHS	1.9	1.9	1.8	1.7	1.6
River Island	2.1	1.9	1.7	1.8	1.8
Gap	1.0	1.0	1.2	1.4	1.5
Ciro Citterio*	0.8	1.3	1.3	1.3	1.3
Littlewoods	1.6	1.4	1.1	1.0	1.1
Grocers	3.8	1.9	2.0	2.1	2.2
ASDA	1.6	1.9	2.0	2.1	2.2
Tesco	0.5	0.5	0.6	0.6	0.7
Sainsbury	0.4	0.4	0.4	0.4	0.4
Dept stores	12.5	13.6	14.6	14.7	14.9
Debenhams	4.0	4.1	4.0	3.9	3.9
H of Fraser	1.9	1.9	1.8	1.9	2.0
John Lewis	1.1	1.2	1.1	1.1	1.2
Mail order	13.2	13.7	13.2	12.7	11.9

†C&A withdrew from the UK market at the end of 2000.
*Ciro Citterio has gone into administration with debts of £30m.
Source: Verdict (2001).

Intensity of rivalry

The intensity of the rivalry between retailers in a particular sector depends on a number of general market-related factors, and factors related to the firms competing in the market. For instance, slow market growth, high concentration, maturity of markets, low differentiation, and high exit costs of leaving the market are likely to lead to intense competition between retailers. The relative balance between competing retailers and their competitive retail marketing strategies also influences the intensity of competition. For instance, competition is likely to be fiercer where there are a number of roughly similar sized competitors pursuing a similar strategy.

⬤ Strategic Groups

A group of stores (competing in similar ways) with similar target markets and similar marketing strategies is referred to as a strategic group. The aim of

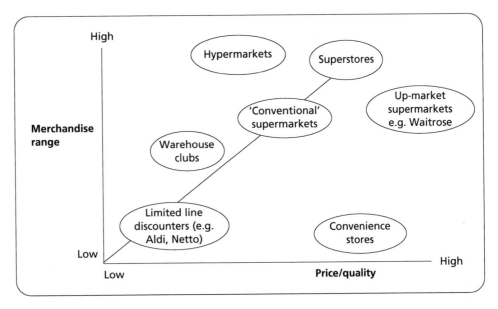

Figure 3.3 Strategic groups in the UK grocery market

strategic group concept is to simplify analysis of competitive strategies and make predictions about competitive behaviour within and between strategic groups. For example, because of the relative homogeneity of the groups, members within them are affected similarly by changes in the environment.

The dimension(s) chosen to define strategic groups relate to shoppers' choice of store – price of goods, merchandise assortment (range), location of store, and service. The actual variables chosen depend on the retail sector concerned. In the clothing sector for instance, quality, fashion orientation and selection could be used to identify strategic groups in the sector. These dimensions can then be used to map the competitors within the industry/sectoral competitive space (see Figure 3.3).

The intensity of competition between firms in different strategic groups depends on the 'distance' between the strategic groups in the competitive space. Competition between neighbouring groups is likely to be most intense as there is likely to be some overlap between their respective target markets. Conversely, competition is least intense between firms belonging to strategic groups furthest apart. Also, where a strategic group is placed between two other groups it will face competition from both.

Although the strategic groups are relatively stable due to mobility barriers that limit the degree of movement between groups, they are constantly evolving due to rivalry and the emergence of new types of retailing. In fashion retailing for instance, mid-market retailers such as Marks and Spencer have lost market share both to specialists (such as NEXT and Gap) and the new discount retailers such as Matalan, New Look, and TK Maxx. Marks and Spencer has found it difficult to compete in these circumstances as its cost base is too high to compete with the discounters and its merchandise is not sufficiently fashion-oriented to compete with the specialists. As a result,

Marks and Spencer's market share declined from 14.0 per cent in 1997 to 11.3 per cent in 2000 (Verdict Research, 2001, see Table 3.2).

Competition is most intense within a strategic group because members pursue similar strategies on the relevant competitive variables such as target markets, merchandise assortment, pricing, location and so forth. These similarities lead to consumers not being able to distinguish between retailers and making decisions based on price. For example, in petrol retailing consumers cannot distinguish between the quality of petrol offered by different retailers and will therefore tend to purchase petrol from the cheapest retailer. Hence, where petrol stations are located near to each other, prices tend to be the same to prevent loss of business to the neighbouring retailer. Also, when prices are changed by one retailer, there is a reaction from competing retailers.

In order to gain competitive advantage, therefore, retailers need to differentiate themselves from other members of the strategic group. The major methods of differentiation in retailing in addition to price are location, sales promotions, store atmospherics, merchandise assortment, and service. However, once a store is built, the location of the store is fixed and can only be changed in the long term. As price is easily imitated and has direct impact on profitability, retailers are more likely to rely on merchandise assortment, promotions, store atmospherics and service to differentiate themselves from competitors. Nevertheless, discount retailers use price as their main differentiating feature.

Competition Regulation

In order to ensure that there is fair competition between competing retailers, and that consumers are not exploited because of their weak buying power, competition needs to be regulated. In the UK, it is regulated by the Office of Fair Trading, which has the power to refer anti-competitive practices to the Competition Commission for a ruling.

For instance, too close a relationship between retailers and suppliers can lead to anti-competitive practices. The practice of obtaining differential discounts (that is, receiving goods at prices lower than competitors) and exclusive supply arrangements (that is preventing suppliers from dealing with other retailers) can give a retailer a big advantage over existing competitors and can make it very difficult for new competitors to enter the market. Regulatory authorities in the UK have taken a fairly lax attitude to these practices preferring to allow them as long as they were not against consumers' interests. In the USA, however, the Robinson–Patman Act actually prohibits price discrimination (differential discounts) unless it can be justified by differences in costs or product differences.

Retailers can also improve their competitive advantage in the market by mergers or acquisition of competing retailers. Dixons, the UK high-street-based electrical goods retailer, for instance, acquired Curry's the out-of-town/edge-of-town electrical superstore, in 1984 to increase its presence in out-of-town locations. Similarly, Tesco acquired the Wm Low chain of supermarkets in 1994 to give it more presence in Scotland. Acquisitions and mergers have the advantage of not only increasing market share, but also of improving buying and other economies of scale. Where a merger or acquisition is likely to significantly affect the competitive balance (or have a negative impact on consumer interest) the regulatory authorities can prevent such mergers or impose conditions on the merger before it can proceed.

Summary

Retailers are facing an increasingly competitive environment due to the relatively slow growth of the retailing sector, increasing maturity and concentration of many retailing sectors, the emergence of new retailing formats such as the internet, changes in consumer expectations and expenditure, and competition from international retailers. Retail competition can take the form of intratype, intertype, vertical and systems competition. In addition, local competition can add to the complexity of decisions regarding competitive action.

The major drivers of competition within the industry are the threat of new entrants, the threat from substitute forms of retailing (that is, intertype competition), the bargaining power of producers, the bargaining power of shoppers, and the intensity of rivalry between firms. The relative balance between competing retailers and their competitive retail marketing strategies also influences the intensity of competition. For instance, competition is likely to be fiercer where there are a number of roughly similar-sized competitors pursuing a similar strategy. Such a group of firms is referred to as a strategic group. Strategic group analysis is used to simplify analysis of competitive strategies and make predictions about competitive behaviour within and between strategic groups. For instance, it predicts that competition between neighbouring groups is likely to be most intense as there is likely to be some overlap between their respective target markets. Conversely, competition is least intense between firms belonging to strategic groups furthest apart.

In order to gain competitive advantage, retailers need to differentiate themselves from their competitors. The methods that are likely to be most successful are likely to rely on merchandise assortment, promotions, store atmospherics and service. Competition is regulated by government bodies to ensure that it is fair, and to prevent the exploitation of consumers.

Questions

1 Describe the main methods used for measuring retail competition and discuss their relative advantages and disadvantages.
2 Outline the differences between intratype and intertype competition.
3 Outline the differences between vertical and systems competition.
4 What major barriers are potential entrants likely to face when entering a retailing sector such as the grocery market?
5 How far do you agree that shoppers are relatively powerless in relation to retailers?
6 What is a strategic group? How useful is this concept for analysing retail competition?
7 How can retailers best achieve competitive advantage in an increasingly competitive environment?

References and Further Reading

Nielsen (2001) *Retail Pocket Book 2001* (Henley-on-Thames: *NTC Publications*).

Competition Commission (2000) *Supermarkets: A Report on the supply of Groceries from Multiple Stores in the United Kingdom*, Cm 4842 (London: The Stationery Office).

Lewison, D. M. and Delozier, W. M. (1986) *Retailing*, 2nd edn (Columbus, Ohio: Merrill Publishing Co.).

London Economics (1997) *Competition in Retailing*, Research Paper no. 13 (London: Office of Fair Trading).

Monopolies and Mergers Commission (1981) *Discounts to Retailers: A Report on the General Effect on the Public Interest of the Practice of Charging Some Retailers Lower Prices than Others or Providing Special Benefits to Some Retailers Where the Difference Cannot be Attributed to Savings in the Supplier's Costs*, Select Committee Report to the House of Commons, HC 311 (London: HMSO).

Office of Fair Trading (1985) *Competition and Retailing* (London: OFT).

Ogbonna, E. and Wilkinson, B. (1996) 'Inter-Organizational Power Relations in the UK Grocery Industry: Contradictions and Developments', *International Review of Retail, Distribution and Consumer Research*, vol. 6, no. 4, pp. 395–414.

Porter, M. (1980) *Competitive Advantage* (New York: The Free Press).

Robins, T. (2000) 'Shoppers Pay Extra in Store Monopolies', *The Sunday Times*, 27 February.

chapter four

Customers

Learning objectives

- To define the role of retailing within the general arena of personal consumption.
- To explore the nature of changes in consumers and reflect on their likely effect on retailing activity.
- To appreciate the various levels of impact that changing consumer profiles can have on retailers.
- To understand the complexity of retailing as a socioeconomic activity, and the way consumers interact with retailing activity.
- To appreciate that consumers have different motivations for shopping.
- To understand the role a retailer plays in the consumer decision-making process.
- To understand the different factors used by consumers when making choices between retail outlets.

Introduction

Retailing activity is, as we saw in the first chapter, defined as selling goods and services to final consumers for their personal, or their family's, consumption. It is therefore in the interest of any retailer to gather as much information about the final consumer as they can in order to check that the goods and services offered remain relevant to consumers. All consumers are potential customers to a retail business, however what is more appropriate for retail managers is the identification of a group of consumers who are likely to become actual customers or purchasers within their own outlet. These groups of people may be defined in terms of their geographical location, for example, or they might be more conveniently grouped according to product or service need. Questions retailers might ask about their customers could be: Who are they? Where are they? What do they need? What do they like? How old are they? How much can they spend? How do they like to shop?

There may also be questions to ask about customers' relationship with all retailers in the sector (see also Chapter 3, retail competitors). For example: Who are our current customers? Who are our competitor's customers? In a saturated marketplace, can we convert them? Would this be economically viable (given that converting new customers is much more costly than keeping existing ones)? Who will be our customers in the future? Are customers changing? Does that change have a positive or negative effect on our business? Are there different customers that have poor retail provision?

Retailers who are in touch with their customers and their needs and wants are more likely to find retail formulae that are relevant to consumers. For example, in the late 1990s, the electrical retail group Dixons launched The Link, a new chain of stores that focused on personal communication products and services, in response to the growing market. Although there was a degree of overlap in this product category with the existing Dixons stores, the new stores allowed the retail group to respond positively to an opportunity presented by a change in consumer lifestyles.

⬤ Retailing and Consumption

A retailer's role in the arena of personal consumption is that of distributor and facilitator, as outlined in Chapter 1. A retailer provides a convenient point for a consumer to obtain goods and services, either by being in a location that is closer than that of the producer and by selling in quantities appropriate to the needs of the consumer, or by providing added value in the offer, such as range assortment or additional services. In a developed society, retailers play a greater role than the distribution viewpoint would imply. They provide an information service, they provide an environment in which new products can be discovered, new fashions followed and lifestyle patterns endorsed. Retailers have the benefit of a direct interface with the final consumer, therefore they should have an advantage over producers when it comes to gathering information about customers in terms of who they are and how and what they buy. However, all too often retailers make too many assumptions about their customers and do not have a thorough and researched awareness of how their customers' needs, wants and preferences can change over time.

⬤ The Changing Consumer

It is claimed that modern societies are increasingly organized around consumption (Abercrombie, Hill and Turner, 1994) and so the trends in the patterns of consumption that emerge over time are very important for retailers to observe and understand. Consumer trends describe how the body of consumers changes over time and make predictions about how those people will consume in the future. The retailer can therefore build up a 'customer profile' that gives an indication of who might 'typically' use their outlet. A retail customer profile is affected by the macro (general) business environment; for example the macro-economic policies a government pursues in relation to personal taxation and interest rates affects the spending power of retail customers, and the extent to which we are familiar with technology will affect our propensity to use technologically based retail formats to undertake shopping activity.

A retailer's customer profile is also influenced by the microenvironment, the specific business arena in which the individual retailer operates. For example, the entry of Amazon.com into the book retailing market gave traditional retailers like Waterstones and Ottakars new competition, not only in the form of a new company, but also a whole new way of shopping (see Chapter 3). Subsequently, store-based retailers have put more effort into creating a pleasant store environment, conducive to browsing and sampling a book over a cup of coffee, something that internet retailers are unable to offer. Book retailers might therefore be able to group their customers according to the ways they like to shop for books, and address their needs accordingly. Some of the most radical changes in consumers in developed economies like Europe and the USA are those that emanate from the changes in society itself; the changing nature of a population's age profile, the changes in the numbers and type of activity of the working population, and the way in which lifestyles themselves are changing. The resulting manifestations of alterations in shopping behaviour and product preference are of interest to the retailer, as they may require some adaptation to the retailer's business in order to maintain an adequate customer flow.

Demographics

One of the most fundamental changes to the consumer body is that concerning demographics. This is the study of populations in terms of measurable aspects such as birthrate, age profiles, working patterns and occupations, family and household structures, education levels, and total income and expenditure levels (Brassington and Pettitt, 2000). These changes are generally out of a retailer's control, depending very much on the social and economic development of a given population, and they are usually relatively slow-moving changes. However, retailers must be aware of the implications of such changes, so that they can be accommodated in a retailer's long-term strategic planning. Some of the demographic changes that are likely to have an impact on retailers are now explored in more detail.

Age profile

The age profile of the consumer market can be extremely relevant to a retail business. Although out of a retailer's control, the deathrate and birthrate influence the 'bulges' in generation cohorts, which may have positive or

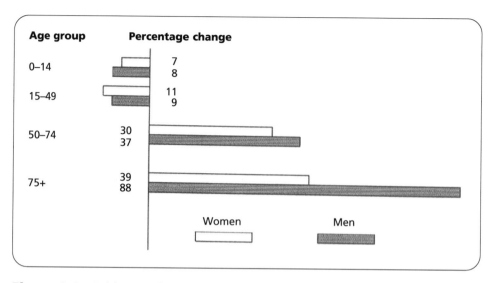

Figure 4.1 Evidence of an ageing population, 1994–2004

Source: Fernie (1999) *The Future for UK Retailing.*

negative effects on the potential customer base. Retailers of young fashion may struggle due to a falling population of teenagers, at the same time as children's wear retailers are thriving due to an upturn in the birthrate. Clearly, some retailers are more directly influenced by changing age patterns than others, when their product range is directly linked to the age of the consumer. For example, prams and buggies have a direct link to babies; after the first four years of a child's life, retailers of this type of product cease to be relevant to the consumer (whether they are parents or grandparents). However, the market for personal computers is much wider, with income rather than age being a more relevant criterion for the identification of customers.

One key challenge for retailers in the early part of the twenty-first century is how to adapt to the ageing population. Figure 4.1 shows the significance of the shift towards older age groups in the UK population; however, unlike most other consumer groups the 'grey market' is both time and cash-rich in spite of being less mobile.

Levy and Weitz (2000) suggest a number of ways in which retailers can adapt to a more elderly clientele. These include training staff to recognize the needs of senior people, and respond to them with clarity and respect; designing the store environment with the older customer in mind (good lighting, consistent layouts, rest areas); providing information in large print and in forms that customers can take away to study; and finally to employ older people who may be better able to empathize with the customer base.

Working patterns

The trend for more women to enter the workplace is continuing in Europe and occupations have moved from the traditional manufacturing industries to the service sector. This type of employment, characterized by part-time and flexible working hours and 'lighter' work (such as keyboard and telephone operators, catering and shop work) generally suits female employees, and with the growth of communication and information technology, many job roles can actually be carried out from the 'home-office' (Fernie, 1999). At the same time, the proportion of time spent by individuals in the workplace is increasing.

The trend for more women to work both in part-time and full-time occupations has had a number of very important influences on the way the retail industry has developed. Some of these are highlighted below:

The influence of working women on retailing:

- The growth of convenience products in the grocery market, for example ready-prepared meals was a product category initially pioneered by Marks and Spencer, and now most supermarkets have take-away food bars.
- The increased offer of products and services under one roof – the one-stop shop, or perhaps more accurately the one-stop household service. Many superstores offer pharmacies, dry cleaning, photograph processing, shoe repair and post-office services, alongside the extensive food and non-food household product range.
- The increased choice of retailers offering a 'working wardrobe' in the clothing sector. UK clothing retailer NEXT has been particularly successful in this market, and the repositioning of 'casual' Chelsea Girl to 'smarter', River Island in the mid-1980s (Lea-Greenwood, 1993) was a response to the opportunity to sell young women their work attire alongside more fashionable items.
- Child-orientated facilities to ease the burden of shopping with children, for example crèches, changing facilities, parent and child car parking places, trolleys with baby carriers.
- Retailers have expanded product offerings to include more services, such as health and beauty-related services and menu-planning services.

Other demographic trends that might affect retailers include geographical shifts, and ethnic diversity. For example, inner-city regeneration schemes are attracting childless single and partnered people into luxury city-centre residential developments, who might have previously migrated to suburban areas. Retailers like Tesco use geomarketing techniques to ensure that their store formats and product ranges are tailored to local catchment areas. It may be important for retailers to provide customer information in alternative languages in order to reflect the ethnic character of the local market.

Income and expenditure

Although the feeling of being better-off is influenced by our level of wealth relative to those we come into contact with, rather than our actual income level, the majority of consumers in developed societies such as Europe and the USA have enjoyed an increasing level of personal disposable income since the Second World War. We now spend a smaller proportion of our income on what might be termed 'the essentials' of life, such as housing and food, whereas the proportion of our income spent on discretionary purchases such as fashion goods, household appliances, eating out, holidays and entertainment has increased. This means that retailers and manufacturers are able to benefit by encouraging consumers to 'trade-up' in their essential purchases, and make discretionary purchases appear to be 'essential'.

Demographics are the measurable outcomes of societal change. For example, the UK has experienced a fall in the size of families and households over the last two decades as the result of a number of variables, many of which are interrelated: the increased availability and acceptability of contraception; an increased number of women having a 'career' and so starting a family later or deciding not to have a family; an increase in the divorce rate, resulting in more households and 'irregular' family groups (for example a couple may live on their own in the week, with an influx of children from two previous marriages at the weekends); and more elderly people living independently, often single, for longer periods of time. Retailers need to be aware of these changes in terms of how they affect the number of consumers in different demographic categories, but equally important is to be able to have an understanding of how the changes influence the lifestyles of groups of people in the various demographic categories.

● Lifestyle Changes

A complete and thorough exploration of societal influences on consumption is beyond the scope of this text. However, some of the lifestyle changes that have occurred in the recent past and have had a significant effect on retailers are the following:

- Time poverty and therefore a resulting convenience orientation, particularly for working women (see earlier section on working patterns).
- Car dependency, resulting in a growth of edge-of-town and out-of-town shopping centres.
- Cellular families, resulting in a growth of spending on personal appliances; households with teenage children are likely to have multiple television sets, telephones, music players and personal computers.
- Informality, as a possible result of the weakening influence of traditional bodies of authority such as the church, the police, the state and the family. In particular, clothing retailers have been challenged by this trend, but it has also had its effect on home furnishings. IKEA, for example, has used informality and fun as a theme in its customer communications, with traditional and formal styles being portrayed as old-fashioned.
- Home style changes resulting in the growth of spending on the home and garden. The media have fuelled this interest with programmes like 'Changing Rooms' and 'Ground Force', and retailers like B&Q and IKEA have been the beneficiaries.
- Increased focus on leisure time. Longer working hours puts a brighter spotlight on the quality of leisure time and consumers are prepared to purchase items and services that will enhance their precious free time.

Labour-saving appliances like dishwashers and microwaves have a high penetration in UK households, but retailers in general have to respond to the fact that shopping is increasingly regarded as a leisure pursuit which should be enjoyable, entertaining, interesting and hassle-free, with service offerings such as restaurants, bars and coffee shops, sporting facilities and entertainment venues in close proximity.

There have also been changes in attitudes within the general body of consumers, which again has influenced the way they shop and the products they choose. These would include the weakening influence of traditional authority indicated above, environmental awareness and consciousness, health consciousness and value orientation.

Within this general appreciation of the nature of consumers as a living changing, adapting, and thriving body of potential customers, retailers need to audit the consuming population in order to establish the rate and impact of change on their own individual businesses.

● **The Consumer Buying Process**

As well as understanding the retail consumer from the point of view of the masses, or total potential market viewpoint, the study of consumer behaviour is also very much concerned with how we consume as individuals. Established theory suggests that each time we purchase something we go through a process composed of a number of key stages as indicated in Figure 4.2.

It has also been suggested that consumer buying behaviour is influenced at least as much by retailers as manufacturers (Knox and Denison, 2000), and so

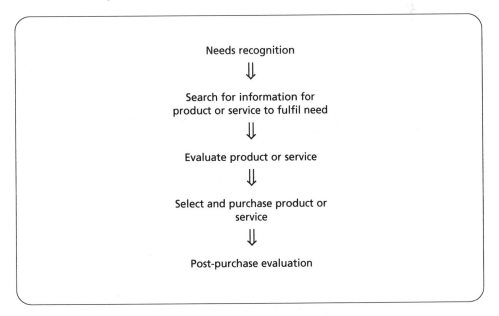

Figure 4.2   The consumer purchase decision-making process

a retailer needs to be aware of the extent to which they can contribute to the purchase decision-making process. Each of the factors of Figure 4.2 are briefly considered below.

Needs recognition

To begin with, the retail environment itself can be used to draw attention to products and stimulate impulse purchases (see Chapter 10). In this case the need is generated during the shopping process rather than prior to it. In other instances, the recognition of need may be closely associated with the retail outlet that has become strongly connected to particular items. For example, an empty refrigerator is more likely to prompt the thought 'I must visit the super-market', than the specific product-related thought 'I must buy a box of eggs'.

Information search

In the second stage, consumers use retail outlets extensively for information about goods and services. Retailers provide information in many forms, includ-ing point-of-sale information, leaflets and catalogues, websites, interactive prod-uct trials such as food tasting, trying on garments or listening to music, and in the one-to-one advice given to customers about their intended purchase by sales personnel. In particular, a sales person can help to move a customer from the stage where they are searching for information about products, to the point at which they start to evaluate the alternatives on offer and make a choice.

Evaluation

During the search and evaluation stage the retailer itself rather than simply the product may become the focus of a consumer's evaluation. Customer loyalty and the value of the retailer's corporate brand may encourage a consumer to restrict their search and evaluation activity. It is in the retailer's interest to progress a consumer to the purchasing stage efficiently in order to prevent them taking their custom to a competitor's outlet. In a saturated retail market, ensuring that customers keep returning to your store or website is a vital ingredient of a retailer's strategy, and as European markets have matured, increasing focus has been placed on customer loyalty. Defining loyalty in retailing is not straightforward because it can be measured in more than one way; frequency of visit, extent of switching and expenditure levels all contribute to the extent to which a customer can be considered to be loyal (Knox and Denison, 2000). Irrespective of the way loyalty is measured, loyal customers are more profitable to retailers than other types of customers, and therefore every effort should be made to maximize their satisfaction. This is a growing challenge; as consumers face increasing choice through their own mobility and gain experience as shoppers, their loyalty levels are likely to fall.

Select and purchase

The extent to which a retailer can influence this stage of the process is closely linked to the type of product being purchased. In low-involvement products, the consumer may be influenced by some in-store promotional activity, whereas in medium involvement products, such as beauty products, the matching of product benefits to customer needs by sales associates will play an important role. In high involvement purchase decisions, such as a carpet, the shopper may revisit alternative retailers a number of times to gather information on product attributes such as price, quality, colour, payment methods and delivery before making a final decision.

Post-purchase evaluation

Again, the extent to which the product or the retailer is judged after the sale will depend on the type of purchase. For high involvement purchases, high levels of post-purchase customer service can help to alleviate any worries about installation and use, whilst clear and generous return and exchange policies can help to reassure the customer in the purchase of all types of product.

● Shopping Behaviour

The model of the consumer purchase decision-making process assumes that the consumer is a rational and economic person, whose evaluation is strictly geared to physical benefits of the product bought. In fact the activity of shopping is tied up with a whole host of human emotion and behaviour, involving benefits sought to satisfy myriad psychological needs. Product needs vary from the functional (for example a vacuum cleaner) to the psychological (for example a FCUK t-shirt); however, most products offer both functional and psychological benefits. For example, the Dyson vacuum cleaner is designed with a transparent dust-collection cylinder providing the user with the psychologically satisfying view of all the trapped dirt! Shopping also fulfils functional and psychological needs, and can vary from a chore to the most favoured leisure pursuit. A retail outlet can be designed to make the functional shop easier and less of a chore:

- By locating the outlet in the most convenient situation, considering travel time, congestion, ease of parking and accessibility.
- By providing a logical layout (applies to both store and non-store outlets).
- Ensuring POS information is clear and easily understood.
- Providing good customer service.
- Ensuring good stock availability.
- Providing fast and flexible payment facilities.

A retail outlet can also be designed to encourage customers to view shopping as a pleasurable leisure pursuit:

- *Ensure customer service levels are high.* Staff/customer interactions should be pleasant, cheerful and courteous. Staff should appear interested in and knowledgeable about the products(s) that they are selling.

● *Provide eating-places.* Customers should be comfortable and well-fed. The provision of restaurants, cafes and tasting bars all help to keep the customer relaxed, and encourage prolonged shopping activity.

● *Entertain the customer.* There are various ways in which customer can be entertained. For example some supermarkets have introduced 'live chef' sessions, and many clothing stores arrange fashion shows (on video if the store is too small). The store environment itself can be designed to provide entertaining features, for example children's wear retailers have used talking trees, hissing snakes and push-button interactive information points to help keep their short attention span customers in a good frame of mind!

● *Make the store environment enthralling.* An inspiring store is likely to encourage customers to browse, whereas one that is dull and badly laid out will do the opposite! The store design and the displays, together with music, lighting and even aromas can create an atmosphere that makes shopping 'an experience'.

● *Choose an outlet location that combines retail and leisure activities.* Many modern shopping centres combine retail outlets with other leisure destinations, such as cinemas, sport facilities, cafés and bars, and tourist attractions. This encourages customers to view the shopping activity as part of a 'day out'. The proximity to other retailers in a centre can also be important in terms of generating high footfall (see Chapter 9).

Vignette 4.1

The Glasgow Outdoor Experience

The 40-year-old retail company Tiso, which has been leader of the outdoor sports market in Scotland for many years, has rewritten the rules of adventure sports retail. The company chairman Chris Tiso recognized the need to service two different types of sporting goods customers. Some customers were more interested in sports clothing as a fashion statement, with sports brands becoming increasingly popular in mainstream shopping centres. Others were enthusiasts, whose concern for the performance of clothing and equipment was paramount. The opening of The Outdoor Experience store in Glasgow finds a way to offer sporting goods to all types of customers, in an entertaining and relaxing environment. The store has a straightforward philosophy: try before you buy and enjoy yourself while doing so. The store covers 7,500 square metres, and houses a café with internet access, a kids' discovery area, and a number of interactive features such as the 'Goretex Fabric Wet Zone' for trying out waterproof clothing and the stove-testing unit. Special sports features include a mountain bike track (including waterfall, pond and bridge), and an ice-climbing wall, encouraging customers to have fun and to try out alternatives in what can be a very high value purchase. The interactive areas also allow sales personnel to demonstrate the benefits of the product, and encourage customers to trade up in their equipment purchases, without having to resort to the 'hard sell'. This unique retail outlet encourages anyone with an interest in sporting gear to browse, have fun, learn, try and then, when they are ready, buy.

Source: Based on J. Young, 'The Outdoors Grows Up', *Retail Interiors*, July 2000, issue 7.

Shopping missions

Another limitation of the consumer purchase decision-making model is that the way we shop can be influenced by the shopping mission. The following accounts of shopping for essentially what could be described as square sheets of absorbent paper, illustrate how different missions have implications for the way a consumer shops, and for the retailer concerned with the purchase:

- *Emergency situation.* Suffering from hayfever, Ms X is in need of a packet of tissues fast! She will buy them from the nearest outlet that has product availability, and product attributes such as price, brand, quality and design are not relevant in this situation. Convenience stores are therefore able to apply high profit margins to this type of product.
- *Routine buying.* On a visit to a supermarket to do the weekly household shop, Ms X purchases a family pack of tissues. She assumes the current pack at home will not last much longer. She may be influenced by promotional offers (such as 2 for 1) and may use other product criteria such as colour and use of recycled materials in her purchase decision. However, her overall involvement in the purchase is low.
- *Destination shopping.* Ms X is organizing a dinner party. She needs to buy some table napkins and she is concerned that the quality of the napkins reflects her excellent cookery skills, and that the design complements the décor in her dining room. She heads for a department store located within a nearby regional shopping centre where she knows she will find a wide selection of designs to choose from. She is not price sensitive in her purchase, although she believes this reputable retailer provides good value for money.
- *Browsing.* Later in the year Ms X is doing her Christmas shopping. Whilst browsing through a variety store she notices some novelty tissues with cartoon characters printed on them. She decides that these would make a good stocking-filler present for her 9-year-old daughter. She then moves on to the male toiletries section to find an equivalent gift for her 11-year-old son.

Shopping motivations

Tauber (1972) was one of the first researchers to ask the question 'why do people shop?', appreciating that there were reasons other than the simple necessity to purchase physical products. He found that consumer's motivations for shopping are derived from many factors, some of which are less related to the buying of products, and more related to personal and social motivations of individuals. He went on to suggest that retailers need to consider the satisfaction that a consumer gets from the shopping activity itself, as well as the utility obtained from product bought if they are to fully understand consumer's motivations for shopping.

Further consumer research has uncovered other psychological motivations for shopping, and Table 4.1 provides a summary of reasons why people go shopping other than to purchase a product to satisfy a physical need, such as running out of an item or something wearing out!

Table 4.1 Shopping motivations

Personal stimulation	The need for 'an experience'; the enjoyment of being in an interesting or different environment
Social experiences	The need to be with people; to go shopping with friends, to talk to people with similar interests, to have contact with a peer group
Learning	The need to acquire new knowledge in order to become an 'educated shopper'; finding out about new products, following fashion trends, talking to 'experts' in stores
Status and power	The need to exert authority, to gain attention from retail personnel, to have somebody 'serve' and show respect
Self-reward	The need to treat oneself, or to put oneself in a positive frame of mind
Diversion	The need to alleviate boredom, to provide a break in the daily routine, to get out and about
Exercise	The need to move about and get some fresh air
Role-play	The need to reinforce a role or to play a role to which one aspires; for example the role of the provider (in the gathering of the weekly family needs)
Bargain hunting	The need to show expertise in finding value in purchasing; the need to have 'beaten' the retailer by buying at discounted prices

As a generalization, the shopping process can be broken down into two separate categories. The first is sometimes referred to as 'chore shopping', and is a reflection of how many people feel about, for example, grocery shopping. It is the kind of shopping that has to be performed in order to replenish food and household goods, or to replace worn-out items. Although many people love shopping for clothes, there is a significant section of the population (many of whom are male) who would consider clothes shopping to be a chore. However, a key feature of chore shopping is the low-involvement, routine nature of the task and therefore it can be separated from clothes shopping. The main objective with chore shopping, for most people, is to perform the task as efficiently as possible.

The second general category of shopping activity is the one that usually involves high-involvement or 'one-off' purchases, and for these the consumer will go through all of the stages in the consumer purchasing process, and may spend a long period of time in the early stages gathering together information and trying out alternatives. The key difference in the two types of shopping from the retailer's point of view is that for low involvement (chore) shopping it is in the consumer's interest to establish a routine in order to maximize efficiency, and one of the ways of doing this is to choose one store and buy as many things from that store as possible. When a consumer buys a high involvement product they will like to consider many alternatives, whereas in the routine process a customer will generally be happy with a smaller number of alternatives, and in many instances will have already decided amongst alternatives based on previous experience. How consumers choose between alternative stores is therefore as important to retailers as how consumers make decisions about what product to buy. As a consumer gains experience within a product classification, such as clothing or household appliances, decisions regarding store choice hold more weight than those regarding the products themselves. Although in the early stages of adoption as a form of shopping, the choice of website from which to order is likely to be subject to a similar process of decision-making.

Retail Outlet Choice

There are many factors that influence how we as consumers feel about a retail outlet. Clearly in the light of the previous discussion, the product range offered is one of those factors. However, in a saturated retail market there may be a number of outlets offering very similar product ranges, and so other means of differentiation become important in the retail offer. The following factors were considered important by more than one-quarter of respondents in a study of why customers chose one grocery store over another:

- Attractive prices.
- Location.
- Quality of products.
- Wide range of products.
- Measures to reduce queues at checkout.
- Fresh food service (e.g. delicatessen, fresh fish, etc.).
- Longer opening hours.
- Good own-label range.
- Cashpoint facilities.
- Express checkout.

(*Source*: Mintel, Food Retailing Report, *Consumer Shopping*, August 2000.)

Attempts have been made to model the process of store choice decision-making, and these models can help retailers to carry out their own research in order to understand what is really important to customers (and potential customers) when choosing one outlet for their shopping over another. The multi-attribute model has been used widely in retail studies in order to measure the relevance of a retail outlet's attributes to the selection criteria used by shoppers (Gonzalez-Betino *et al.*, 2000), and the following hypothetical illustration shows how this type of store-choice modelling can be used.

The multi-attribute store-choice model

The first stage of using the model is to identify stores that are in a customer's set of alternatives. The set may include outlets that compete on an intertype or an intratype basis, and in this example we will use intratype competition and consider the process of choosing between three different grocery super-stores located within a five-mile radius. Table 4.2 lists a number of store attributes (characteristics) and makes a qualitative assessment of each store according to their performance in relation to these attributes.

Table 4.2 Store attributes and individual store performances

Superstore	X	Y	Z
Price level	Average	Above average	Average
Price offers	Few	Few	Many
Car parking	Unrestricted	Unrestricted	Sometimes difficult
Speed through checkout	Slow	Fast	Fast
General product assortment	Average	Vast	Below average
Organic produce	No	Yes	Very limited
Store environment	Average	Excellent	Average
Pharmacy	Yes	No	No

Customers can then be asked to score the three stores according to these characteristics, and these scores can be summarized under general attribute groupings as shown in Table 4.3.

Table 4.3 Superstore scores according to attributes (top score =10)

| | Superstore | | |
	X	Y	Z
Prices (level, offers)	7	5	9
Convenience (parking, checkout speed, pharmacy)	8	7	6
Product range (general assortment, organic produce)	6	9	6
Store environment	7	9	6
Totals	28	30	27

The total scores indicate that all three stores are performing well, scoring between 26 and 30 out of a possible 40 points.

Even though different customers may rate these three stores similarly in terms of their general attributes, there may be particular characteristics that have a greater importance to different individuals, and therefore have a bearing on the store choice that they personally make. So, by asking individual customers to attach an importance weighting to the general attributes, we will gain a better insight into how different groups of customers choose stores. Table 4.4 shows the importance weights put onto the general attributes by two different customers. Customer A is 55, with grown-up children and a professional occupation. Customer B is a parent with three children and a low disposable income. By multiplying the importance weighting by the scores for the general attributes, we can see that different stores gain top scores for these two individual customers, and so they are likely to choose different superstores for their weekly shop (Table 4.5).

Table 4.4 Importance weightings given by two different customers

	A	B
Price	5	10
Convenience	9	6
Assortment	10	7
Shopping environment	7	2

Table 4.5 Weighted store attribute scores

	Customer weighting		Store attribute score		
	A	B	X	Y	Z
Price	5	10	7	5	9
Convenience	9	6	8	7	6
Assortment	10	7	6	9	6
Shopping environment	7	2	7	9	6
Total weighted scores			A 216	**A 241**	A 196
			B174	B 174	**B 180**

Although this model provides a useful framework for researching how customers make choices between alternative retail outlets using a multi-attribute scoring system, our decision-making is not always transferable into numeric scoring. For example, the parent (customer B) may need to use a pharmacy regularly, and so the presence of this single attribute might outweigh all others. Similarly, customer A may have made a decision to eat only organic foods, and so store Y would be the only acceptable choice for them, no matter how much stores X and Z improved other parts of their offer.

● **Retail Segmentation**

The result of the type of research outlined above could indicate to retailers where loyalty might be generated within a specific customer group and many retailers gear their offerings to particular groups of individuals who they have identified as being accessible enough and viable enough to support a business. For example, their level of need and willingness to be loyal provides a flow of income that maintains the operation. This process is known as segmentation and targeting: the retailer splits up the total population of the consumer market into a number of segments, into which individuals are placed according to their own physical or psychographic characteristics, and then the retail offer is aimed at a the 'target' segment. A number of retailers have gained success by targeting a narrow segment, but for general retailers, the customer group served might be quite broad.

A deep understanding of the consumer is a prerequisite to successful segmentation. Some of the more common methods used by retailers to segment their markets are:

● *Demographic*: age, gender, family size, family life-cycle, income, occupation
● *Psychographic*: social class, lifestyle, personality, attitudes
● *Behavioural*: benefits sought, loyalty status, usage rate
● *Geographical*

It is useful to separate the last variable out because it can be used either from the point of view of where the customer lives, or from the point of view of where the buying activity actually takes place. For example, some consumers can be geographically grouped according to their travel routes, or where they carry out their work. Boots, for example, target 'lunchtime' shoppers with their takeaway food range and lunchtime deals. Yet, two of those lunchtime shoppers may live in very different suburbs of the town in which Boots is located, and therefore be considered in a very different customer segment by a different retail company; indeed, to a convenience store one of the customers may be a viable target, but the other who lives on the opposite side of town is completely irrelevant.

Segmentation based on shopping behaviour

Some attempts have been made to group consumers on the basis of their shopping behaviour, which can generally be viewed as a combination of psychographic and behavioural segmentation. Categories have been developed such as: the convenience shopper; the bargain hunting or economic shopper; the environmental/socially concerned shopper; the personalizing or innovative opinion-leading shopper; the fashion follower; the traditional shopper; the creative shopper; the recreational shopper; and even the apathetic or uninvolved shopper (Stone, 1954; Stevenson and Willett, 1969; Shim, Gehrt and Lotz, 2001). In an era of multi-channel strategies, retailers may increasingly use the customer's preferred method of shopping as a basis for segmenting customer markets. For example, internet shopping might appeal to customers that are time-poor, lack mobility, or dislike the social aspects of shopping, whilst store shopping is more likely to appeal to those with more time who enjoy browsing and impulse purchasing.

Segmentation has traditionally been very important to retail businesses. The viability of the segmentation process depends on the identification and separability of accessible, measurable and viable groups of potential customers. If a target customer segment is no longer viable, or another segment looks more attractive, a retailer may need to use new criteria for segmentation and 'reposition' the business. For example, in the late 1990s Iceland, who had previously focused on low-price frozen food products, attempted to reposition their business to attract a more upmarket, environmentally concerned customer by banning genetically modified food products and introducing organic products. Some larger retailers, however, will segment their customers *within* the outlet; for example New Look's 9–15 range for teenagers, or Marks and Spencer's designer-created Autograph range for customers with higher disposable incomes and fashion orientation.

Summary

In this chapter we have outlined the importance to retailers of getting to know their customers, both as a group of people within a population, and as individuals. Having an in-depth knowledge about customers' product and store preferences allows retailers to gear their businesses towards the customer and make their product and service offerings more attractive than those of competitors. Customers exist within a society, and are subject to a whole host of influencing factors that shape the way they shop. Customers are complex human beings, they may act differently according to the type of shopping trip they are on, seeking value during one shopping mission, and then indulging themselves on another. This gives rise to the notion of a hybrid customer, within a market of customers who seem to be increasingly less predictable as groups. At the same time, international retailing activity reflects an acceptance of global brands in a worldwide market in which needs and tastes converge.

Questions

1. For a retailer of your choice, discuss how elements in the product/service offer reflect the lifestyle of their customers.
2. Discuss the demographic changes that are taking place within your country. Identify retailers who stand to gain and those who may lose out because of these changes.
3. Review the buying process that you went through when you last purchased a high-involvement product. To what extent did the retail outlet (rather than the product itself) influence your choice of product and store? Can you think of anything further retailers could have done to get you to purchase within their outlet? What would definitely put you off buying this product in a particular retail outlet?
4. Review the different motivations for shopping. Give an example of a shopping incident that would illustrate each one.
5. Compare and contrast the concept of a shopping mission and a shopping motivation.
6. Referring to the vignette on the Glasgow Outdoor Experience, describe how retailers can enhance the leisure aspects of shopping.

References and Further Reading

Abercrombie, N., Hill, S. and Turner, B. S. (1994) *Dictionary of Sociology* (London: Penguin, London).

Brassington, F. and Pettitt, S. (2000) *Principles of Marketing* (Harlow: Financial Times, Prentice-Hall).

Fernie, J. (1999) *The Future for UK Retailing* (London: *Financial Times* Retail and Consumer Reports).

Gonzalez-Benito, O., Greatorex, M. and Munoz-Gallego, P. A. (2000) 'Assessment of Potential Retail Segmentation Variables. An Approach based on a Subjective MCI Resource Allocation Model', *Journal of Retailing and Consumer Services*, no. 7, pp. 171–9.

Knox, S. D. and Denison, T. J. (2000) 'Store Loyalty: Its Impact on Retail Revenue. An Empirical Study of Purchasing Behaviour in the UK', *Journal of Retailing and Consumer Services*, no. 7, pp. 33–45.

Lea Greenwood, G. (1993) 'River Island Clothing Co.: A Case Study on Changing an Image', *International Journal of Retail and Distribution Management*, vol. 21, no. 3, pp. 60–4.

Levy, M. and Weitz, B. A. (2001) *Retailing Management* (New York: McGraw-Hill).

Mintel (2000), *Food Retailing* (London: Mintel).

Shim, S., Gehrt, K. and Lotz, S. (2001) 'Export Implications for the Japanese Fruit market: Fruit-Specific Lifestyle Segments', *International Journal of Retail and Distribution Management*, vol. 29, no. 6, pp. 298–314.

Stevenson, D. and Willett, R.P. (1969), 'Analysis of Consumers' Retail Patronage Strategies', in P. R. MacDonald (ed.), *Marketing Involvement in Society and Economy*, AMA, Chicago, pp. 316–22, cited in McGoldrick, P. J. (1990) *Retail Marketing*, McGraw-Hill.

Stone, G. P. (1954), 'City Shoppers and Urban Identification: Observations on the Social Psychology of City Life', *American Journal of Sociology*, vol. 60, pp. 36–45.

Tauber, E. M. (1972) 'Why Do People Shop?', *Journal of Marketing*, vol. 36, no. 4, pp. 46–9.

Young, J. (2000) 'The Outdoors Grows Up', *Retail Interiors*, July, issue 7.

part two

Formulating and Implementing Retail Strategy

chapter five

Formulating Retail Strategy

Learning objectives

- To understand what is meant by strategy.
- To appreciate the difference between corporate, business and functional strategies in retailing.
- To understand the strategic planning process and its components.
- To explore the alternative competitive strategies available to retailers and understand how retailers can use the value-chain concept to implement those strategies.
- To understand and evaluate the various growth strategies available to retailers.
- To understand what is meant by a retail mix and its role in developing positioning strategies.

Introduction

Retailing strategy outlines the goals and objectives a retailer wants to achieve and a plan that determines how it will achieve them. It provides an overall framework for dealing with its operating environment, customers and competitors, given the retailer's resources and competencies. Strategic management is relatively new to retailing and has emerged with the growth of large multiple chain stores and the resulting complexity of retail organizations. In the past, retailers tended to be largely reactive to changes in the business environment, but this is no longer viable as competition in all retail sectors is intense, and changes in consumer behaviour, technology and other environmental variables are happening very fast. Long-term analysis and planning are therefore required to ensure that growth opportunities are not missed and action is taken in good time to avoid the impact of negative trends in the retail business environment.

Strategy sets direction and scope of an organization over the long term, and creates sustainable competitive advantage through the configuration of its resources to meet customers' needs and expectations of stakeholders in a changing environment (Johnson and Scholes, 1997). This requires the development of a corporate mission that defines the scope of a retailer's activities, matching those activities to its business environment, building the organization's resource capability and competences, and allocating or reallocating resources between business activities to achieve the retailer's organizational objectives.

● Levels of Strategic Planning

Before discussing the nature of strategy it is necessary to discuss the levels at which strategic planning occurs in retail organizations. Many large retailers consist of a number of different business units. For instance, in addition to its supermarkets business, Sainsbury's operates Savacentre, its hypermarket business, as well as Shaws in the USA, and Sainsbury's Bank. Each of these businesses caters to a different set of customers, faces a different set of competitors, and develops and executes its own marketing strategy. Such businesses are called strategic business units (SBU). A SBU is a unit within the overall corporate entity for which there is an external market for its goods and services which is distinct from other SBUs; it is treated as a separate profit centre and is responsible for its own strategy. In multi-business organizations, such as Sainsbury's (see also Figure 5.1), there is a need to distinguish strategic planning at three levels, namely corporate strategy, business-unit strategy, and functional or operational strategies.

In businesses consisting of two or more SBUs, corporate strategy is responsible for setting overall organizational objectives and objectives for each of the SBUs such that they contribute to the achievement of overall organizational objectives. Corporate strategy is also responsible for allocating resources among the SBUs and coordinating their activities to maximize synergy between the SBUs.

A business-level strategy deals with how a particular SBU intends to achieve the objectives assigned to it in the corporate plan. This means, in effect, that business-unit strategy is concerned with how the SBU will compete in its particular market and create sustainable differential advantage. This necessitates decisions on the customers that the SBU intends to target, retailers that it intends to compete against, and how it intends to deliver value to its customers. The distinction between corporate and business-level strategy is only relevant to multi-business organizations; for single-business retailers, such as the fashion retailer New Look, corporate and business-level strategies are the same.

Functional strategy specifies how each of the operational areas of the business (for example human-resource management, finance, marketing, logistics and buying) contributes to implementation of the overall business-unit strategy.

It is also worth distinguishing between strategic and operational management. Operational management is routine, limited to specific

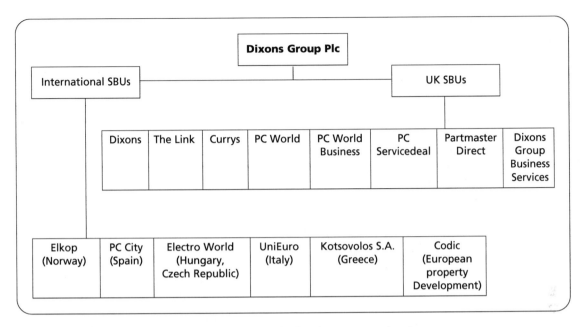

Figure 5.1 Organization of SBUs in a multi-business organization

areas, deals with small-scale change, and is resource-led. Strategic management, on the other hand, deals with non-routine issues with long-term, fundamental, organization-wide implications and is driven by the environment or expectations rather than existing resources and competences.

● **The Strategic Retail Planning Process**

In order to develop retailing strategies, retailers need to follow a systematic procedure or planning process. The planning process describes analysis of the current state of the business, the formulation, choice and evaluation of alternative strategic directions, and the implementation of the chosen strategies. Given the importance of strategic decisions for the future success of the business a systematic approach is vital. The strategic planning process consists of the following major steps:

1 Defining the business philosophy and mission
2 Setting corporate objectives
3 Situation analysis
4 Identification and evaluation of strategic opportunities
5 Development of marketing and positioning strategies
6 Development of suitable retailing mix strategies
7 Implementation and control

⬭ **Defining the Business Philosophy and Mission, and Corporate Objectives**

The strategic planning process starts by identifying the *firm's mission* or purpose for its existence and hence the scope of the business. A mission statement needs to identify the products and services to be offered and the customers to be served. It also needs to indicate how the resources and capabilities of the firm will be used to create customer satisfaction and how the firm intends to compete in its chosen markets. An example of a mission statement is that of Sainsbury's (see Figure 5.2), whose mission for its supermarkets business is '*to be the UK's first choice for food, delivering products of outstanding quality and great service at a competitive cost through working "faster", simpler and together*' (J. Sainsbury Plc *Annual Report*, 2001, p. 4).

The mission also indicates the firm's philosophy for the way it intends to conduct its business. For instance, Tesco's mission is to 'create value for customers to earn their lifetime loyalty'. This is supported by Tesco's core values of 'No-one tries harder' and to 'treat people, how we like to be treated'. This reflects not only the way it intends to treat its customers, but also how it treats its employees and what it expects from them in return.

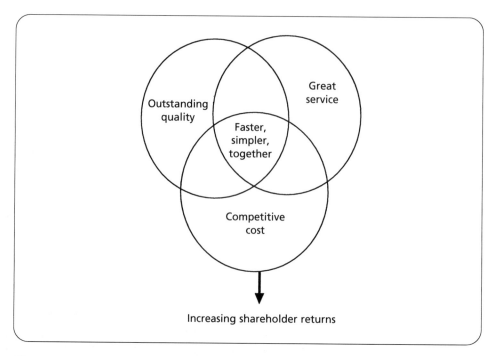

Figure 5.2 Sainsbury's mission for its supermarkets

● Situation Analysis

The purpose of situation analysis (also referred to as situation audit) is to determine where the organization is at present and to forecast where it will be if existing strategies are pursued. The difference between the forecast and where the firm is likely to be if the current strategy is pursued is called the planning or strategic gap. The purpose of strategic management is to bridge this gap. Situational analysis can be divided into two broad components, namely external (or environmental) analysis and internal analysis. The purpose of external analysis is to identify opportunities and threats in the environment, and that of internal analysis to identify the key strengths and weaknesses of the organization.

External analysis

The major components of external analysis are the *macroenvironment* and the *task environment*. The macroenvironment consists of economic, political and legal, sociocultural and technological forces that affect all retailers and over which they have very little control. The task environment, on the other hand, can be influenced directly by a retailer's own strategies and includes competitors, suppliers and customers.

The macroenvironment

Changes in the economic environment affect the ability and willingness of consumers to purchase goods and services and the costs of doing business for retailers. Important indicators of the economic conditions include rate of economic growth, rates of inflation, the unemployment rate, changes in incomes, changes in corporate and personal debt, interest rates, and changes in consumer expenditure patterns.

Legal changes and changes in governmental policies can also increase or decrease the attractiveness of a market. For instance, changes in planning regulations can affect the attractiveness of the locations that are available to retailers. Competition policy, for example, can determine whether acquisition can be used in pursuit of a growth strategy. In the 15 European Community countries, retailers are affected not only by national legislation but also by EU legislation. For instance, the recent launch of the euro has meant that all EU countries excluding the UK, Sweden and Denmark have had to switch to trading in euros instead of their national currencies. The switch has meant that there is transparency of prices across the EU and has led to increasing cross-border shopping. Even in the UK, Marks and Spencer and some other large retailers have decided to convert their tills to accept euros (particularly in large cities such as London) in order to make shopping easier (and cheaper) for European tourists.

Sociocultural changes, for example in demographics, lifestyles, attitudes and personal values, can also create threats and opportunities for retailers. For instance, the increasing emphasis on health and physical fitness has resulted in the growth of sports retailers and growth in sports fashion merchandise generally. Retailers also need to develop strategies to accommodate demographic changes such as an ageing population and an increasing number of single-person households. Consumers are also increasingly taking an ethical stance on the way products are produced and sold and retailers need to respond appropriately to these concerns. Demographic changes can also impact on employment practices. For instance, in the UK the decline in numbers of those of school leaving age has led to the revision of employment practices of many retailers to draw from a wider pool of the workforce.

Technological changes and innovations can create new retail markets, reduce the cost of doing business, improve the shopping process, and create new and more efficient ways of managing retail businesses. Changes in technology can make retailers vulnerable to competition from new retailers, and existing competitors may be willing and able to exploit the new technology faster than them. In the past 20 years, information technology has transformed all aspects of retailing beyond recognition. The impact of IT can be seen in the now ubiquitous use of EPOS and EFTPOS terminals, loyalty cards improving service for shoppers in store, to EDI (electronic data interchange) and improved communication between suppliers and retailers. The internet is the latest IT innovation to transform retailing in all its aspects creating new retailing channels, competitors, and new ways of cooperating and communicating with suppliers (see Chapter 8 for an extensive discussion on the application of IT in retailing).

The task environment

The task (or operating) environment has direct impact on the retailer but, unlike the macroenvironment, can also be influenced by the retailer's own strategies. Major factors in the task environment include competitors, suppliers and customers.

Competitive factors and the influence of suppliers have been discussed at length in the Chapter 3, therefore we concentrate here on market development and customer-related factors. Large markets are attractive to large retailers because they are more likely to generate the sales required to cover the large capital investments and the profitability required by these organizations. Growing markets are also more attractive than mature markets because competition is less intense and profitability is higher in growing markets. Hence, the strategies pursed by retailers need to be appropriate to the level of market development.

Many retail markets are seasonal, which requires accurate sales forecasting to ensure that the most is made of the sales opportunities and that resources are used efficiently. For instance, fashion retailing is highly seasonal and requires an accurate knowledge of the latest fashion trends to ensure that the merchandise sells and that there are no stockouts. Retailers can influence customers through their marketing strategies, but the ability to react quickly to changes in customer needs and competitors' marketing strategies is essential for survival in fast-moving retailing markets.

Internal analysis

The purpose of internal analysis (or an internal audit) is to assess the strategic capabilities of the retailer by examining the quality and quantity of resources available, how effectively they are used and the extent to which they are unique and difficult to imitate by competitors. Resources can be grouped into physical assets, human resources, financial resources, and intangible resources. Intangible resources include goodwill embodied in the retailer's own brands and the retailer's image.

The following is an illustration of the type of questions that should be asked when conducting an internal audit of resources:

- *Finance.* What is the cash flow from existing activities? What is the ability of company to raise debt or equity financing? This will depend upon the financial standing of the company and the current levels of the debt-to-equity ratio (or gearing). What is the quality of financial management within the company?
- *Merchandising.* How good are the knowledge and skills of buyers? How good is the company's relationship with its suppliers? How successful is the company at developing and managing own brands?
- *Marketing.* What is the marketing capability within the company? To what extent is the firm market-oriented. How good is the marketing research function? How good is the competitor intelligence system? How effective is marketing at generating new custom? How effective is marketing at maintaining customer loyalty?
- *Management capabilities.* What is the capability of the company's management? Are the capabilities and experience of the top management team adequate? What are the capabilities of middle management? Is there sufficient depth? Is the management committed?
- *Store management.* What are the capabilities of the store managers? What is the quality of sales assistants? Are the non-management-grade employees adequately trained and motivated? Is the staff turnover rate amongst employees at acceptable levels?
- *Operations.* What is the overhead cost structure? What are the capabilities of the logistics/distribution system at delivering merchandise to stores? How good are the information systems? How effective are stock-control systems? How good are the loss-prevention systems?

The effectiveness with which resources are used is often assessed by comparing present performance with historical performance, or with the industry norm. A problem with historical analysis is that the focus of analysis is internal and does not take into account performance of competitors. This is rectified by comparison with industry norms. However, problems with industry analysis include lack of comparative information as well the fact that the industry as a whole could be performing poorly. For this reason there is increasingly a search for best practice and benchmarking relative to best practice. Best practice seeks to assess performance against 'best-in-class' performance wherever it is found, and not merely in the sector in which the retailer operates.

Differences in performance between retailers are usually due to more than just differences in resources deployed. Difference in performance also results from the way the resources are deployed to create competences within the organization. Certain competences created by the organization will be such that they enable the retailer to be more efficient than its competitors or provide its customers with better value. These core competences need to be difficult to emulate in order to provide long-term advantage.

⬤ **Competitive Advantage and Competitive Strategies**

In order to survive over the long term, retailers need to build sustainable competitive advantage (SCA) over their rivals in the market. SCA can be built in many ways and in essence any activity that a retailer undertakes can form the basis of competitive advantage. However, this competitive advantage must be such that it allows the retailer to fulfil customer's needs significantly better than its competitors and be sustainable over the long term (that is, difficult for competitors to emulate). Major methods of creating SCA include convenient locations, building customer loyalty, building close relationships with suppliers, efficient logistics and supply-chain management, good information systems (including customer database management), exclusive merchandise (including own brands), buying economies of scale, superior customer service, and a knowledgeable and motivated sales force.

SCA is most likely to be achieved through multiple approaches rather than any single approach. It is the specific combination of skills and competencies of the organization that gives a retailer its specific advantage in the market. Essentially, however, there are two basic competitive strategies – differentiation and low cost. If these strategies are combined with the competitive scope of the firm (the width of the market targeted), this produces three generic strategies – namely, cost leadership, differentiation and focus. The focus strategy can be further subdivided into differentiation focus and cost-focus strategies. Each of the strategies requires specific skills, resources, and business and organizational systems. A differentiation strategy, for instance, requires strong marketing capabilities, a reputation for quality, and innovative products. This can take the form of exclusive or fashionable product ranges, convenient locations, store design and atmospherics, and high levels of service. Cost leadership requires that all business systems and strategies are designed to control costs – requiring, close supervision of labour, efficient store operation, low-cost distribution systems and strong buying. A focus strategy attempts to achieve differentiation or low costs but is directed at a particular market segment (see Figure 5.3).

Porter (1980) suggests that a firm must either pursue a differentiation or low-cost strategy; it cannot pursue both or it will find itself 'stuck in the middle' and suffer from below-average profitability. However, evidence suggests that firms following a hybrid strategy may be more profitable in the long run than those following pure differentiation or low-cost strategies. The reason for this appears to be the fact that firms following hybrid strategies are better able to cope with changes in the business environment. Furthermore, in an environment in which customers want good value products without

Competitive scope	**Competitive advantage:** Lower cost	Differentiation
Broad target (assortment)	*Cost leadership* Wal-Mart Currys	*Differentiation* Harrods Marks and Spencer
Narrow target (assortment)	*Cost-focus* Aldi	*Differentiation focus* Body Shop Benetton

Figure 5.3 Generic competitive strategies

Source: Based on Porter (1980), *Competitive Strategy: Techniques for Analyzing Industries and Competitors* (New York and London: The Free Press).

having to pay high prices for them, even retailers known for their differentiated offer cannot afford to ignore the cost side of the business. Also, some firms deliberately attempt to position themselves in the 'middle'. For instance, Sainsbury's have used the advertising message 'Making life taste better, for less'. Previously, Sainsbury's had also used the slogan 'Good food costs less at Sainsbury's'. Sainsbury's advertising is clearly designed to indicate that high-quality products do not necessarily mean high prices.

The value chain and competitive strategies

The idea of a competitive strategy suggests that specific systems, or a value chain, need to be set up to achieve particular competitive objectives. A value chain consists of a set of activities ranging from design, production, marketing, distribution and support of the product that a firm markets (see Figure 5.4). The activities in the value chain can be divided into what are called primary activities (operational activities) and support activities (or corporate functional activities). In retailing the primary activities consist of logistics and supply-chain management, merchandising, marketing, store operations, and service. The support activities consist of human-resource management, technology, buying, and property management. It is the specific interrelationships between primary and support activities and the ways in which they are performed that gives the firm its particular competitive advantage in the marketplace. Implementation of specific strategies requires consistency between the various elements of the value chain. For example a low-cost strategy would require that all elements of the value chain emphasize the reduction of costs.

Vignette 5.1

IKEA: high quality at low prices

The global furniture retailer IKEA's stated business mission is to offer a wide range of home furnishings with good design and function at prices so low that as many people as possible will be able to afford them. IKEA'S offer can be summed up as 'affordable solutions for better living'. In other words, it offers differentiated products at low cost. IKEA's products are easily recognizable by their high-quality functional Scandinavian design. Consistency and clarity of design is achieved by centralizing the design function at its HQ in Älmhult, Sweden. Products are also designed to be low-cost and easy to manufacture.

Prices and costs are kept low in a number of ways but mainly by producing furniture that can be flat-packed and transported and assembled by the customer at home. Costs are also kept low by working closely with manufacturers to reduce costs, and using global sourcing and bulk buying to purchase raw materials at the best prices. The product range of around 10,000 SKUs (stock keeping units – product lines), is kept the same around the world which helps IKEA to benefit from huge economies of scale. This is supported by an efficient supply chain that provides an effective system for ordering from its suppliers and integrating them with the stores. This has been accomplished by setting up a network of 14 warehouses in strategic locations around the world, which has helped to reduce logistical costs, and minimized inventory holding costs.

Store location and operation are areas of further major cost savings. IKEA stores are located in out-of-town locations and provide little service in comparison with traditional furniture stores (except for a free supervised playroom for children). However, by use of coordinated displays (where products are displayed in room-like settings), product information on sales tags, and a comprehensive product catalogue, customers are assisted in making their purchasing decisions. Adjacent to display areas is a warehouse or self-serve hall where customers collect the merchandise themselves. The large store format (stores in the UK range from 170,000 sq ft to 300,000 sq ft) with a combined warehouse allows direct delivery to the store and avoids the need for centralized warehousing, enabling further efficiencies to be gained. The success of IKEA's business formula is evident in the fact that it has 175 stores in 31 countries and generated sales of 11 billion euros in 2003.

Source: Norman and Ramirez (1993), 'From Value Chain to Value Constellation: Designing Interactive Strategy', *Harvard Business Review*, vol. 71, no. 4, pp. 65–77. IKEA website http://www.ikea.com.

Identification and Evaluation of Strategic Opportunities

Having conducted internal and external analyses, the retailer should be able to identify its key strengths and weaknesses and the major opportunities and threats that it faces. This is often termed SWOT analysis – Strengths, Weaknesses, Opportunities and Threats. It is also sometimes referred as TOWS analysis emphasizing that analysis of the external environment (threats and opportunities) should take place before internal analysis (strengths and weaknesses). Ranking of the issues in terms of importance helps to provide a focus for the strategic issues upon which the retailer should focus on.

Firm infrastructure					
Human resources	Training	Quality training	Marketing research training	Sales assistant, customer service training	Customer service training
Technology/ systems	Handling and sorting, computerised warehousing	Feedback/ control	Marketing information generation & distribution	Feedback/ control systems	Customer service support systems
Buying	Supply chain management	Buying systems, buying cycle management	Supporting marketing objectives	Budget control	
Property management	Warehouse location	Store design, store atmospherics		Store location	
	Central warehousing Third party logistics management	Product range Product mix	Retail branding Advertising, sales promotions Returns policy guarantees	Presentation Stock management, Check-out service, Financial services	Complaints management, Returns handling, Repairs/service agreement management
	Logistics/ distribution	**Merchandising**	**Marketing**	**Store operations**	**After sales service**

> **Margin**

Figure 5.4 Value chain for retailers

Source: Based on McGee (1987), 'Retailer Strategies in the UK' in Johnson (ed.), *Business Strategy and Retailing* (Chichester: John Wiley) pp. 89–106.

After conducting the situation analysis the retailer needs to decide on the strategic direction for the organization. The main strategies available are growth, consolidation and harvesting. For example, retailers in the mature or declining phase of the life-cycle need to consider productivity improvements or even withdrawal from the market. In such a situation major injections of capital are difficult to justify; instead, the focus is on making as much profit as possible from the venture.

Productivity strategies aim to improve earnings and increase the efficiency of current resources through cost reductions, higher turnover and margins through an improved assortment and higher prices. Strategies for improving efficiency include increasing inventory turnover by utilizing store space more effectively, reducing costs of labour, credit, logistics and other operating costs.

Consolidation means making specific changes in the way the company operates, although the merchandise assortment and the customers remain the same. It does not, however, mean doing nothing. In a growth market, the retailer may seek to maintain its market share as the market grows; a failure to do so may mean that it does not benefit from economies of scale to the same extent as its competitors and thus make it uncompetitive. Recovering market share in the mature market is extremely difficult. In mature markets retailers are likely to consolidate their position by increasing emphasis on building customer loyalty, improving service quality, increasing marketing activity and/or increasing emphasis on productivity improvements.

● Strategies for Growth

There are four main growth strategies that are available to retailers, namely market penetration, market development, assortment/format development and diversification. This is illustrated by the matrix in Figure 5.5 which suggests that growth can come from either existing or new customer segments using either the existing merchandise assortment or a newly developed assortment package.

Market penetration involves targeting existing customers with the existing retail assortment/range of products, and increasing market share by attracting a larger proportion of the total sales generated within the trading areas of existing stores. This can be achieved either by getting existing customers to visit the store more often, or buying more on each trip, or attracting customers from competitors. Market penetration involves increasing retail marketing activities including:

- Improved visual merchandising to increase impulse buys
- Store extensions/revamps

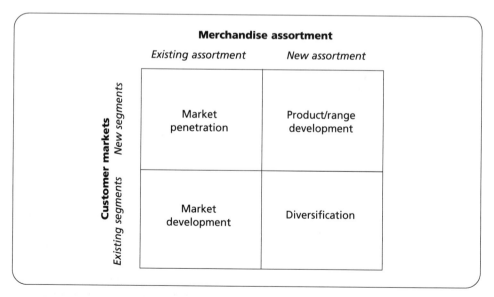

Figure 5.5 An assortment–market growth matrix

Source: Based on Ansoff (1965) and Kristenson (1983).

- Increasing customer loyalty
- Price reductions
- Increasing promotions
- Increasing convenience, for example by longer opening hours

Market penetration strategies are most appropriate where the target market is still growing. In mature markets, consolidation via productivity gains may play a more important role. Market penetration strategies are most likely to succeed when they are based on the retailer's strengths that its competitors cannot match. For instance, price reductions can be easily copied by competitors and are unlikely to succeed in the long run unless they are based on low cost structures.

Market Development involves targeting new market segments using the existing merchandise assortment. This can take the form of either geographic expansion within the domestic environment, or targeting segments of the market not previously targeted by the retailer. Targeting new segments inevitably involves some repositioning of the retail offer in order to appeal to the new segments. It involves the use of more capital and greater risk than the market penetration strategy.

Product/assortment development involves increasing sales from existing target markets by developing new products/service mixes to cater for the wider needs of customers. This can take the form of old lines being replaced by new ones, or the addition of new product lines and items, or both. This strategy has been used very effectively by the large grocery retailers who have added numerous non-food lines to their stores including stationery, books, CDs, clothes and electrical goods, amongst others.

Diversification involves targeting new markets with new products/retail formats. Diversification can be either related or unrelated to the current business. Related diversification involves undertaking activities that share some similarity with current business processes, marketing or technologies. The similarities might, for instance, involve using the same logistics/distribution system, or information systems. The Arcadia Group, for example, has developed a diversified set of stores focusing at various segments of men's and women's fashion. The stores include Burtons, Topman, Wallis, Miss Selfridge, Evans, Topshop and Dorothy Perkins. The group in essence constitutes a set of branded stores.

Vertical Integration or the undertaking of activities further up the distribution chain, such as wholesaling or manufacturing, is a form of diversification as both activities involve different operational skills and competencies compared with retailing. Examples of backward integration include retailers such as Benetton and IKEA, both of whom manufacture as well as retail their products.

Unrelated diversifications have no commonality with the existing retail business. The ISP (internet service provider) operation set up under the Freeserve brand name was an unrelated diversification by the UK electrical retailer, Dixons. Similarly, Tesco and Sainsbury's have diversified into banking.

Range extension, market extension and internationalization

A more realistic view of product/assortment development and market development suggests that retailers do not move from current to new market segments in one step, nor do they move from existing merchandise assortments to new assortments in one leap. Such strategies would involve considerable risk. An intermediate strategy is to adapt current merchandise assortments and to extend market coverage by targeting closely related segments before targeting more difficult market segments and segments unrelated to the current ones. For instance, domestic geographical expansion would precede international expansion; this is illustrated in Figure 5.6.

Figure 5.6 suggests that in addition to market penetration, market development, product/range development and diversification a further three growth strategies are available to retailers. These are range extension, market extension and internationalization. Range extension involves the addition of some new lines not previously offered by the retailer. For instance, a clothes retailer may add shoes to its current lines, aimed at existing customers as a complementary purchase to clothes. It may also start offering own-branded products to its customers. Again, the own-branded products would offer more choice to customers without changing the overall merchandise offer.

Market extension involves development of related market segments with a modified but related product offer. Hence, market extension is more than just

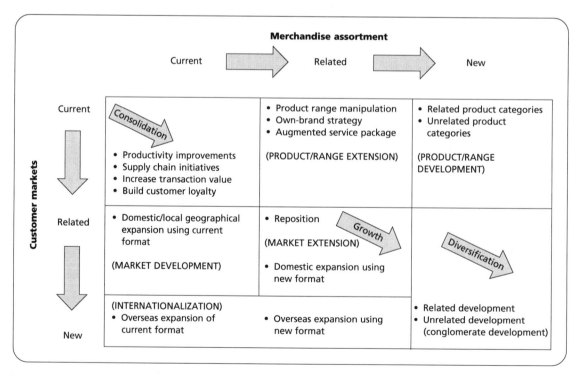

Figure 5.6 Retail strategy – merchandise assortment/market options

Sources: Adapted from Knee and Walter (1985), and Omura (1986).

geographical expansion of the retail network An example is the development of convenience store formats by large supermarkets in the UK – for example Tesco's Express and Sainsbury's Local formats. In both cases the stores are smaller, sell a more focused set of lines aimed at the convenience shopper, and are located in more convenient high-street locations or petrol forecourts for added convenience.

The introduction of the internationalization strategy allows us to distinguish market development in domestic markets from market development in foreign markets. This is necessary because international activities are much more risky than domestic activities because the retailing environment is very different to the domestic one.

Vignette 5.2

Growth strategy at NEXT

The first NEXT store opened in February 1982 with an exclusive coordinated collection of stylish clothes, shoes and accessories for women. By the end of July 1982 there were 70 shops. This was followed by collections for men (1984), NEXT Interiors (1985) and childrenswear (1987).

NEXT Directory, the mail-order catalogue shopping division was launched in 1988 with 350 pages. The new larger format now has over 800 pages. Online shopping was introduced in 1999 and now the entire catalogue is available on the internet – a first in home shopping in the UK. In September 2001 NEXT launched its own online flower retail service through http://www.nextflowers.co.uk. The site is also accessible from the NEXT Directory website. With sales of around £500 million, NEXT Directory now accounts for around a quarter of the company's total turnover.

At the start of 2003, NEXT was trading from over 330 stores in the UK and Eire and 49 stores overseas. In recent years NEXT has sought to achieve growth through the development of larger stores and expansion of product ranges particularly in the home furnishings area. Since 2001, a number of larger format stores have opened in the UK, including Bluewater Park, Middlesbrough, Bromley, Norwich, Belfast and Liverpool. The largest NEXT store to date opened in Cardiff in July 2002. New store locations have tended to be in out-of-town retail parks. At present NEXT has Interiors departments in only 94 of its stores, and the development of the larger stores are seen as opportunity to increase its share of the home furnishings market.

Sources: Various NEXT Annual Reports and the NEXT Plc website http://www.next.co.uk

Evaluating Alternative Retailing Strategies

Having delineated the strategic options available, the retailer needs to decide on specific strategic action. This requires the evaluation of the strategies in terms of how they help to bridge the strategic gap, profitability, risk and the ability of the organization to undertake the particular strategy. One useful method of doing this is to compare the attractiveness of the market opportunities with the possible competitive advantages of the retailer. The technique suggests that the highest amount of resources should be invested in opportunities where the retailer has the strongest competitive advantage. For instance, a retailer targeting a new segment would evaluate the attractiveness of market opportunity in terms of:

● Market size.
● Market growth rate.
● Degree of competition and competitive structure.
● Profitability of the segment.
● Technology requirements.
● Legal and regulatory issues.
● Human-resource requirements.
● Environmental issues.

This information must be compared with the retailer's strengths relative to that of competition on factors such as:

● Current market share.
● Merchandising skills.
● Buying strength.
● Supply-chain management and supplier relations.
● New product development.
● Own-label reputation.
● Financial resources.
● Salesforce.
● Managerial competence.
● Fit with current retailer image in terms of breadth and depth of product lines, quality and reliability, customer service.

To operationalize the technique the retailer rates each product area (or SBU) on each of the factors. The ratings are then combined into indices of market attractiveness and retailer strength and plotted on a two-dimensional matrix. Each dimension is usually divided into three categories – high, medium and low. The position of the product reflects its attractiveness and suggests a course of action. For instance, where the market attractiveness and business position are strong then the retailer should invest aggressively and grow the opportunity. Where the market attractiveness and business position is weak, the recommended strategy is either to harvest or divest unless the product category is to be vital to the overall success of the business. In the intermediate situation, where the opportunities are moderately strong on both dimensions, or moderately strong on one and weak on the other, firms are recommended to invest selectively.

● ## Development of Marketing and Positioning Strategies

By this stage the retailer has set general objectives and analysed a number of opportunities and decided on a specific direction for the organization and the opportunities it wishes to take advantage of. For each of the opportunities chosen the retailer now needs to set specific objectives and allocate resources to achieve the objectives. In order to achieve the set objectives, marketing strategies have to be devised. These are normally developed for specific market segments rather than the market as a whole, as this makes more effective use of resources. After selecting the target markets a positioning strategy must be developed.

Retail positioning

A positioning strategy is a plan of action for how the retailer will compete in the targeted markets and how it will differentiate itself from competitors in those markets. Retail positioning is the process of creating and maintaining a distinctive and valued image of the retailer in the target customer's mind relative to its competitors. This emphazises the fact that positioning is a relative concept and understanding consumers' perceptions is the key to effective positioning in the market. Positioning can be a deliberate attempt to differentiate from the rest of the market (for instance Harrods), or an attempt to be as close as possible to the average shopper's view of the attributes of an ideal retailer in a particular market segment.

Walters (1989) suggests that positioning should be either merchandise or service-led. Wortzel (1987) suggests that another basis for positioning strategies is to distinguish between symbolic and functional merchandise, and whether it attracts high or low margins. The reason here is that people are motivated to buy the two categories and shop for them in different ways. Wortzel suggests three main positioning strategies, namely product differentiation, service and personality augmentation, and price leadership.

- *Product differentiation* is achieved through unique or exclusive products or brands, own-branded products, and unusually broad or deep merchandise assortments.
- *Service and personality augmentation* can be achieved in many different ways, including high levels of personal service, convenient locations, long opening hours, generous returns policy, home delivery and so forth.
- *Price leadership* can be established through offering low or discounted pricing, and good value or price promotions on key items.

Positioning is not a once-and-for-all decision. Because of changes in the market (consumers and the competitors) the positioning may need to be adjusted. Repositioning needs to be considered where there is a big discrepancy between consumers' perceptions and management perceptions. This is usually reflected in poor performance and declining market share. Repositioning can also be used to target a new set of customers.

The retail mix

The retail marketing and positioning strategy is put into effect by the retail mix – the set of controllable variables that the retailer can use to satisfy customers' needs and to influence their buying behaviour and compete effectively in the market. To implement a specific retailing strategy, managers must decide the best combination of retail-mix variables and coordinate the activities of the different elements of the mix such as:

● Merchandise assortment.
● Location.
● Price.
● Visual merchandising.
● Store atmosphere.
● Customer service.
● Advertising.
● Promotions.
● Personal selling.

Walters (1989) suggests that positioning is the result of interaction between the four main areas of the retailing marketing mix; namely, trading style/format strategy, merchandise strategy, customer service, and customer communications strategy.

● Implementation and Control

Without effective implementation, strategies are nothing. Effective implementation requires that appropriate resources be allocated to required tasks, which requires budgeting in respect of specific elements of the retailing mix, personnel and so forth. Effective implementation also requires scheduling and coordination of retailing activities. It requires the translation of retailing strategies into tactics. Functional strategies lead to the establishment of long-term objectives that must be translated into day-to-day operational decisions. For instance, when to advertise, what media to use, and the length of promotion campaigns are tactical decisions influenced by the competitive environment and the communication strategy.

The implementation of new retailing strategies inevitably requires changes in working methods and responsibilities which can lead to resistance from employees, and organizations need to develop strategies to reduce this resistance to a minimum and to actively sell the new strategies to their employees.

In order to assess how effectively strategies are being implemented and how far the strategic objectives are being achieved, control procedures need to be established to determine whether the objectives set are being achieved in the specified time periods. Such procedures allow unsatisfactory performance to be identified at an early stage, and remedial action or the reevaluation of retailing strategies and objectives to be instigated (see Chapter 6 for further discussion).

● Emergent Strategy versus Planned Strategy

The discussion of the strategic management process above has emphasized a systematic top-down planning approach that suggests that strategy formulation precedes strategy implementation. This suggests that organizations systematically create strategies that they pursue, but some strategy writers reject this view and argue that rather than strategies being deliberately created by organizations, strategies can emerge without formal planning. Mintzberg (1990), for instance, is particularly critical of the rational planning approach to strategic management. He argues that strategies can emerge without the explicit intention of managers as a result of the cumulative effect of operational, day-to-day decision-making, and only in retrospect is the strategy identified from the pattern of actions taken. In practice, it is more than likely that the realized strategies are some combination of planned and emergent (or unplanned) strategies. However, the planning approach has the advantage that it suggests that senior retail mangers should be proactive in formulating retailing strategies rather than waiting for strategies to emerge. In the fast-moving retailing environment, proactive strategic management is indispensable for long-term survival.

Summary

This chapter has explained the nature of retail strategy and the strategic management planning process. In broad terms, strategy determines the long-term direction and scope of the organization. Developing retailing strategy involves defining the company's mission, setting objectives, situation analysis, identifying and evaluating strategic opportunities, developing marketing strategies to take advantage of the opportunities, developing a retail mix to meet customers needs and compete effectively in the market, and effective implementation and control. Situation analysis or (SWOT analysis) identifies the strengths, weaknesses, opportunities and threats facing the organization. It determines where the organization is at present and where it will be if it continues with its current strategies. The difference between where it wants to be and where it is forecast to be is the strategic gap. The chapter has also discussed the generic strategies (differentiation, cost leadership and focus) available to retailers. The concept of the value chain as an essential prerequisite for implementing competitive strategies has also been discussed. Strategies available to the retailer to close the strategic gap include growth, consolidation and harvesting, and framework for analysing the major growth strategies has been presented. Those discussed include market penetration, market development, product/assortment development, diversification, range extension, market extension and internationalization. For each of the opportunities selected marketing strategies have to be devised to target specific markets and to position the retail offer relative to the competition. The retail marketing strategies are implemented using a suitable combination of the retail-mix variables. Strategic analysis and strategy formulation can be undermined by poor implementation, and hence it is essential that mechanisms are in place to ensure effective implementation and control so that timely remedial action can be taken, if necessary.

Questions

1 Explain the distinction between corporate strategy, business-unit strategy and functional strategy.
2 What is meant by 'strategic gap'?
3 What are the major growth strategies available to a retailer? Give examples of retailers that have used each of the strategies.
4 Explain the value-chain concept using a major fashion retailer as an example.
5 How far do you agree that 'stuck in the middle' is not viable as a long-term competitive strategy?
6 Explain what is meant by the retail mix and how it can be used for retail positioning purposes.

References and Further Reading

Ansoff, H. I. (1965) *Corporate Strategy* (New York: McGraw-Hill).

Johnson, G. and Scholes, K. (1997) *Exploring Corporate Strategy: Text and Cases*, 4th edn (London: Prentice Hall).

Knee, D. and Walters, D. (1985) *Strategy in Retailing: Theory and Application* (Oxford: Philip Allan).

Kristenson, L. (1983) 'Strategic planning in Retailing', *European Journal of Marketing*, vol. 17, no. 2, pp. 43–59.

McGee, J. (1987) 'Retailer Strategies in the UK', in G. Johnson (ed.), *Business Strategy and Retailing* (Chichester: John Wiley and Son), pp. 89–106.

Mintzberg, H. (1990) 'The Design School: Reconsidering the Basic Premises of Strategic Management', *Strategic Management Journal*, vol. 11, no. 6, pp. 171–95.

Norman, R. and Ramirez, R. (1993) 'From Value Chain to Value Constellation: Designing Interactive Strategy', *Harvard Business Review*, vol. 71, no. 4, pp. 65–77.

Omura, G. S. (1986) 'Developing Retailing Strategy', *International Journal of Retailing*, vol. 1, no. 3, pp. 17–32.

Porter, M. E. (1980) *Competitive Strategy: Techniques for Analyzing Industries and Competitors* (New York and London: The Free Press).

Porter, M. E. (1985) *Competitive Advantage: Creating and Sustaining Superior Performance* (New York and London: The Free Press).

Prahalad, C. K. and Hamel, G. (1990) 'The Core Competence of the Corporation', *Harvard Business Review*, May/June, pp. 79–91.

Robinson, T. M. and Clarke-Hill, C. M. (1990) 'Directional Growth by European Retailers', *International Journal of Retail and Distribution Management*, vol. 18, no. 5, pp. 3–14.

Walters, D. (1989) *Strategic Retailing Management – a Case Study Approach* (London: Prentice Hall).

Walters, D. and White, D. (1987) *Retail Marketing Management* (London: Palgrave Macmillan).

Wortzel, L. H. (1987) 'Retailing Strategies for Today's Mature Marketplace', *Journal of Business Strategy*, vol. 7, no. 4, pp. 45–56.

chapter six

Implementing Retail Strategy

Learning objectives

- To understand the structural organization of a retail business and how this supports the implementation of a retail strategy.
- To appreciate the responsibilities of the outlet manager within a multiple retail organization, and the key role that they play in the implementation of a strategy at the customer interface.
- To gain an overview of the various departments that are likely to be found in a centralized multiple retailer, and an appreciation of the functions that they perform within the business.
- To understand the concept of taking an integrated approach towards monitoring and controlling the strategic plan.

Introduction

In the previous chapter we looked at the way in which 'the retailer' should go about formulating retail strategy. Formulating a retail strategy is a planning process; it is about establishing where a company is going to go in the future and allocating resources in order to reach the company objectives within that plan. The strategic plan must find a balance between the risk associated with the goals pursued, and the resources deployed in the attainment of those goals. Implementation of the strategy requires an orchestration of human resources, financial resources and assets, which includes tangible ('bricks and mortar') assets like outlets, distribution centres, IT systems, head offices and stock, as well as intangible assets such as brand values, reputation and the image of the retailer.

Within a small retailer, the planning and operation of a retail strategy may be carried out by a single or small number of people who have broadly defined roles. However, as organizations get larger, tasks will be divided, so that the use of individuals' talents and experience can be maximized. This chapter considers the various ways in which tasks can be divided and how roles can be allocated so that the retail business runs as effectively as possible. It also explores how retailers go about introducing mechanisms for monitoring and controlling the activities of the various parts of the business, to ensure that the strategy is 'on track'.

● Managing a Retail Outlet

We have emphasized the need to be customer-focused in the formulation of a retail strategy, and it therefore makes sense to start at the customer interface when considering how a retail business might be managed in order to achieve the objectives it sets for the strategic plan. Whether a retailer uses a store or non-store format, the way customers are dealt with is a real priority in the management of any retail business. In Chapter 15 we consider all aspects of retail service, and it is those members of the business who are employed as 'sales advisers, sales associates, sales consultants or customer services operators' who take on the task of implementing the customer-service strategy. Whether the general level of personal service is low, for example within a supermarket, or more involved as in a speciality store, the contribution of service to the overall strategy is supported at the outlet level. It is also at this level where customers will make judgement of a retailer's strategy.

Customer-focused retailers will ensure that support is given to the teams of customer sales employees in order that they can concentrate on the task of maximizing sales. This support might come in the form of a sales supervisor who organizes the sales team to ensure that the availability of sales staff is matched to the rate of customer flow, and to provide advice on any problems team members may have. The supervisor is likely to be a more experienced sales employee, who is prepared to take on the extra responsibility of leading the team. In a small retailer, the supervisory role may be taken on by the store or outlet manager, as one of many tasks in a multifaceted role.

● The Outlet Manager

The main objective for the outlet manager is to meet the targets set for the successful running of that outlet. These targets are often instigated in the form of financial aims, based on sales turnover and/or profitability. However, other targets that could be set include the number of customers or the number of transactions. In addition, more specific targets such as the number of customers recruited for a store card, or sales of a particular type or brand of product, might be used during a marketing campaign.

The larger the store, the more likely it is for the responsibility of the store manager to increase, as numbers of staff and complexity of product range normally grow relative to store size. The diversity in a store manager's role will depend on the extent to which a central organization such as a head office or company headquarters takes on specific tasks, but the list below shows areas of responsibility that are common in the store manager's remit.

- ● *Managing staffing levels.* This includes the general management of sales personnel and support or auxiliary staff (cleaners, maintenance, financial clerks and so on). It includes scheduling, recruiting, developing and, if necessary, disciplining employees. According to Fraser and Zarkada-Fraser (2000), staffing in the retail industry is complex and problematic because of the need for flexibility (multiskilling) and the need to balance seasonal customer flow patterns with the availability of employees (both part-time and full-time).

- *Organizing the sales environment.* This involves implementing store layout plans, managing the allocation and replenishment of stock, and overseeing the implementation of visual merchandising (display) plans. A certain degree of interpretation of plans communicated from a central department may be necessary in the light of specific store characteristics. However, the outlet manager is ultimately responsible for the way the store appears to customers, and therefore supports the corporate image of the retailer.
- *Supporting marketing initiatives.* This means implementing the marketing tactics devised in order to pursue strategic marketing aims; for example, organization of point-of-sale display materials, allocating space to promoted items, overseeing price amendments, and raising awareness of marketing campaigns with the sales team.
- *Staff development.* It is the outlet manager's responsibility to ensure that the training needs of the outlet staff team are met, by using either in-house or external training provision and to identify potential candidates for promotion. Also, implementing the company's health and safety policies and providing induction training for new staff is part of this process.
- *Monitoring performance.* This involves analysing sales and profit reports – these might be orientated towards product performance (at department or item level), or towards the performance of members of the sales staff (employee productivity). The outlet manager needs to accommodate detailed knowledge about how the outlet is performing in order to identify any problem areas for further investigation.
- *Minimizing costs.* In order to maximize outlet profitability, the store manager needs to keep the costs of running the outlet as low as possible. This involves the elimination of waste, including overstaffing and the reduction of shrinkage (such as theft and damages). This aspect of a retail manager's job is especially important when a low-cost strategy is being pursued.
- *Forecasting and budgeting.* The outlet manager is best placed to predict future performance by estimating sales through the outlet, estimating future costs, and setting budgets. Agreeing forecasts with line managers (typically a regional retail operations manager, or a central retail operations department) and setting performance targets for the outlet based on forecasts are part of this process. They also need to provide feedback to and communicate with centralized departments, such as the buying department or human-resource management department regarding specific issues.
- *Team leadership.* The outlet manager has the responsibility for motivating a team of colleagues and reducing any resistance to change in working methods that may be required when new strategic directions are set. They may be involved in setting targets and will be responsible for reviewing and appraising of team members' activities in accordance with the strategic objectives of the organization.

In a large retail store, such as a multi-department superstore, a team of deputy managers and/or department managers will support the store manager. These subordinates will have partial store management responsibilities, and in this instance the amount of time the store manager spends collating information and liasing with the management team will increase and the tasks of managing staffing levels and organizing the sales environment will be delegated.

● The Centralized Retailer

The notion of a centralized retail structure was introduced in Chapter 2. In essence, any retailer that has more than one outlet, but carries out functions on behalf of the outlets collectively as opposed to individually, is operating a centralized structure (even though in terms of retail industry definitions a retailer is only termed a multiple retailer if there are 10 or more outlets). As a retail organization grows, the more specialized aspects of retail management tend to become the responsibility of individuals and then dedicated departments, which are often then transferred to a separate location. The benefits a retailer derives from centralization are essentially based on economies of scale and specialization. Many retail decisions that need to be made for one outlet need to be made for all outlets, and so a central body of employees becomes responsible for decision-making for all outlets.

Figure 6.1 illustrates the relationship between a retailer's central head office, the stores network, the distribution centre, the call centre and suppliers in terms of product flow and information flow. The majority of employees at the head office work in departments dedicated to a particular aspect of retail management. Effectively, they are the departments who carry out the first stages of the strategic plan, while the personnel located within the outlets continue the implementation at the customer interface. Most central retail organizations will include the following departments:

- Buying and merchandising (product/category management).
- Marketing (may be separated into corporate marketing and store marketing).
- Logistics (distribution) – concerned with deliveries to store and also deliveries from suppliers.
- Human-resource management (personnel).
- Finance.
- Property.
- Non-store operations.
- International operations.

An explanation of the operational responsibilities of each of these follows.

● Buying and Merchandising (Product/Category Management)

The section of the central organization concerned with bringing the right products into the retail organization in order to satisfy the needs and desires

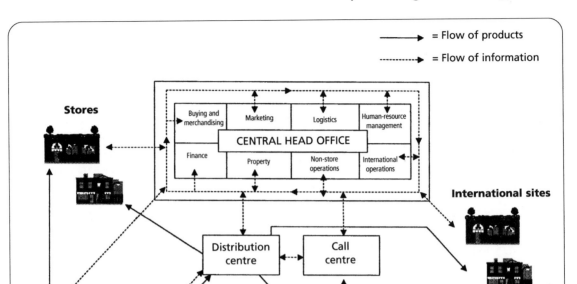

Figure 6.1 An international multichannel retailer

of customers (often referred to as the buying office) is usually the largest section of a central organization in terms of number of employees. Teams of highly specialized experts with regard to particular products and their supply markets are responsible for allocating large sums of the retailer's money to products with the view to gaining an acceptable profit margin on those products when sold, which will be the life-blood of the organization. Many of today's large multiples have been built on the back of talented 'traders' who developed a knack of buying the right thing and being able to sell it on well to consumers. Both Tesco and Marks and Spencer, for example, are retail empires founded by market traders. However, contemporary retail product management is a highly analytical task, involving the management of the supply base in response to changes in consumer demand. A more detailed discussion of the buying and merchandising function can be found in Chapter 11.

● Marketing

Although retailers are in essence carrying out one of the key functions of a marketing mix by providing the 'place' where consumers can locate products, successful retailers are often highly marketing-orientated organizations in their own right. A retailer may have marketing objectives that complement those of the producer or supplier, but they may have others that are of no concern to, and may even conflict with those of, suppliers. For example, when Sainsbury developed and marketed their own-brand drink, Classic Cola, this was not at all in the interest of Coco-Cola or Pepsi and it created conflict between the retailer and their manufacturer brand suppliers. However, an advertisement that communicates the opening of a new store is relevant to all suppliers to that retailer as this represents one more channel of distribution for their product. Co-operative marketing, where suppliers and retailers fund and develop a marketing campaign together, is likely to result in more effective campaigns as the two companies pool their expertise for mutual benefit.

Marketing has such a wide remit with regard to the implementation of a retailer's strategy that a number of more specialized departments may make up the marketing section. In particular, it makes sense to divide marketing communications into those that are corporate in nature (such as improving the overall image of the store, changing the retailer's market positioning, or reinforcing the retail brand values), and those that are more specific in nature (such as store opening information, or product/price offers). Another way of organizing for retail marketing communications is to have one section devoted to the marketing needs of the individual outlets (store marketing), and another that deals with communications that are storewide in nature. The advantage of this approach is that the relationship between the central marketing organization and marketing initiatives that use local marketing service providers (such as the local press) is strengthened. In some retail organizations the individual outlets are responsible for their own local marketing. The drawback with this approach concerns control and consistency of the message across the retail organization.

Historically, it has been traditional for marketing departments and buying departments to operate separately within the central organization. Often the buying department had little or no responsibility for a product once initial orders had been placed. However, new buying approaches like category management (see Chapter 11) force the two functions together in order to achieve product-orientated objectives. Within the category, product developments and introductions have to be managed alongside established products and promotions so that the performance of the entire range is maximized. The buyer or product manager must therefore use marketing as a way of supporting the objectives set for the product category and the individual product items within it.

⬤ Logistics (Distribution)

The logistics department is responsible for providing stock service to the retail outlet or, in the case of direct retailing, to the customer. The department manages arrangements for deliveries from suppliers through what is called the retail supply chain (involving transportation, warehousing and sorting) to the customer. The logistics department liases closely with both the buying and merchandising and the marketing departments to ensure that supply-chain operations support the product and marketing strategy of the organization. In some retail organizations, the departments are merged, for example in the case of fresh produce, because the logistics of food supply are so vital to the success of the product offer. A more detailed discussion of the contribution that logistics makes to the running of a retail business can be found in Chapter 7.

● Human-Resource Management

Personnel are essential to a retail organization, even in the virtual shopping world (at least at the time of writing!). Given the complexity of the consumer and the consumer decision-making process (see Chapter 4), only other people can come close to fully understanding needs and desires of customers, which can involve irrational, non-economically-driven and emotional decision influences. Even though information systems provide a plethora of data on sales, that data is only useful when interpreted by the retail buyer or sales consultant and used to match customer needs and desires to product solutions. In addition, retailers provide a social arena; the local post office, for example, may provide a focus for exchange of information in a community and indeed might provide a therapeutic service for the off-loading of a moan or piece of gossip! Personnel employed for the many tasks within a retail business have to be 'people'-orientated. No matter what powers of analysis an individual may have, unless they have the personal communication skills to convince others of their views, then the retail organization will be unable to benefit.

Human-resource management may be decentralized or controlled by head office, but it makes sense to recruit for the outlets locally, operating within strict company guidelines. For example, wages for retail staff may vary across the country; unless a retailer is offering a competitive rewards package, they will not be able to recruit the best calibre staff (see Vignette 6.1). Like the marketing department, the human-resource department may be divided up with one section dealing with managerial and head office personnel, whilst another oversees the management of the sales teams within the outlets. Many large multiple retailers operate a system of regional human-resource managers who monitor staffing levels and offer support and advice to store management on human-resource issues. Where a retail outlet is large and employs a greater number of sales staff, then a personnel manager may be dedicated to and based at that outlet.

Career paths

In recent years the retail industry has offered increasingly dynamic and lucrative careers. In a fast-moving and competitive business environment, only high-quality management can survive. Retail outlets are getting bigger, and with increased space the diversity of product offered has also expanded, and so the responsibility placed with store managers has also increased in size and complexity. In addition, opportunities in specialist departments such as buying, merchandising, marketing and logistics have also grown as retailers have become more sophisticated in their operations and approaches

Vignette 6.1

The problems of high employment

Whilst politicians view high employment figures enthusiastically, the same cannot necessarily be said for retailers. A low rate of unemployment, the competitive retail arena and higher customer expectations of service, all put pressure on the retailer at the customer interface level where retailers will want to attract and retain the highest possible calibre of people. The fact that areas where retailers would ideally like to locate stores to take advantage of affluent populations are precisely the kind of areas where employment is at the highest levels can compound the problem. Although money is a motivating factor, a competitive hourly rate goes only part of the way to keeping workers happy. Problems that can cause retail employees to seek an alternative employer include poor management cultures, being undervalued, and poor training opportunities. Government initiatives like Investors in People can help retail organizations understand the importance of teamwork, communications and the sharing of corporate objectives in the development of a positive company culture.

Source: Based on Porter (2001).

to business. Although a number of retailers have always recruited high-level graduates, some of the industry could be criticized for 'mopping up' graduates from any discipline, and then expecting them to develop the necessary skills by placing them on a long and uninspiring 'retail management scheme' chiefly orientated towards stock allocation!

In response to the growing demand for more appropriate managerial skills and knowledge, training and development within the UK retail industry has improved and is supported by a number of key organizations such as the British Institute of Retailing, the Distributive National Training Organization (DNTO), BSSA (an association for small retailers) and the Consortium of Retail Teaching Companies (CORTCO – see Vignette 6.2). The number of retailing courses offered at higher-education institutions has also proliferated, and so the profile of a career in retailing has been raised.

As well as the development of retail managers, human-resource management encompasses the 'Personnel' function, which specifically deals with issues relating to people as employees of the retail organization, such as employment terms, wages and salaries, job descriptions, incentives and promotions. It also needs to be concerned that the retailer meets (or exceeds) its legal and moral obligations concerning Health and Safety, employee welfare, grievance procedures and so on.

● Financial Organization

Retailing is all about the exchange of money for goods and services. Funding the products entering the business and receiving income from sales are a perpetual aspect of the financial management of a retail business, and essentially determine the cash flow of the company. However, financial management is

Vignette 6.2

CORTCO

The Consortium of Retail Teaching Companies was formed in 1986 to promote to graduates the diversity and quality of career opportunities in retailing. Much of their work is done through collaboration with training and education service providers. By 2001, membership of CORTCO included Arcadia, Boots, Debenhams, John Lewis Partnership, Marks and Spencer, J. Sainsbury, Tesco, and Waitrose, thus representing a large and sector-wide part of the UK's retailing industry. Over time, the group has developed the following set of personal competencies, which are considered to be of prime importance to retail managers, and in particular graduate retail managers.

CORTCO competencies

1 *Business focus.* Customer focus, commercialism and business awareness and job motivation.
2 *Personal effectiveness.* Personal presence, emotional resilience, assertiveness, self-confidence, task management, flexibility/adaptability and self-development.
3 *Relationship management.* Team-working and awareness, team-leading, communication skills, managing and coaching for performance.
4 *Critical thinking.* Planning and organizing, forward planning, critical thinking and analytical consideration, decisiveness, innovation and strategic thinking.

Readers should consult the CORTCO website for a fuller description.

Source: CORTCO website, http://www.cortco.co.uk, 17 January 2002.

also concerned with the deployment of resources; making decisions about the spending of the profit generated on sales after the incoming stock has been paid for. In order to monitor the deployment of resources, spending needs to be managed at the outlet level, and centrally. At the outlet (store) level the costs of running the outlet need to be balanced against the income generated by the store, and so sales targets, ordering forecasts, staffing budgets and running cost allowances can be used in the process of maintaining the balance sheet of the outlet. The extent to which the financial management is centralized varies. Some retailers may give their store managers financial autonomy and responsibility, whilst others may require stores to defer all decisions regarding spending to a head-office department. The Appendix provides more detail on the pursuit of profit within a retail organization.

At the central level, the performances of stores and product departments are reviewed on a regular (at least annual) basis, in order to identify trends that may require specific management attention. Any decision to change the outlet (for example to close it down, extend it or refurbish it) is strategic in nature. For example, a particular store may currently be performing relatively poorly, but new retail developments in the town centre in which that outlet is located point to a better future for that store in years to come, therefore the outlet is kept within the portfolio with the view to improving performance in the future. Likewise, changes to product ranges within the store are strategic decisions, taking into consideration the needs of the local catchment area, the presence of competitors (which may include different retailers according to product area) and the characteristics of the store itself.

Decisions regarding the funding of assets within the organization, for example building a new distribution centre or purchasing a new computer system, are also strategic decisions, concerning the deployment of considerable company resources from which the retailer hopes to generate a good return on their investment. This kind of investment therefore has to be sanctioned by the highest authorities, and monitored centrally.

The extent to which an organization puts pressure on individual departments and outlets to constrain costs is also strategic in nature. If a retailer is pursuing a cost-leadership strategy, then all decisions about running the organization have to be taken in the light of this strategic aim; spending at outlet and department level is likely to be severely restricted and heavily scrutinized.

The relationship between the money flowing out of the business to pay for stock, and the money flowing in from the sale of products, is usually managed by merchandisers (or stock controllers) who work with the buyers. They will schedule deliveries so that enough stock is ordered to meet anticipated sales, but they will also try to ensure that the retailer does not have too much stock. This ties up company capital and runs the risk of the products becoming obsolete (especially fresh produce and high-fashion goods). Many recent supply-chain initiatives have reduced the levels of stock kept within a retail business, and this has helped retailers to improve their operational efficiency (see Chapter 7).

● Property

As a retail organization grows, it may become necessary to devote an individual or a team of people to the task of finding suitable locations for new outlets. Over the years, a retailer may become increasingly involved in property management and development as a way of supporting their other areas of operational management. In fact many large retail organizations are asset-rich when it comes to the ownership of retail property. This may make them less efficient in other operational functions, simply because they can be, as they are not having to pay back the investment put into a new site or pay an expensive lease.

Some retailers become heavily involved in the ownership and management of retail centres and this can supplement the revenue that they receive from their trading operations. For example, shoe retailer C. & J. Clark had significant investments in factory outlet retail centres, which it sold off in the late 1990s in order to concentrate on its retail trading activities (Mintel, 2001). The importance of a retailer's location to its overall success is highlighted in Chapter 9, and so having a team of specialists who have the expertise to evaluate new sites, manage the site acquisition process (through architectural design, planning applications, tendering for leasehold, construction, refurbishment and so on), as well as liase with property developers and local authorities and monitor the performance of the outlet within the overall property portfolio, is a valuable resource to a growing retailer.

Non-store Operations

The extent to which the operations of store and non-store operations are aligned can vary. In recent years many retailers have developed new retail channels, and in the initial stages this type of new operation can be managed on a specific project basis, but as it grows it will become necessary to integrate it within the overall organizational structure. For example, having treated its direct-mail retail format originally as a separate entity, Tesco subsequently amalgamated the catalogues within the store-based operations in order to maintain corporate consistency. In contrast, Tesco's internet shopping format was operationally integrated with the stores right from the start. Rather than having a dedicated distribution system, the stores were used for collating the grocery home deliveries.

International Operations

Due to the complexity of running retail outlets in non-domestic markets, international operations are usually supported by a dedicated team that works in close communication with other sections within the head office. For an in-depth discussion of retail internationalization, please refer to Chapter 16.

An Integrated Approach

Today's rapidly changing business environment necessitates a retail management approach that integrates the efforts of the different sections of a business, whether they are broken down into separate departments or not. Only by taking an holistic approach to tackle the challenges and opportunities that are faced, can a retailer optimize the efforts of the total organization. According to Walters and Hanrahan (2000, p. 117), 'effective strategic planning relies upon a planning and control approach which embraces all interests of the business'. One such approach is the so-called 'balanced scorecard', which is a framework that takes the strategic objectives that a retailer sets itself and translates them into operational objectives that can be measured. The concept of the balanced scorecard was devised by Kaplan and Norton (1996) and has been interpreted in a retailing context by Walters and Hanrahan (2000). Figure 6.2 shows the relationship between the strategic direction and operational implementation from various perspectives of a retail business, and suggests how these retail operations can be measured.

The balanced scorecard approach is important because it includes the consideration of qualitative (non-financial measures) as well as quantitative measures. For example, it considers the way in which customers will evaluate a retailer' strategy (such as number of repeat visits, or image perception), which cannot be measured unless customer research is carried out. This can be set against the financial evaluation that a shareholder may make, based purely on the performance of company shares. Even though shareholders and customers take different perspectives in terms of their evaluations of the retailer's performance, both are useful measures when it comes to monitoring

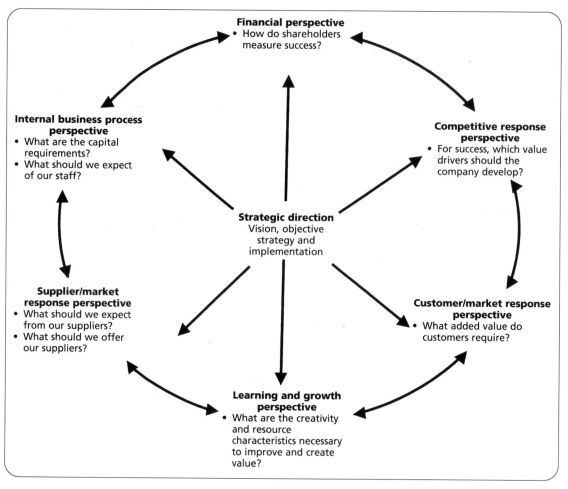

Figure 6.2   The balanced scorecard

Source: Walters and Henrahan (2000), p. 117.

the effectiveness of a strategy. By using such a broad range of performance indicators the balanced scorecard integrates the goals set at board executive level and the activities carried out at outlet level and within the centralized specialized departments. It also helps to communicate those goals to the people who are ultimately depended upon for their attainment (Fraser and Zarkada-Fraser, 2000).

Summary

Managing a retail business is a complex task, requiring a blend of diverse knowledge and skills to meet the challenges presented by customers, products, employees and financial resources. This chapter has moved from the strategic retail planning stage to the implementation of that plan at the organizational level. In particular, the roles and responsibilities of the outlet manager and the centralized departments have been examined in order to give an understanding of the relationships between the departments, and how they support the directional development of the retail corporate strategy.

Having gained an appreciation of how retail companies are organized to operate, we now move on to explore how logistics and information technology, two specific areas of retail operations underpin the smooth running of a retail business. Part 3 of the text will concentrate on the various elements of the 'retail mix' that contribute to a retailer's overall strategic market positioning; it is in this section of the book that a detailed analysis of the activities attributed to the specialized departments of marketing, property, and buying and merchandising can be found.

Questions

1 Explain how the organizational structure of a retailer supports the implementation of a retail strategy.
2 Suggest personal characteristics that a retailer would look for when recruiting retail outlet managers.
3 Briefly describe the functions performed in the following centralized departments within a retail organization:

   (a) buying and merchandising
   (b) marketing
   (c) logistics

4 Although the notion of a multiple retailer is one of a centralized structure, there are instances when decentralized decision-making in the areas of human-resource management and financial management are more appropriate. Explain, using examples to illustrate your answer.

Appendix: The Pursuit of Profit Within a Retail Organization

The achievement of profit is essential to survival, and the level of profit is an indicator of the success and health of an organization. In order to explore the management of profitability at store level the case of a single outlet retailer will be considered.

Given that profit is the surplus after deducting the cost of goods sold and running costs, profits can be increased by raising the gross margin on products (by increasing prices or reducing the cost of the goods from suppliers), increasing the quantities of goods sold to customers, or reducing the costs of running the outlet.

The opportunities for increasing prices or increasing sales volumes may be limited by the competitive arena and the geographic location of the retailer, and while all the elements of the retail mix should be explored (see Chapter 5), it may be more appropriate to consider reducing the costs of running the business (the operating costs) as a means of increasing profits.

The most significant everyday costs at store level for a retailer are wages/salaries, accommodation costs (rent, rates, heating and lighting) and the costs of products sold. The opportunities to reduce product costs will depend on the relationships between retailers and their suppliers (see Chapter 11 on buying) and the negotiating skills of the retailer, however the opportunities are unlikely to be great, especially in the case of the single-outlet retailer. It can therefore be concluded that control of labour, accommodation and administration costs is extremely important.

One way of managing the operation of a business is through budgetary control, which involves three essential stages. The first is to forecast the retailer's activity (such as sales and costs); the second is to monitor that activity, and make a comparison with the forecast; and the third is to investigate why the actual performance varies from that forecasted, and to undertake managerial action to put the company back on track.

Having put the budgeting and monitoring procedures in place, the task of the retail manager is to investigate any variance between planned and actual performance. Even if performance is better than the level planned, it is important to find out why this has happened so that opportunities are exploited as efficiently as possible. Part of the reviewing process into variances between planned and actual figures takes the form of 'ratio analysis', which is essentially a study of relationships between certain values within the financial make up of the business (which are indicated in financial accounting summaries). The most useful ratios for retailers are:

- *Return on capital employed (ROCE)*. This compares the amount of profit (e.g. pre-tax net profit) made with the amount of money being invested to make that profit (e.g. the issued shareholding together with company reserves).
- *Liquidity*. This compares the amount of current assets that a retailer has with their current liabilities. It provides an indication of how easily the retailer would be able to meet their current financial obligations, should they need to.
- *Stock turn rate*. This compares the amount of sales revenue to the amount of stock held to create those sales (using an average stockholding figure).

Whilst these measures indicate the overall health of the retail business, a deeper analysis of a retailer's performance as part of the management process may require the use of additional quantitative information. For example, a commonly used performance measure in the retail industry is sales per square metre, often referred to as sales density. In some instances it might be appropriate to measure employee performance, for example by using sales per employee, or sales per checkout as indicators.

In addition to the day-to-day operating costs associated with running a retail outlet, from time to time significant additional expenditure may be required in order to maintain or improve the overall level of business activity. Equipment such as tills and fixtures may need to be updated, or the whole shop may need to be redecorated, and so it makes sense to put some financial resources aside for this type of exceptional expenditure and build it into the budget for operational costs. The overall financial situation of the retail business can be summarized in the usual financial statements, such as the periodic profit and loss summaries and the balance sheet (see Figure 6.3).

In a multi-outlet retailer the costs of running a central organization will need to be built into the budget for operating costs and be subject to its own budgetary control. Given that a central organization does not earn sales income, it can only be considered as a cost, which then needs to be allocated to the income-earning sections of the business. This might take the form of a flat rate charged per store, for example, or it might be a small percentage allocation covered by the profit margins attached to each individual product. The detailed financial planning involved in running a multi-product, multi-outlet retailer is extremely complex and is not within the scope of this text. Nevertheless, it is important for an outlet manager to understand the accounting principles that are used within their businesses so that they understand the financial implications of their own decision-making.

Profit and loss account for the 52 weeks to 31 March 2003

Sales	840,000
Cost of sales	490,000
Gross profit	350,000
Expenses (salaries, advertising, running costs etc.)	266,000
Operating profit	84,000
Interest charges	21,000
Profit before tax	63,000
Taxation	5,000
Profit after tax	58,000
Profit retained	58,000

Balance sheet as at 31 March 2003

Fixed assets		238,000
Current assets	140,000	
Creditors	80,000	
Net current assets		60,000
Total assets		298,000
Capital and reserves:		
Share capital		240,000
Unappropriated profits		58,000
Total liabilities		298,000

Figure 6.3 Profit and loss account and balance sheet for V&R stores

References and Further Reading

Cortco (2001) 'Fit for Retail' http://www.cortco.co.uk_fit_for_retail_page.htm, 17 January 2002.

Fraser, C. and Zarkada-Fraser, A. (2000) 'Measuring the Performance of Retail Managers in Australia and Singapore', *International Journal of Retail and Distribution Management*, vol. 28, no. 6, pp. 228–42.

Kaplan R. S. and Norton, D.P. (1996) *Translating Strategy into Action: The Balanced Scorecard* (Boston, Mass.: Harvard Business School Press).

Mintel (2001) *Factory Outlet Centres*, Mintel Retail Report, March.

Oldfield, B.M, Schmidt, R. A., Clarke, I., Hart, C. and Kirkup, M. H. (2000) *Contemporary Cases in Retail Operations Management* (Basingstoke: Palgrave Macmillan).

Porter, J. (2001) 'Ooh recruits you, Sir', *Retail Week*, 20 April.

Walters, D. and Hanrahan, J. (2000) *Retail Strategy: Planning and Control* (Basingstoke: Palgrave Macmillan).

chapter seven

Retail Logistics

Learning objectives

- A familiarization with the structure of 'typical' retail supply chains, and the roles of the components of that chain.
- To understand the way in which logistics support the objectives of retail activity.
- To understand the importance of controlling supply-chain costs.
- To appreciate the importance of achieving logistical efficiency.
- To understand the enabling role of information technology in retail logistics.

Introduction

As sellers of merchandise to the final consumer, retailers are dependent on the supply of that merchandise in order to provide a high level of service to their customers. In some instances manufacturer may deliver goods that they produce directly to the retail outlet, but in many cases a product item will travel through a complex route encompassing transportation, warehousing and various handling devices in order to get from the production location to the consumer's home. Some products, such as fresh grocery, have the complication of specific requirements needing to be met during this process, such as a chilled environment, and so the whole organization of what is commonly called 'the supply chain' needs to be integrated with the requirements of the retailer, and ultimately the consumer. The range of activities involved in the physical distribution of products through the supply chain is often referred to as retail logistics.

Logistics is a key support area for any retail operation, and in most large multiple retailers its importance is reflected in the organizational structure of the company. However, logistics has not always had such a central role in the eyes of the retailer (Fernie and Sparks, 1999). Over the last two decades, more and more retailers have turned to view their logistical arrangements as a potential area for making 'efficiencies' that simultaneously save costs and improve the stock service to the outlet, and therefore to the final customer. However, many of the efficiencies that have been introduced have only been possible because of advancements in information technology systems upon which the logistics arrangements depend, and so the development of logistics has gone hand in hand with development in technology applications.

Retail Supply Chains

Figure 7.1 illustrates different supply chains that can be found within the retail industry, and shows how products move through various stages between the supplier's factory and the customer. Many retailers have a global supply base, in which case extra stages in transportation that incorporate sea or air-freight will be required to bring the product into a distribution centre. Retail logistics are further complicated with the issues of the ownership of the goods, and the supply of the logistics service. In some situations, the goods may be made exclusively for a particular retailer, and from the point at which they leave the factory gates they are owned by the retailer and taken through a logistical set up that is run by the retailers themselves. On the other hand, in some retail supply chains the ownership of the goods may pass from manufacturer to broker or agent, to wholesaler, before reaching the retailer. Even when there are no other intermediaries in the supply chain, the logistical

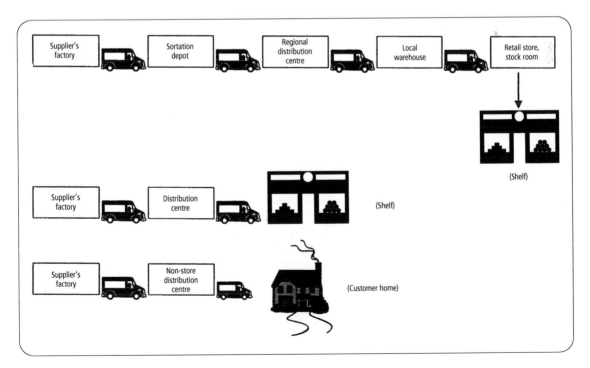

Figure 7.1 Retail supply chains

operations may be contracted out to a 'third-party' logistical service supplier (for example Christian Salvesten, Exel, or Tibbett and Brittain) who provide transportation and warehousing and distribution management facilities for their retailer clients.

The actual product involved has a great bearing on the way a retail supply chain is run. For example, for fresh produce and other short-shelf-life articles, it is vital that the supply chain is geared up to very fast transportation, to ensure that the retailer's customers receive the product in good condition. Fragile products have extra requirements in terms of packaging and handling arrangements, so that the risk of damage is reduced. Frozen and chilled produce requires very specific handling, warehousing and transportation throughout the supply chain, in order to ensure that the stringent food safety legislation is complied with and that the produce is at its best for the consumer. Clothing products are often taken through their supply chain on hangers, rather than in boxes.

The Role of the Distribution Centre

The distribution centre plays a key part in the retail supply chain of all large multiple retailers, and so a deeper insight into the role that it plays in support of the overall retail strategy is necessary. Its main functions can be broken down into: breaking bulk and storing products, providing a vital link in the distribution channel, and amalgamating and preparing stock for stores.

Breaking bulk and storing supplies

One of the benefits of large-scale multiple retailing is the scale economies derived from collating store orders and placing large quantity orders with suppliers. However, this gives retailers the challenge of breaking those 'bulk' orders down again so that they can be fed in manageable quantities to the retail stores. The distribution centre therefore provides the facility to receive stock in bulk, provide some temporary storage space for large quantities of product, and then collate assortments of products that are appropriate in quantity and characteristics for individual stores.

Distribution

Having suppliers deliver in bulk to one or a number of regional distribution centres means that the distribution of produce is more efficient. Figure 7.2 is an extension to the earlier Figure 1.2 and shows how distribution centres provide an intermediary service in the distribution channel between producers and consumers.

Amalgamation of product assortments for stores

The stock requirements of individual stores will differ according to their size and the demand patterns generated by their own customer sales. The

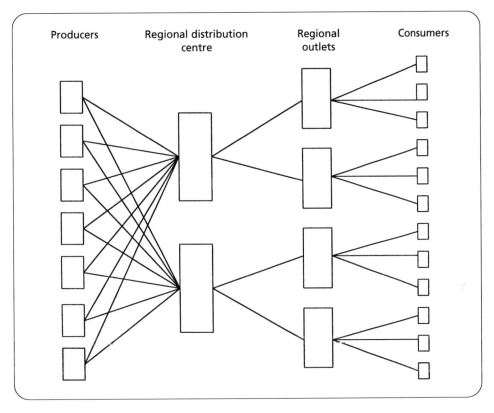

Figure 7.2 The role of the distribution centre within a multiple retailer

distribution centre can therefore prepare an assortment of products from all the different suppliers tailored to the needs of the store, which can be delivered, in some cases a number of times daily, to the stores. The stock service level to stores is therefore extremely high, both in terms of getting the right products and getting them delivered quickly.

Preparation of merchandise

In addition to the collation of store deliveries, distribution centres often carry out processes that are involved with the preparation of stock for the stores, so that products can go straight from the delivery lorry onto the shopfloor to replenish shelves. Merchandise preparation can include the following activities:

- Removing all packaging.
- Putting price tickets on the products.
- Cleaning and dusting the products, hanging and pressing garments.
- Collating products by department and organizing according to a store's requirements (according to store or stockroom layout for example).

● Other Elements within the Supply Chain

Sortation depot

In the supply chains of large retailers, who require vast quantities of products from their suppliers, it is sometimes necessary to introduce another link between suppliers and distribution centres. This is effectively a large-scale warehousing operation which breaks down supplies into appropriate quantities for the regional distribution centres.

Regional warehouse

Sometimes a link is introduced between the distribution centre and the retail store. For example, where a retail outlet is limited for space, and yet the distribution centre is located a long distance from the outlet, a warehouse near to the outlet can store supplies and provide a more efficient replenishment service. Effectively, it is providing additional storeroom space for the retailer, located in a lower-cost site.

Transportation

In any logistics operation, goods have to travel from one location to another. Supplies may have to be carried from different sides of the globe, and then transferred from the air or sea freight to a land-based transport system (rail or road) for onward delivery. An extensive discussion of transportation issues is not within the scope of this text, however one issue that is steadily rising up the strategic agenda is the environmental impact of retail logistics (see Vignette 7.1).

Vignette 7.1

Green supply chains

Since the early 1990s, retailers and their supply-chain partners have been under increasing pressure to become more responsible towards the environment. The objective of providing a better service to the customer can directly conflict with a corporate objective to reduce the impact of retail logistics on the environment in areas like vehicle emissions and congestion, fuel usage, packaging, and land use for warehousing. Retailers are facing pressure from a number of sources: European and UK legislation, industry peer groups, local authorities, green campaign groups and the media, and while companies must be seen to be financially successful, stakeholders and customers are also demanding that companies take social and environmental responsibility too. Retail companies that have initiated environmental policies include Body Shop, Safeway, Sainsbury's, and Marks and Spencer. The companies that set trends and anticipate legislative pressure could well have a competitive advantage in the future over those companies that ignore the environmental issue, run the risk of causing customer unease and have to be reactive in their compliance with environmental legislation.

Source: Adapted from Worsford (2001).

Suppliers

Any retail logistics system starts with suppliers whether they are the immediate producer, or whether they are acting in the capacity of agent for a producer. Suppliers can play a passive role in the supply chain, with their involvement restricted to waiting for orders, packing the goods up and handing them over to a carrier, or they may become highly involved in logistical arrangements in partnership with their retail customers. The benefits of taking a partnership approach to logistics are explained in more detail later in the chapter.

● Costs in the Supply Chain

In Chapter 6 we acknowledged the importance of containing costs at the retail outlet level. However, an outlet manager in a multiple retailer has no control over the costs involved with getting produce into the outlet. These are essentially incurred and controlled centrally, but can be analysed further according to the activities involved with the procurement of goods. Each link in the supply chain incurs its own individual costs and it is the detailed analysis of these costs that is the basis of much of the work on logistics efficiency. Figure 7.3 gives a breakdown of logistics operations, the likely costs involved, and the factors that directly affect costs, which can be viewed as a starting point for a logistics cost analysis.

Although cost analysis is fundamental to achieving efficiency, decisions about logistics are not made on costing information alone. Other factors that have to be considered are the ability to move products very fast through the supply chain, the ability to provide a reliable service, and flexibility. Any stock that is in the supply chain is, as far as the retailer is concerned, tying up capital that is only released when the goods are sold. Therefore the less time a product spends in the supply chain the lower the costs of financing 'pipeline' stock. A supply chain should ideally be without

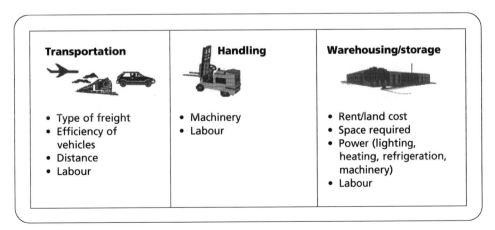

Figure 7.3 Logistics operations

any forms of inaccuracy which can hold up the flow of stock. Defects can originate in many ways:

- Damage to stock
- Shortages (for example the actual quantity in the carton does not comply with the stated number on an invoice).
- Assortment inaccuracy (incorrect quantities in terms of product variation such as colour, flavour, size and so on).
- Information inaccuracy (wrong barcode for example).
- Non-conformance with packaging specification (for example the wrong size carton may mean the goods cannot be automatically received onto a conveyor belt in the distribution centre).

Retailers and their supply chains should ideally be able to react quickly and easily to any changes in consumer purchasing patterns that switch demand from one product to another, or result in surges or downfalls in demand. The inability to apply resources flexibly can result in additional costs in the long term and a lowering of service efficiency in the short term.

In the pursuit of cost and service efficiency in the supply chain, it becomes apparent that scrutinizing the retailer's own internal costs is often not enough. Suppliers and logistic service suppliers also need to be considered. Many of the initiatives that have saved costs in the supply chain, which can eventually be passed on to the consumer in the form of lower product prices, have been the result of extensive collaboration between retailers and their suppliers. By working together on supply-chain management issues, cost and waste have been reduced and leaner stock levels achieved across business organizational boundaries.

● Logistics and Information Technology

As in the case of many technological innovations, retail logistics systems were revolutionized on the basis of a relatively simple application – the barcode. By converting product codes to a system of monochrome bars, which could then be read by an infra-red scanning device, the capture of information about products sold within a retail business became both fast and accurate. Feeding barcode data into computers provided the means by which retailers could count electronically, rather than manually, how many products had been sold, how many had been taken into the business, and therefore the level of stockholding (and if required, the level of stockholding in the various parts of the retail supply chain) quickly established. As computer systems grew in sophistication, their ability to read, analyse and transmit data increased, and so the quality of information fed to retail decision-makers improved. In terms of retail logistics, the systems highlighted areas of inefficiency, such as goods waiting to be processed, or unsold stock being held in various locations in the supply chain.

Another technological innovation that has underpinned retail logistics information-systems development is electronic data interchange (EDI) via internal company networks. This provided the means to link stores, head offices, distribution centres and suppliers electronically and enabled the immediacy of electronically transmitted information. This cut out the need for hours of manual sales reporting over the telephone, or in a written format; with EDI it became possible to transmit sales data directly from the electronic point of sale (EPOS) in real time allowing immediate reaction to those sales to be made. Here, technology has greatly facilitated the conversion of retail supply chains from product-push-based systems to customer-pull-based systems.

● Product-Push and Customer-Pull-Based Logistics Systems

The product-push system is based on the concept of a quantity of goods being brought in according to a level forecast in advance, and then placed on the shelf to wait for a customer to buy. Suppliers make goods according to orders placed by the retailer, but after sending the goods into the retailer' supply chain, have no further involvement in the process. If the goods sell well, the retailer reorders when stocks are diminishing; if they do not, the retailer has to lower the price to shift the unwanted stock.

The customer-pull system is based on the concept of responding to each customer's purchase, where the recording of the sale of a product triggers a sequence of events in the supply chain. Firstly the sales data is sent electronically to all members of the supply chain. The distribution centre responds by automatically replenishing the item sold. The lowering of the stock level at the distribution centre may then trigger an order suggestion to the buying office to call more product in from suppliers. In the meantime, the buying office will have received sales notification, and will have already started to consider their response to those sales, either by calling more product from suppliers or (if the product is seasonal, for example) to let the stock run down. The supplier, who also obtains the sales information in real time, can get ready to make more of the product in anticipation of another call from the retailer. The customer-pull system is therefore centred around responding to customer purchasing, unlike the product-push system which is based on the notion of holding stock and waiting (or hoping) for sales.

Although both approaches to logistics have the same aim, which is to provide a good service to customers, there are a number of factors that have encouraged more and more retailers to adopt a responsive retail logistics system.

● The system of automatic replenishment allows the retailer to maintain low stock levels at the store, and this has enabled retailers to reduce the number of products on the shelf, and to increase product variety. It has also allowed retailers to convert stockroom space to sales space, as there is no need to hold stock in a storeroom at the outlet.
● The sharing of sales information with suppliers allows them to see sales patterns emerging, so they can gear their production up for the fast-selling lines, and cut back on slow-selling items. This has the effect of reducing the number of products needing to be marked down to sell, and

helps to maximize the sales of good sellers by keeping them in stock, leading to more profits for both retailer and supplier.

- The elimination of slow-selling stock from the supply chain means that less money is invested in stock, stock turnover improves and so the return on capital employed is raised.

The success of responsive retail supply chains has led to the development of a whole new philosophy within retail organizations, and that is efficient consumer response (ECR). In addition to the key benefits of a responsive system outlined above, combined with the use of increasingly detailed information systems, retailers have found that they have been able to take a very close, analytical view of their supply chain and logistical operations in order to cut out unnecessary costs. This led to a business philosophy that not only aligns all logistical operations to customer response, but runs through all aspects of the product management process.

Efficient Consumer Response

Figure 7.4 outlines the scope of ECR. The outer circle represents activities that are concerned with the management of supply within a retail organization, whilst the inner circle represents activities that are concerned with the management of consumer demand and the initial response to it. The management of

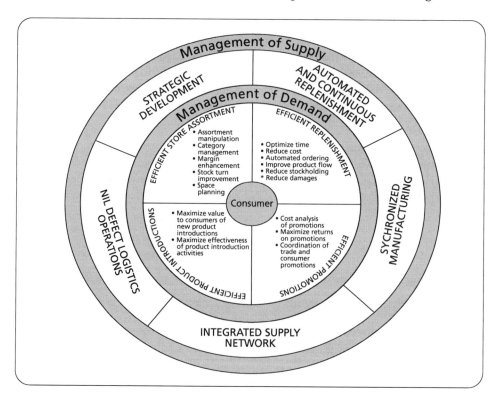

Figure 7.4 The scope of efficient consumer response

supply relates to activities that often fall within the remit of logistics and buying and merchandising departments, whilst the activities concerned with demand management are generally more marketing and outlet-orientated. However, ECR makes this kind of departmental boundary somewhat redundant, because of the totally integrated approach that the ECR system requires. The critical success factor in an ECR system is the satisfaction of the final consumer, and this becomes the driver for all retail activities (shown in the central position in Figure 7.4).

Collaboration with suppliers

In addition to the integration of activities within the retail organization, ECR is also dependent on an integrated approach to the business right through the supply chain, and into supplier organizations. In order to achieve maximum efficiencies, all parties need to work together to identify problems, and agree on initiatives to overcome them. Only then can the necessary seamless interface from consumers' purchasing patterns to suppliers' production schedules be achieved (Lowson *et al.*, 1999), and the benefits of ECR derived. Figure 7.5 illustrates how both retailers and their suppliers benefit from ECR initiatives.

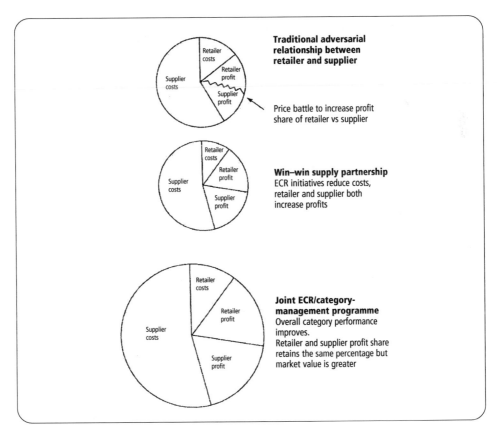

Figure 7.5 Benefits to retailers and suppliers of adopting ECR systems

Logistics and the non-store retailer

By their nature non-store retailers have a simpler logistics requirement than store retailers. Orders for goods are taken remotely, and the goods sent directly to the customer from a distribution centre. In the case of direct marketing facilitated by internet technology, goods do not need to move down a supply chain at all but move in a customer-specific delivery system, from producer to consumer. However, a major drawback of non-store retailing is the high level of returned goods. When a product is represented rather than real, and the customer is unable to test or try the product in-store, there is a much higher risk of product dissatisfaction. The distribution centre for a non-store retailer therefore acts as a two-way receiving station, with bulk orders arriving from suppliers, and individual returns from customers. The returned products have to be checked and reprocessed before being returned to saleable stock, and any faulty goods have to be returned to suppliers or scrapped. In non-store retailing, the condition in which a package arrives at a customer's home is likely to impact upon their perception of the product and the retailer, and so the quality level of the packaging and delivery service must be in line with the overall retail image.

Reverse logistics

In an era where retailers have generous and flexible returns policies across sales channels, the disposal of unwanted merchandise is a growing, costly and complex problem. This has given rise to the concept of 'reverse logistics' which is concerned with managing returns in the most efficient way. For example, third-party service-providers can set up a dedicated system which captures data on customers' returns that are ready to be collected from stores, and arranges for them to be collected and taken to a 'reverse logistics' site where the goods are assessed for damage. The goods are then categorized by type and/or supplier, and then collated for redistribution either back to suppliers for repair, back to stores for resale, or to be disposed of through non-conflicting channels (for example, factory outlets or market stalls) or, if all else fails, to landfill sites (Clements, 2002).

The advantage of non-store retailing is that a whole layer of operational costs can be avoided; the costs of running a store are removed, and the order-fulfilment operation can be positioned in a low-cost location. In order to achieve a good delivery service to customers, however, non-store retailers have to hold stock from which to fulfil customer orders. NEXT, for example, promise a 48-hour delivery to customers from the receipt of order. As a way of helping to keep fashion products in stock, some mail-order companies issue a preview catalogue ahead of the season to a group of loyal customers, whose purchasing helps the company to forecast the demand for products in the main catalogue. In a similar way, multi-channel retailers can use sales reaction in one format (for example a website) to plan product availability in another (stores for example). 'Pure-play' retailers, who trade exclusively on the internet, in theory do not need to hold stock but do need a highly developed information system in order to keep track of customer orders, suppliers' stock positions and order fulfilment, and customer deliveries, in order to ensure that their customer stock availability service is operating at an acceptable level (see Vignette 7.2).

Vignette 7.2

SimplyOrganic

SimplyOrganic is the epitome of a modern niche retailer. It provides specialist products to a narrowly defined and lucrative customer base. At the heart of the company is an integrated information system that provides a window from cyberspace to view the realities of retail logistics. On receipt of an order, received by web, fax or phone, the details are entered into the trading system and then automatically matched to customer details held on a database. An ID number represents the customer, so that their personal details remain secure within the database. Stock is allocated to the customer order, and an order is then generated for the supplier, according to quantities needed and the time of delivery. SimplyOrganic have web-linkages with many of their suppliers so that they can gain automatic access to product information, such as harvesting and organic certification information. If necessary, suppliers can e-mail digital photographic representations of the goods that are being purchased by the retailer, so that quality checks can be made 'virtually'. By developing a history of individual customers' purchases, SimplyOrganic can tailor meaningful and personalized one-to-one offers to customers. The application of technology allows the online retailer to maintain a high level of customer service, without the need for stockholding to cover inefficiencies; achieving better profitability and providing added value to customers.

Source: Adapted from de Klerk (2001).

● **Limitations of Efficient Consumer Response**

The principle of efficient consumer response appears to be so logical that the reader may be surprised to learn that not all retailers are able or willing to organize their supply chains in this way. However, there are a number of reasons why ECR may not be applicable.

Logistics and the small retailer

Small retailers do not have the resources to get heavily involved in supply-chain management, nor would it be cost-effective for them to do so. In addition, the opportunities for them to collaborate with suppliers may be severely limited. However, they still need to make decisions regarding logistics arrangements on a small scale. For example, is it more cost-effective to collect orders from suppliers, or have them delivered? How often do they need to visit a wholesaler, and to what extent can they risk running down stock levels between visits? In a competitive and saturated retail market, customers are intolerant of stock-outs; therefore small retailers must manage their stock to the best of their ability. Periodic review (Figure 7.6) is a simple but effective stock control system appropriate for small and medium-sized

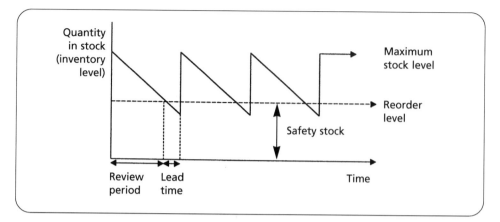

Figure 7.6   The periodic review system

retailers, where items sold have a relatively predictable demand pattern. The essence of this system is that the stock position in a retail outlet is reviewed on a regular basis. When stock falls to a predetermined minimum level, a replenishment order is placed. Between the time of order placement and delivery (called the 'lead time'), demand for the item is met by an amount of 'safety stock'.

The periodic review system helps the small retailer to ensure that their product range is maintained with an adequate stock service. However, it may be necessary for the retailer to make further decisions based on the trade-off between the feasibility and costs associated with holding larger amounts of stock and ordering (or collecting) less frequently, and the feasibility and costs associated with taking in less stock on a more frequent basis.

Seasonal products

One of the problems concerned with both periodic review systems and automatic replenishment systems is that they are geared to a situation where the demand for a product item is relatively consistent. However, many products are highly seasonal and therefore have a demand pattern consisting of rises, peaks and falls. A stock control system that goes some way to helping retailers cope with fluctuating sales patterns is the Open-to–Buy (OTB) system. The basis of the OTB system is a sales forecast, which is based on the previous year's sales, taking into consideration any relevant external variations. The sales forecast then determines the stock-level requirement for those sales to be made. As the season progresses, a sales level that exceeds the forecasted level allows a higher purchasing budget, whereas when sales fall below expectation the purchasing budget is reduced. The effect is that the overall stock level is managed according to the level of sales.

● Sales Forecasting

In an ideal world, stock would be replenished into a retailer's outlet exactly at the rate at which stock left the store in customers' shopping bags. However, retailers do not exist in this kind of utopia, and so retail managers have to use their experience and entrepreneurial skills to manage stock in order to fulfil the needs and desires of the fickle consuming population in a manner that is most profitable in the long term. For many products it is necessary to use some degree of forecasting in order to ensure that stock levels are high enough to cope with customer demand. Most forecasting techniques use previous sales figures as a base from which future sales are estimated, however simply looking to the past is a rather narrow way of anticipating future performance. More sophisticated forecasting methods take into consideration external factors that are likely to have a negative or positive impact on sales. By allocating numerical values to these factors, which are then applied to the basic 'past-sale indication' a more accurate forecast emerges. Factors that might be quantified include weather patterns, promotional activity, competitors marketing activity, market or seasonal growth in a particular product category, and so on. It is particularly difficult to match supply and demand for seasonal products; for example, it would not be in a retailer's interest to replenish the stock of Christmas wrapping paper at the rate it was sold in the week commencing 18 December, in the following week, whilst a shortage of this item in the week prior to Christmas would lead to considerable customer frustration. It is therefore necessary to build stock levels of seasonal items high enough to allow customer demand to be fulfilled at the peak of the season. For some products, like gifts, or dresses, customers like to have a wide choice from which to make a purchase, which again pushes up the stock requirement.

Fashion products

Many fashion products combine a situation of a short shelf-life (before becoming outdated) and long chains involved in their manufacture and supply (for example, for a pair of trousers yarn has to spun out of fibres that have to be produced, cloth has to be woven from yarn, garments have to be cut out, sewn and pressed). This situation has led fashion retailers and their suppliers to investigate ways of aligning fluctuating customer sales as closely as possible to manufacturing and supply systems, an approach termed Quick Response (QR) (Fiorito et al., 1995). Fashion retailers such as Benetton, Oasis, Gap, Zara and Mango are all known for the use of QR systems in order to respond faster to sales of fashion items; for example Benetton have a system of dying ready-knitted sweaters to the fashion colours that are selling well, instead of knitting up precoloured yarn. This means that the introduction of the fashion element (colour) happens at a later stage of the process. Other companies have also found ways of introducing flexibility in their design and manufacturing systems that allow production to quickly switch from slow-selling styles to 'hot items'. Vignette 7.3 illustrates how UK fashion retailer New Look used logistical competitive advantages to gain a foothold in a stagnant retail market sector.

Vignette 7.3

New Look

In 1969, a young entrepreneur named Tom Singh opened a women's clothing shop in a small town in Somerset, in the south-west of the UK. The store quickly became successful and by 1995, when the company was floated on the stockmarket, there were 250 outlets spread across the country. The retail formula that had led to this growth was, at the time, relatively unique. On the one hand the company traded on a low cost basis, using secondary locations, basic but functional store design, high stock densities, and a great deal of in-store promotion. Their product offer, however, was one that made high-fashion clothes accessible to the mass market, by introducing the 'new look' quickly and at affordable prices. The company does not attempt to be 'fashion forward', which would involve a much greater degree of risk taking, but they follow trends and translate catwalk ideas into commercial garments, with 'newness' being offered via a styling detail, a fabric design or a new silhouette. Those items that sell well are reordered and promoted, while the poorer sellers are quickly marked down. The store then attracts customers with its blend of key looks at reasonable prices, together with heavily discounted bargains.

New Look use a number of operational approaches that allow them to respond fast to fashion change, and maintain freshness in the product offer. Clothing retailers have traditionally found it very easy to become overstocked with lines that are not appealing, and out of stock of the best-selling lines because of the long lead times for repeat orders. By cutting down on the time it takes to introduce new products and the time it takes to reorder, New Look can take steps to avoid these common problems in the clothing sector. One system they introduced was to send lorries from stores that they had just delivered to, straight on to supply points to collect merchandise for the distribution centre. Not only did this speed things up, but more efficient use of vehicles was obtained. New Look have powerful information systems which analyse sales overnight and provide information which can be used for immediate decision-making, such as taking a mark-down or reordering a product; many other clothing retailers only make a full review of sales on a weekly basis. Internet-based tracking systems to locate merchandise at any point in the supply chain, and a dedicated modern distribution centre near the company headquarters, are other elements in the supply chain. Quick response starts early in the supply chain; New Look designers turn catwalk ideas into commercial garment patterns in a matter of hours, and their small and committed supply base quickly moves prototypes down the critical path from design room to factory floor. In some cases New Look may source the base fabric for garments themselves and then send it to manufacturers who convert the cloth into styled garments at the very last moment, so that the latest styling details can be incorporated.

Sources: New Look (1999) and Whitehead (1998).

Summary

Retail logistics play a central role in the implementation of a retail strategy. Without the support systems that move products into outlets and/or customers' homes, a retailing strategy is pointless. If a retailer is unable to deliver or make available adequate supplies in good condition of what customers want, when they want it, they will find that a competitor soon will! Poor logistics can therefore place a retailer at a significant competitive disadvantage. The enormity of the logistical arrangements for large multiple retailers means that any change in operations can have a major cost implication, and so customer-service levels, total logistics costs and total benefits to the retailer have to be finely balanced (Collins et al., 2001). In a competitive and saturated retail market like the UK, the approaches that have made supply chains more efficient are moving forward into the management of customer demand, and so the integration of marketing operations and logistical operations support the customer-responsive organization in the pursuit of its overall strategic objectives.

Questions

1 Provide an analysis of the role of the distribution centre within a multiple retail organization.
2 Multi-channel retailing provides some additional logistics challenges to retailers. Discuss the nature of these challenges.
3 Lowering costs is one, but not the only, objective of efficiency in the supply chain. Discuss other objectives that retailers may seek to achieve with their logistics systems.
4 Explain the benefits that a retailer might accrue from a customer-pull distribution system.
5 ECR not only involves taking on a new operational alignment in logistics, but also a new company philosophy. Discuss.
6 Identify specific products that might present particular challenges for retail logistics systems, and discuss ways in which these challenges might be tackled.

References and Further Reading

Collins, A., Henchion, M. and O'Reilly, P. (2001) 'Logistics Customer Service: Performance of Irish Food Exporters', *International Journal of Retail and Distribution Management*, vol. 29(1), 6–15.
Clements, A. (2002) 'Return Ticket', *Retail Week*, 1 November.
De Klerk, N. (2001) 'Sowing the Seeds', *Retail Week Supply Chain Guide*, October.
Fernie, J. and Sparks, L. (1998) *Logistics and Retail Management* (London: Kogan Page).
Fiorito, S. S., May, E. G. and Straughn, K. (1995) 'Quick Response in Retailing: Components and Implementation', *International Journal of Retailing and Distribution Management*, vol. 23(5), pp. 12–21.

Gattorna, J. L. and Walters, D. W. (1996) *Managing the Supply Chain* (London: Macmillan).

Lowson, B., King, R. and Hunter, A. (1999) *Quick Response: Managing the Supply Chain to Meet Consumer Demand* (Chichester, Sussex: John Wiley).

New Look (1999) *Company Report* (Weymouth: New Look).

Whitehead, D. (1998) 'The DIY Man Gives Fashion a New Look', *Draper's Record*, 5 September.

Worsford, F. (2001) *The Green Logistics Company* (Kingston upon Thames: Croner CCH).

chapter eight

Information Technology and Retailing

Learning objectives

- To understand how EPOS, EFTPOS, and EDI can be used to improve customer service and retailer efficiency.
- To explore how loyalty cards can be used to improve store performance.
- To appreciate the role of IT in improving marketing and merchandising.
- To understand data warehousing and data-mining concepts.
- To explore the different types of information systems used by retailers and their role within retailing organizations.

Introduction

Information is a key resource that retailers need to manage effectively in order to satisfy their customers' needs and to remain competitive in the industry. The number of products carried by a retailer and the large number of customers and suppliers means that retailers generate huge amounts of information. The advent of information technology has given retailers the means to harness it and enabled them to improve the efficiency of their businesses and the service that they provide to customers. Information technology is ubiquitous in retailing today, with its most obvious manifestation in the electronic point-of-sale (EPOS) cash register and the laser scanner used at checkouts by the vast majority of retailers. EFTPOS (electronic funds transfer at point of sale) systems also allow customers to pay either by credit or debit cards at checkouts without cash. Many retailers also use electronic loyalty cards to add incentives. In the background, store retailers use the information provided by the EPOS system and direct communication with their suppliers through electronic data interchange (EDI) to allow automatic reordering and replenishment. The internet has also changed how retailers communicate with their suppliers, and retailers use information technology in general to improve their marketing and merchandising performance.

Despite the above, retailers were relatively slow to adopt information technology. Although computer technology has been used by retailers since the 1960s, it was not until the early 1980s when computer technology became relatively cheap that retailers began to seriously consider its widespread use within stores. One study estimated that in 1991 the expenditure on IT by major European food retailers, the lead sector in terms of IT use, amounted to only around 0.5 per cent of sales. And more recently it has been estimated that expenditure of US retailers amounts to only around 1 per cent of sales compared with 5 per cent of sales for industry as a whole. Nevertheless, information technology is now integral to the operation of retail stores.

IT has been used by retailers for three main purposes: item identification, improvement of communication internally and externally, and information processing and analysis. EPOS systems are a direct outcome of item identification. The development of internal networks, intranets and EDI and the internet represent attempts to improve communications internally and externally. Retailers have gone beyond simply using information technology to collect information; increasingly they are using it to analyse and better to understand the needs of their customers, to improve retail business processes.

This chapter examines the use of information technology and its impact at store level. Internet retailing which is revolutionizing retailing and shopping is discussed separately in Chapter 19.

⬬ Electronic Point-of-Sale Systems (EPOS)

An EPOS system consists of a laser scanner capable of reading a universal product code (the black-and-white stripes or barcode found on most merchandise today), attached to a computer that can recognize the product, with, in addition, a price look-up table of all products sold in the store. The EPOS terminal is itself connected to the company computer which collates information from all stores in the chain. On scanning a product, the computer records the sale and displays the price for the customer to check, and at the end of the transaction an itemized receipt is produced for the customers.

EPOS systems provide retailers with up-to-date information on how fast goods are moving and hence when stocks need replenishing. A major saving to retailers, such as supermarkets, in adopting EPOS systems is that items do not need to be priced individually, with resulting savings in labour costs. Also, by monitoring changes over time retailers are in a position to detect changes in customer behaviour to which they can respond more quickly than non-EPOS based systems. In fact, the availability of this information has given retailers extra bargaining power as they frequently have more information about the popularity of goods than the manufacturers.

EPOS systems are particularly useful in the fast moving consumer goods (FMCG) area both from the customer's and the retailer's perspective. From the customer's perspective, the major benefit of is that checkout time is reduced, and hence there is less queuing, and an itemized list also gives them the opportunity to check their receipts in detail. Another major benefit to both customers and the retailer is that stockouts are less frequent, and the increased efficiencies help to maintain low costs or allow the provision of extra services for customers. For instance, many supermarkets now provide

Vignette 8.1

Sainsbury's adoption of EPOS

Although the first barcode scanning trials were conducted in the early 1970s by Albert Heijn (Holland), Migros (Switzerland) and Shaw's in the USA, Sainsbury's did not rush into adopting the new technology. The main reason for this was the fact that Sainsbury's management felt that the cost of adopting the system was too great in terms of improved customer service. The main stumbling block was the small number of products that carried barcodes. By 1980 only 3 per cent of products carried barcodes and Sainsbury's estimated that this figure would need to rise to 85 per cent before the scanning system became viable.

Sainsbury's started its own experimentation with scanning in 1979, but was not until 1984 that it felt it had a sufficiently reliable system to go for full conversion to scanning. It invited ICL to develop a tailored system, and the first fully scanning branch was opened in October 1985. The system was quickly rolled out to the branches and by 1988 more than half of its stores were equipped for scanning and 75 per cent of all food scanned in UK supermarkets passed through Sainsbury's. By 1990, all Sainsbury's stores were equipped with scanning systems. It is estimated that Sainsbury's was two to three years ahead of its competitors in adopting scanning technology, which gave the company a significant advantage over competitors in having accurate information about sales and stock movements. It also allowed the company to introduce new innovations such as 'multibuys', and to introduce weighing scales linked to scanning terminals at checkout so that customers did not need to queue several times. Around this time the company also began experimenting with electronic loyalty schemes.

Sainsbury's took advantage of the point-of-sale information provided by the new system and integrated it with its ordering system. In 1992 it introduced the ordering sytem called SABRE (SAles Based REplenisment), using current sales figures to calculate the amount of stock required, rather than using previous years' sales for instance. The system provided stores with up-to-the-minute information on sales, stock levels, goods on order, and when the orders were to be delivered. A big advantage of sales-based ordering systems is that they reduce stockouts and the amount of inventory carried.

In October 1988 Sainsbury's also became the first big supermarket to commit itself to EFTPOS when it signed an agreement with Midland Bank to accept the Switch debit card, implemented a year later at all Sainsbury's stores and filling stations. Similar agreements followed leading to the acceptance of all major banks' debit cards, and by 1991 EFTPOS accounted for 25 per cent of all sales and exceeded payments made by cheques. However, Sainsbury's did not begin to accept credit cards until November 1991 when the credit card companies reduced their handling fees which Sainsbury's had previously felt were too high.

Sources: Williams (1994) *The Best Butter in the World: A History of Sainsbury's* (London: J. Sainsbury); Rafiq (1997) 'Developing Customer Loyalty: The Savercard Experience', in Hart *et al.* (eds), *Cases in Retailing: Operational Perspectives* (Oxford: Blackwell Business), pp. 43-61.

help with packing. To increase benefits to consumers even further, some retailers have introduced self-scanning into their stores. The UK food retailer Safeway makes the most extensive use of self-scanning in its stores (see Vignette 8.2), although others such as Sainsbury's, Tesco and Waitrose are also experimenting with the system. With self-scanning the shopper scans the merchandise that they want to purchase as they move around the store. This is done either by using a hand-held scanner provided by the store or a scanner fitted to the shopping trolley. At the till the shopper simply pays the bill without having to unload the shopping and wait for it to be scanned, thus considerably reducing the time spent queuing which is the most disliked aspect of food shopping.

Vignette 8.2

Self-scanning at Safeway

Safeway was the first UK supermarket to launch self-scanning in March 1995 at its Solihull store, which has proved very popular. Safeway has branded its self-scanning service as 'Shop & Go', which by 1999 was available to Safeway cardholders in 169 stores.

The system is simple to use and involves customers using a hand-held scanner, 'Handiscan', to scan their own shopping as they go around the store. The Handiscan is obtained from a dispenser using the Safeway ABC loyalty card. The customer scans the product barcode by pushing a 'plus' button on the Handiscan (or if they change their mind, a 'minus' button), with a running total obtainable at any time by pressing the 'equal' button. Once the shopping is completed, the scanner is returned to its dispenser and a barcoded receipt is automatically generated. The receipt is taken to the Shop & Go pay point where it is scanned, an itemized bill printed and payment made without unpacking. Rescanning occurs the first time a customer uses the system and then randomly to ensure that the system is accurate and works efficiently and to prevent theft.

To maximize the benefits of self-scanning to shoppers, Safeway provides shoppers with Greenboxes to aid them whilst shopping. These are sturdy plastic boxes designed to fit a specially designed shopping trolley and allow shoppers to pack their groceries as they shop, The boxes can be transferred straight into a car and used again on the next trip. The reusable nature of Greenboxes means that they are also environmentally friendly. To increase customer convenience, by 1999. Safeway has also introduced self-serve automatic pay points into 15 of its stores, the automatic pay points, branded Easi-pay, allow customers to scan their Shop & Go total slip and pay for their groceries in a single transaction. The Shop & Go and Easi-pay systems allow customers to avoid traditional checkouts altogether. At the beginning of March 2003, however, Safeway announced a halt to the roll-out of its self-scanning service. The Shop and Go service is currently offered from 150 stores, but Safeway has no plans to introduce it at further locations.

Sources: Various sources including information on the Safeway website, http://www.safeway.co.uk.

● Electronic Funds Transfer at Point of Sale (EFTPOS)

An EFTPOS system is basically designed to facilitate cashless payment by customers. An EFTPOS terminal connected to the sales till is connected not only to the retailer's central computer, but also to the computers of participating high-street banks, building societies and credit card companies. The system allows customers to pay for their shopping using debit or credit cards swiped through a scanner on the till. The details of the transaction are instantly transmitted to the customer's bank or credit-card company which checks to see if there is enough money in the customer's account to pay the bill, and authorizes the retailer to proceed with the transaction and debits the customer's account within three days of the transaction. At the same time, the retailer's account is credited. For the customer, EFTPOS is convenient; for the retailer, it is quicker and less open to fraud than cheque card-based systems and there are savings to be gained from the reduced handling of cash.

● Electronic Data Interchange

Electronic data interchange is the electronic exchange of information between the retailer's computer and that of its supplier. The exchange can consist of orders, delivery notices, invoices, returns and even sales data. Retailers have found that EDI links with suppliers considerably reduce the lead times required for deliveries, and hence large savings can be made by the consequent reduction in inventory required. Additional benefits include a huge reduction in paperwork and consequently an increase in productivity. The constant exchange of information between the retailer and its suppliers also helps retailers assess more accurately suppliers' performance, accuracy and quality of service. This information can also be used in price and contract negotiations.

Initially, EDI systems were proprietary, that is owned either by the retailer, the supplier, or an independent third-party provider known as a value-added network (VAN). The proprietary systems were very expensive to develop and needed considerable investment both by retailers and suppliers to develop communication and business protocols, and thus could only be afforded by larger retailers and suppliers. Small suppliers were particularly vulnerable to exclusion as retailers began to insist on EDI compatibility. One advantage of using VAN networks is that retailers and suppliers with different EDI protocols can communicate with each other through the VAN provider translating the data from each party before transmitting it to the other.

With the development of the internet, however, data is now being transmitted either directly to suppliers/retailers or via an extranet. An extranet is an internet-based collaborative network linking suppliers and their customers. An advantage of such systems is that the cheap and uniform internet communications platform means that small suppliers are not excluded from the network and the networks are potentially global in scope. Sainsbury's, for instance, uses an internet-based extranet, SID (Sainsbury's Information Direct), to communicate a variety of information other than orders with its supply-chain partners (see Figure 8.1). An example of a global

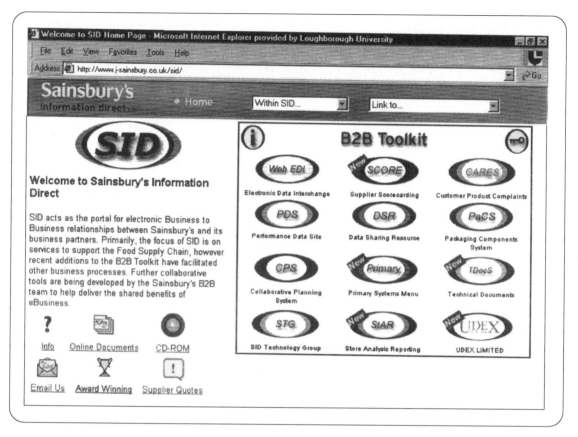

Figure 8.1 Sainsbury's uses the internet for more than just EDI

retailing extranet is GlobalnetXchange (http://www.gnx.com), whose members include Carrefour (France), Sainsbury's (UK), Sears (USA), Kroger (USA) and Metro (Germany).

A rapidly emerging application of extranets is reverse auctions. This is where a retailer specifies merchandise details on the extranet and invites interested suppliers to submit proposals/bids within a specified time period. Reverse auctions mean that the retailer is not limited to existing suppliers for merchandise, and receives a number of competitive quotes for specified merchandise at little extra cost, hence enabling them to reduce their costs further.

● Quick-Response Replenishment Systems

When EPOS systems are combined with EDI, retailers are in effect adopting just-in-time replenishment or quick-response (QR) replenishment methods (Figure 8.2). Ordering of merchandise is thus based on current rather than historical sales. Sales-based ordering systems are now common place. The lead time (the time between placing an order and its arrival in the store)

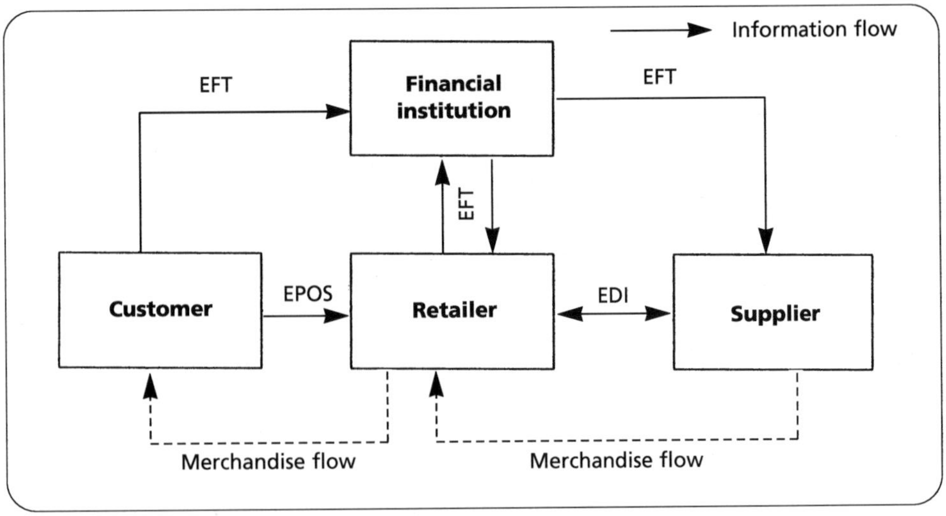

Figure 8.2 A simplified quick-response replenishment system

speed of response of suppliers can be further enhanced if retailers agree with their suppliers the level of sales at which orders are automatically triggered, that is an automatic reordering system. A big advantage of QR systems is in reducing stockouts and the amount of inventory carried, hence improving the service to customers and reducing costs to the retailer.

Collaborative efforts between retailers and their suppliers to reduce inventory costs and improve responsiveness to consumer demand are more generally known as ECR (efficient consumer response), and are particularly popular in the grocery industry. An emerging process that extends the use of EDI to a new level is collaboration, planning, forecasting and replenishment (CPFR). CPFR is an inventory management system designed to improve store-level sales and provide forecasts based on the previous sales history and forthcoming merchandising and marketing activities of the retailer and suppliers. CPFR requires the retailer to send information in real time to a supplier who uses the data to forecast the required inventory and replenishment schedule. The supplier shares the forecast with the retailer before acting on it. Sainsbury's has signed a CPFR agreement with Unilever and Kimberley, facilitated by the GlobalnetXchange extranet.

In an increasingly competitive retail market, a major function of retail marketing is to maintain customer loyalty. Loyalty can be developed by providing customers with incentives to shop at a store, and by ensuring that a store's merchandise is tailored to the needs of its customers. Information technology may help retailers achieve the first aim by the use of electronic loyalty schemes which reward customers based on their store expenditure. The second aim is being facilitated by the ability to analyse information at local and individual level, which has enabled retailers to develop micromarketing strategies or customized marketing and merchandising programmes for each store based on local preferences.

● **Electronic Loyalty Schemes**

A major problem with EPOS data is that it does not carry any information about the customer. Hence, whilst the data is useful for monitoring sales and the impact of sales promotions and so forth, it provides little information as to who is buying the merchandise. Retailers have overcome this problem by setting up EPOS-based loyalty schemes. In order to become members of the loyalty scheme customers are asked to fill in a form with their personal demographic information (name, address, occupation, marital status, income and so on) and some questions regarding product preferences. Customers are given a personalized electronically readable magnetic card. When a purchase is made it is recorded by scanning the card. Customers earn a number of loyalty points (based on the size of their purchase) and these are added to their account and also printed on their till receipt for checking. The points collected are redeemable either against their next shopping bill, promotional gifts, or other promotional offers such as air miles.

The basic rationale behind loyalty schemes is to increase profits by developing long-term relationships with customers, particularly loyal customers. An important underlying reason for targeting existing customers is that it is easier to sell more to existing customers than to recruit new ones. Loyal customers also tend to spend more than the average customer per visit, and hence the loss of loyal customers can have a highly detrimental effect on store profitability. It is widely recognized that Tesco's Clubcard helped it to wrest market leadership, in terms of market share, from Sainsbury's.

A major driver of the current wave of loyalty schemes (see Table 8.1) is that they enable retailers to build up, relatively cheaply, a database of their customers who can be encouraged to remain or become the stores most loyal customers. With electronic loyalty schemes it is also possible to gather data on the shopping habits of customers and to use this information to target specific groups with customized incentives and offers. The data can also be used to define trade areas for stores and to target current and potential customers with marketing promotions. With the emergence of smart cards (electronic cards with a built-in microchip) retailers will be able to capture much more information about customer behaviour than the current swipe cards allow. Of course, an essential prerequisite of electronic loyalty schemes is the existence of an adequate IT network.

Table 8.1 Some examples of loyalty schemes in the UK

Retailer	Loyalty programme	Year launched	Rate of return on money spent	Estimated number of members
Sainsbury's	Reward card[1]	1996	1%	14 million
Tesco	Clubcard	1995	1%	12 million
Boots	Advantage card	1997	4%	10 million
WH Smith	Club card	1997	2%	5.5 million
Shell	SMART card	1994	1.04%	4.5million

[1] Replaced by the Nectar card in 2002.

Vignette 8.3

Loyalty cards

A major impetus to the growth of loyalty schemes was given when Tesco caught its competitors off guard by launching its Clubcard scheme nationally in February 1995, after previously trialing the scheme since 1993 in a limited number of stores. Until Clubcard's national launch, Sainsbury's had been using its own Saver card loyalty scheme in only 15 to 20 of its stores at any one time. Two months later Sainsbury's was operating the scheme in 50 of its stores and by July it was operating in 180 stores. Similarly, Safeway had been using its ABC customer reward card in 25 stores in February but by April 1995 had extended it to 106 stores and then to all its stores in October 1995. ASDA also began trialing its Club card in different versions during this period despite investing heavily in the Catalina system which provides customers with computer generated coupons at the checkout. Sainsbury's eventually replaced its limited Saver card scheme with its Reward card scheme in June 1996.

Loyalty schemes *per se* are not new; they have been used by retailers for a long time. In fact, one of the original loyalty schemes, the trading stamp, originated in the USA in the late nineteenth century. Trading stamps were given by a retailer to customers (usually in proportion to expenditure) which could be redeemed for cash or goods. The idea behind such schemes is to get customers to spend a greater proportion of their expenditure in the store (rather than a competitor's) and to frequent the store more often. A trading stamp-based loyalty scheme popular among UK retailers until the late 1970s was the Green Shield trading stamps scheme, which collapsed in 1977 after Tesco, one of its major supporters, withdrew in its bid to reposition its stores more upmarket.

Whilst manual schemes are effective, they are relatively crude compared to the electronic schemes. Electronic promotional schemes consist of either electronically dispensed, coupons or frequent shopper or loyalty clubs such as Tesco's Clubcard. An example of the former is the Catalina system used by Asda. In this system, consumer purchases trigger the dispensing of coupons for the product bought, or rival manufacturer's products or the store's own products. Unlike trading stamps and similar loyalty schemes, the new loyalty schemes can be branded by retailers to reflect a store's image and values.

Sources: Various sources including Rafiq (1997) 'Developing Customer Loyalty: The Savercard Experience', in Hart et al. (eds), *Cases in Retailing: Operational Perspectives* (Oxford: Blackwell Business), pp. 43–61.

Loyalty cards are, however, expensive to operate. Safeway abandoned its ABC loyalty card scheme in May 2000 after five years of operation, and has estimated a saving of more than £50 million per annum by getting rid of the scheme. There is also evidence that loyalty cards may be becoming less effective as most shoppers now possess more than one. Despite this, retailers operating loyalty schemes feel that the value of the information provided by the schemes outweighs the costs. A new loyalty scheme that addresses some of these concerns is the Nectar loyalty card launched by Sainsbury's, Debenhams, Barclaycard and BP in September 2002, replacing their individual schemes with a single multiparty one. From the retailer's perspective, a multiparty scheme has the advantage that the costs of running the scheme are shared between scheme members and potentially allows retailers to form a more rounded picture of their customers. It also has the advantage that customers can collect loyalty points faster, thus making it more attractive. Six months after the launch of the Nectar scheme it already had 11 million active cardholders and a number of other companies had joined the original consortium.

Customer Relationship Management (CRM)

A more general term for programmes designed to build and manage customer loyalty and to increase sales and profitability from existing customers is customer relationship management (CRM). CRM programmes require the collection and analysis of customer data. Such data can be acquired in a number of ways, including loyalty cards, credit cards, customer guarantee forms, invoices and so forth. For mail-order and internet shoppers, information identifying customers is less of a problem as it is provided by the customer when purchasing products. The purpose of analysis is to identify patterns and trends in customer shopping habits in order to meet customer needs more precisely. The information is used to develop marketing, customer services, and customized merchandise programmes for targeted groups or individuals. The power of CRM programmes is most evident in the area of internet retailing, where the technology is available to personalize webpages and to tailor offers to each customer.

Data Warehousing and Micromarketing

A data warehouse consists of a collection of various internal retailing databases such as EPOS data, loyalty card data, customer payment data and external data such as geodemographic profiles, competitor data, and market research information from third parties. The idea behind constructing such data warehouses (or stores of data) is so that the relationships within and between the databases constituting the warehouse can be analysed for useful patterns and structures for marketing and other purposes. These patterns are identified by using various statistical, database and artificial intelligence data-mining techniques, amongst others. An important facet of data warehousing is that it allows information to be shared with different parts of an organization in the required format, whilst separating analysis from operational activities.

The data warehouses can be used for any number of purposes ranging from forecasting sales trends, pricing, measuring effectiveness of displays and promotions, to tracking customer profitability. One particular use of data-mining is that of micromarketing. Micromarketing is the identification of the needs of store-specific markets and tailoring marketing and merchandising efforts to satisfy those needs. A corollary of micromarketing is micromerchandising or the development of the store-specific product mix required to satisfy the needs of the target market. Wal-Mart is one retailer that has adopted the micromarketing and micromerchandising approach by using data-mining to help each of its stores to adjust its merchandise mix to local preferences, ensuring that the range and prices are in line with local spending patterns. There is no real reason why this approach cannot be extended to one-to-one marketing. Internet retailers in particular have information on individuals and the ability to target them individually. However, the benefits of one-to-one marketing must be weighed against the costs.

For large retailers, in particular, the data collected can take up vast amounts of computer memory. For instance, the world's biggest retailer, Wal-Mart, has a data warehouse considered second in size only to the Pentagon. It was already 43 terabytes (trillions of characters) in size in 1998, but by 2000 it had more than doubled to 101terabytes. Given the size of the investment in terms of time and money, data warehouses need to be actively managed to obtain the best information from them.

● Retail Management Information Systems

Given the quantity of information generated by retailers, it needs to be organized so that management can use it effectively for decision-making purposes. A *retail information system* systematically collects, processes, stores and distributes information to the relevant decision-makers for the purposes of planning, controlling and monitoring business processes. An information system has four basic components: namely information inputs, information processing capability, outputs, and information storage capacity. Information systems also require feedback, which is output that is returned to those dealing with information input so that they can evaluate or modify the data entered at the input stage.

Information inputs are essentially either internal or external to the retailer. Internal inputs are either information routinely collected, or information collected on an *ad hoc* basis such as market research. Routinely collected information includes EPOS sales data, loyalty card data, store card data, returns, customer complaints, coupon redemptions and so on. Other information inputs include costs of merchandise, costs of operations and financial budgets, merchandise plans, product information, inventory, orders, deliveries, pricing, promotions and so forth.

External information is information from external organizations such as market research companies, government sources, suppliers and so on. For instance, Nielsen's Homescan provides panel data on consumer shopping behaviour across all types of retailers and products. The MOSAIC and ACORN lifestyle and geodemographic databases are available from the market-research companies Experian and CACI respectively. Much of this information is available in electronic format and can therefore be easily integrated into retailers' information systems. External information performs an important function in that it provides an external view of the market and fills in gaps in retailers' knowledge of the market.

The type of information input into a system depends upon the purpose for which it is required. For instance, if the retailer wants to estimate the profit that each individual product contributes (DPP) to the overall profitability of a department, information on the revenue generated by each product and the

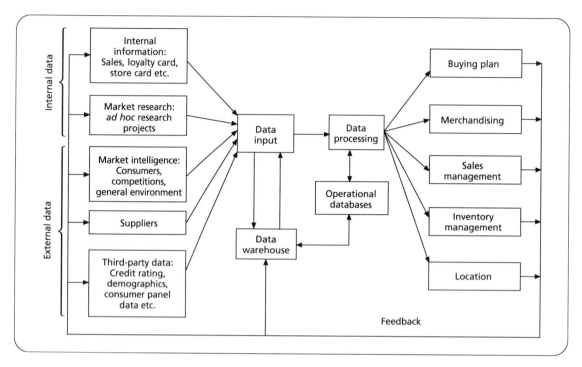

Figure 8.3 A hypothetical retailing information management system

costs associated with selling it will be required. On the revenue side, the sale price, any promotional support from the supplier, and invoice cost are required to calculate the gross profit. On the costs side, transport direct costs, warehousing direct costs, store direct costs (space, labour and so on), promotional costs, and pre-warehousing costs (for example ordering costs) would be required as inputs to calculate the costs associated with each product (see Figure 8.3).

Database management

In order to maximize the value of the information that the organization collects, it needs to ensure that the information from different databases is effectively integrated and actively managed. For instance, a retailer may collect information on customers using its store card, from responses to promotional campaigns, and third-party lists, and maintain separate databases for each. However, to maximize the value of these databases they need to be integrated into a master customer database. Direct marketing campaigns based on such a database are much more likely to be comprehensive and effective than those based on the individual databases. Active management of such a customer database also means that the data are used to analyse the recency, frequency, average spend of customers and the lifetime value of the customer to the organization so that the most valuable customers can be identified and targeted for direct marketing campaigns.

Types of information systems

Retail information systems can be divided into four basic types, namely:

● transaction processing systems (TPS);
● management information systems (MIS);
● decision support systems (DSS); and
● executive support systems (ESS).

Transaction processing systems (TPS) are used to facilitate customer transactions and other routine business processes necessary for the conduct of business on a day-to-day basis. Examples include sales recording by EPOS systems, payroll, and employee record-keeping. A breakdown in TPS is likely to have a severe impact on the operation of the business and thus requires regular monitoring by managers. The information collected by TPS forms a major input into other systems.

The purpose of management information systems (MIS) is to assist middle managers in their monitoring, controlling and decision-making activities. MIS normally provide routine summary or exception reports either in the form of a report or online access. The reports are usually summaries of transaction data from TPS indicating the firm's current performance. The reports provide answers to questions that are pre-specified and usually only contain simple summaries and comparison rather than sophisticated analysis of the data. An MIS report for a store manger, for instance, might consist of a report on weekly sales by each department of a store.

A decision support system (DSS) is an information system designed to assist managers in making non-routine semi-structured or unstructured decisions. A DSS combines use of models with data from various sources including both internal and external data (where relevant). A DSS typically allows the user to conduct 'what-if' analyses by changing the assumptions underlying various components of the decision. In retailing, a DSS may be employed in assisting store location decisions, for instance. Such a system would require internal data on existing locations and criteria that the new store must satisfy. External information, for instance on the demographics of the trading area of the proposed store, would also be required. In addition, the DSS would also incorporate a model (either theoretical or one proposed by management) as to how this information should be combined to arrive at a location decision.

An executive support system (ESS) is designed to support senior mangers responsible for making strategic decisions in the company. As strategic decisions are non-routine and require information about trends in the external environment as well as internally, an ESS incorporates information both from MIS and DSS and external data about competitors activities, the regulatory environment, the economic environment and so forth.

Electronic kiosks

Electronic kiosks are being increasingly used by retailers to support their in-store activities. For instance, they can be used to give customers more detailed information about product features. Car dealers could provide more precise information about the features of car, for example, what features come as standard and what are optional extras and so forth. They can also provide information about items that the branch does not stock but can be ordered for the customer. Kiosks can also be used to check if an item is in stock. Some retailers, such as Sainsbury's, are using electronic kiosks to give loyalty card-holders information about the latest special offers, to dispense coupons, and to provide information about new products.

Kiosks can be linked to the retailer's online store for customers to order merchandise and have it delivered either at home or at the store. Indeed, usage of web kiosks is showing the most expansion; web kiosks act as a doorway to the retailer's online merchandise. Usage of kiosks leads to customers spending more time and hence money in stores. They're relatively cheap as most are just an extension of the in-store intranet. The major advantage of kiosks is that they encourage self-service amongst shoppers, providing them with a higher level of service in stores that employ them. However, they may be less welcome in high-service environments such as department stores where shoppers expect service to be more personally provided by the store.

Electronic shelf-edge labels

Electronic shelf-edge labelling technology has been available for some time but is still at an experimental stage. This technology replaces the need to manually change shelf-edge labels, by using liquid-crystal display (LCD) modules to give customers information about products and prices. The major advantage of this system is that the labour requirement is reduced. The electronic labels are directly linked to the EPOS system thus ensuring that the price charged at the checkout is the same as that displayed on the shelf. It also gives retailers such as supermarkets the ability to change prices several times daily. For instance, prices in the evenings could be lower than during the rest of the day to generate extra traffic. However, the technology is still relatively expensive and requires considerable investment by retailers. Also, depending on the system that is used, the technology may restrict the way in which products are merchandised.

Summary

Whilst retailers were once slow to adopt IT in stores, IT is now integral to all aspects of retail management. The use of EPOS, EFTPOS and EDI has increased store productivity and improved customer service. The combination of EPOS and EDI has allowed retailers to develop quick-response systems which gives them more flexibility, reduces inventory costs and improves customer service. The use of loyalty cards has given retailers not only a way of offering incentives to customers, but the data provided by the schemes gives retailers more precise insight into customer behaviour. Retailers have been able to use this internally generated information and external databases to develop new micromarketing techniques to target customers more precisely with more tailored merchandise. Retailers are also beginning to use sophisticated information systems designed for specific types of management decisions ranging from transaction processing systems for routine decisions, to executive support systems for strategic decisions. In order to make the most effective use of the information available, retailers need to integrate their various information systems to give them an edge in a rapidly changing environment.

Questions

1   What are the benefits of using EPOS systems for retailers?
2   How have shoppers benefited from the use of information technology by retailers?
3   Explain how a QR system can reduce inventory investment and improve customer service.
4   What are the benefits of electronic loyalty schemes for retailers? Why do many retailers not have loyalty schemes?
5   Discuss how retailers can exploit various databases at their disposal.
6   Describe the key elements of a retail information system.
7   Explain the functions of the different types of information systems used by retailers.

References and Further Reading

Burden, R. and Proctor, T. (1997) 'Information Systems Development in Retailing', *Marketing Intelligence and Planning*, vol. 15, no. 2, pp. 106–11;

Clarke, I. and Rowley, J. (1995) 'A Case for Spatial Decision-Support Systems in Retail Location Planning', *International Journal of Retail and Distribution Management*, vol. 23, no. 3, pp. 4–10.

Cohen, B. (1992) 'How Micromerchandising can Work for Big Chains', *Chain Store Age Executive with Shopping Center Age*, New York, vol. 68; no.2 (February), p. 58.

Dawson, J. A. (1994) 'Applications of Information Management in European Retailing', *International Review of Retail, Distribution and Consumer Research*, vol. 4, no. 2, pp. 219–38.

Fisher, M. L., Raman, A. and McClelland, A. S. (2000) 'Rocket Science Retailing is Almost Here: Are YouReady?', *Harvard Business Review*, vol. 78, no. 4 (July/August), pp. 115–24.

Larson, P. D. and Lusch, R. F. (1990) 'Quick Response Retail Technology: Integration and Performance Measurement', *International Review of Retail, Distribution and Consumer Research*, vol. 1, no. 1, pp. 17–35.

Laudon, K. C. and Laudon, J. P. (2000), *Management Information Systems: Organisation and Technology in the Networked Enterprise*, 6th edn (London: Prentice-Hall).

Levy, M. and Grewal, D. (2000) 'Supply Chain Management in a Networked Economy', *Journal of Retailing*, vol. 76, no. 4, pp. 415–29.

O'Brien, L. and Jones, C. (1995) 'Do Rewards Really Create Loyalty', *Harvard Business Review*, vol. 73, no. 3, pp. 74–82.

Pearce; M. R. (1997) 'Succeeding with Micromarketing', *Ivey Business Quarterly*, London, vol. 62, no.1, pp. 69–72.

Rafiq, M. (1997) 'Developing Customer Loyalty: The Savercard Experience', in C. Hart, M, Kirkup, D. Preston, M. Rafiq and P. Walley (eds), *Cases in Retailing: Operational Perspectives* (Oxford: Blackwell Business), pp. 43–61.

Rowley, J. (1995) 'Multimedia Kiosks in Retailing', *International Journal of Retail and Distribution Management*, vol. 23, no. 5, pp. 32–40.

Steidtmann, C. (1999) 'The New Retail Technology', *Discount Merchandiser*, vol. 39, no. 11, pp. 23–24.

Sweeney, T. (2001) 'Web Kiosks Spur Spending in Stores', *Informationweek*, 12 March, issue 828, pp. 126–128.

Wasserman, T, Khermouch, G. and Green, J. (2000) 'Mining Everyone's Business', *Brandweek*, New York, vol. 41, no. 9 (28 February), pp. 32–6.

Williams, B. (1994) *The Best Butter in the World: A History of Sainsbury's* (London: J. Sainsbury plc).

Wright, C. and Sparks, L. (1999) 'Loyalty Saturation in Retailing: Exploring the End of Retail Loyalty Cards?', *International Journal of Retail and Distribution Management*, vol. 27, no. 10, pp. 429–40.

part three

Retail Marketing Management

chapter nine

Retail Location

Learning objectives

- To understand the importance of retail location decision-making.
- To distinguish between different types of available retail locations.
- To explore patterns of retail development.
- To appreciate the importance of defining and estimating a trade area and selecting the best sites.
- To explore the use of geo-demographics in location decision-making.
- To understand the various methods of assessing the potential of retail sites.
- To appreciate the impact of planning regulations on location decisions.

Introduction

Location has long been recognized as one of the prime determinants of success in retailing. It is for this reason that, even in an era where virtual retailing is increasingly commonplace, it is still said that the three determinants of retailing success are 'location, location, and location'. Whilst other aspects of the retail mix can be changed relatively quickly, location decisions are long-term in nature and difficult to change in the short term. Hence, costs of wrong decisions can be high. For instance, a new Tesco store in the UK can cost up to £50 million to open, depending on the store type (Tesco website). A growth-orientated retailer such as Tesco is also looking to expand its store portfolio and hence constantly on the lookout for suitable new locations. For instance, Tesco spent nearly £500m on 55 new store openings in 2001/02 and planned to open a further 75 new stores in 2002/03 (Tesco *Annual Report*, 2002).

Location decisions are complex, as they need to satisfy consumer needs for convenience, accessibility and quality and at the same time provide a competitive advantage for the organization. A chosen location must also take into account other operational needs such as adequate access for deliveries, availability of labour and so on. Also the choice of retail locations is much wider than it used to be. New locations are becoming available all the time. Some of the alternative locations include traditional town centres or 'high streets', major regional centres; out-of-town centres (for example Bluewater); speciality centres such as historical districts, waterfronts, factory outlets, old industry sites; freestanding locations such as greenfield sites; retail warehouse parks; petrol station forecourts; motorway service stations, airports and other transport terminals (rail, sea, ferry, Eurotunnel). At the same time the choice of location is becoming increasingly difficult because of increasing competition and the shortage of large sites due to stricter planning regulations on out-of-town developments.

● Types of Retail Location

One of the first decisions that a retailer has to make is to decide what is the best type of location for its store. The decision may be whether to choose a solus or freestanding location, a site within a planned shopping centre, or one in an unplanned shopping centre such as the traditional 'high street'. Each type of location inevitably has its advantages and disadvantages, and these are discussed below.

Solus or freestanding site

A solus site is a standalone site away from other shopping centres. Such stores are usually purpose built. Generally, retailers that select freestanding sites are seeking either to benefit from spatial monopoly or for reasons of operational efficiency. Typical examples of freestanding stores are grocery superstores and non-grocery stores such as DIY and furniture stores. For grocery stores, it is essential that the store location is convenient for customers and that the trading area is not shared with other competitors. For a furniture retailer such as IKEA the availability of a low-cost, large, flat site for an extensive display and warehouse area and car parking is essential. A major disadvantage of a solus site is that the retailer cannot rely on the 'centre' to attract customers and has to undertake its own promotional activity to generate footfall. Another problem with solus sites is that new sites are likely to require planning permission, which may be difficult to obtain.

Unplanned shopping centre

An unplanned shopping centre is one that has evolved in a gradual, piecemeal manner. Typical unplanned centres include the 'high street' or central business districts (CBDs) in town centres. Suburban centres also tend to be unplanned. A distinctive feature of unplanned locations is that ownership of the centre is fragmented. Unplanned centres rely on customer traffic generated by other attractions to the centre as well as retailing, including business and leisure attractions. A major attraction of such centres is the variety of retailers, which facilitates comparison-shopping for customers. The retail composition of unplanned centres is unregulated and hence, unlike planned centres, there are no quotas on particular types of retailers within the centre.

Planned shopping centre

A planned shopping centre is one that has been deliberately designed and developed for retail use. This may be a single building with one of a number of stores, for example a shopping mall, or a group of physically separate stores with common access and car parking (such as a retail park). Planned centres are designed to serve a specific, geo-demographic segment of customers, are normally under single ownership and are actively promoted by their owners as a single entity. As a result they have the advantage of a consistent image for the centre whereas this is much more difficult for unplanned centres. In order to maintain this image planned centres will restrict retailers' activities, such as the type of store design, and the tenant mix will be carefully coordinated.

The choice between planned and unplanned centres depends on the amount and type of customer traffic a centre generates, and the quality and suitability of the site for specific retailers and retail activity.

● Patterns of Retail Development

A number of theories exist to explain the pattern of retailing locations and the interrelationships between them. These include: the central-place theory which attempts to explain the existence of shopping districts, their size, composition and spacing and the hierarchical relation between them; the bid-rent theory which provides an explanation of internal spatial organization in unplanned shopping districts; and the agglomeration theory that provides explanations for the clustering of similar types of retailers.

Central-place theory

The central-place theory is a model that explains the economic forces that lead to a *hierarchical* supply of shopping facilities in urban areas. It was first proposed by Christaller in the 1930s and further developed by Losch (1954) and others. The theory is based on the premise that as the distance to a retail centre/district increases, demand for a product will decrease due to increased cost of travel. The maximum distance that a customer will travel to obtain a product is known as the market area or *range* of the good. The *threshold* is defined as the minimum population required to make the supply of a good worthwhile. In order to be viable, the range of the good needs to exceed the threshold for the product. Using this framework the theory predicts that low-order (frequently purchased, low priced, convenience) products will require low threshold and low range to be successful, whereas high-order products (infrequently purchased, expensive products) such as comparison goods require larger ranges (market areas) and thresholds to be successful. For these products the shopper is willing to travel a greater distance in order make comparisons and to buy. This suggests that high-order goods are supplied only from large populous 'central' places and lower-order goods are supplied locally, leading to a hierarchy of shopping centres at different levels, such as regional shopping centres, district shopping centres, and neighbourhood shopping centres. Furthermore, as the model assumes identical sellers (that is, they sell a single line of merchandise, and overheads and buying costs are the same for all retailers selling similar goods) and no barriers to entry, it follows that the retailers of each item are equally spaced in a triangular fashion and have non-overlapping hexagonal trade areas, the size of which depends upon the order of the good sold.

This model came to be seen as an ideal arrangement or hierarchy for shopping centres by UK planners (particularly in the 1950s and 1960s) and is one major reason for the comparatively late emergence of freestanding hypermarkets/superstores, and out-of-town and retail parks in the UK.

The central-place theory has come under severe criticism for some of the assumptions that underpin it. For instance, the assumption that consumers have identical needs and undertake single-purpose (product) shopping trips to the nearest centre that supplies the merchandise is no longer tenable. For instance, whilst single-purpose shopping visits may have accurately described a situation in the past when grocery shopping involved buying meat from the butcher, bread from the bakery and vegetables from the greengrocer, in the era of the superstore and hypermarket such a description is not very realistic where all grocery shopping needs are supplied in one location. The central-place theory also implies that the only factor that differentiates one store from another is location, which ignores other factors such as quality and image that also play an important role in store choice.

The relevance of the theory in developed countries today has been almost completely undermined by the transformation of shopping and retailing in the emergence of mass car ownership. One of the major effects has been to turn the accessibility of town centres (or central places) on its head such that they have changed from being the most accessible to the most congested. As a consequence, there has been a huge shift of retailing from town centres to out-of-town locations in the last 30 years in what has been called 'waves of decentralization' by Schiller (1986). This began with the development of grocery superstores in the early 1970s, followed in the mid-1970s by space-hungry specialists such as electrical, carpet and furniture stores. The vast majority of comparison shopping still remained in town centres until the early 1980s, when the first retail parks started to emerge. The 1990s saw the emergence of large out-of-town regional shopping centres large enough by themselves to compete directly with town centres. These developments have fundamentally altered the traditional retailing hierarchies, which led Dawson (1979, p. 190) to comment that:

> Whilst the theory serves to describe and, in part, explain locational patterns developed prior to the 1960s, it can no longer be used as a basis either for the explanation of present patterns or the planning of future patterns.

In a similar vein, Schiller (2001, p. 55) argues that, 'The theory is ... no longer relevant and is indeed positively dangerous as a guide to planning policy or understanding retail location as it exists today.'

Despite the criticisms noted above the central place theory is useful for drawing attention to the fundamental importance of the distance-decay effect, that is the attraction of retail centre/location to consumers declines as the distance to it increases. It is also useful in that it highlights the fact that suitability of location (central place or not) depends upon the type of merchandise that is being offered.

Bid-rent theory

Whilst in planned centres the location of actual stores is largely determined by centre management, in unplanned centres the location of retailers is determined by competition for the sites between different potential users. The bid-rent (or land-use) theory attempts to explain the spatial arrangement of retailers within centres. The theory is based on the premise that accessibility is of paramount importance for explaining patterns of urban land use. In urban settings, the city centre is the focal point of transportation networks and is, therefore, the most accessible and offers the maximum potential and optimum access to customers and labour. Competition is highest for a central location and land goes to the highest bidders; those that can derive the greatest utility from the location. Hence, rents are highest in the centre and decline with distance from the core. Access to consumers is of paramount importance to retailers and they are therefore prepared to pay the high rents that city-centre locations demand. However, only some retailers are able to afford the cost of these prime sites. Invariably prime-pitch locations (those with the highest customer traffic) are more likely to be occupied by department stores, variety stores or speciality fashion stores. Grocery and furniture stores are more likely to be located towards the edge of the centre because of their need for cheap sites with large amounts of surface area and car parking spaces.

Explanations of retail clustering

Bid-rent theory does not explain *agglomeration,* that is the tendency of similar retailers to cluster together. Early explanations of this phenomenon are based on Hotelling's (1929), *Principle of Minimum Differentiation* which suggests that a retailer would be able to maximize profits by locating or relocating closer to a competitor in order to gain a larger market area. Using the example of two similar profit-maximizing firms operating on a linear market (for example, two ice-cream vendors on a beach) Hotelling argued that if one vendor is free to relocate, he would maximize his 'hinterland' or market (and hence his profit) by setting up shop adjacent to the other on the 'long' side of the market. If both sellers are footloose, a process of leapfrogging to the 'longer side' of the market develops, resulting in eventual clustering in the centre of the market (see Figure 9.1).

More recent explanations of agglomeration are based on the existence of positive externalities (benefits) for retailers locating together to attract a

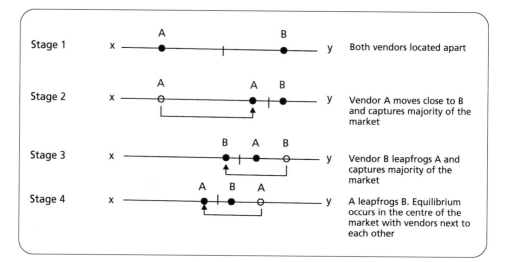

Figure 9.1 Principle of minimum differentiation

Source: Based on Hotelling (1929).

higher flow of customers. For instance, clustering could lead to improved infrastructure, or reduction in costs due to shared car parking and hence improve access for customers of all the retailers. Agglomeration also makes sense where retailers can take advantage of traffic generated by destination stores (such as department stores) by intercepting customers on their way to and from the store. Department and other destination stores are aware of the externalities that they are generating and in planned shopping centres are able to negotiate considerable reductions in their rents. Landlords in these centres recoup these costs by charging higher rents to retailers located near the destination stores. The externalities argument also suggests that clustering of similar stores leads to an increase in the total sales of retailers unlike the arguments supporting the principle of minimum differentiation. There is also evidence that consumers attempt to reduce search and uncertainty costs by undertaking multipurpose, multistop and comparison shopping and therefore prefer shopping where retailers are conveniently clustered. These explanations are better able to explain why, for instance, motorcar dealers tend to cluster together outside of central locations.

● The Retail Location Decision Process

Retail location decision-making is a stepwise process, and it begins with the identification of the most attractive market areas or regions. The *regions* in this context can be towns, cities, metropolitan conurbations, or even geographic regions. Such analysis is necessary as there can be a great deal of variation in demand and competitive conditions between regions. The next step is to identify suitable sites within the market area with a viable trading area (or catchment). The trade area is the geographical area that contains the potential customers for a particular retailer. The third step is the selection of the best site taking into account not just the potential revenue that the site can generate, but also the costs of locating at the site.

Region/market-area decision

Most retailers expand organically, that is by adding additional branches to their existing networks. This usually means that they will expand in a step-wise fashion from their original area of location or region and will only consider other regions when they have saturated the original region. Expansion is hereafter usually into neighbouring regions and not distant ones as this minimizes the need to set up new distribution and logistical centres to support the new stores. However, in later stages of growth, retailers may consider regions more distant from their original location and infill interven-ing regions at a later stage – a strategy that was employed for instance by Kwik Save (Sparks, 1990). More recent examples include Aldi, IKEA and Toys R Us.

Decisions on which regions to locate will depend on a number of factors including demography, economy, competition and infrastructure. For instance, Aldi entered the UK market by opening its first store in the West Midlands region of the UK because the region's socio-demographic profile matched the customer profile of the Aldi customer; that is, households that are likely to be on a tight budget or interested in a value-for-money proposi-tion when shopping for groceries. Even within regions there is a considerable amount of diversity and decisions have to be made regarding which trade area(s) within the regions to target.

Trade-area decision

The trade area (or catchment) is defined as the geographic area from which a particular store or shopping centre draws its customers, and essentially deter-mines the potential sales for a store. The extent of the trade area is determined by the type of store (and consequently the type of merchandise and the total size of the assortment sold by the retailer) and the degree of mobility of the customer and relative location of competitors. For instance, the trade area of convenience store is likely to be less than a mile, whereas that for an IKEA store may extend more than 20 miles. The difference is due to fact that customers are not willing to travel long distances for convenience items such as bread and milk, but will travel much longer distances to stores that offer speciality and comparison goods and large assortments. Other major influ-ences on trade area-size are:

● Population density/distribution.
● Socioeconomic status of consumers.
● Distance and time to travel (actual and perceived).
● Transport/communication networks.
● Level of car ownership.
● Business attractions of the centre where store is located.
● Social attractions of the centre where store is located.
● Competition from neighbouring stores/centres.

● Presence of complementary retailers.
● Geographical barriers (for example a river).

The exact shape and size of the trade area will be determined by the interaction of all these factors. A consequence of this is that stores do not draw trade from all areas of their catchments in equal proportions. In fact trade areas can be divided into primary, secondary or tertiary zones. The *primary trade area* is designated as the area from which the store attracts 60 to 65 per cent of its customers and is the area closest to the store. This area has the highest density of customers and generates the highest expenditure per head. The *secondary trade area* generates around 20–30 per cent of the stores' sales, and the remainder of the sales come from the *tertiary trade area*. Its customers may shop at the store when they are in the vicinity, for example on their way to or from work. It also includes shoppers who lack adequate retailing facilities closer to where they live and the site is served by excellent transport connections.

Figure 9.2 shows the trade areas of supermarkets in the UK. Research by the Competition Commission (2000) has shown that for large supermarket operators such as Sainsbury's, on average 73 per cent of customers come from within a radius of three miles (designated as primary trade in Figure 9.2), a further 15 per cent travel come from a distance of four to five miles from the store (secondary trade area), and the remaining 12 per cent from more than five miles away (the tertiary trade area). The research further showed that shoppers living in highly urbanized areas (for example London) tended to travel shorter distances than the average, and that those living in rural areas tended travel further than the average.

The question arises whether it is more appropriate to describe trade areas using distance travelled, or the travel time to a store. Given that the majority

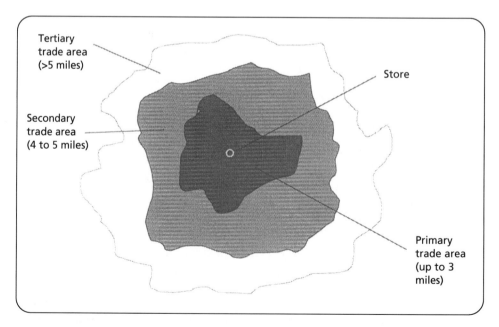

Figure 9.2   Trade areas for a large supermarket

of shoppers are car-borne (particularly in the case of grocery shopping), it is common practice to use drive-time isochrones to delineate trade areas. Isochrones are contours on a map representing equal travel time (usually drive time) from the store. An advantage of drive-time isochrones is that they take account of traffic conditions as well as distance. The Competition Commission research found that 66 per cent of food shoppers travelled 10 minutes or less to a supermarket, a further 25 per cent travelled between 11 and 20 minutes, and 7 per cent between 21 and 30 minutes. Therefore, when considering potential sites for new stores, the majority of UK food multiples use a 15–20 minute drive-time-based measure as the main factor in determining the size of a store's trade area, as 80 to 90 per cent of customers are likely to come from this area. Local demographics and the presence of competitors and own stores are then used to refine the initial estimate.

Determining trade areas

There are two main techniques for determining trade areas; namely, 'spotting' techniques and mathematical models. The first technique is used by retailers to determine the extent of trading areas for existing stores, whilst quantitative techniques are used with new stores. Essentially, 'spotting' attempts to spot the customer's origin on a map. The technique allows retailers to determine the extent of trading area as well as the major areas within the trading area from which customers originate. Some common spotting techniques include customer surveys, customer records (for example customer credit, service and delivery records) loyalty schemes, and sales promotion techniques such as contests and sweepstakes. The most commonly used mathematical models for determining the catchment areas of a store are the so-called gravitational (or spatial-interaction) models. The models are loosely based on the physical laws of gravity, and attempt to measure the pull or attraction of each of the locations. Two of the more widely used models are Reilly's Law and Huff's probability model.

Reilly's Law

Reilly's Law is named after William Reilly who, in 1931, proposed a mathematical formula for determining a trade area known as the 'law of retail gravitation'. Reilly's Law provides a measure of the relative power of two competing towns to attract customers to shop there from the area between them. Reilly proposed that a town's ability to attract shoppers depended on the size of its population and the distance between it and the outlying area. More formally, the proportion of retail trade attracted from an intermediate area between two competing communities is *directly* proportional to the populations of the two towns and *inversely* proportional to the square of the distances between them.

Converse (1949) restated Reilly's Law in the form of a 'breaking point', which is defined as the point up to which one location is dominant and beyond which the other is dominant. In other words, the breaking point defines the point between competing centres where the probability of a consumer visiting either centre is the same. The relationship is stated in the form of a formula as follows:

$$BP_a = D_{ab} \div \left(1 + \sqrt{P_b \div P_a}\right)$$

where BP_a is the distance of the breaking point from town A (that is the catchment of town A); D_{ab} is the Distance from A to B; P_b is the population of town B; and P_a is the population of town A.

As an illustration consider the case of two small towns located eight miles apart. Town A has a population of 10,000 and town B a population of 40,000. Substituting into the formula gives the boundary between the two towns as follows:

Distance from breaking point to town B = 8/(1 +√10,000/40,000)
= 8/(1+0.5) = 5.3miles

Thus the breaking point in this example is 5.3 miles from town B and 2.7 miles from town A. The model can be easily modified to measure the breaking point between shopping centres by replacing the town populations by the size of the shopping centres. A trading area can be determined by computing the breaking point between one retail centre and all competing centres. The formula assumes that the attractiveness of a centre can be represented by the size of the population and that shoppers are deterred by distance. Specifically, that the further away a retail centre is, the more likely that the shopper will be deterred from visiting it. This is mainly due to increasing travel costs. Gravitational models assume that competing centres are equally accessible and that retailers in both areas are equally effective and do not have any significant competitive advantage over each other. The model can be modified to measure the breaking point between shopping centres by the replacement of distance by travel time as consumers are more likely to perceive distance in terms of time due to the widespread availability of personal transport and given that consumers are time poor. The size of the population of a destination can also be replaced by the total retail floor space of a centre, which is more likely to reflect the attractiveness of the centre to potential customers.

According to Huff (1964), a major weakness of the gravity models is that they do not provide interval estimates of the likelihood of attracting customers above or below the breaking point between two centres. This is particularly important, as the form of the breaking point equation will vary according to the type of shopping trip. For instance, shoppers are likely to travel furthest for speciality goods, least for convenience goods and moderate distances for comparison (shopping) goods. As discussed above, from the retailer's perspective a given store will have primary, secondary and tertiary (or fringe) trading areas:

- Primary trading area – closest to the store, attracts 60–65 per cent of sales; within this area the store has the best competitive advantage.
- Secondary trading area – attracts around 20–30 per cent of sales; in this area the store has to compete with other stores to attract customers.
- Tertiary trading area/fringe area – area from which the store occasionally attracts customers (5–10 per cent); the competitive position in this area is weakest as competing stores are more accessible.

The physical extent of the zones depends on the type of store, accessibility, competition, and the mobility and willingness of customers to travel, and can be defined in terms of physical distance or drive time. The shape of the trading area is determined by transportation networks, the physical geography of the area and the location of competitors. The store may also attract transient customers who patronize the store either because they are in the vicinity, are variety seekers, or are very loyal to the store.

Huff's probability model

To overcome the difficulties of Reilly's model, Huff proposed a model to predict the trade area of individual stores rather than towns. Huff proposed that the trade area of a store is determined by its relative attraction; relative, that is, to all other similar stores in the area. Hence, to estimate the trade area of a DIY store, its attraction relative to all other DIY stores in the area must be assessed. Huff further proposed that the value or the attraction of a store to a customer depends on its size and the distance the customer has to travel to shop there. In the model the attraction of a store to a customer is given as:

$$A_{ij} = S_j^a / D_{ij}^b$$

where A_{ij} is the attraction of store j to customer i; S_j is the size of store j; D_{ij} is the distance or travel time of customer i from store j; a is a parameter reflecting the sensitivity of the customer to store size; and b is a parameter reflecting the sensitivity of the customer to distance.

Given the above, the probability that a customer is attracted to a particular store, P_{ij}, can be expressed as a ratio of the attractiveness of a given store to the sum of the attraction of all competing stores:

$$P_{ij} = \frac{\text{Value of store } j}{\text{Sum of the values of all stores}}$$

Given the number of competing stores, n, the above formula can be restated as:

$$P_{ij} = \frac{S_j^a}{D_{ij}^b} \div \sum_{j=1}^{n} \left(\frac{S_j^a}{D_{ij}^b} \right)$$

The values of the parameters can be used to reflect the relative importance of store size, a, and distance, b, in a given shopping situation. For instance, a high value for b can be used to reflect the deterrent effect of distance in the case of convenience shopping. In the case of comparison shopping, the distance parameter is likely to be lower and the size parameter higher. Hence, accurate estimates of the parameter values are an important determinant of the accuracy of the predicted trade areas. The parameter values are usually determined by surveys of shopping patterns for the particular type of store. Alternatively, estimates based on similar locations may be used.

Example 9.1 An illustration using the Huff model

Consider an individual who has the choice of shopping at two supermarkets in a town. The distances from the customer's home and the sizes of the two supermarkets are as follows:

Store	Distance (miles)	Size (square feet)
A	3	20,000
B	4	40,000

If the parameter $a = 1$ and parameter $b = 2$, the relative attraction of each of the three stores to this individual can be calculated as follows:

Attraction of store A = $20,000/3^2 = 2,222$
Attraction of store B = $40,000/4^2 = 2,500$

The probability of this individual visiting store A is:

$$\frac{\text{Attraction of store A}}{\text{Sum of attractions of all stores in the area}}$$

$$= 2,222/(2,222 + 2,500) = 0.47 \text{ or } 47 \text{ per cent}$$

Similarly, the probability of the consumer shopping at the store B is:

$$2,500/(2,222 + 2,500) = 0.53 \text{ or } 53 \text{ per cent}$$

Index of retail saturation

The attractiveness of an area to a retailer depends not only on the potential demand within an area but also the degree of competition. An area with high demand may not be suitable because of high levels of competition. The index of retail saturation (IRS) measures demand relative to the supply of retail floor space within a specified area. IRS is the demand for a product category divided by the total retail floor space for that product category:

$$IRS_i = \frac{C_i \times RE_i}{RF_i}$$

where C_i is the number of customers in area i for the product category; RE_i is the average customer spend in area i for the product category; and RF_i is the total retail square footage in area i allocated to the product (including proposed store).

A low value of IRS indicates overstoring in the area, for the specified category of store, and a high value indicates understoring. The relative attractiveness of different areas can be obtained by ranking different areas by their IRS scores. However, the IRS figures need to be compared with a retailer's organizational norm to ensure that a proposed store meets minimum sales expectations. The IRS figure provides an average sales per square foot figure across all retailers. The actual sales per square foot achieved by a particular retailer will differ from that depending on the retailer's competitive advantages in the market-place including size of store, location, pricing strategies and so forth. Also, IRS reflects existing demand and supply in an area. However, a new retailer coming into a market may expand demand due to its marketing activities. Demand may also expand due to agglomeration effects; that is, demand expands due to more retailers being located near to each other.

Vignette 9.1

ASDA's unrestricted entry and expansion scenario in Birmingham

An application of the index of retail saturation is illustrated by ASDA. In its submission to the Competition Commission (2000), ASDA estimated that there were an average of 671 people for about every 90 sq mtrs (1,000 sq ft) of supermarket floor space. It then used this average as a benchmark to assess whether different areas of the country were under- or overstored in terms of grocery provision. For instance, in the Birmingham postal area it estimated that there were an average of 857 people for about every 90 sq mtrs (1,000 sq ft) with a total supermarket floor space of 0.2 million sq mtrs (2.1 million sq ft). Given the population of Birmingham, ASDA estimated that the floor space necessary for the Birmingham postal area to have average levels of provision was 0.25 million sq mtrs (2.7 million sq ft). The difference between the actual provision (0.2 million sq mtrs) and that necessary to achieve average national levels of provision (0.25million sq ft) of +0.05 million sq mtrs (+ 0.6 million sq ft), gives the relative underprovision of grocery facilities in Birmingham. This is equivalent to 12 superstores of around 50,000 sq ft, roughly the average size of an ASDA store. The analysis is somewhat crude but gives an indication of the number of new superstores that might appear if there were no barriers to entry. However, new entry is affected by the ability to obtain planning permission (likely to be difficult in out-of-town locations in the current climate), but also depends on the availability of suitable sites at reasonable cost. The analysis also assumed that the 'average' level of provision was the correct level of provision; however, it may be that the average is not the right benchmark for determining which areas need more food retailing provision.

Geo-demographic information systems

In order to ensure the success of stores, retailers need to know not only the size of the trade area but more precise information on the location and demographics of potential customers. This is provided by *geo-demographics*, which is a system of classifying customers by linking demographic data (for example age, income) to geographic areas of residence using postcodes or census enumeration districts. Postcodes are more precise for location purposes as they represent on average 14 to 15 households compared with census enumeration districts which average 148 households, and therefore they used more frequently these days. This information is computerized and enables location analysts to visualize the information on a digital map. Digital maps can provide additional information on road networks and traffic flows and hence facilitate the accurate calculation and depiction of trade areas.

The demographic data are based on a combination of census and market research data, and this information is used to classify individuals into meaningful socioeconomic groups using clustering statistical techniques. A number of commercially available systems exist on the market. The earliest system, ACORN (A Classification of Residential Neighbourhoods) was developed by CACI and consists of 54 neighbourhood types (http://www.caci.co.uk). Another widely used system is Experiàn's MOSAIC system, which consists of 52 neighbourhood types (http://www.uk.experian.com). All geo-demographic classification systems are based on the assumption that people living in similar neighbourhoods are likely to have similar behavioural and lifestyle patterns and hence purchasing patterns. Each system divides neighbourhoods into groups based on similarities in income, education, household type and other available data (such as attitudes and product preferences). Retailers can enhance the geo-demographic information with their own information (such as that derived from loyalty cards or store cards) to develop a geo-demographic information system (GIS) to help target markets more accurately.

Site Assessment Techniques

There are a number of techniques that retailers can use to help them assess the potential of new sites and to select the best specific site for their business. This section discusses techniques that are frequently used by retailers, namely checklists, ratio of space method, analogue method and multiple regression.

Checklists

The checklist is most commonly used to assess the potential of retail sites. It attempts to identify the most important locational factors for the success of a store, and is usually based on previous experience and/or judgement of retail managers. A typical list of factors will include demographics, accessibility, competition and costs. More sophisticated methods use a weighted checklist where each identified factor is rated in terms of its quality, and according to its overall importance in the location decision, with a weighted rating obtained for each identified factor by multiplying the rating by its importance factor. An overall rating or index is obtained by summing all the weighted ratings. Alternative sites may then be ranked according to the weighted rating. The retail organization may also require a minimum overall score before considering a location. Checklists have the advantage of simplicity and require little expertise. Their major disadvantage is that the relationship between different factors is not usually known (or articulated) and it is therefore difficult to estimate their precise effect on the location decision. Checklists are therefore used as a starting point for store location and evaluation decisions.

Ratio of space method

Here, sales are allocated to a proposed store in proportion to its share of competing space in the trade area. This is a fairly crude method and can be used in the absence of reliable data. The method assumes equal productivity amongst retailers, which is not a tenable assumption given the different market positioning of different retailers.

Analogue method

The analogue method for estimating the sales potential of a new store was pioneered by Applebaum (1966) and involves measuring the market share of the trade area of one or more existing stores that are similar to the proposed store, and then using the data as 'analogues' to extrapolate turnover estimates for new sites. The procedure for using the analogue method is as follows:

1   Identify stores within the current network that are similar to the proposed store in terms of store size, the size of the trade, demographics, competition, merchandising policies, pricing and so forth.
2   Divide the trade area into drive-time zones.
3   Estimate the sales generated from each drive-time zone using either internal store data or customer surveys.
4   Use the sales estimates from each zone to calculate the per capita expenditure for each zone by dividing the sales generated by the population in the zone.
5   Use the per capita expenditure estimates for each zone of the analogue store to estimate the sales forecast for the proposed store by multiplying it by the total population of each zone of the proposed store.
6   Adjust the estimate up or down to take into account factors specific to the new location.

A major advantage of the analogue method is that it is based on actual shopping patterns and it is relatively easy to implement. However, the choice of the analogue store is critical in the accuracy of the forecast, but, inevitably, a certain amount of subjectivity is involved in the selection of the analogue stores. However, the degree of subjectivity can be reduced by using more than one analogue store and taking the average of the estimates as a sales forecast. A further problem with the analogue approach is that forecasting becomes more difficult as the number of stores grows and more complex patterns of relationships are identified. At this stage it is more appropriate and viable to use multiple regression techniques.

Multiple regression

Unlike the analogue procedure, multiple regression uses data from a large number of existing stores to forecast the sales of a new store. Regression is a statistical technique for establishing the relationship between a dependant variable (such as turnover) and a set of independent variables that affect it (for instance, catchment population, competition, store size and so on). The technique estimates the line of 'best fit' that minimizes the variance between individual data points, that is the stores being analysed. Multiple regression requires a minimum of 30–40 cases (stores) and at least 15–20 cases (or stores) per variable used in the regression. Regression models are, therefore, mainly used by large multiple/chain retailers with large numbers of branches.

When using this technique, it is first necessary to identify all variables that influence store sales. In order to be able to use a variable within the regression equation it must be independent of other variables in the equation (that is, it must not be highly correlated with other variables as, for example, is the case with car ownership and income). If a number of variables are correlated with each other, one solution is to use factor analysis to identify a common factor underlying the variables. The key variables are then used in the regression model to forecast, for example, expected sales. The general form of the regression model is:

$$Y = a + b_1X_1 + b_2X_2 + b_3X_3 \ldots + b_nX_n + E$$

where Y is a dependent variable (e.g. sales); X_1, X_2, $\ldots X_n$ are various independent (explanatory) variables (e.g. competition, size of store); a is a constant (or intercept term estimated by regression procedure); and b_1, $b_2 \ldots$ b_n are regression coefficients that measure the impact of the independent variables on the dependent variable and E is an error term.

The regression coefficients represent the degree of impact of the independent variables on the dependent variable. The signs of the coefficients indicate the direction of influence (positive or negative). The explanatory variables will differ by the type of store. For instance, for a convenience store the main determinants of sales performance are likely to be the trade-area population and the number of competitors in the area. For a DIY store, on the other hand, owner–occupation and household income are likely to be more important variables. Although the precise variables differ between retailers and store types, most regression models used for predicting sales performance include store attributes, location factors (shopping-centre characteristics), demographics and competition variables.

Whilst regression models are relatively complex to develop, once developed they are easy to use. Their use simply involves entering values for a new site on the relevant predictor variables, multiplying them by their associated regression coefficients, and then adding the resulting values to arrive at the forecast for store sales. However, in order for the forecast to be accurate and meaningful, the model should be built using a sample of similar stores to the proposed store. For example, it would be inappropriate for Sainsbury's to forecast sales of a new central store (usually located in town centres and averaging 7,000 to 20,000 sq ft) using a model that is built on a sample of Sainsbury's edge-of-town stores averaging over 40,000sq ft. This also highlights the necessity of developing a number of different models where a retailer operates a number of different types of stores aimed at different market positions and different target segments.

The advantage of regression models is that they allow a large number of factors that influence store performance to be considered together. The models indicate which factors are most important in predicting sales and

Table 9.1 Advantages and disadvantages of regression models for forecasting store sales

Advantages	Disadvantages
• Systematic framework/objective discipline • Quantitative measure • Purpose-built • Allows what-if scenarios to be constructed • Can identify underperforming/overperforming stores	• Complex and costly to develop • Minimum number of observations (~ 30) required for statistical validity • Needs to be redeveloped for changed circumstances • Not suitable for diverse portfolios of stores • Can only predict within range

hence allow managers to focus their efforts. Analysis of residuals (the difference between forecast and actual sales) allows retail managers to assess the performance of their current portfolio of stores by identifying underperforming or overperforming stores and the factors behind the performance of stores. The major problem with regression models is that they are costly and complex to develop, and the need for statistical and practical retail know-how for the proper specification of the model. The models need to be regularly reestimated to take account of changes in the retailing environment, the accuracy of regression is critically dependent on the quality of data. Advantages and disadvantages are summarized in Table 9.1.

The techniques discussed above are usually used in conjunction with each other rather than in isolation. In fact, research on location techniques employed by major UK supermarket operators employ a combination of approaches which reduces the risk involved in store-location assessment by comparing the different predictions. The use of checklists reduces the cost and time required to assess a large number of stores before using the analogue approach and regression modelling. Whilst these techniques provide more accurate estimates they are more expensive. There is no single 'best' technique for assessing retail location. The techniques employed will depend upon the amount of information available, costs in terms of time and money, and the sophistication of the retailer.

Selecting the specific site

The exact location of a store within a shopping centre/district is extremely important, as a few yards either way can be the difference between success and failure. This is because customer flows vary greatly within centres, for example customer traffic can be very different on the two sides of the same shopping street.

Within any centre, one specific location will have the highest level of customer traffic. This will usually be where there are one or more anchor stores, accessibility is easy due to close proximity of transport terminals, and other attractions are located nearby. This area is known as prime pitch and is given a 100 per cent rating. The remaining locations are rated in relation to the prime pitch. Hence a site rated as 60 per cent pitch would have 60 per cent of the customer traffic of the prime-pitch location.

Factors that need to be considered when assessing specific sites include:

- The relationship of the site to the main shopping centre.
- The strength of interception – the ability to intercept customers as they move from place to place within the centres. Shops located on routes popular with shoppers (for example routes between car parks, bus or railway stations and the shopping centre) will have stronger ability to intercept shoppers than other locations. Shops located between anchor stores will also benefit from additional traffic as shoppers move between them.
- Cumulative attraction – the degree of pull that results from similar and/or complementary retailers locating together. The existence of leisure, social, business and other attractors is also important as they have the ability to generate additional impulse trade for stores.
- Compatibility – the degree to which stores in close proximity are likely to interchange customers. This is more likely to occur where the merchandise mix of the stores is complementary, as in the case of a clothes store, shoe shop and jewellery outlet. The degree of compatibility is enhanced if the stores also have similar pricing strategies. Competing stores may also be considered compatible where they satisfy the need for comparison-shopping for customers.
- Competition – not all competition is benign, and therefore it is important to take into account the size, number and type (inter- or intratype) of competing stores and their relative locations to a proposed store as they are likely to directly impact on the sales potential of the store.
- Accessibility – a key determinant of customer patronage, and hence new sites need to be evaluated in terms of their closeness to (and size of) car parks, transport terminals and traffic arteries. Customer safety and security are also important considerations as close proximity of road traffic and lack of pedestrian crossings may deter many potential customers.
- Suitability – for the purpose of business. As mentioned above, the cost of sites within centres varies depending on their distance from the centre. Whilst high customer traffic may increase sales, high-rent leasing, purchasing price or building costs may make the store unprofitable. Retailers need to take into account acquisition costs, operating and fitting costs of any site.

● Planning Regulations and Location

In addition to market-related factors, retail location is greatly influenced in most countries by government regulation and planning policies. In fact, planning policies can be so influential that Davies and Bennison (1978) complained that in the UK the spatial organization of shopping districts was more the result of planning polices than market forces. In the UK, local authorities are responsible for administering requests for planning permission, with appeals being administered by central government. Local authorities consider planning applications in the context of the Unitary Plan for the district which they are required to produce by the Town and Country Planning Act 1990. These plans incorporate national planning guidelines and indicate major areas of action such as development, redevelopment and improvements in retailing over a 10-year period. Hence it is essential for

Leasing in retailing

Although some retailers own the freehold of their properties, most retailers are more likely to lease a property than to buy it. This frees up capital and gives the retailer more flexibility to respond to the changing environment. In many cases it is not possible to purchase a property, particularly in the case of shopping malls. Leasing retail properties is a fairly complex business and retailers need to make sure that the type of retailing agreement that they undertake is suitable for their needs. Relevant factors and terminology include:

- *Straight lease* – an agreed sum paid over life of lease.
- *Percentage/turnover lease* – rent is linked to sales.
- *Net lease* – retailer is responsible for maintenance and utility charges.
- *Prohibited use clause* – prohibits the landlord from leasing to tenants who may affect image of the business.
- *Exclusive use clause* – prohibits landlords from leasing to direct competitors.
- *'Zone A' rental* – rent paid per sq ft on the first 20 feet back from the store front.
- *Upward only reviews* – rents can only rise in periodic reviews.

retailers to understand these plans when they are proposing new developments, as they are likely to be rejected if they do not fit the structure plans for the district. Refusal of planning permission usually relates to issues of suitability of land use for retailing, traffic generated, and impact on existing centres.

Until about 1970, the maintenance of existing retailing hierarchies was the prime concern of planning authorities in the UK, with comparison shopping being clustered in large shopping centres and convenience shopping more widely spread out. This policy was relaxed a little in the 1970s and saw the spread of stores in the UK, although comparison shopping remained in city centres. However, further relaxation of the regulatory framework in the 1980s led to a rapid development of out-of-town retailing in the form of retail parks and regional shopping centres, with many comparison retailers moving out of city centres and undermining the traditional retail hierarchies. In the late 1990s the government issued stricter guidelines (PPG6 and PPG13) for out-of-town retail developments to prevent the further erosion of high-street retailing. This has necessitated retailers to reconsider their location policies. Retailers such as Tesco have responded by developing specific high-street concepts (for example Metro stores) to comply with the new regulatory framework.

● Internet Retailing and Location

It is self-evident that store-based retailers are likely to lose a proportion of their sales to virtual retailers. Additionally, most established retailers are setting up their own transactional internet sites (varying in scope) in addition to their physical stores. The combination of these developments and the increasing penetration and acceptance of the internet will mean that an increasing proportion of retail sales are likely to be e-commerce-based; and so many retailers will require fewer stores in the future to service their customers. This will inevitably mean some rationalization of retail networks and the greater importance of getting the location of the remaining stores right. On the other hand, as it increasingly appears that hybrid strategies are like to be more effective than internet (or store-based) only strategies, some demand for stores may be created by internet retailers to facilitate deliveries and returns. Alternatively, they may seek alliances with existing retailers to achieve the same ends.

Some retailers are more likely to be affected than others. For instance, the growth of internet sales of books, records, wines and computer products suggests that retailers specializing in these products are most likely to have to review their store portfolios. At the same time, some retail locations are more likely to be affected than others. Locations with a wide mix of retailers and social attractions that provide more than shopping are likely to remain strong destinations for shopping and prime locations for retailers. Secondary locations are likely to come under severe pressure.

Whilst internet retailing takes distance out of the equation, accessibility is still crucial to its success. Internet stores need to be easily located on the World Wide Web, which means having a unique, easily remembered website address. This also needs to be further enhanced by multiple linkages from other websites of related businesses as well as search engines. Decisions also need to be made as to whether the virtual store should be a standalone site or part of a virtual mall. Clearly, many of the location principles discussed in this chapter can also be applied to internet retailing.

Summary

This chapter has emphasized the importance of location decisions given that they are long term in nature and therefore difficult to change quickly and consequently the costs of wrong decisions can be high. Location decisions are also complex, as they need to satisfy not only consumer needs for convenience, accessibility and quality but must also provide a competitive advantage for the retailer.

Retail location decision-making is a stepwise process beginning with the identification of the most attractive market areas or regions and followed by the identification of suitable sites with a viable trading area. The most commonly used models for determining the trade areas of a store are the so-called gravitational (or spatial interaction) models, namely Reilly's Law and Huff's probability model of retail attraction. The final step is the selection of the best site taking into account not just the potential revenue that the site can generate but also the costs of locating at the site.

Retailers need precise information on the location and demographics of potential customers. This is provided by geo-demographics information systems (GIS), which enables location analysts to visualize the information on a digital map. Techniques that are frequently used by retailers to estimate the potential of a specific site include checklists, the ratio of sales to space method, the analogue method and multiple regression. In addition to market related factors, retail location is greatly influenced by government regulation and retail planning policies as evidenced by the impact of PPG6 and PPG13. In the future, the Internet is likely to have a major impact on the number of retail outlets required and how stores are integrated with online operations.

Questions

1 Distinguish between the main types of retail locations available to retailers. What advantages do planned locations have over unplanned locations?
2 Discuss why some retailers prefer to cluster together and others do not.
3 Discuss the main factors that influence the size of a store's trade area.
4 How can GIS assist retailers in their location decisions?
5 Explain the circumstances under which the analogue approach may be used to estimate the potential demand for a new store? Outline the steps involved in using this method.
6 Explain the multiple-regression approach to estimating demand for a new store. What variables might be included to predict the demand for a supermarket? A DIY store?
7 Explain how planning regulations influence store-location decisions.

References and Further Reading

Applebaum, W. (1966) 'Methods for Determining Store Trade Areas, Market Penetration and Potential Sales', *Journal of Marketing Research*, vol. 3, no. 2, pp. 127–41.

Applebaum, W. (1968), *Store Location Strategy Cases* (Reading, Mass.: Addison-Wesley).

Birkin, M., Clarke, G. P., Clarke, M. and Wilson, A. (2002) *Retail Geography and Intelligent Network Planning* (Chichester: John Wiley).

Brown, S. (1993) 'Retail Location Theory: Evolution and Evaluation', *International Review of Retail Distribution and Consumer Research*, vol. 3, no. 3, pp. 185–229.

Christaller, W. (1933) *Die zentrale Orte in Suddeutschland*, translated by C. Baskin (1966) as 'Central Places in Southern Germany', (Englewood Cliffs, NJ: Prentice-Hall).

Clarkson, R.M., Clarke-Hill, C.M. and Robinson, T. (1996) 'UK Supermarket Location Assessment', *International Journal of Retail and Distribution Management*, vol. 24, no. 6, pp. 22–33.

Competition Commission (2000), *Supermarkets: A Report on the Supply of Groceries from Multiple Stores in the United Kingdom*, Cm 4842 (London: The Stationery Office).

Converse, P.D. (1949), 'New Laws of Retail Gravitation', *Journal of Marketing*, 14, pp. 379–84.

Craig, C.S., Ghosh, A. and McLafferty, S. (1984) 'Models of the Retail Location Process: A Review', *Journal of Marketing*, vol. 60, no. 1, pp. 5–36.

Davies, R.L. and Bennison, D.J. (1978) *The Eldon Square Regional Shopping Centre – the First Eighteen Months*, Retailing and Planning Associates, Northumberland.

Dawson, J.A. (1979) *The Marketing Environment* (London: Croom Helm).

Ghosh, A. (1990) Retail *Management*, 1st edn, (Chicago: The Dryden Press).

Hotelling, H. (1929) 'Stability in Competition', *The Economic Journal*, vol. 39, no. 3, pp. 41–57.

Huff, D.L. (1963) 'A Probabilistic Analysis of Shopping Centre Trade Areas', *Land Economics*, vol. 39, pp. 81–90.

Huff, D.L. (1964) 'Defining and Estimating a Trading Area', *Journal of Marketing*, vol. 28, pp. 34–8.

Jones, K. and Simmons, J. (1990) *The Retail Environment* (London: Routledge).

Losch, A. (1954) *The Economics of Location* (New Haven, Conn.: Yale University Press).

Morphet, C. S. (1991) 'Applying Multiple Regression Analysis to the Forecasting of Grocery Store Sales: An Application and Critical Appraisal', *International Review of Retail and Consumer Research*, vol. 1, no. 3, pp. 329–51.

O'Malley, L., Patterson, M. and Evans, M. (1997) 'Retailer Use of Geodemographic and Other Data Sources: An Empirical Investigation', *International Journal of Retail and Distribution Management*, vol. 25, no.6, pp. 188–96.

Reilly, W. J. (1931) *The Law of Retail Gravitation* (New York: Knickerbocker Press).

Rogers, D. (1992) 'A Review of Sales Forecasting Models Most Commonly Applied in Retail Site Evaluation', *International Journal of Retail and Distribution Management*, vol. 20, no. 4, pp. 3–11.

Schiller, R. (1986), 'Retail Decentralisation – the Coming of the Third Wave', *The Planner* (July), pp. 13–15.

Schiller, R. (2001), *The Dynamics of Property Location: Values and Factors which Drive the Location of Shops, Offices and Other Land Uses* (London: Routledge).

Sparks, L. (1990) 'Spatial – structural relationships in retail corporate growth: a case study of Kwik Save Group Plc', *Service Industries Journal*, vol 10, no. 1, reprinted in Akehurst, G. and N. Alexander (eds.) (1995) *Retail Structure*, Frank Cass: London.

Tesco plc (2002) *Tesco Annual Report 2002* (http://www.tesco.com)

chapter ten

Retail Design and Visual Merchandising

Learning objectives

- To understand the role of design in retailing and how it can be used to differentiate a retail offer.
- To explore areas of the retail outlet where design can be used to contribute to an overall retail identity.
- To understand the scope of visual merchandising as a specialized area of retail management concerning layouts, displays and product presentation.
- To appreciate that different types of layouts, displays and fixturing are appropriate for different types of retailers.
- To gain an understanding of the need for retail space to be productive, and the various ways in which space productivity can be measured.
- To understand the key principles of planning and allocating space to the various product categories that makes up a retailer's offer.

Introduction

Having finalized decisions regarding the location and type of outlet from which the retailer is going to run their business, it is then necessary to consider in detail how that business will appear to potential customers, irrespective of whether it is a store-based or a non-store retail organization. The environment in which the retailer–customer interface takes place needs to be designed so that target customers feel comfortable, interested and encouraged to purchase. Managing the selling environment is a two-stage interlinked process beginning with the design of the outlet itself, and then moving on to the presentation of the product-service offering within. Choosing a design for most types of retail outlet is a long-term decision; store development and refits are large investments with a long and indirect payback. Retail designs are also completely integral to a retailer's strategy, communicating strong messages about who that retailer is, the positioning they are seeking within the market, and what their retail brand stand for. At the same time, a retailer needs to provide space in which customers can comfortably and conveniently carry out their shopping process. The way that products are displayed on fixtures, and how those fixtures are placed around the outlet are also key elements in the overall design of the selling environment. Those aspects of the retail environment that are more able to change according to variations in the merchandise assortment are often referred to as visual merchandising, and provide a strong link between the retail identity and the management of the product range.

● Design in Retailing

Design in retailing has always been important. An outlet that is aesthetically pleasing and logically laid out is appealing to customers, whilst the efficient use of space makes a major contribution to the running of a profitable retail business. In saturated and mature retail markets, innovative design is a way of keeping the retail offer fresh and providing differentiation from competitors. It is also a means by which the retail brand can be strengthened by forging links between the selling space, the corporate identity, product design and display. In a small business, retail managers may have to concern themselves with all of these aspects, as well as being responsible for the day-to-day running of the business. In large multiple retailers, design management may involve teams of specialists or they may recruit the services of a third party such as a retail design agency. Whether or not the retail management remit has any direct involvement in design or not, an appreciation of the role of design in retailing is a key part of a manager's personal development. Retail design input must reinforce and support the strategic aims of the retailer whilst facilitating the practicalities of strategy implementation. In addition, the design of a retail outlet can have a significant impact on staff morale, influencing how employees feel about working for a company, and the extent they feel to be 'brand ambassadors' for it (Lamacraft, 1998, p. 1).

● The Corporate Identity

The selling environment is a very useful vehicle for reinforcing a retailer's corporate identity. This begins with the initial impression the retailer makes with the exterior of the store or the cover of the catalogue for example, and then moves on to the interior of the outlet. The retail fascia, which includes external features above and around any windows and doors into the outlet, communicates the name of the business, and may also incorporate a logo that helps customers to recognize the retailer from afar.

Fascias usually use distinctive corporate lettering and colours, which can then be linked to other elements within the outlet, such as instore signage, point-of-purchase materials and carrier bags. The corporate identity may be extended further to own-label packaging, and product information sources like leaflets. It is easier to reinforce a corporate identity within a store environment, but that does not mean that non-store retailers should overlook this area. For example, the use of corporate colours and lettering within a website or a catalogue can be linked to the packaging used in home delivery. Multi-channel retailers like NEXT frequently use the same or a similar corporate identity across all formats in order to transfer the positive associations built up in traditional channels to new shopping methods.

● Store Design

Although the design of the retail website is receiving more intense attention as the novelty of internet retailing is replaced by the need for the website to create a desirable shopping environment (see Chapter 17), this discussion will initially consider the design of stores, and then move on to discuss other retail formats and make some comparisons.

A store can usually be considered as a combination of five key elements: the exterior, the interior space, fixtures, merchandise and people. The first two elements are relatively static, and so they need to be designed within a longer-term framework. The third element should be considered at least as a medium-term factor, but the last two elements undergo changes such as the type of merchandise changing according to season, and the number of customers varying according to the time of day. The way these changing elements impact on the store means that some degree of flexibility needs to be built into the design.

The exterior

The exterior of most stores includes the fascia, mentioned above, the store entrance, the architectural features of the building and windows. The contribution of these parts of a store's exterior to an overall design can vary in importance according to the type of store format and the products on offer. For example, superstores, hypermarkets and category killers rarely use window displays, but have bold fascias and easy to access entrances. Stand-alone stores may have to conform to strict architectural guidelines imposed by government planning authorities, whilst the centre management team may control the exterior of stores in a planned regional shopping centre. Entrances can be designed to be open and welcoming, or closed and exclusive. A key consideration for retailers is the need to be accessible for all members of society.

The interior

The interior of a store can be viewed in a similar way to living space. It comprises ceiling, walls, flooring and lighting, but instead of furniture a retail outlet houses fixtures for the presentation of merchandise, and fittings for equipment such as tills. In choosing the materials used for the interior, retailers have to consider the type of product being sold, costs, store traffic and health and safety. For example, the store interior for a food retailer needs to be easy to clean and hygienic, but able to withstand high levels of customer footfall; high quality materials are therefore likely to be a worthwhile investment. Alternatively, a young fashion retailer will place more emphasis on less expensive but fashionable furnishings materials, in the knowledge that an updated refit is likely to be necessary in less than five years. All retailers have to conform to heath and safety trading standards such as those set out under the Health and Safety at Work Act 1974, and the Offices, Shops and Railway Premises Act 1963.

Atmospherics

There are many ways in which retailers can try to enhance the appeal of their stores by stimulating the senses. Creating an aura or an atmosphere in a store can include the use of different aromas, sounds, colours, lighting, textures and temperatures. Some examples of elements that can be used for atmospheric purposes are listed below. It is up to the retail designer to choose appropriate elements in order to create an effect that is suitable for the product being sold, and the type of customer. Vignette 10.2 describes how beauty retailer Sephora blends materials and atmospheric elements to create a unique retail environment.

- *Aromas*: bread, coffee, chocolate, floral, pine (for Christmas).
- *Sounds*: popular music, classical music, 'mood' music, voice (announcements, shop radio).
- *Colours*: neutrals such as black, grey, white; natural materials, warm colours (reds, oranges, pinks, yellows), cool colours (blues, pale greens, white) earthy colours (browns, greens, oranges).
- *Lighting*: cool lighting (blue, bright), warm lighting (orange, yellow, pink, subdued), spotlights (to pick out and highlight), ambient (general) lighting, sculptural light (in alcoves, behind panels and so on), illuminated panelling and signage, neon.
- *Texture*: shiny and smooth (chrome, gilt, marble), metallic (brushed, galvanized, embossed), textile (carpet, fabric, fur, sacking), wood (polished, raw, smooth, knotted), stone/brick.

● The Strategic Role of Store Design

Most of the UK's largest retailers have a huge investment or asset tied up in their store portfolio. It is therefore in their interest to keep a high level of customer traffic moving through the store in order to maintain an adequate return on that investment. Good use of design in stores helps to keep customers interested in store-based shopping. When consumers have a high level of choice, they will visit places where they feel comfortable, inspired and even entertained. Customers are nowadays more design literate; the plethora of interior style media offerings has created a body of consumers that are not willing to tolerate badly designed and poorly decorated space. Competitive threats from home shopping means that the store environment has to have something special to offer, and international competition can also force retailers to pay more attention to their selling environments. As discussed in Chapter 1, Spanish fashion retailers Mango and Zara, who use clean-cut and modern store interiors, have been able to threaten domestic retailers in the UK middle-market women's clothing sector.

Store design has always been used to reinforce other elements of a retail strategy. For example, plush carpeting and marble used in a store denotes high-quality merchandise and may suggest a high-price positioning. Strip lighting and dump bins for merchandise brings the word 'bargains' to mind. However, as retail markets mature, the design of retail space is increasingly being used as a means by which strategic aims are reached. For example, in 2001 Safeway introduced a new store design to reinforce their position as a good-value fresh and quality grocery retailer. Wood panelling, slate tiling and pendent lighting were used in the wines and beers section to create the impression of an upmarket wine cellar; baskets and barrels were used in the fruit and vegetable section to give the impression of 'market freshness' and chalkboard signage to foster the impression of good prices. It is these small details that help to refocus the attention of the shopper onto revised core values, providing a struggling grocery chain with a new lease of life to compete against other forceful players in the market (Atkinson, 2001).

● Design in Non-Store Retailing

Although non-store retail formats place some significant restrictions on the use of design in the selling environment, innovative approaches have often paid off as a source of competitive advantage. For example, when NEXT launched their NEXT Directory it was unlike anything customers had previously encountered in the UK home-shopping market. The format was more like a coffee-table book than a catalogue, with hard covers and a much higher proportion of full-page spreads than used by other mail-order retailers, and the bold and neutral corporate identity of the stores is clearly reflected in the pages. Early editions even included small swatches of material to allow customers to get a 'feel' for the garments prior to purchase. The catalogue was aimed at a more upmarket customer than the typical mail-order catalogue profile, with a narrowly targeted, all retailer-branded range of products.

● Retail Website Design

Many retail entrepreneurs have tried to use sophisticated design as a way of overcoming the shortcomings of virtual retailing, and whilst many of the ideas have been innovative and attention-grabbing, their incorporation into a fully

Vignette 10.1

Flagship Stores

Although there is no accepted definition of the term, the concept of a 'flagship' store is one that all multiple retailers will be familiar with. They are found in prestigious, high-footfall locations, and are viewed as the pinnacle of the retail chain. Flagship stores are likely to be large, refurbished according to the latest store design concepts, and house a full or 'top-end' product range. Many flagship stores can be found in international city centres like London, Paris and New York, or within large regional shopping centres like the Bluewater Centre in south-eastern England, where the strategic reinforcement of the retailer's brand is as important as the financial performance of the store. The maintenance of a flagship store in a high-profile site may need to be viewed as an investment that the rest of the retail chain (including multi-channel outlets) pays for. For example, in 2000 the House of Fraser department store group spent £18 million overhauling and rebranding the Oxford Street (central London) store previously named 'D. H. Evans', an operation that provided the whole of the House of Fraser portfolio with an injection of vitality. Flagship stores perform a public-relations function, providing a convenient location for trade and popular press to view new store concepts and product ranges, which is especially important for retailers who are entering new international markets, or changing strategic direction.

A new store opening or a major refurbishment is an important corporate communications opportunity for retailers. French Connection, the young fashion retailer famously advertised their Oxford Street flagship opening in October 2000 as 'The world's biggest fcuk'. Flagship stores are not restricted to fashion retailers; supermarkets, variety stores and category specialists also use 'model' stores to introduce new design concepts, demonstrate new visual merchandising plans and trial new product lines. Neither are flagship stores restricted to companies that are classified as retailers; many manufacturers use retail flagships to raise the profile of their brands, NikeTown (in London, New York and Chicago) being perhaps one of the best well-known examples.

Source: Morrell (2000).

operational transaction site has not always been successful (see Vignette 17.1 on retailer http://www.Boo.com). On the other hand, according to Gerdes and Nachtwey (2000) many retail web sites follow a set formula. This moves from opening page, to company information, to categories of product available, which then open up to pages of tiny product photos that can be clicked on for a closer look, finishing with the ordering facility. Whilst this type of standardized navigation does help the user to become familiar and functionally proficient, it does not provide much opportunity for differentiation.

A successful retail website needs to balance visual interest with ease of navigation and use. The whole attraction and competitive advantage of website shopping is based on convenience, and so reminding the customer of the frustrations incurred in store shopping such as not being able to locate items, or waiting (for downloaded images as opposed to in checkout queues) is bound to cause shopper dissatisfaction.

Virtual retailing does provide some additional opportunities to stretch the concept of the selling environment to new dimensions. For example, food retailers can display recipe ideas in dining settings; sporting goods retailers can provide celebrity endorsements and information alongside products; and speciality and leisure product retailers can offer advice tips and chat-room opportunities for customers who have similar interests (see Vignette 15.1).

● Visual Merchandising

Visual merchandising is concerned with presenting products to customers within the retail space. It is a term sometimes used as an alternative to merchandise display, but these days is generally understood to have a wider definition encompassing all activities concerned with the presentation of the product within the retail outlet, including the choice of store layout, the method of product presentation, the choice of fixture and fittings, the construction of displays, and the use of point-of-sale material. It also has a very close connection with the allocation of space within the outlet. Visual merchandising is more important in some retail sectors than others. For example, fashion and home furnishing retailers have always devoted considerable resources to displaying products in a visually appealing way, whilst discount grocery retailers are much more concerned with space efficiency. However, the need to adapt to style-conscious twenty-first-century customers is as relevant to the way products are presented as the way a store environment is designed.

The implementation of a visual merchandising strategy within a retail business is not standardized across the industry. Lea-Greenwood (1998) found that visual merchandising could be the responsibility of directors of corporate communications, promotion or marketing, whilst some retailers gave the function the status of a specific directorship. Often a multiple retailer will employ a team of regional visual merchandisers who rotate through a number of stores in a given area. The creative aspect of the visual merchandiser's role attracts people with a design training or background, although specific training for visual merchandising is becoming more common. One of the advantages of using a centralized team is that the retail brand identity can be controlled across all outlets, and visual merchandising can tie in with other corporate communication themes and messages. There is, however, a danger that the centralized approach may prevent the retailer from adapting to local themes, preferences and competition in the visual merchandising activity.

Store layouts

There are a number of different types of layouts commonly found in retail stores (Figure 10.1). The layout used will be dependent on the width and depth of the product range, the nature of the product categories sold, the type of fixturing used and the constraints of the outlet in terms of size and shape. The objective of a store layout is to maximize the interface between customers and merchandise.

One of the most common store layouts is that of a grid. This layout is used with fixturing in a shelving format (the gondola), separated by aisles through which customers flow. The grid layout provides logic and space efficiency, but it is inflexible and standardized and therefore not useful for creating interesting product displays. Supermarkets tend to use the grid layout for most of their store layout, as it is a good way of displaying an extensive range of products.

Some retailers have experimented with variations on the grid theme. Woolworths, for example, have trailed a 'fishbone' layout, where the grids are angled rather than straight; however, space utilization is less efficient with this method. Other retailers use layouts that combine grid areas with other formations in order to provide variety and more appropriate layouts for merchandise. ASDA, for example, have used a freeform layout for the 'George' clothing range, with a grid layout for the rest of the merchandise. A freeform layout is less systemized and can accommodate a wider variety of fixturing. It is also more conducive to browsing. Whilst providing increased flexibility, freeform layouts can result in customers feeling 'lost' in a mass of merchandise and fixturing, and so in larger stores the merchandise areas are often broken down by a series of walkways and/or partitions. This helps customers to orientate themselves within the store and allows a certain degree of departmentalization.

Where a retailer has a limited range of merchandise, or in situations where a high level of personal selling is required, a number of alternative approaches can be used. The first is to surround the customer with merchandise; which is sometimes referred to as the boutique layout. Alternatively, the store may be divided up into 'service stations' where a customer and sales person sit down to discuss the purchase, with the merchandise conveniently nearby to refer to. This type of layout is used in personal communications stores such as Carphone Warehouse. Another approach is to house the merchandise behind a counter, a technique used in high-value merchandise stores because of the security risk.

As well as exposing customers to as much merchandise as possible, layouts can also make a contribution to the selling process by placing complementary merchandise categories adjacent to one another, and seasonal and impulse product categories near to areas of high footfall. Decisions on the allocation of space within the general outlet layout will be discussed later in the chapter.

Product presentation

There are essentially two ways of presenting merchandise in a store. The first is to place or stack a product on some kind of fixture; stacked merchandise can be neatly arranged or, as in the case of promotional items, it can be 'dumped'. The second way is to hang the product; either directly onto a hanger, or onto a prong, using some kind of specially designed packaging. Having decided on the type of presentation to be used, it may then be necessary to use a specific method of organizing the product presentation in order to provide logic in the offering, or to enhance the visual appeal of the merchandise. For example, clothes are often presented according to colour themes, and greetings cards are presented according to end use. Other techniques include grouping according to price, technical features and size.

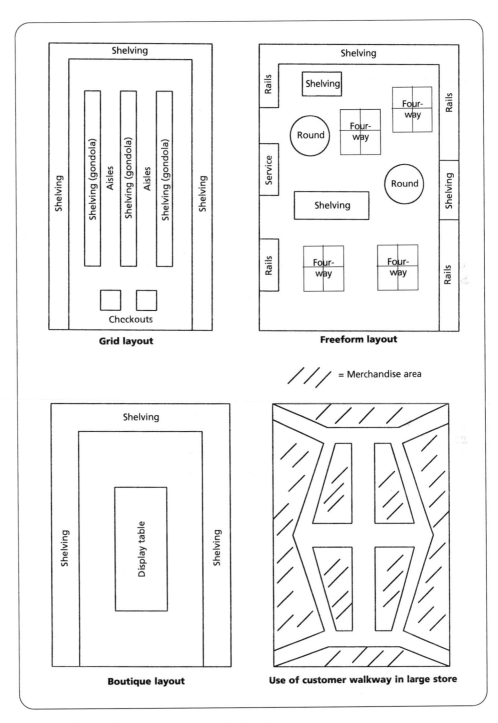

Figure 10.1 Alternative types of store layout

Table 10.1 Alternative Fixture Types

Fixture	Merchandise example	Presentation
Shelving	Home accessories	Stacked/placed
Gondola	Grocery products	Stacked
Railings	Clothing	Hanging (front or side view)
Four-ways	Clothing	Hanging (front and side view)
Round	Stationery	Bubble-packed
Bins/baskets	Small DIY products	Dumped
Tables	Gifts	Placed

Fixturing

Fixturing is necessary to display merchandise to customers, whilst making best use of the retail space. Fixtures can be obtained from a shopfitting wholesaler, or they may be custom-built to tie into a specific retail design. The following fixtures are commonly found in retail stores: shelving, gondolas, railings, four-ways, round fixtures, bins, baskets and tables. The type of fixturing used will depend on the product and its presentation method; examples are shown in Table 10.1

In order to create a consistent look within the outlet, it is sensible to choose fixturing that is coordinated in terms of the type of material and style. An array of different types of fixturing may provide flexibility, but it can make a store appear cluttered and untidy. It is generally the merchandise rather than the fixturing that should be noticed, although some fashion stores do use unique designs for fixtures that help to reinforce the retail brand image.

Displays

Fixturing is generally concerned with the housing of merchandise in what is sometimes termed 'on-shelf' displays. This is the routine display of goods from which customers are expected to make their selection. 'Off-shelf' or feature displays are used to create a visual impact with the merchandise, or to show how the product might be used. They might also be used to introduce and promote new products or to support supplier promotions or trade initiatives (such as Fair Trade). As they are not intended to be used in the routine selling of the products they can be artistically arranged and situated in parts of the store that are not useful for selling purposes, such as high up on walls or within an alcove (although the closer to the selling stock the better, in order to encourage customers to respond to the display). Often, more than one product is used in an off-shelf display, for example to suggest complementary purchases or to show the depth of offer in a particular product category; mannequins are used for displaying complementary or coordinated clothing products in this way.

Feature displays often follow a theme to add interest within the selling environment. Themes for displays include seasonal, colour and lifestyle orientations. Within the calendar year there are a number of seasonal opportunities over and above the general 'weather'-dictated seasons of Spring, Summer, Autumn/Fall and Winter; for example New Year (celebrations and resolutions), Valentines Day, Mother's Day, Easter, Father's Day, Holidays, Back to School, Halloween and Christmas. Lifestyle themes can take an extensive variety of forms, and follow some kind of preference in terms of personal consumption or time expenditure. Lifestyle themes that retailers could use include sporting interest or participation, health interests, musical preference, home entertaining, hobbies, occupations, and so on.

Another type of off-shelf display is the promotional display. This is a technique frequently used in grocery stores and features a display comprising a large amount of stock of one item, often housed on a dedicated fixture. This type of display is often found at the end of the gondola (on 'end caps'), where the sheer volume of one product item catches the shopper's attention.

For many retailers, the most important display space is their windows, as they are the means by which customers are attracted into the store. The window communicates the type of product the retailer sells and is also used to indicate market positioning. Window displays can be open, where the customer can see behind the merchandise into the store, or the window may have a closed back which allows the retailer to create a more elaborate display. Destination stores like department stores often use closed window displays, but many retailers are of the opinion that the backed window can act as a barrier between customer and store, and therefore is less welcoming to customers. Diamond and Diamond (1999) suggest that effective displays follow one or more of the general principles of design, which are: balance, emphasis, proportion, rhythm and harmony. Figure 10.2 gives a graphical illustration of these.

● Space Allocation

The allocation of space to products within a retail outlet links the designed selling environment to the financial productivity of the retail space. Space management has to consider the long-term objectives concerning market positioning and customer loyalty, alongside short-term objectives concerning stockturn, sales and profits. A retail outlet that looks beautifully spacious will not stay that way if there are not enough products selling to sustain the business, yet if the store is full to bursting with merchandise some customers may choose not to enter the foray. Retail space is costly and increasingly scarce (see Chapter 9), and so whatever the visual merchandising strategy is, an adequate return must be made.

The usual method for measuring retail performance is according to the amount of sales (or profits) generated by a given amount of space. Sales per square metre are a commonly used method of assessing the value of retail space, but linear and cubic measures can also be appropriate. Space planning needs to take account of not only the amount of space allocated, but also the quality of space; for example, the space nearest the front of the store and the till areas are usually the most productive. Certain practicalities also have to be taken into consideration, such as the size and weight of the merchandise.

Space-allocation decisions usually need to be made at various levels of

178

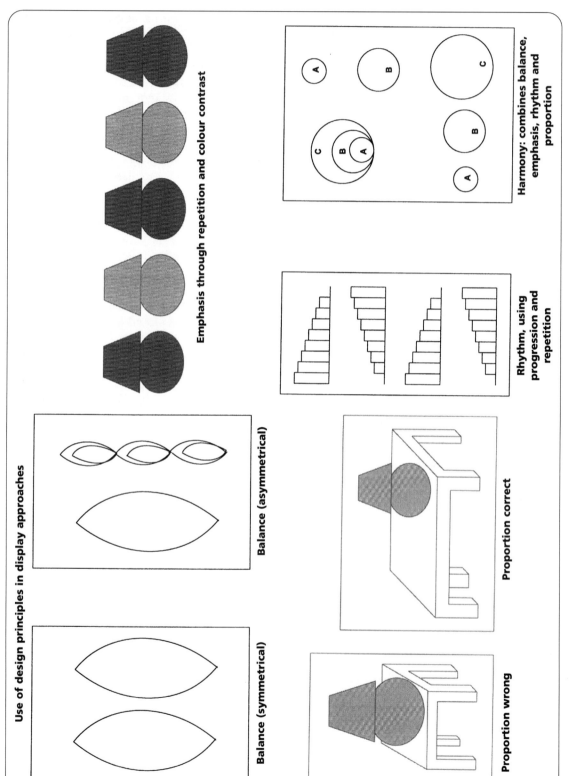

Figure 10.2 Principles of design within the context of retail display

merchandise classification, for example at departmental level, product category level and SKU (stock keeping unit) level. Retailers usually have some historical data that can act as guidance in the allocation of space, for example a similar store's performance, or historical department sales figures, but the need for the maximization of financial objectives means that space planning and allocation is under constant review and refinement at individual store level. The allocation of space can be geared towards different objectives, for example achieving the highest sales turnover, maximizing product profitability or maximizing customer satisfaction, and a retailer may be faced with making trade-off decisions in order to achieve those objectives. Those products that generate the highest sales value may only achieve low profit margins, but concentrating on high-profit items may put unnecessary emphasis on products that are less of concern to customers, thereby decreasing their levels of satisfaction. The matrix in Figure 10.3 suggests alternative space allocations according to whether a product has high profitability or high sales.

Consideration of the financial implications of allocating amounts of space must be conducted within the framework of an outlet plan that is geared to making the shopping experience of the customer a satisfactory one. Too much emphasis on the retailer's financial objectives could result in a store being laid out illogically and make products difficult to find. Long-term profitability is dependent on customer satisfaction and loyalty, and so space planning must incorporate factors other than individual product sales and profitability. Aspects such as seasonal goods, the physical size and weight of the product, the type of fixturing required and the need to display complementary goods in close proximity should all have a bearing on the overall plan.

The complexity of space-allocation decisions has encouraged the use of computer-based systems as a retail management aid. Modern space-allocation systems are able to synthesize a plethora of quantitative and qualitative data

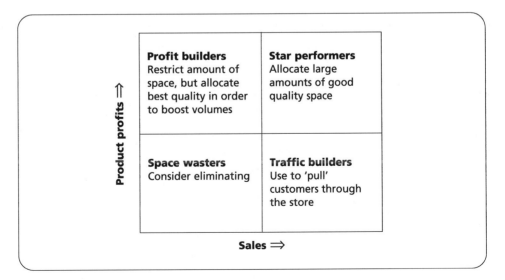

Figure 10.3 Space-allocation alternatives

such as product costs, sales forecasts, product sizes, complementary purchasing potential, fixturing details and so on. The output of these systems is a space-allocation plan or planogram that shows exactly how the products should be displayed on the fixturing, including the number of facings of each product that the customer should see.

Although space-allocation systems have resulted in retailers using space in a much more productive way, they do have limitations. Most large multiple retailers have a portfolio of stores that differ in size and shape, and so unless that retailer has access to individual store input data and the system is capable of producing customized plans for each store, the planogram will have to be subject to a certain degree of interpretation at store level. Many retailers have tackled this problem by grading their stores by size and producing a set of plans for the different store grades. However, grading by size is a very crude method of assessing different stores. Recent advances in micromarketing have shown that the profile of a store's catchment area gives a better indication of the type and amount of merchandise required than the size of the outlet (Ziliani, 2000). As retail management-information systems become increasingly sophisticated (see Chapter 8), this type of store performance analysis and customer-profile customization will become more widespread. Space allocation systems are expensive, and may be beyond the means of the smaller retail organization.

Vignette 10.2

Sephora

Sephora is a beauty retailer who has used store design and visual merchandising in a bold and innovative way to carve out a distinctive positioning in a crowded marketplace. Sephora faces many strong direct and indirect competitors. The retail market for beauty products in the UK encompasses department stores, health and beauty specialists like Boots, Superdrug and Body Shop, fashion retailers like NEXT and Karen Millen and Miss Selfridge, who have extended their product ranges, and even supermarkets. Traditionally, beauty-store environments have used polished materials like marble, glass, gilt and mirrors to create a luxurious and clean feel, with pale and cool colours such as white, cream, grey and pale green used to relax the customer and provide a neutral backdrop to the colourful merchandise. Sephora, however, have taken a very different stance, combining a bold and rich colour theme with distinctive design features in both the store's architectural design and the presentation of the products themselves.

The two most prominent features of the store's interior design are the deep-red plush carpet, which covers the floor of the store, and the bold black and white tiling that is used on pillars to break up expanses of space within the store and on the floor to create a sharp edge around the red carpet. The black and white theme is reflected throughout in the fixturing, the signage, carrier bags and the outfits that the sales associates wear.

In addition to this unique store design, Sephora have devised some extremely clever attention-grabbing product design and presentation combinations. One of these involves the display of beautification tools such as nail files and make-up brushes in glass cubes full of tiny metal balls. The resulting display method allows ungainly objects to be housed neatly and effectively, with the repetition in the size and shape of the containers providing a creative impact. The use of extensive colour blocking is also used; for example in the bathtime products where circular bottles of bath foams, oils, soaps and novelties provide shape and colour impact as soon as the customer enters the store, and the vast spectrum of lip, eye and nail colours displayed on low level counters.

Sephora's strategy is concentrated on the product and the selling environment. The company does not advertise and prices are competitive and displayed discreetly. The stores play loud, dramatic and atmospheric music, there is a Hollywood-style make-up demonstration area in the centre of the store, and staff wear a black glove on one hand which continues the dramatic theme right to the point of sale. Yet, the store atmosphere is far from intimidating, the accessibility of the product encourages involvement and trial, combining a sense of fun and theatre within the store. In the words of the company:

> we seek to defy the traditional 'selling methodology' to give you what you want – Freedom, Beauty and Pleasure. Freedom in the form of a hands-on, self-service shopping environment where you are free to touch, smell and experience each and every product. You are also free to choose the level of assistance you desire, from individual experience and reflection, to detailed expert advice. Beauty comes to you through a splendid international array of unique and luxurious beauty products. Pleasure comes through an environment designed to stimulate your senses – a blend of expert advice, personal freedom and special service displays bringing you the latest beauty tips and treatment breakthroughs (http://www.Sephora.com, 2002)

Sephora has a chequered history, starting out as a small specialist chain in its home country of France, owned for a short time by Boots who then sold the chain in 1997 to luxury branded-goods conglomerate LVMH. The backing of this multinational company has grown Sephora into a major international force, with 70 outlets in the USA, 150 stores in France and around 90 stores in the rest of Europe in 2002.

Sources: Clements, 2000; Sephora.com 2002.

Summary

In a retail industry where the consumer is growing increasingly style-literate, the 'persona' of the retail outlet, whether it is a store, a catalogue or a web page, needs to connect with the customer, both functionally and psychologically. Customers must be attracted to and then enticed into the retailer's space. Once inside they need to be filled with positive emotions and associations, and their shopping needs both in terms of the product and the process have to be understood and fulfilled. The design of the retail outlet has to find a balance between creating an original and enthralling arena, and a place where shopping is carried out efficiently. The objectives of store design and visual merchandising may be different according to the role that individual outlets play within the retailer's portfolio, with flagship stores and internet sites frequently taking brand-building rather than productivity-orientated roles.

Store design and visual merchandising in most retail businesses however, have very clear objectives concerning the enhancement of products, generation of sales and the augmentation of profitability. This all revolves around an understanding of the relationship between customers, space and the product range. According to Webb (2001) superstore retailers, who have been traditionally focused on space allocation and its impact on sales and profits are now widening their horizons to consider visual merchandising from the viewpoint of the total store environment, and its ability to interest, enthral and entertain. At the same time, fashion retailers who have been traditionally adept at using the store environment to encourage shopping as a leisure pursuit, are now becoming more disciplined about making retail space more productive.

Questions

1 Explain why retail design is a strategic issue for organizations operating in mature retail markets.

2 Outline the aspects of retail management that come under the umbrella term 'visual merchandising'. Explain why the term may have a different emphasis in different product sectors, such as grocery retailing and fashion retailing for example.

3 By using observational research in your nearest shopping centre, make a critical analysis of the use of design in a retailer that you think has a pleasant shopping environment. Then find a shop you do not feel comfortable in and try to analyse why you feel that way.

4 Retail stores have been referred to as a form of free advertising. Discuss the extent to which you agree with this description.

5 Discuss the main considerations retailers would have when embarking on a space-allocation exercise.

6 Using a large multi-channel retailer of your choice (one that you can visit), compare and contrast the design and visual merchandising found in the various store and non-store outlets that are used. To what extent is the retail brand reinforced and supported by the different retail formats.

References and Further Reading

Atkinson, K. (2001) 'Carlos's Way', *Retail Interiors*, issue 14, February.

Clements, A. (2000) 'Scents and Sensibility', *Retail Week*, 12 May.

Diamond, J. and Diamond, E. (1999) *Contemporary Visual Merchandising* (Englewood Cliffs, N.J.: Prentice-Hall).

Din, R. (2000) *New Retail* (London: Conran Octopus).

Doyle, S. and Broadbridge, A. (1999) 'Differentiation by Design: The Importance of Design in Retailer Repositioning and Differentiation', *International Journal of Retail and Distribution Management*, vol. 27, no. 2, pp. 72–82.

Gerdes, C. and Nachtwey, J. (2000) *Cybershops* (London: Thames & Hudson).

Lamacraft, J. (1998) *Retail Design: New Store Experiences*, FT Retail and Consumer Reports, London.

Lea-Greenwood, G. (1998) 'Visual Merchandising: A Neglected Area in UK Fashion Marketing?', *International Journal of Retail and Distribution Management*, vol. 26, no. 8, pp. 324–9.

Morrell, L. (2000) 'The Flagship Enterprise', *Retail Week*, 15 December.

Sephora.com 'About Sephora', 25 March 2002.

Webb, B. (2001) 'VM – Is It Working for You?', *Retail Interiors*, issue 21, September.

Ziliani, C. (1999) 'Retail Micromarketing: Strategic Advance or Gimmick?', in *Proceedings of the 10th International Conference on Research in the Distributive Trades*, Institute for Retail Studies, University of Stirling, August.

chapter eleven

Retail Buying

Learning objectives

- To understand a retailer's objectives that guide the buying process.
- To appreciate the complexity of a buying task, and the impact a buying situation has on that complexity.
- To explore retail-buying organization structures.
- To understand product-management approaches, including category management and lifestyle retailing.
- To appreciate the extensive number of product and supplier selection factors involved in retail buying decisions.
- To understand the different types of relationships that can occur between retailers and their suppliers, and how those interactions may affect the buying process.

Introduction

The products that a retailer sells are the mainstays of the business. The outlet may be within reach of a viable catchment population, the outside of the store may look very inviting and the interior may look interesting and well-appointed, but if the products are not what the customer wants to buy when they walk into the store, then a retailer will not be able to implement other areas of management and will be unable to meet its financial objectives in terms of profits made on sales. Products are an important aspect of a retailer's corporate strategy, as discussed in Chapter 5, as they are a means by which a retailer is able to differentiate itself from its competitors. The operations that are used to acquire a superior product range, and the ways in which retailers organize themselves to carry out these operations, are key areas of retail management and are the subject of this chapter.

● **The Buying Task**

Managing the product offer within retail businesses has traditionally been the task of 'buyers', who work from buying offices located at a flagship store or at an entirely separate head-office location. It is the buyer's responsibility to negotiate with suppliers to obtain products for the entire retail organization, in sufficient quantities to meet consumer demand, and at the time of year, week or day that consumers wish to purchase. Buyers have to ensure that the deals they obtain from suppliers enable the retail organization to sell products at a suitable level of profit. They also have to be concerned with the logistical arrangements for the products that they buy. The larger the retail organization, the more complex the buying task becomes, and so buying is usually carried out by teams, or departments, rather than individuals, with their activity being supported by the logistics or distribution operations within the organization (see Chapter 7).

● **Retail Buying Objectives**

Like most other organizational purchasing tasks, the process of retail buying is guided by the need to meet the following objectives (Baily *et al.*, 1994):

● *The right product.* Retailers need to be sure that the product range includes the kind of products customers want to buy. This involves recognizing consumer needs, tracking consumer purchasing patterns, being aware of changes in fashion and tastes and introducing new products to customers. It also involves brand management, whether the brand strategy of the retailer is all own-brand or a blend of producer and retailer brands (see Chapter 12).

● *The right time.* Different products are needed and wanted at different times, and a retailer must manage their stock so that the product offer reflects the requirements of customers at any particular time. For example, a confectionery, tobacco and newspaper (CTN) retailer must make sure that the latest edition of a newspaper is available as soon as possible, as the shelf-life of a daily newspaper is only a few hours. Other products such as chocolate and suncream have seasonal sales patterns, whilst staple products such as salt have a more constant demand pattern. Shelf-life, season and fashion are the key factors in the time aspect of retail buying, which is often referred to as 'stock control' (see Chapter 7).

● *The right quantity.* Closely linked to the timing aspect, buyers must manage the quantities that are bought into the retail business. There is nothing a customer dislikes more than a retailer running out of stock of their favourite items, yet too much stock is extremely problematic to a retailer for a number of reasons. Not only does excess stock tie up capital, it also uses up space that would be better devoted to a faster-selling product. Too much stock inevitably means a reduction in price to speed up the sell-through process, and this means a reduction in profits for the retail business.

⬤ *The right place.* Large retail organizations such as J. Sainsbury are not only selling ranges of products on a wide geographical spread, they are also selling products in a variety of formats which have their own characteristics in terms of size, location and customer profile. The product range sold in each outlet should ideally reflect these characteristics, and so buyers have to consider where they will be selling products when buying for the retail business. Logistical concerns may also influence how a buyer orders from suppliers, for example whether store or warehouse delivery is required.

⬤ *The right price.* Much of the focus of a retail buyer's activity will be on negotiating the 'right' price for the product they wish to purchase from a supplier. A retail buyer needs to consider the role of the product in terms of its contribution to the overall profitability of the retail business. A retailer may be happy to make a very small profit margin on a frequently purchased item, but may expect a higher level of profit from a less-frequently purchased product. The different levels of profit will be determined by the price that the retailer sets and the cost price of the product that the retailer pays to suppliers, and the overall profitability will be determined by the rate of sales of the whole product range and the profit margins set within the product range. The rate of sales is influenced by the price level the consumer is willing to pay, and so the setting of prices becomes another area of complex decision-making for retail buyers (see Chapter 13 on retail pricing).

⬤ **Retail Buying Decisions**

The complexity of buying decisions varies enormously. On the one hand an owner-manager of a small convenience store may notice that there are only three tins of baked beans left on the shelf, and only two left in the box in the stockroom. He or she therefore adds beans to the list of items they are planning to pick up at the cash and carry wholesalers the next day. They know that the demand for beans is quite high but regular, and, from years of experience, that two boxes of 12 cans each will be enough until the next visit to the wholesalers. Consider on the other hand the kind of buying decisions that have to be made for a knitwear garment from a major retailer like BhS. First of all the characteristics of the garment itself have to be determined, the composition of the yarn it is knitted in, the style, the colour(s) and so on. Then a supplier has to be chosen who has the machinery and enough production capacity to make the product in the kind of quantities that BhS would need. A price that enables both the supplier and the retailer to make satisfactory levels of profit has to be negotiated, and in order to reach a particular selling price, the buyer may need to make compromise decisions such as using cheaper raw materials, or simplifying the style. Then the stock-control decisions have to be made. Will the garment be sold in all stores, or just some? How many of each colour should be ordered for the initial delivery? Should all the colours on offer be ordered in the same quantity? None of these questions can be answered without further considerations. Who is the intended customer for the product, and what are their purchasing habits?

Table 11.1 The buying process

New task buy	Buying decision process	Reorder
Yes	Determine customer requirements	No
Yes	Search for, or develop product to meet customer requirements	No
Yes	Source supplier (existing or new) to make/supply product	No
Yes	Establish, by negotiation, price for product	No
Yes	Specify order details (quantities, delivery time and place)	Yes
Yes	Monitor delivery and sales	Yes

Source: Adapted from Webster, Faris and Wind (1967).

Will coordinating garments, such as trousers, be offered at the same time? Quickly, it becomes apparent that buying situations can vary from a simple restocking task to an entirely new and complex task. Table 11.1 shows how two different buying tasks involve different stages in the buying decision process.

Retail Buying Organizations

In large retail organizations the buying task is extremely complex, involving large teams of people and often several layers of management. In this section we describe the ways in which such larger organizations are structured for the buying process.

Centralization

Most multiple retailers carry out their buying operations through a central organization. Centralization has been a key feature of the evolution of the retail industry through the last half-century; smaller retailers have gradually been taken over by larger retailers and buying operations have been amalgamated, leaving central buyers in control of larger volumes of goods with increased financial responsibility. A centralized approach brings the advantages of scale economies and augmented buying power, as well as the opportunity to employ product specialists. It also allows the product offer to be centrally coordinated, supporting the corporate retail brand. Between 1960 and 1970, the number of buying 'points' controlling 80 per cent of the grocery market dropped from 1621 to 647 (De Chernatony and McDonald 1992, p.190) and by 2001 over 70 per cent of the grocery market was controlled by just seven retailers (Nielsen, 2001).

Buying departments and teams

The buying offices of multiple retailers are usually managed on the basis of splitting the total product range into manageable subsections and allocating a team of people to manage a part of it. In order to maximize the use of product expertise, the product range will be divided on the basis of similarity of product characteristics, so that for example in a department store the same buying team may be responsible for coats and dresses, but a separate team are likely to be used for stationary and gift-wrapping. Some buying organizations allocate buying responsibility according to the turnover of the department, so that each department handles roughly the same proportion of the total buying budget. To some extent the larger the retail organization the more narrowly the buying areas will be defined because of the larger volumes of product and cash flowing through the organization.

Rarely, in large retail organizations, are all the buying decisions for a product range left to an individual. The buying team may consist of a number of people carrying out different roles. The Burton Group (now Arcadia) were one of the first retail companies to implement the buyer/merchandiser buying-team structure which is the basis of many buying-team formations. Within this arrangement the buying function is broken into a selecting role which is chiefly concerned with the 'right product and price' functions and a merchandising or stock control role that is concerned with all the other factors' (time, quantity, place). The people who carry out these tasks however, work interdependently, working together towards the same departmental goals. They are also likely to have one or more assistants each. The buying teams will be overseen by senior management whose titles may be merchandise manager, buying director, or similar.

Buying committees

A highly complex buying decision, such as introducing a new product line, will have an impact on all areas of retail management. The buyers have to consider the supply side; the merchandisers have to consider the stock levels and the space allocation for the product; and the store management has to concern themselves with how the product should be displayed and how it should be sold to customers. Ultimately the most important person in this process is the consumer, in terms of the ability of the new product to meet unsatisfied needs or desires. Retailers therefore have to have some mechanism by which all the needs of the people involved with the product are considered in the buying decision-making process.

One way in which these various concerns can be considered is by using a group of people to make buying decisions. These groups are often referred to as buying committees; representatives from all the areas of the retail business get together on a regular basis to consider product ranges. The advantages of this system are that the committee represents a considerable wealth of product expertise, and whatever decision is made has the backing of all members. However, gathering the committee takes time and the group may not be able to reach a consensus view, which may result in some buying opportunities being lost.

Decentralized buying

Whilst most buying decisions and operations are carried out within the central buying organization within a multiple retailer, it may be more efficient to carry out some buying on a regional basis, or even at store level. Fresh produce such as meat and vegetables is sometimes bought by regional buyers because of the geographically fragmented nature of supply. Likewise, it makes sense to manage regionally-specific products such as newspapers or heritage-orientated gifts by store personnel. As catchment areas are increasingly saturated with retail provision, catering for regional preferences is a way of achieving an effectively differentiated product range (see Vignette 11.1).

Regional buying has been seen to be more appropriate when the catchment areas of stores show marked differences, for example in the case of Fenwicks who had stores in central London, Brent Cross, Tunbridge Wells and Newcastle. However, modern sales information systems are likely to show that a high percentage of goods can be bought centrally, giving the organization the benefits outlined earlier.

Vignette 11.1

Local buying within a large centralized organization

In 2001 it was reported that J. Sainsbury plc was stocking nearly 2,500 regional product lines from over 350 regional suppliers. Sainsburys initiated the local sourcing policy when they opened stores in Northern Ireland. In that particular market, Sainsbury's own-brand did not have the heritage and appeal that had been built over the years of the retailer's development, firstly in the south-east and then throughout England. The move proved to be successful, and so was replicated in Scotland, Wales and then into south-west England. In order to support the use of local and regional suppliers, Sainsbury's collaborate with government organizations to encourage potential suppliers to undergo development programmes which help them to understand the needs of retailers and their customers. Using local and regional suppliers sits well with the development of premium product ranges like their 'Taste the Difference' items, and the regional products can be highlighted in store, for example by using the dragon motif from the Welsh flag in Wales.

In early 2003, Sainsbury's built further on their positive image for authentic food by launching a new store format. The 'Market' format (trialed initially in King's Road in south-west London) goes right back to the roots of grocery shopping, with products grouped along traditional lines with a greengrocer, baker, butcher, fishmonger and so on. The products are displayed in a more traditional way, using sacks, racking and crates rather than the huge 'gondola' shelf with never-ending aisles in between. Heads of the food departments are allowed to source their own produce and adapt the signage and fittings accordingly. There is more focus on seasonal produce within a range that moves away from breadth and scale and towards edited product quality.

Sources: Faithfull (2003) and Abdy (2001).

⬤ Product Range Management

Decisions about single product items have to be made within the context of the product range offered by a retailer. The decisions regarding the knitwear garment mentioned earlier on in the chapter will be taken within the framework of the knitwear product range, and ultimately the whole of the clothing product range. A retailer like BhS has a wide product range and so the number of knitwear styles will be relatively small compared to a specialist knitwear retailer like Benetton. Product ranges can therefore be wide, covering a large number of product types (or categories), but with limited choice within those categories. At the other extreme, a very small number of categories or a single category may be stocked, but the choice within that category is seemingly endless. Tie Rack, for example, offer enormous depth in neckwear merchandise categories, but little else is stocked in their outlets.

Product ranges have traditionally been determined by product area, so that customers know which retailer to visit for certain products. However, as retail choice increases, retailers are becoming more adept at tailoring their product ranges to a particular customer type; this is often referred to as lifestyle retailing. Another term for the total range of products on offer within a retail outlet is the product assortment, and we now describe strategies for managing that assortment.

● Product Assortment Strategies

Width and depth

Product assortment strategies tend to be determined by the store format used, so that for example a neighbourhood supermarket offers a wide assortment of many different product categories to fulfill the majority of basic grocery needs, but little choice is offered within each category. A specialist retailer like Sock Shop, however, offers a very deep assortment in a relatively narrow band of categories. Department stores generally offer both width and depth in their product assortment. The name 'category killer' applied to larger specialist retailers such as IKEA, Toys R Us and Homestyle, is derived from their assortment strategy, which is to constrain the categories of merchandise on offer but to explode the depth of choice within those categories, effectively killing off any nearby competition in those categories. Figure 11.1 illustrates the concepts of product range width and depth (assortment).

Service level

Part of the assortment strategy must be the stock service a retailer wishes to offer, and for each SKU (stock keeping unit) within each category, a stock-holding level must be decided. This level may vary according to whether a product item is considered to be a core line, which should have a service level close to the ideal of 100 per cent, or whether it is non-core. For the latter, a service level of 80 per cent may be sufficient, which means that most customers will be satisfied most of the time. The higher the service level, the higher the stock investment, so an appropriate service level is an important part of range planning.

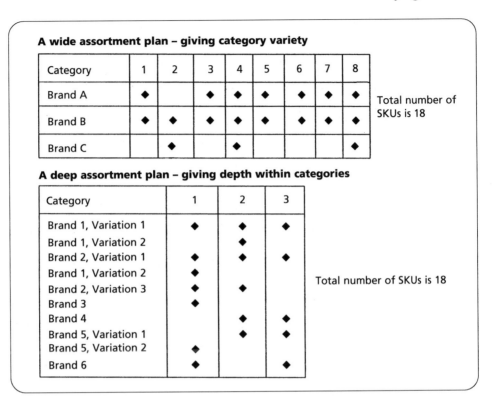

Figure 11.1 Contrasting wide and deep assortment strategies

Consistency and flexibility

Samli (1998) considers these two further dimensions to range planning. Consistency relates to the level of compatibility between merchandise within and across buying departments, in terms of product attributes such as quality and price level. The merchandise on offer in Harvey Nichols, for example, is consistent because the products on offer in all departments are high- quality, stylish, directionally fashionable and premium priced. New Look, on the other hand, is consistent with its mainstream, value-orientated, reasonable quality merchandise. Inconsistency within a product range is confusing for customers and damaging for the retail brand image. Consistency must also be considered in relation to the congruence between the merchandise and the store environment that surrounds it, an aspect of retail management discussed in Chapter 10. A clear merchandise strategy and good communication between departments are key requirements for a consistent approach.

Flexibility refers to the extent to which a product range reflects regional sales opportunities, buying opportunities and seasonal variation. Pumpkins, for example, are only stocked by supermarkets in October. Product categories such as gifts, chocolate, lingerie and slippers are offered in increased depth in the Christmas period. Flexibility allows retailers to improve cash flow by maximizing short-term sales opportunities, but it may conflict with the aim to be consistent.

Lifestyle retailing

Selecting products for a lifestyle retailer requires a detailed knowledge of a particular customer type, in terms of their attitudes and opinions and the activities they choose. In this way the retailer is able to offer a choice of products determined by a living pattern, which is not easily described by more traditional segmentation variables such as age, income level or geographical location. Planet Organic, for example, offers a wide range of organic products, appealing to the customer who would choose organic produce over other products irrespective of brand, price or product design. The Gadget Shop offers a product range which is geared towards people who readily adopt new ideas and gadgetry into their living patterns. Lifestyle retailing has enabled some specialist retailers to extend their product ranges without losing sight of the core business. Internacionale, for example, introduced a range of gifts and home accessories to its core range of young, budget, fashion clothing and personal accessories. The range, including clocks, candles, frames, pottery and inflatable chairs, is geared to the needs of the customer; it is fun, fashion-orientated and inexpensive.

⬤ Product Selection

The task of selecting products for a product range can involve decision-making at two main levels. Firstly, the buyer has to decide whether there is a place for the product in the retailer's offer at all. This level of decision-making is all about getting the product range right, and ensuring that whenever a customer enters the outlet the product offer is interesting and relevant to them. The second area of decision-making concerns the detail of the product itself; the buyer has to be sure that the product reflects the image the retailer is trying to portray in every respect.

Product range (assortment) decisions

Space is an expensive commodity in retailing. Retailers have to make sure that their outlet space is producing maximum benefits to the organization, and the products that occupy that space should therefore reflect the needs and desires of the customer at the moment they choose to enter the outlet. Retail buyers should be constantly reviewing the product range on offer. It may be time to delete a product item; it may be time to scale down the offer in a particular product category. On the other hand, customers may have requested a product item, or a buyer may have seen a new product when visiting a supplier and decide they would like to offer it to their customers. Ranging decisions should be made with the lifecycle of the product category in mind. Figure 11.2 illustrates the product life-cycle, and the related buying decisions are as follows:

- *Introduction phase* – trial product; Restricted offer in limited number of stores.
- *Growth phase* – increase store distribution; increase product variation (colour, flavour, pack size, brand choice).

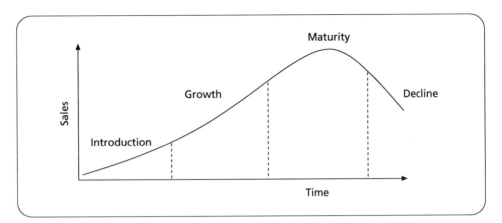

Figure 11.2 The category life-cycle

- *Maturity phase* – all-store distribution; core product offer with additional variation according to store profile.
- *Decline phase* – Reduce product variation to core lines; determine store distribution according to branch sales; phase out product category completely.

The product assortment plan (the model stock list)

The assortment plan is an aid to product management that considers the selection of products from a physical, rather than a financial viewpoint. It therefore complements the stock-planning systems outlined in Chapter 7. It is a written representation of the ideal product selection that a customer should face at any one time, indicating the colours/style/flavour, size and price-level variations. The grid shown in Figure 11.3 illustrates the use of an assortment plan within the context of a towel range for a department store.

New assortment plans will be drawn up in line with seasonal changes, and to reflect the expansion or contraction of a product category.

Product selection criteria

Within the framework of the product range, selecting products is also concerned with getting the detail of the product correct. Products represent a blend of a number of features, all of which need to be considered by the buyer so that customers' needs are met most closely and satisfactorily. Table 11.2 presents a generic list of product features that may bear upon a product's ability to satisfy a consumer.

Price/value as a product feature

The ability of a product (represented by the relevant features taken from the list in Table 11.2) to provide customer satisfaction will be determined

Standard price		Premium price		Children's		Adult patterned	
Blue	Bath Hand Face	Royal	Bath Hand Face	Seaside motif	Bath Hand	Brights design	Bath Hand
Pink	Bath Hand Face	Burgundy	Bath Hand Face	Cartoon character 1	Bath	Pastels design 1	Bath Hand
Peach	Bath Hand Face	Cream	Bath Hand Face	Cartoon character 2	Bath	Pastels design 2	Bath Hand
Aqua	Bath Hand Face	Fashion colour	Bath Hand Face				
White	Bath Hand Face						
Fashion colour	Bath Hand Face						

Figure 11.3 Assortment plan for towels

Table 11.2 Product features: a generic list

Feature	Indicators/considerations
Physical properties	Size, weight, volume, components, ingredients
Packaging	Aesthetic, protection, added value, promotional vehicle
Product quality	Raw materials, production processes, social and ethical issues, product standards
Brand	Trademark, certification, association approval, designer
Style	Design, taste, fashion, sensory factors
Utility	Functions, maintenance, durability, versatility, health and safety, environmental issues

Source: Adapted from Cash, Wingate and Friedland (1995).

in the light of the price tag. Price will be considered as one of the product features, and, like style or quality, different customers will perceive a price differently. When the retailer is making satisfactory profit margins *and* the collection of product features represents good value to the majority of customers, a buyer will have made good selection decisions, although a price which represents value will have some flexibility (see Chapter 13 on retail pricing).

Product development

Selecting products by retail buyers can involve different levels of involvement in the development of the product itself. Retail buyers may buy a product from a supplier exactly as it is shown to them, for example products that carry a manufacturer's brand (for example Cadbury's chocolate) are bought in this way – a retail buyer simply decides the quantity of the product they wish to stock. Many retailers, however, offer products that are branded with a retailer's own label, and in this instance the retail buyer has more control over the way the product is made and presented. Some retailers get involved with the development of products at a very early stage, making choices about raw materials and components and methods of production. Marks and Spencer operate in this way and have been referred to as the manufacturer without factories (Tse, 1985). The main advantages for retailers in developing their own products are:

● A unique product range can be created and controlled.
● Products can be developed according to the retailer's customer needs.
● Repetition or gaps in the overall product range can be avoided.
● Higher profit margins are generated.

An extensive discussion on retailer brands can be found in Chapter 12.

However, not all retailers have the resources to operate in this way. In order for a retail buyer to be competent in product development, they not only need the business skills of a keen negotiator, they also need the specific technical product knowledge of their particular product area. The buying quantity also has to make it worthwhile for a retail supplier to enter into a product development arrangement with a retailer. In addition, access to a particular supplier may only be possible by buying supplier-branded products. Kellogg's, for example, have visibly promoted the fact that they do not supply own-label: 'If you don't see Kellogg's *on* the box . . . it isn't Kellogg's *in* the box'.

Buying cycles

In Chapter 7, various techniques to help retailers forecast demand for products were discussed. Forecasting demand for consumable, fast-moving consumer products with a relatively stable demand pattern is challenging, but with the use of sophisticated computer programmes the task has been greatly facilitated and fine-tuned. Managing product ranges that change with the seasons, or with fashion (often combined!) pose additional problems. Demand forecasting can only be based on a similar, rather than the same product item. New products invariably have long lead times (the time between ordering and delivery) because the supply company has not had the benefit of experience, and set up times need to be added to the normal production times. In order to achieve the five rights (see pp. 185–6) of buying for seasonal/fashion-orientated products, buyers need to adhere to a critical path within a buying cycle. A simplified buying cycle for fashion products is shown in Figure 11.4.

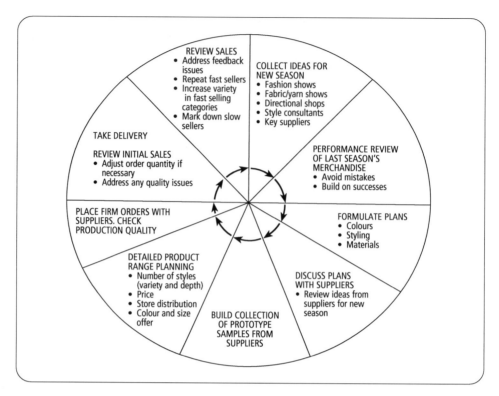

Figure 11.4 Buying cycle for fashion products

It must be remembered that Figure 11.4 represents the cycle for one season. Fashion products have two and in some cases three seasons, and so at any one time a buyer could be working on different sections of three cycles. For example, in September a footwear buyer will be concerned with current Autumn sales and deliveries, be in the process of finalising the range of Spring/Summer styles, and will be starting to gather new styling ideas for the next Autumn range.

⬤ Category Management

In product areas that are fashion-orientated, customers have a high expectation of change within the product range. They expect the product offer to change with the seasons and to be presented with a continuous array of new product ideas. In other product areas, for example grocery products, frequent changes to the product ranges would be confusing and irritating. Many products and brands have a loyal customer following and a constant demand, and should such a product not be available customers are likely to show high levels of dissatisfaction. At the same time, however, customers of the twenty-first century like to try new product variations and new product ideas, and so product ranges have to be managed so that the popular items can always be found, but at the same time advantage can be taken of consumers' tendencies to seek variety.

Table 11.3 Category management within the confectionery product area

Product category	Countline	Boxed	Bagged
Typical need	Instant gratification, reduce hunger	Gift	Sharing, relieve boredom
Likely user	Self	Friend, family	Family, self
Price level (comparative)	Low	High	Medium
Purchase frequency	High	Low, seasonal	Low/medium

An approach to the buying process that allows for this type of product-range management is category management. A merchandise category is the term used for an assortment of product items that a customer sees as reasonable substitutes for each other. Each product unit (SKU) is able to satisfy the same basic need, but the category would include a number of product variations which satisfy individual preferences. For example, the product area 'confectionery' can be broken down into three distinct categories: boxed, bagged and countlines (bars). A countline bar (such as a Snickers or Mars) fulfills a need which is different to products in the other two categories, as shown in Table 11.3.

Rather than planning the profit margins of individual items, products are managed as a group to obtain maximum category performance. Decisions regarding product development, pricing and promotions are made with a view to maximizing the profitability of the category, rather than the individual SKU. Each category therefore effectively has its own retail marketing mix. The buyer's role is extended to a category-management role, with responsibility to manage the category right through the organization from 'cradle to grave'. The category manager would be involved with new product development within the category, working with suppliers on new product innovations and managing product launches. A large part of category management is concerned with in-store marketing; ensuring that the category is supported with point-of-sale materials and appropriate space allocation. The category manager also has to be concerned with logistical arrangements, customer service and aftersales issues, as these all impact on the performance of the product category. One of the keys to success in the category-management approach is close collaboration with suppliers. It is in the interest of leading suppliers (sometimes referred to as 'category champions') to work with a retailer to make a merchandise category as successful as possible, because the retailer's success will mean higher sales volumes for the supplier. Category management is an integral part of the ECR (efficient consumer response) approach to retailing discussed in Chapter 7.

● Retail Suppliers

Throughout the retail industry, supply sources come in many different guises, from the individual craftsperson to the sprawling factory. Supplies can be purchased directly from a manufacturing unit (small or large), or the retailer may use another intermediary such as an agent, a wholesaler or a broker. Retailers will use supply sources that are appropriate to their needs. A supplier's ability to meet a retailer's needs will be determined by the following factors:

- Product range – design, quality and brand recognition.
- Price level – negotiation opportunities, discounts and payment terms.
- Capacity – volumes, lead-times, available capacity (other customers).
- Service – delivery service, sales service, and aftersales service.
- Flexibility – ability to manufacture different products and make fast changes to production planning.
- Technology – use of technology in production, and information systems.
- Approach – understanding of retailer's needs; partnership; opportunistic.
- Location – local, domestic or global.

Retailers will have a set of suppliers that they currently order from. Some suppliers might be used on an intermittent basis; others may be supplying on an ongoing basis. Either way, suppliers that are current are termed 'active' suppliers. Alongside the list of active suppliers will be a set of 'inactive' suppliers that a retail buyer will keep as their consideration set. This set of suppliers might include those who have recently made approaches to the buyer but offer a similar product proposition to an existing supplier, and it may include suppliers who have been used in the past. Buyers who work for large retail organizations very rarely have to search out suppliers, as they are frequently approached by producers who wish to increase their distribution coverage. However, if a retailer is planning to enter a new product area, or is keen to supply a new type of product, then a supplier search might be necessary. Smaller and specialist retailers may also need to search for suppliers.

Sources of information on suppliers include the following: trade journals and magazines, local and international trade associations, trade fairs and exhibitions, and catalogues. Although it is time-consuming, buying teams should always be open-minded when reviewing suppliers who make approaches to the retailer, because the supply environment can change as well as the needs of the retailer. It is often the task of an assistant buyer to screen supplier representatives for the departmental buyer. New product ideas and new suppliers very often go hand in hand, but it is not uncommon for new product ideas to be quickly 'interpreted' by retailers, using existing supply sources. For a wider discussion on the ethics of sourcing retail products, readers are referred to Chapter 18.

Buying groups and buying alliances

Earlier in this chapter, the advantages of centralized buying were outlined. Some small retailers become members of a third-party buying organization in order to gain some of the advantages of centralization. In this situation, the orders of a large number of smaller retailers are amalgamated so that lower prices can be negotiated with suppliers, and a wider range of supply sources used. AIS (Associated Independent Stores), for example, represents a group of smaller department store retailers in the UK. The organization acts like a retail head office, offering not only buying expertise, but also training on merchandising, marketing, customer service and so on. Membership to buying groups may be at a flat rate, or it may be paid on a commission basis. Symbol groups (such as Nisa) operate in a similar way, although members may be bound by certain buying agreements, and they may be required to display the symbol group's trademark (for example on the shop fascia). Some larger retailers also collaborate in order to tap into each other's buying expertise. The internet has led to the development of e-commerce trading networks which offer the opportunity for retailers to combine their buying power. The World Wide Retail Exchange, for example, includes Tesco, Marks and Spencer, Casino, Ahold and Kmart within its membership. This type of collaboration can be used for non-resale sourcing, for example for shopfitting or office equipment, as well as for stock for resale.

Retailer–supplier relationships

In a previous section of this chapter, the ideas of intermittent and ongoing supply sources were introduced. Some retailers have a relatively small number of suppliers who provide large quantities of products in many merchandise categories; others tend to 'shop around' between a large number of suppliers. Over the last decade, however, many of the large multiple retailers have gone through a process of supply-base rationalization, resulting in smaller numbers of suppliers who are responsible for larger order quantities. This type of approach to buying is often termed the 'partnership approach', because the suppliers are considered to be partners in the success of the retailer, even though there is no financial ownership linking the two companies.

Partnerships

Partnerships are highly developed retailer–supplier relationships and are usually the result of a long-term association between the two companies. They are characterized by a 'corporate approach' to the relationship, where contacts are formed at all levels of the organization, not just at the point between retail buyer and supplier sales representative. Figure 11.5 illustrates how retailer–supplier partnerships involve the whole of the retail organization.

Benefits of the partnership approach to supplier management include:

● Suppliers gain a deep understanding of the retailer's operational organization. They are therefore able to offer a better quality service to the retailer and meet stringent standards, for example in delivery requirements, whilst simultaneously driving down costs (Bowlby and Foord, 1995).
● Suppliers gain a better appreciation of a retailer's positioning and aims. They will understand the retailer's customer profile and the retailer's strategic objectives (Hogarth-Scott and Parkinson, 1993).

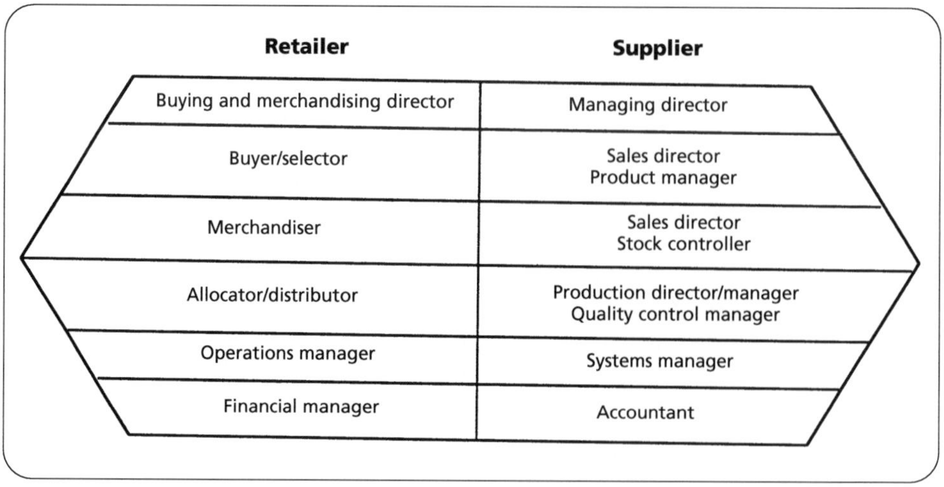

Retailer	Supplier
Buying and merchandising director	Managing director
Buyer/selector	Sales director Product manager
Merchandiser	Sales director Stock controller
Allocator/distributor	Production director/manager Quality control manager
Operations manager	Systems manager
Financial manager	Accountant

Figure 11.5 The retailer–supplier partnership

Source: Adapted from Davis (1993), p. 74.

● Corporate supplier management means that supplier contact is not 'lost' when a buyer leaves the retail organization (Miller, 1997).
● Suppliers will be more willing to make adaptations to their own businesses to accommodate the needs of the retailer. This is particularly relevant to information technology. The use of certain systems (such as EDI) may be a prerequisite to the formation of a trading relationship with some retailers (Bowlby and Foord, 1995). More effective systems facilitate faster reactions to market opportunities.

Although partnerships are very common in retail buying, there are dangers involved with this approach. Partners may become interdependent, which certainly encourages commitment, but it can also breed complacency which is a dangerous state in a fast-moving environment like retailing. Concentrating on existing supply partners may also cause a buyer to overlook product opportunities offered by other supply sources. For this reason a buying department may be using a portfolio of different suppliers, with varying types of relationships amongst them (Figure 11.6).

Transactional buying

A partnership approach is not appropriate for all retail buying situations. Small retailers, and those who are not concerned with developing their own retail branded products, may find that a transactional approach is more profitable. In this situation the supplier that offers the best deal at the time of purchase is the supplier that is selected for the order. Here, suppliers do not expect continuity, but neither will they be willing to change the way they operate to accommodate a retail customer. This type of relationship is sometimes referred to as the 'arms-length' relationship, and may demonstrate

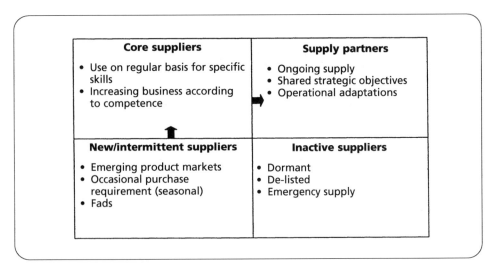

Core suppliers	Supply partners
• Use on regular basis for specific skills • Increasing business according to competence	• Ongoing supply • Shared strategic objectives • Operational adaptations
New/intermittent suppliers	Inactive suppliers
• Emerging product markets • Occasional purchase requirement (seasonal) • Fads	• Dormant • De-listed • Emergency supply

Figure 11.6 A portfolio of supplier relationships

adversarial characteristics because of the focus on the short-term gains for both parties.

Summary

This chapter has been concerned with the pivotal (McGoldrick, 2002) role of the retail buyer. The chapter introduced the main objectives associated with any retail buying task and then outlined how the complexity of a buying decision might vary according to the familiarity of the task. The way in which retail organizations tend to be structured for the buying process was explored followed by some approaches to product-range management.

What becomes clear in this discussion is that a retail buyer needs to possess a unique set of attributes in order to cope with the changing facets of their organizational role. It has been suggested that a retail buyer should be educated to graduate level, be enthusiastic, analytical, articulate, product knowledgeable, objective, dedicated and flexible (Diamond and Pintel, 1997). However, the buying function is so central to the organization's success, that retailers should ensure that these innate personal characteristics should be combined with specific skills development, such as negotiation, leadership and communication skills (Swindley, 1992).

Retail buying operations play an exceedingly important role in the implementation of a retail strategy. Buying objectives, however, are unique to each retail organization and will depend on its positioning strategy. This chapter has provided a discussion of the structures and decision-making processes which are likely to be included in one form or another in any retail business as they go about buying merchandise, but the interpretation of these generic approaches will be dependent on the individual internal organization and operation of each retailer.

Questions

1 Using a manufacturer-branded product and a retailer of your choice, outline the various buying process stages that would be necessary for the retailer to introduce an own-label version of the product, assuming the original manufacturer is not interested in supplying under a retail brand. Make a list of the product and supplier selection factors that would be important for the chosen product. Some suggestions are given below:

Product	*Retailer*
Gucci-style fashion bag	Marks and Spencer (variety store)
Oasis fruit drink	Co-operative retail stores (supermarket)
Sharp electronic personal organizer	W. H. Smith (variety store)

2 Describe the assortment strategies that would be appropriate for the following retail organizations:

- A general department store (for example John Lewis).
- A convenience store in a village.
- An out-of-town home furnishings retailer (for example MFI).
- An audio specialist retailer, operating from a secondary site within a town centre.
- A lifestyle retailer.

3 Outline the principles of category management, and discuss why partnerships between retailers and suppliers are necessary for this approach to product retail management.
4 Explain why many buying decisions within multiple retailers are made by groups of people rather than individuals.
5 Outline the main benefits of a centralized approach to retail buying. Discuss instances when a decentralized approach would be more appropriate.

References and Further Reading

Abdy, M. (2001) 'Pros and Cons of Keeping it Local', *Retail Week*, 31 August.

Baily, P., Farmer, D., Jessop, D. and Jones, D. (1994) *Purchasing Principles and Management*, 7th edn (London: Pitman).

Bowlby, S. R. and Foord, J. (1995) 'Relational Contracting between UK Retailers and Manufacturers', *International Review of Retail, Distribution and Consumer Research*, vol. 5, no. 3, pp. 333–60.

Cash, R. P., Wingate, J. and Friedlander, J. S. (1995) *Management of Retail Buying* (New York: John Wiley), p. 84.

Davis, G. (1993) *Trade Marketing Strategy* (London: Paul Chapman).

De Chernatony, L. and McDonald, M. (1992) *Creating Powerful Brands* (Oxford: Butterworth-Heinemann).

Diamond, J. and Pintel, G. (1997) *Retail Buying*, 5th edn (Englewood Cliffs, N.J.: Prentice-Hall).

Faithfull, M. (2003) 'Market Trader', *Retail Interiors*, April.

Hogarth Scott, S. and Parkinson, S. T. (1993) Retailer–Supplier Relationships in the Food Channel: A Supplier Perspective', *International Journal of Retail and Distribution Management*, vol. 21, no. 8, pp. 11–18.

Jackson, T. and Shaw, D. (2001) *Mastering Fashion Buying and Merchandise Management* (Basingstoke: Macmillan).

McGoldrick , P.J. (2002) *Retail Marketing* (Maidenhead: McGraw-Hill).

Miller, L. (1997) 'The Changing Role of Buyers', *Drapers Record Focus*, October.

Neilson (2001) *Retail Pocket Book 2001* (Henley-on-Thames: NTC Publications).

Robinson, P. J., Faris, C. W. and Wind, Y. (1967) *Industrial Buying and Creative Marketing* (Boston, Mass.: Allyn & Bacon).

Samli, A. C., (1998) *Strategic Marketing for Success in Retailing* (Westport, Conn.: Quorum Books), p. 295.

Swindley, D. (1992) 'The Role of the Buyer in UK Multiple Retailing', *International Journal of Retail Distribution Management*, vol. 20, no. 2, pp. 3–15.

Tse, K.K. (1985) *Marks and Spencer: Anatomy of Britain's Most Efficiently Managed Company* (Oxford: Pergamon Press).

Varley, R. (2001) *Retail Product Management* (London: Routledge).

Wills, J. (1999) *Merchandising and Buying Strategies: New Roles for a Global Operation*, Financial Times Retail and Consumer Reports, London.

chapter twelve

Retail Brands

Learning objectives

- To understand the reasons for the emergence of retailer brands.
- To identify the different types of own brands used by retailers.
- To understand the own-brand development strategies employed by retailers.
- To explore the use of lookalike brands and their impact on brand manufacturers.
- To understand consumer perceptions of quality and the difficulties associated with trading-up brands by retailers.
- To understand how brands can be used in the overall retail brand-building strategy.

Introduction

Retail branding has developed to such an extent that, today, retailers are perceived as being brands in themselves rather than as distributors of manufacturer brands. Many retailers have developed such a strong consumer franchise that customers are more loyal to the retailer than they are to the manufacturer's brand. This shift is mainly due to the extensive development of own brands and a more marketing-orientated approach to retailing. Retailers have been rewarded for their focus on customer needs and aspirations by increased levels of trust from customers.

This chapter examines the branding strategies of retailers and the contribution of brand management to the overall retail positioning. The chapter begins with an examination of the growth of own brands. This is followed by a discussion of the different types of retailer brands and own-branding strategies used by retailers, with particular emphasis on the controversy over copycat/lookalike own brands. The chapter also examines the problems that retailers face when they attempt to position their own brands upmarket.

204

Growth of Retailer Brands

The growth of retailer brands, variously known as own brands, own labels, private labels, and store brands, has paralleled the growth of multiples, particularly in the grocery sector. It was in the 1960s that the major multiple retailers began to realize that they could increase their margins significantly if they did not have to pay for manufacturers' branding overheads. The substantial costs associated with the task of branding mean that branded products are unable to compete on a level price basis with own-brand lines. A 1994 survey by the Consumers' Association magazine *Which?* concluded that consumers could save more than 25 per cent of a weekly shopping bill if they purchased the own-brand equivalents of branded goods (Hobson, 1994), although this survey did not include budget own-brand lines, such as Tesco's 'Value' range. Given this price positioning, it is not surprising that own brands have proved popular with consumers, particularly during periods of economic difficulty when value for money is becoming increasingly important to consumers.

Retailer brands are now a dominant force in the grocery sector of the UK retailing industry (Table 12.1). The share of grocery sales allocated to own-brand products has increased rapidly during the last 20 years, with Simmons and Meredith (1984) estimating an own-brand turnover of just 20.5 per cent in 1975, but increased to 26 per cent 1983. More recently, according to Taylor Nelson AGB's Superpanel, which regularly monitors the purchases of a sample of 28,000 consumers, 37 per cent of all grocery sales in the last quarter of 1994 were of own-brand products (Nielsen, 1994). In March 1998, Taylor Nelson estimated the share of own labels to be 40.5 per cent (*The Grocer*, 1998). As would be expected, the level of own-brand sales was even higher within the major multiple retailers. Sainsbury's led the way, with nearly 48.8 per cent of the chain's sales being own-branded products, followed by Tesco (44.7%), and Safeway (41%). However, by 2001 the own-label share of packaged grocery sales had fallen to 38 per cent, according to Taylor Nelson Sofres. This is partly explained by aggressive promotional activity by brand manufacturers, particularly in the area of sales promotions.

Table 12.1 Percentage of own-brand products sold in the large UK grocery multiples: packaged groceries and toiletries

	Quarter ending March				
	1995[a]	1996[a]	1997[a]	1998[a]	2001[b]
Tesco	45.6	45.1	45.8	44.7	42.0
Sainsbury	53.8	53.3	51.2	48.8	45.0
ASDA	37.0	40.6	46.2	47.6	44.0
Safeway	41.0	40.9	41.4	41.5	34.0
Somerfield	38.6	38.1	37.8	36.7	34.0
Kwik Save	9.9	13.1	12.8	18.7	16.0

Sources: (a) Figures for 1995 to 1998 are for the quarter ending March for each respective year and based on Taylor Nelson AGB Retailer Sharetrack; (b) Figures for 2001 are for the 3rd quarter and based on TNS Superpanel.

The size of the retail brand market in the UK is greater than anywhere else in the world, the USA, for example, has an own-brand share of just 20 per cent. Recent research into own brands in Europe by Euromonitor shows that across Europe as a whole, the UK has the highest private-label sales, valued at over US$87 billion in 1998, giving it a 31.4 per cent market share of the US$277 billion European market for own labels. Germany and France rank second and third with sales of US$58.7 billion and US$47.4 billion respectively.

Perhaps unsurprisingly, the product categories that are now dominated by retailer brands tend to be those where traditionally there have been few (if any) strong brands. According to Nielsen (1995) the own-brand market share was strongest in categories such as prepacked salads (86%), prepacked sliced meats (72%) and cream (70%). Conversely, where brands are strong, for instance in confectionery and hair care, own-brand market share is considerably lower (1.3% and 17.9% respectively, see Table 12.2). As retailers have gained greater confidence in the sales potential of their own-branded lines, they have ventured into new product categories, including some where there has always been a strong manufacturer brand presence. Up until relatively recently, for instance, there were but two big players in the cola market – Coca-Cola and Pepsi-Cola; they have now been joined by a whole host of own-brand colas (most notably, Sainsbury's Classic Cola).

Table 12.2 Percentage penetration of retailer-branded goods by product category

| | Quarter ending March | | | |
	1995	1996	1997	1998
Bakery	58.8	62.2	62.1	61.8
Dairy	50.0	51.0	52.0	53.5
Prepared frozen food	46.3	45.0	46.0	47.5
Soft drinks	40.0	40.6	42.5	41.9
Canned goods	32.3	34.4	37.2	39.2
Household & cleaning products	32.2	36.2	36.1	36.8
Packet & other foods	29.9	31.8	33.2	35.1
Pickles, sauces & ketchups	28.5	31.2	32.8	33.7
Biscuits	29.6	32.8	33.5	31.5
Healthcare	14.7	15.0	22.6	28.1
Other toiletries	24.1	22.7	24.6	26.3
Hot beverages	24.5	24.9	26.5	25.7
Bathroom toiletries	22.2	22.9	23.5	23.7
Oral care	16.6	20.1	20.2	22.1
Pet foods	13.7	16.6	18.7	18.3
Hair care	16.9	19.1	16.7	17.9
Confectionery	1.1	1.3	2.8	1.3

Source: *The Grocer* (1998).

Table 12.3 Retailer brands by product sector in Europe, 1995/97

	Percentage share	
	1995	**1997**
Food	34.7	34.8
Clothing & footwear	18.3	18.0
Drinks	14.0	14.1
Household goods	10.8	11.4
Cosmetics, toiletries	6.3	6.5
DIY	6.1	6.1
Electrical appliances	4.4	4.4
Others	5.4	4.8

Source: Euromonitor,' *Private Label in Europe*', March, 1999.
Note: Figures may not sum due to rounding.

Although in the past, own-brand products were positioned as cheap alternatives to manufacturers' brands, in recent years retailers have upgraded the quality of their own-branded goods. Hence, many shoppers now accept that own-brand products are of an equal quality to their branded rivals. Individual multiple retailers have also made their own-brand ranges more consistent, and are, in effect, now making a brand statement of their own (Caulkin, 1987). One of the main reasons why such a strategy has been implemented is because multiple retailers are now competing head-on against other multiple retailers; the independent sector has been reduced to an insignificant size, and most future growth of a multiple retailer must be at the expense of other multiples.

An examination of own-brand development in Europe also shows that food retailing has been the leading sector for own-brand development with a percentage share of 34.8 per cent in 1997 (see Table 12.3). Considerably behind are the clothing and footwear sectors with a share of 18 per cent and the drinks sector 14.1 per cent. The least-developed sectors are electrical appliances, DIY, and the cosmetics and toiletries sector. Given the high penetration in food retailing, own brands are unlikely to experience much higher levels of growth, with the growth of non-food own brands outstripping those of food. Own brands are therefore likely to become an integral part of retailers' strategies in all sectors of retailing.

⬤ A Typology of Retail Brands

Retail brands now play a much more strategic role than they have done in the past, as is clear when one examines the different types of own brands on the market. In fact, given the existence of so many different types of retail brand, the term is too general and it is necessary to use more precise terminology to understand the role of particular categories of own brands in retailing strategies.

Pellegrini (1993) proposes a six-fold typology based on the degree of identification of the product name with the retailer, the positioning of the retailer brand *vis-à-vis* the manufacturer brands, the width of the range of products covered by the brands, and the extent of backward integration required (see Table 12.4). Pellegrini identifies generics, controlled brands, counter brands, produits drapeaux ('flag products'), house brands, and fascia brands. By *produits drapeaux* Pellegrini is referring to 'commodity-like, low priced' products with common packaging stressing the name of the goods and carrying the colours of the retailer. These brands were introduced in the mid-1970s by the French hypermarkets as an offensive strategy against manufacturers. More recently, in the UK grocery market context Sainsbury's, Tesco and Safeway developed 'Essentials', 'Value' and 'Saver' ranges, or 'budget' own brands, to combat hard discounters such as Aldi and Netto. This is a similar strategy to brand manufacturers using what are termed 'price brands' or 'fighting brands' where a producer introduces lower-priced brands with minimal advertising and promotional support to compete with a retailer's own brands and generics, maintaining the price premium of the main brand. Hence the term 'fighting' own brands is used in preference to Pellegrini's 'produits drapeaux' because of its parallel usage with regard to manufacturer brands. An omission from Pellegrini's typology is copycat own brands which offer the same or similar quality of product as the manufacturer brands and imitate many of the visual features (or cues) of the manufacturer brands. In the UK these brands came into prominence with the launch in the UK of Sainsbury's Classic Cola in April, 1994 when it attacked the market leader head on.

Another type of own brand that is not included in the Pellegrini typology is the exclusive designer label. These are products specifically commissioned by a retailer from a leading designer and sold exclusively by the commissioning retailer, bearing the designer's name to demonstrate authenticity. Such a strategy is more likely to be used by a middle to upmarket retailer. For instance, Debenhams, the department store, commissions a number of designers including Jasper Conran and Ozwald Boateng to produce exclusive designer products (see Vignette 12.2). However, ASDA provides an interesting example of how a value-positioned retailer can use exclusive ranges in its own branding strategy with its George Collection.

An additional dimension can be added to Pellegrini's four criteria, namely that the type of own brand utilized depends upon whether it is a tactical response to market changes or a longer-term strategic development. In the typology presented above, generics, controlled brands and fighter brands are largely tactical responses by retailers, whereas copycat brands, house brands and fascia brands represent long-term branding strategies.

● Retail Brand Development Strategy

The typology also suggests an own-brand development strategy, namely that retailers can start own-brand strategies by beginning with generics and then moving up the own-brand ladder as they gain experience and confidence in own-brand development. Wileman and Jary (1997) suggest a similar staged development of own brands over time in which retailers trade up in terms of

Table 12.4　A typology of retail own brands

Own-brand type	Description	Identification with the retailer	Positioning	Range of products	Degree of backward integration
Generics	Non-branded merchandise sold in plain packaging with low-price positioning; now replaced by budget own brands (see below)	Limited	Low	Limited	Low
Controlled-brands/ exclusive manufacturer brands	Brands owned by a manufacturer but exclusive to a retailer in a given market e.g. Proctor and Gamble's Physique hair-care brand sold exclusively through Tesco	None	Low/ medium	Limited	None
Counterbrands	Brands owned by a retailer, differentiated by product category, which do not identify the retailer and little attempt is made to associate the brand with the retailer; e.g. Matsui brand sold in Currys and Dixons outlets	None	Low/ medium	Limited	Low
Fighting/budget brands	Products identified with the retailer but stress name of the good itself, sold in relatively simple packaging and with low-price positioning; e.g. Tesco Value brands	Strong	Medium	Limited	Low
Copycat brands: *Reengineered brands*	Low-cost retailer-owned brands offering the same functionality of the branded product; e.g. Beaumont coffee sold by Aldi	Strong	Low/ medium	Wide	High
Lookalikes	Offer similar quality and imitate many visual features of manufacturer brands; e.g Sainsbury's Classic Cola	Medium	Medium	Limited	High
House brands	Name of retailer appears together with a separate brand name for different product groups or segments; e.g. Tesco Finest range	Strong	Medium	Wide	High
Exclusive designer labels	Products designed exclusively for the retailer and carrying the designer's name; e.g. Jasper Conran at Debenhams	Strong	High	Limited	High
Fascia brands	The trade name of the retailer (or a name strongly associated with the retailer e.g. St. Michael and Marks and Spencer) identifies all products sold as private brands; e.g. NEXT	Very strong	Medium/ high	Wide	High

Source:　Based on Pellegrini (1993).

quality and relative price *vis-à-vis* manufacturer brands, beginning with generics, followed by cheap store brands which are a step above generics but still of inferior quality, offering a large discount against manufacturer brands. Reengineered low-cost brands are the next step up where a retailer proactively examines the product and packaging to see how costs can be reduced, whilst offering the same functionality of the branded product. The retailer makes no real attempt to pass off the product as a copycat of the branded product. For example, discount retailer Aldi has developed a set of 'exclusive' brands that allows it to deliver a price differential across the range of 20–30 per cent in comparison with supermarkets. The next stage is to offer par quality store brands, which are aimed to match manufacturer brands in terms of quality and performance but at prices 10–25 per cent lower. The price discount is possible because retailers' marketing expenses are considerably lower and they can subcontract production of the store brands to manufacturers with excess capacity. In the final stage, retail brands take on a leadership role through positioning and innovation with a price parity or price premium relative to manufacturer brands, and hence better margins than traditional own labels (Dunne and Chakravarthi, 1999).

Whilst this development sequence is generally accurate for retailers who start off by selling only manufacturers' brands, fascia retailers are more likely to adopt an own-brand leadership strategy from the beginning rather than to evolve into one. That is, fascia retailers such as Marks and Spencer, NEXT and Gap have occupied that position from their inception. Similarly, discount supermarkets have adopted a policy of offering reengineered own brands from the beginning and do not intend to evolve their own brands into positions of leadership *vis-à-vis* manufacturers' brands. Some retailers (for example Tesco and Sainsbury) have developed a tiered own-brand strategy; they have created budget own-label lines (fighting brands) aimed at price-sensitive shoppers, standard own labels that offer par quality designed to take market share from existing manufacturer brands, and premium own brands (for example Tesco's Finest range) aimed at the top end of the market. The rise of premium own labels suggests consumers' acceptance of retail brands as being on a par with manufacturers' brands and the ability of retailers to deliver innovative quality products.

The discussion above suggests that the key dimensions for own-brand development are the degree of innovation, positioning (that is, the degree of identification with the retailer and its market positioning), and the strategic role of the own brand. These dimensions are used in Figure 12.1 to develop a matrix of own-brand development options which moves away from a simple descriptive typology. The matrix provides a clear rationale behind own-branding strategies. The matrix suggests that certain strategies are not viable, namely low positioning and high innovation, and low innovation and high positioning.

⬤ Lookalike Own Brands

Copycat own-brand products are increasingly common on supermarket shelves these days and are perceived as a major threat by owners of leading brands (see Vignette 12.1). The scale of the problem can be judged from the fact that in one survey of 100 brand managers, over a half had seen their brands copied by supermarkets, and 80 per cent of these had seen their sales decline as a result (*Marketing*, 1994). Some manufacturers and brand-owners were sufficiently concerned that they formed their own lobby group – the British Producers' and Brand-Owners' Group (BPBOG) – to press for changes in the law in order to help protect their brands.

What is of particular concern to the brand-owners is that recent lookalike own labels resemble their products so closely that they imitate not only the

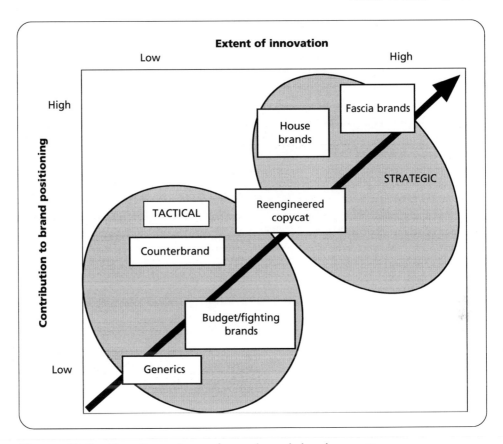

Figure 12.1 Key dimensions of own-brand development

trade marks, graphics, colours, lettering, words and packaging, but also the names of the branded products. They argue that the close resemblance of the copycat own-label product to the original brand confuses consumers and that retailers are attempting to ascribe by association the qualities of the imitated brands to the own-label product, if not the source of the product. The possibility of confusion is increased by placing brands and the lookalike own brands side-by-side on supermarket shelves. Retailers, meanwhile, have claimed that similarities in packaging design are essential in enabling consumers to recognize own-brand products and that consumers are quite adept at distinguishing between brands and own-brand products.

What constitutes a 'lookalike'?

Own-brand copycat products are considered to be retailers' products *with one or more visible attributes that is/are similar to that of a better-known product, to the extent a consumer paying an average amount of attention in the process of shopping is likely to confuse the two.* Even this relatively simple definition needs to be used carefully because 'similarity' and 'average amount of attention' are relative concepts. For instance, consumers make certain 'associations' with various

Vignette 12.1

Sainsbury's Classic Cola

In April 1994, the issue of own-brand copycat branding was dramatically brought to the fore with Sainsbury's launch of Classic Cola, with remarkable resemblance to the leading cola brand Coca-Cola. According to AGB's data, Sainsbury's Classic Cola took a 15 per cent share of the market in the week ending 24 April 1994, which compared with an own-brand share of 2.5 per cent – 3 per cent for Sainsbury's previous own-brand cola, which was replaced by Classic. The chain's overall cola turnover grew from around £1.1 million in a normal week to a staggering £1.6 million, lifting its share of the total cola market sales from 20 per cent to 25 per cent. In value terms, Coca-Cola's share within Sainsbury's halved from 63 per cent to 33 per cent, while the own-brand share increased dramatically from 17 per cent to 60 per cent. This example graphically illustrates the potential gains to retailers and the losses to brand-owners as a result of the introduction of lookalike own-brand products.

Sources: Various, including *Supermarketing* (1994a) 'No Confusion Over Own-Label', 4 March, p. 14; *Supermarketing* (1994b), 'Quarrel Over Brands v Own-Label Hots Up', 22 April, p. 5; *Supermarketing* (1994c), 'Classic Cola Boosts JS Own-Label Sales by 50%', 13 May, p. 16.

types of product, which it would be unreasonable to expect own-brand lines not to use. As an example, in the UK, lemon-scented washing-up liquid is expected to be found in a yellow-coloured container, whilst plain and milk chocolate are easily differentiated with the use of red and blue packaging respectively. The use of many visual images (such as a picture of salad on a bottle of salad cream) can hardly be construed as copycatting; however, it is questionable whether some visual images are acceptable (for example the use of a red mug on several coffee jars which was originally used on Nestlé's Nescafé coffee jars – not all coffee mugs are the same colour!). The factor that differentiates own-brand copycats from non-controversial *'acceptable to manufacturers'* own-brand products is the level of confusion likely to be caused by the design of their packaging, or by the name of their product.

How confused are consumers by lookalikes?

The research that has so far been undertaken in the area of copycat branding has proved somewhat inconclusive. Two surveys by NOP (*Supermarketing*, 1994a) and MORI (*Supermarketing*, 1994b) concluded that 78 per cent of consumers were not confused by copycat branding; meanwhile, a third survey (commissioned by the BPBOG) discovered that 42 per cent of shoppers had confused own-brand with branded products, because of similar packaging design (*Marketing*, 1994). Uncles (1993) suggests that consumer confusion is not as big a problem as manufacturers make out given that we are all now experienced customers routinely buying packaged goods. In any case consumers are promiscuous in their behaviour and quite often buy branded as well as own-brand goods. Kapferer (1995a), on the other hand, using an experimental technique employing a tachystoscope (a device for projecting images for short durations), suggests that the danger of confusion between brands and own brands is very real. Kapferer's research further suggests that the majority of consumers tend to ascribe the qualities of the brand to the lookalike own-brand product due to the similarities in packaging. A survey by Rafiq and Collins (1996) into the level of confusion for five grocery product groups (cola; instant coffee; shampoo; breakfast cereal; yogurt) found moderate levels of confusion. 17.9 per cent of respondents agreed or strongly agreed that confusion can occur when purchasing similarly packaged products. The level of confusion varied by retailer, as Safeway shoppers were three times more likely to agree/strongly agree that confusion could occur than Tesco and Sainsbury shoppers. The survey also suggested that frequent purchasers of own-branded products were the least confused, while those who shop most often were most likely to be confused.

Brand-owners' versus retailers' views of copycat products

Manufacturers and brand-owners argue that copycat products are an attempt to steal the goodwill built up by a leading brand over a considerable period of time. They claim that retailers are taking advantage of the reputation that brands have built themselves, and that producing lookalike products is an attempt to trick consumers into believing that the own-brand products are sourced from the same manufacturer as the brands. The retailers are also attempting to associate the quality and the attributes of the brand to the own brand. They are effectively trying to gain a good brand name without the levels of advertising and promotional outlay normally required to achieve such a status.

Brand-owners warn that the increasing presence of own-brand lookalike products will diminish consumer choice in the future, and that the emergence of copycat products will act as a deterrent to innovation on the part of manufacturers and brand-owners. They further argue that whilst brand manufacturers invest heavily in new product development, packaging design, marketing and advertising, retailers incur none of these costs when launching lookalike own-brand versions. Hence the incentives to manufacturers to develop new products are clearly diminished by the likelihood of retailers subsequently copying the products, nullifying expected future benefits. Furthermore, if manufacturers lose sales as a direct result of own-brand lookalike products, then they will be able to invest less in new product development in the future.

Retailers, on the other hand, argue that they have different reasons for introducing copycat products. They generally agree that the brands have become synonymous with the categories of products that they are trying to sell, and argue that an own-brand product that looks nothing like a brand will not be recognized by consumers. They maintain that similar-looking products are useful because they help consumers to make price comparisons within stores. Retailers accept that their own-brand products are packaged similarly to brands, but refute claims that they have been copied from brands. They feel that their own-brand products provide a fair form of competition to the traditional brands. The viewpoints of retailers are typified by the following quote from James May, Director-General of the British Retail Consortium:

> The customer expects certain products to come in certain shapes and containers. In a supermarket with 17,000 different lines on the shelves a customer with a shopping list of perhaps 20 products would want to be able to find these without having to discard the other 16,980. The use of visual signposts and visual cues is part of the process. (Drummond, 1995)

A question that naturally occurs is why don't manufacturers take legal action to counter infringements by retailers? There are two main reasons for this reluctance, namely:

● the difficulties associated with proving 'Passing-Off' claims in court; and
● the need to maintain a favourable working relationship with the retailer.

The difficulties associated with 'passing-off' claims

The process of taking legal action against an imitator is far simplified if a trademark has been registered. If an unregistered mark has been 'copied' – as is the case in virtually all instances of copycatting – then the victim has to establish to the court's satisfaction that he has a reputation and a degree of goodwill in that mark. Furthermore, the chance of a manufacturer obtaining an injunction to stop lookalike products is only 40 to 50 per cent under current legislation in the UK (Lewis, 1994). This clearly does not provide much incentive for a brand owner to implement expensive legal action. Nevertheless, a number of successful cases have been brought against retailers. For instance, in 1997 United Biscuits successfully brought a case against ASDA, contesting the similarity of ASDA's own-label Puffin chocolate biscuits to its Penguin biscuits. More recently, Ragdoll Productions, the creators of the popular Teletubby characters, filed a lawsuit against the world's most powerful retailer, Wal-Mart, and successfully forced it to remove stocks of 'Bubbly Chubbies' toys – which bore a striking resemblance to the Teletubby characters.

The need to maintain a favourable working relationship with the retailer

The overriding reason why manufacturers and brand-owners have been wary of taking legal action against retailers is their need to maintain a good working relationship with them given that the balance of power in the British retailing industry is now firmly in the hands of a small number of dominant multiple retailers. Whilst retailers' own-branded products are competitors to the traditional brands, the retailers themselves are effectively customers to the manufacturers, and consequently manufacturers need to maintain good terms with them. Manufacturers and brand-owners cannot afford to risk being delisted from any of the multiple retailers. Instigating legal proceedings against a multiple retailer would severely jeopardize the working relationship, and diminish the bargaining power of the manufacturer, particularly if that manufacturer is also an own-brand supplier to the retailer.

However, there is a limit to the power of the large retailers. For instance, retailers, by the very act of incorporating similar packaging designs onto their own-brand products, are acknowledging the fact that particular brands are very strong within their respective categories. In such circumstances, delisting a particular brand would also adversely affect the credibility of the retailer in question. Martin Glenn, the director of new products at Walkers, is fully aware of the importance of successful brands to retailers:

> Retailers need big brands because they help drive the categories. What they don't need is a lot of small brands which don't do much for the category and have no real point of difference. (Barrett, 1994).

The credibility of Sainsbury's would clearly be diminished if it no longer stocked Coca-Cola, which explains their willingness to effect some design modifications in the face of strong representations from their CCSB, Coke's franchisee in the UK.

New Developments in Own-Brand Strategy

The result of copycatting and the proliferation of own brands across product categories has created a lack of consistency of values projected about store brands. Hence, retailers are now developing their own-brand packaging to project a clear corporate signature that can be seen, for example, in super-markets' sub-brands that cross categories with distinct identities of their own. In terms of the typology used in Table 12.4, own brands are moving towards the house-brand phase.

The precursors of this trend are the economy and value lines which make a bold unmistakable statement suggesting they are the cheapest products. Such clear positioning has allowed supermarkets to move the rest of their own-brand offer upmarket. Examples of this upward movement and extension of branding across categories is provided by Tesco's Finest line of chef-quality meals, which now includes fruit and vegetables and features the characteristic silver labels, small images and typeface across categories. This allows shoppers to instantly recognize that the products are of premium quality anywhere in the store. The increasingly sophisticated use of branding by retailers and their closeness to the customer means that own brands will increasingly become leaders in many product areas.

Retailer's sub-brands are also being used to segment product ranges according to criteria other than simply price. Marks and Spencer have moved away from the generic use of the St Michael fascia brand on their clothing and have introduced a number of house brands to differentiate alternative 'lifestyle' ranges including Autograph (designer clothing), Per Una (younger fashion), Classic Collections (traditional), Blue Harbour (casual menswear), and ViewFrom (sportswear).

Trading-up and the consumer perceptions of own-brand quality

In order for retailers to successfully position themselves against manufactur-ers' brands, as own brands trade up, they need to communicate the improved quality of the products to customers. Until recently, research has shown that consumers rate own labels as inferior in comparison with national brands on a number of important product attributes including quality. This is despite the fact that in many cases the quality of the ingredients of own labels is the same or higher than manufacturer brands. This suggests that other informational cues such as price and product positioning, packaging are being used by consumers to assess quality. One study (Richardson, Dick and Jain, 1994) has experimentally demonstrated that consumers evaluate brands and brand quality mainly by extrinsic cues (for example price, advertising, packaging, brand name and warranty), rather than by intrinsic cues (such as ingredients and taste).

⬤ Own Brands and their Impact on the Retail Brand

Implied in the own-brand typology of Table 12.4 is the fact that own brands have an impact on the retail brand itself. With some own-brand strategies (such as generics, counterbrands) the retailer attempts to maintain a distance between itself, that is the retail brand, and the own brand. With other strategies such as house brand and fascia brand strategies, the own brands are an integral part of the retail brand itself. Hence, retailers have to be clear about where the own-branding strategy fits in with their overall branding strategies for the store (see Figure 12.2). This also implies that retailers must constantly monitor the relative contribution of own brands and manufacturer brands to their overall retail brand image. For instance, it is widely regarded that one of the factors in Sainsbury's loss of UK grocery market leadership to Tesco was that the proportion of own brands in its stores had become too high (O' Sullivan, 1995). A similar experience befell the American retailer Sears in the late 1980s when its excessive concentration on own brands led to consumer perceptions that its assortment was incomplete with a consequent negative

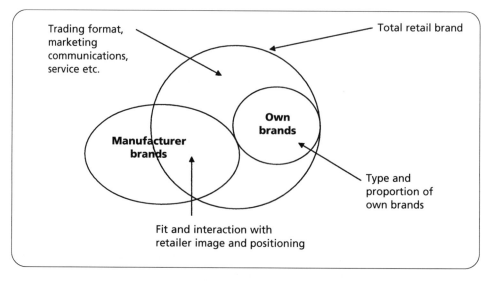

Figure 12.2 Factors contributing to total retail brand image and positioning

impact on store traffic and profitability (Quelch and Harding, 1996). Retailers also need to monitor and control their portfolio of own-brand types as they can impact on each other. In fact one of the arguments advanced by retailers for withdrawing generics is that their association with the retailer can have a negative impact on the retailer's own labels (Burt, 1992). Category management, the process of managing products as categories rather than individual brands or products lines, can help retailers manage the balance between own brands and manufacturers more effectively. However, problems are still likely to arise if there is too much emphasis on category profits or categories are managed in isolation and without reference to the overall retail brand.

From a customer perspective, it is generally accepted that brands have four main functions – identification, information, guarantee of product quality, and symbolic associations. Whereas identification and informational aspects of brands increase shopping efficiency, guarantees reduce consumer risk. Symbolic associations, on the other hand, provide psychological utility to consumers and allow them to make a social statement about themselves. In the main, the success of own-label products has occurred because retailers have demonstrated that they can perform the first three functions just as well as the brand manufacturers. However, except for fascia own brands, it is

Vignette 12.2
Retail branding at Debenhams

Since around 1995 Debenhams has launched in excess of 50 own brands across key product areas which have accounted for approximately 50 per cent of total turnover. These ranged from well-established names such as *Maine New England, Casual Club, Trader, Hyphen, Red Herring* and *ID:X*. Since 2000 Debenhams extended its *Maine New England* own brand even further with the addition of *Maine Golf* and *Maine Ski*.

At the same time, Debenhams has a policy of offering leading brand names including YSL, *Reebok, Elle, Denby* and *Le Creuset*. These national and international brands complement Debenhams own brands and offer customers more choice. Catering for the growing trend towards brand names Debenhams has also recently introduced labels such as *Berghaus, Nancy Ganz* and *Karrimor*, and claim to be the number-one UK retailer of international fashion brands such as *Ben Sherman* and *Kangol*.

Debenhams now works with over 25 leading British designers including Jasper Conran, Philip Treacy, Lulu Guinness, John Richmond and Ozwald Boateng. These designers are contracted to create clothing, accessories and homewares exclusively for Debenhams, offering customers real designer merchandise at high-street prices.

As with other department stores, concessions play an important role in providing more choice within Debenhams' merchandise offer and currently account for around 25 per cent of total sales turnover. Key concessions at Debenhams include *Alexon, Royal Doulton* and *Dorma Plus*, as well as *Morgan* and *Country Casuals* at selected stores. Debenhams has to manage its own brands, manufacturer brands, its exclusive designer brands and concessions in order to maximize consumer choice, store profitability and project a distinctive brand image.

Sources: Debenhams *Annual Reports* and website http://www.debenhams.co.uk.

extremely difficult for own brands to compete with manufacturer brands in terms of symbolic associations. Also, manufacturer brands are much more likely to be innovative than retailers' brands. This is particularly likely to occur where a retailer offers a large number of own brands, as it is unlikely to be able to support research and development costs in all of them.

The foregoing suggests that manufacturer brands have an advantage relative to own brands (excluding fascia brands) where symbolic associations and/or product innovation are important to customers. Conversely, where symbolic associations and product innovation are less important there is an opportunity for retailers to compete successfully with manufacturer brands if they can demonstrate comparable product quality and provide value for money.

Summary

This chapter has examined the growth of own brands in retailing. A typology has been presented which identifies the type of role that the own brand is required to perform in a retailer's overall branding strategy. Retailers have to make decisions on the balance between manufacturer brands and own brands as they affect the overall positioning of the retail brand image. Retailers are now considered brands in themselves rather than just purveyors of manufacturers products, and are becoming very sophisticated in their use of branding techniques and innovative in their development of new products, leading the market in a number of product areas.

Questions

1 What are the pros and cons of manufacturer and own brands for retailers?
2 'Own-brand lookalikes amount to theft of goodwill built up by established brands'. Discuss.
3 Discuss the methods which manufacturers can employ to protect their brands.
4 Why do some retailers sell 100 per cent own brands and others do not?
5 How can retailers improve customers' perceptions of own-label quality?
6 How do own brands and manufacturers brands contribute to the overall image of the retail brand?

References and Further Reading

Barrett, P. (1994) 'Another Fine Mess', *Supermarketing*, 22 July, pp.14–16.
Blackburn, J. (1994) 'Unique Branding is a Thing of the Past', *Marketing*, 23 June, p. 20.
Burt, S. (1992), *Retailer Brands in British Grocery Retailing. A Review*, University of Stirling, Institute for Retail Studies, Working Paper no. 9204.
Burt, S. (2000) 'The Strategic Role of Retail Brands in British Grocery Retailing', *European Journal of Marketing*, vol. 34, no. 8, pp. 875–90.

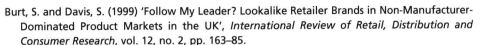

Burt, S. and Davis, S. (1999) 'Follow My Leader? Lookalike Retailer Brands in Non-Manufacturer-Dominated Product Markets in the UK', *International Review of Retail, Distribution and Consumer Research*, vol. 12, no. 2, pp. 163–85.

Caulkin, S. (1987) 'The Fall and Rise of Brands', *Management Today*, July 1987, pp.44–49.

Drummond, G. (1994), 'The Real Thing', *Supermarketing*, 30 September, pp. 20–2.

Dunne, D. and Chakravarthi, N. (1999) 'The New Appeal of Private Labels', *Harvard Business Review*, vol. 77 (3), pp. 41–8.

Glancey, J. (1994) 'The Real Thing Put to the Test', *The Independent on Sunday*, 24 April, p. 5.

The *Grocer* (1998) 'Imitation has Limitations', 25 April, pp. 45–6.

Hobson, S. (1994) 'The Year of the Own-Label', *Supermarketing*, 14 January, pp. 22–3.

Hoyer, W.D. (1984) 'An Examination of Consumer Decision Making for a Common Repeat Purchase Product', *Journal of Consumer Research*, vol. 11 (December), pp. 822–9.

Kapferer, Jean-Noel (1995a) 'Brand Confusion: Empirical Study of a Legal Concept', *Psychology and Marketing*, vol. 12 (6), pp. 551–68.

Kapferer, Jean-Noel (1995b) 'Stealing Brand Equity: Measuring Perceptual Confusion between National Brands and "Copycat" Own-Label Products', *Marketing and Research Today*, vol. 23, no. 2, pp. 96–103.

Lewis, J. (1994), 'Lords back owners against retailers', *Marketing*, 3 March 1994, pp. 16–17.

Marketing (1994) 'Brand Managers Back Lookalikes Crackdown', *Marketing*, 3 March, p. 1.

Nielsen (1994) *The Retail Pocket Book 1995* (Oxford: NTC Publications).

Nielsen (1995) *The Retail Pocket Book 1996* (Oxford: NTC Publications).

O'Sullivan, T. (1995) 'Sainsbury's Scores an Own Goal', *Marketing Week*, vol. 18, no. 11, p. 21.

Olashavsky, R.W. and Grandbois, D. (1979) 'Consumer Decision Making: Fact or Fiction? *Journal of Consumer Research*, vol. 6 (September), pp. 93–100.

Pellegrini, L. (1993) 'Retailer Brands: A State of the Art Review', *Proceedings of the 7th International Conference on Research in the Distributive Trades*, Institute for Retail Studies, University of Stirling, 6–8 September, Stirling, pp. 348–63.

Quelch, J.A. and Harding, D. (1996) 'Brands versus Private Labels: Fighting to Win', *Harvard Business Review*, vol. 74, no. 1, Jan.–Feb., pp. 99–109.

Rafiq, M. and Collins, R. (1996) 'Lookalikes and Customer Confusion in the Grocery Sector: An Exploratory Survey, *International Review of Retail, Distribution and Consumer Research*, vol. 6, no. 4 (October), pp. 329–50.

Rafiq, M. and Kirkup, M.H. (1999) 'Role of Own Brands in Retailer Branding Strategies", in L. Hildebrandt and D. Annacker (eds), *Proceedings of the 28th EMAC Conference*, Humboldt University, Berlin (May).

Richardson, P.S., Dick, A.S., and Jain, A.K. (1994) 'Extrinsic and Intrinsic Cue Effects on Perceptions of Store Brand Quality', *Journal of Marketing*, vol. 58 (October), pp. 28–36.

Simmons, M. and Meredith, W. (1984) 'Own Label Profile and Purpose', *Journal of the Market Research Society*, vol. 26, pp. 3–27.

Supermarketing (1994a) 'No Confusion Over Own-Label', 4 March, p. 14.

Supermarketing (1994b) 'Quarrel Over Brands v Own-Label Hots Up', 22 Apri, p. 5.

Supermarketing (1994c) 'Classic Cola Boosts JS Own-Label Sales by 50%', 13 May, p. 16.

Uncles, M.D. (1994), 'Just How Different are Retail Lookalikes from Traditional Me-Toos? *Journal of Brand Management*, vol. 2, no. 4, pp. 204–7.

Uncles, M.D. and Ellis, K. (1989) 'Own Labels: Beliefs and Reality', in L. Pellegrini and S.K. Reddy (eds), *Retail and Marketing Channels* (London: Routledge), pp. 274–86.

Wileman, A. and Jary, M. (1997) *Retail Power Plays: From Trading to Brand Leadership* (Basingstoke: Macmillan Business).

The website http://www.martex.co.uk/marques/ is the website of the Association of European Trade Mark Owners. The website is useful for information on trademark cases drawn from the courts and Trade Mark Registries in Europe.

Retail Pricing

Introduction

Pricing is a highly sensitive issue, for both retailers and consumers. In an era where pricing regulation has diminished, and price changes can be implemented almost instantaneously, retailers have considerable control over the prices that they offer to their customers. On the other hand consumers are knowledgeable and confident, and when they can, they will seek out alternative retail outlets if they feel that they are paying over the odds. Pricing is a marketing tool; it has a considerable part to play in both the formation of the retail brand identity and in retail promotional activity. Pricing is also a management issue, because of the unavoidable relationship between pricing and profitability.

● **Setting Retail Prices**

Unless a retailer is setting extremely aggressive promotional prices, the prices of goods sold in a retail outlet are higher than the price paid to the retail supplier. The difference between the two is the gross profit margin, often referred to as the mark-up. The gross margin can be expressed as a percentage of the cost price of the product, or more commonly as a percentage of the selling price. The gross margin level varies greatly between retail outlet types and between product categories. For example a supermarket may only apply a mark-up of a fraction of a per cent to some of their grocery product lines, whereas designer clothing retailers frequently operate on the basis of a gross margin of more than 100 per cent. The reasons for these variations will become clear in this chapter.

Retail costs

The prices that retailers pay for their supplies are only one of the many costs that have to be covered by the selling price of the product. Unless a retailer has other sources of income, the gross profit margin has to cover the costs of wages, the costs of distribution for multiple retailers, the running costs of the outlet including rent, rates and maintenance for store-based retailers and customer ordering centres for non-store retailers, the costs of running a central office and the costs associated with marketing activity such as advertising costs. The higher these costs are, the more pressure there is on the retailer to raise their gross profit margins to be able to contribute a net profit margin, which can then be used for reinvestment into the business, for example to pay for more outlets and refurbishments or for rewarding shareholders. Different approaches to costing and profit assessment are discussed later in this chapter.

● **Price and Demand**

Traditional economic theory places great emphasis on the relationship between the price charged for a product and the resulting demand for that product, and whilst an understanding of these general principles is important for retailers, the theories concentrate on individual product items rather than viewing pricing within the context of a product range, thus ignoring the complexity of retail pricing from both the retailer and the consumer viewpoints.

The economist's view

In most product categories, demand rises as prices fall, whilst less is bought if prices rise, giving an inverse relationship between price and quantity demanded, as shown in Figure 13.1.

Some products are more sensitive to price changes than others. For example, even if the price of salt doubled, it is unlikely that the demand for salt would alter much. Likewise if the price for salt fell, it is unlikely that

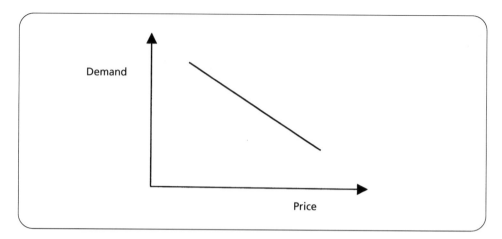

Figure 13.1 The relationship between price and demand

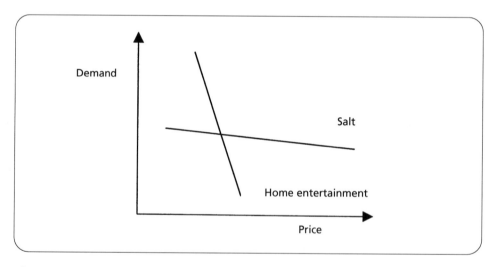

Figure 13.2 Demand elasticity, according to product

customers would buy much more (apart from perhaps on a temporary basis in order to stockpile). Salt therefore has a demand that is said to be inelastic, and unresponsive to price changes. Other products, however, have much more 'elastic' demand, where sales are responsive to price fluctuations. Demand for discretionary purchases such as home entertainment systems is highly sensitive to price fluctuations. Figure 13.2 illustrates these differences.

⬤ **Price in the Retail Marketing Mix**

Ever since the abolition of the Resale Price Maintenance legislation in 1964, UK retailers of most consumer goods have had the freedom to set their own

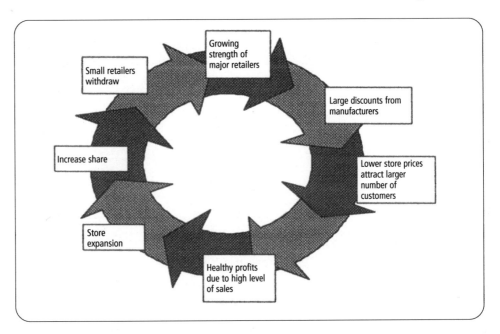

Figure 13.3 The wheel of increasing multiple retailer dominance

Source: Adapted from De Chernatony and McDonald (1998).

prices, and have therefore been able to use pricing as a powerful marketing weapon. The Wheel of Increasing Multiple Retailer Dominance (Figure 13.3) shows the combined effect on the industry of retailer-controlled pricing and the acceptance by consumers of lower-cost retail formats like the self-service supermarket (De Chernatony and McDonald, 1998).

Price and value

Prices are a visible and highly sensitive part of the retail marketing mix, and have a direct relationship with a retailer's profitability. However, prices are subject to individual interpretation in terms of value representation, and so are deeply affected by consumer behaviour. Value is an individual's interpretation of worth, and therefore measures the relationship between the price being charged for an item and the benefits received.

When it comes to making a purchase, most consumers work within price thresholds (Figure 13.4); if the price of an item rises above the upper price threshold, the consumer will not buy, perhaps choosing a substitute product or making do without the benefits that the product would bring. On the other hand, the consumer will normally work to a lower price threshold, under which they would not purchase a product because of concerns about product quality.

The benefits a consumer derives from a product bought in a retail outlet include physical attributes such as quality and functional features, which are relatively tangible and measurable. However, value is also put on less measurable product benefits such as the brand, the environment in which the product is sold, and the service received during the purchasing process. A retailer's

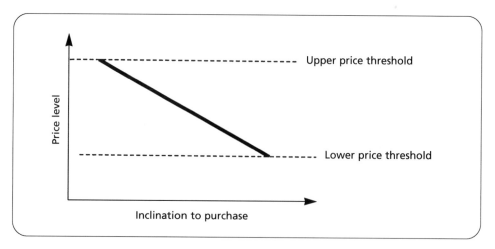

Figure 13.4 Price thresholds

pricing strategy must therefore be fully integrated with the overall marketing strategy, in order for a value appreciation to take place and the price positioning of the retailer to be understood.

⬤ **Price Competition**

Whilst an unregulated economy allows retailers to set prices as they see fit, a saturated retail market exerts considerable competitive pressure on retail pricing strategies. Where customers have a choice of outlet, offering the lowest price is an easily understood and effective marketing strategy. It is, nevertheless, a strategy that is easy for competitors to match, particularly in the short term. Price competition on a large scale can lead to price wars, where retailers cut their margins very low in order to maintain a competitive edge; however, price wars have a negative effect on the profits of all players in the industry, and are therefore avoided by retailers. In fact highly concentrated retail sectors such as grocery in the UK have been accused of maintaining a price cartel in order to prevent price competition (see Vignette 13.1).

Vignette 13.1

Government intervention on pricing

Early in 1999, the supply of groceries from multiple retailers was referred to the Competition Commission by the Director General of Fair Trading, under the monopoly provisions of the Fair Trading Act (1973). The origins of the move lay in a number of areas of concern:

- Public perception that the price of groceries in the UK tended to be higher than in other comparable EC countries and the USA.
- The apparent disparity between farm-gate and retail prices, and the suspicion that grocery multiples were profiting from a crisis in the farming industry (mainly caused by oversupply and cheaper imports).

- The continuing concern that large, out-of-town supermarkets were contributing to the decay of the high street in many towns.

Twenty-four grocery retailers were included in the inquiry, which looked at pricing practices and a range of practices in relation to suppliers. The scope of the inquiry included:

- Price trends within the industry.
- International comparisons.
- Decline in wholesale prices.
- Profit margins.
- Consumer satisfaction with supermarkets.
- Relevant planning regulations.
- Social and environmental issues relating to the growth of supermarkets.

The main findings of the report, issued in 2000, are summarized below:

- The majority of the retailers investigated persistently sold frequently-purchased products below cost, and because of the negative effect that this could have on smaller operators, it was deemed to operate against public interest.
- There was some evidence of geographical price variation, which was related to local market competition rather than local costs, and this was viewed as against public interest because customers had no comparable choice in the area in many cases.

However, because the remedies for the removal of these practices was considered to be too complex and difficult to regulate, no recommendations were made for remedial action.

- All the large grocery multiples adopted pricing strategies that focused price competition on a relatively small proportion of their product lines. However, whilst this distorts competition, it was not deemed to be against public interest because of the overall competitive nature of the retail sector.
- The report also found no evidence of excessive profits being made on retailer's own-label products, or any excessively slow reaction to changes of prices (downwards) in wholesale markets. The commission justified their recommendation for no remedial action by stating that they found the grocery market to be generally competitive and that the costs of any government intervention would be disproportionate to the benefits sought.
- In relation to retail suppliers, the Commission investigated a number of practices (such as requesting non-cost-related payments or discounts, imposing charges and making changes to contractual arrangements without adequate notice, and unreasonably transferring risks from the retailer to the supplier. Taking into consideration the market power of retailers in relation to suppliers, they concluded that such practices were evident and against public interest and recommended that the retailers draw up a Code of Practice which could be approved by the Office of Fair Trading and become a standard for the industry.

Source: Competition Commission (2000).

● Pricing Strategy

A retail pricing strategy usually operates on two levels. The first is the general approach to the overall pricing level, which positions the retailer in the market. For example, consider the price positioning of Netto, Tesco and Selfridges Food Hall. Each retail outlet has a clear position when it comes to price: Netto is a 'discount supermarket' offering extremely low prices; Tesco operate a medium-level 'value-for-money' approach to prices; and Selfridges is clearly in the category of retailers that takes a premium-pricing approach. Of course, these retailers have completely different retail marketing strategies and do not compete with one another; however, it is possible to buy food in all three outlets and it is their long-term pricing strategy that most clearly sets them apart.

The second level of a retailer's pricing strategy is tactical. This usually relates to the need to manipulate prices to achieve specific short-term objectives such as an introductory price for a new product line, a defensive price cut in reaction to competitive threat, or price discounts to clear redundant stock. The general, long-term pricing strategies will be considered first, followed by a discussion of tactical pricing techniques and short-term pricing considerations.

● Long-Term Pricing Strategies

Premium pricing

Retailers that operate a premium pricing strategy use sources other than price as differentiating factors in their retail marketing mix. High product quality and augmented customer services often go hand in hand with a premium pricing strategy, and consumers who value these aspects of the retail mix will not be deterred by the higher prices that need to be charged to cover the extra costs incurred by the retailer. In fact, many customers will gain psychological benefits associated with the symbolic status of shopping in such retailers. Retailers that use premium pricing include the department store Harvey Nichols (upmarket and fashion forward); the specialist store Fired Earth (tiles and furnishing fabrics); and the food store Cullen's (high-quality convenience foods).

Seasonal pricing

Retailers who sell goods with a seasonal factor, such as clothing, will often need to add a seasonal dimension to their pricing strategy. Where products have a tendency to become obsolete quickly, it is important for retailers to sell them while they still have some value to customers. Making decisions about when to drop prices is one of the most difficult areas of retail management, balancing the need for higher turnover with a reduction in profitability. Seasonal pricing strategies involve selling products at 'full price', and then 'marking down' or reducing the standard price of the product in an 'end-of-season sale'. The sale period will often attract an entirely different customer profile to that which the store normally has, as a wider band of consumers are able or willing to pay the reduced prices. This strategy is often referred to as a high–low pricing strategy.

Markdowns

A markdown is a reduction in the selling price, where the original price is displayed alongside the new price. By law the product must have been on sale at the original price for a period of 28 consecutive days in the previous six months in order for the markdown to be referred to as a price 'reduction' in the UK (the Consumer Protection Approval Order, 1988). Markdowns inevitably mean a reduction in profitability for the retailer, however the extent of the loss is a product of the markdown taken and the volume of product requiring markdown. For example, it is difficult for a clothing retailer to avoid having a few odd sizes and colours left at the end of the season, and a small markdown is likely to shift those that are left; but if a garment does not fit properly it may be necessary to take a large markdown on a very large volume of product items, cutting deeply into the retailer's profits.

Promotional purchases

In contrast to a markdown or price reduction, some items are sold at a very low price from day one. These offers may be referred to as a 'special purchase', and are usually the result of a supplier offering a retailer a special price for an item, which in turn is passed on to the consumer by the retailer. This type of product is sometimes offered alongside reduced price merchandise in an end-of-season sale so that the retailer can capitalize on a high volume of bargain-seeking store traffic.

Everyday low pricing

Everyday low pricing (EDLP) is a pricing strategy that has become increasingly popular in the last decade. Retailers who operate this policy strive to offer very competitive prices on all of their product range, all of the time. Instead of the high–low variation of seasonal pricing, prices are kept low all the time and are normally only discounted when the product line is discontinued. EDLP is a popular strategy with the majority of retail customers because they feel they are receiving a fair deal; the pricing message is straightforward rather than being bound up in a complicated array of product/price offers. It is not, however, an appropriate strategy for retailers who take risks with their product range, when it makes more sense to skim off profits on winning product items to pay for the markdowns on losers. EDLP makes it necessary for retailers to keep their selling costs low in order to maintain the pricing strategy as well as make a profit, and so they are less able to offer added value in terms of additional services and the store environment. The introduction of internet retailing has put an additional emphasis on the need to be competitive, with sites like ShopSmart offering customers a highly convenient price comparison service.

The popularity of EDLP has given rise to a new category of retailers called

Value Retailers, who concentrate on offering good value to the customer. The clothing retailer New Look grew in a stagnant market sector through the 1990s by virtue of a 'value' offer. Prices are kept low, but the product offer is kept lively by using sophisticated sales analysis and buying systems (see Vignette 7.3).

Discount pricing

Discount pricing is different from everyday low pricing, in that the retailer offers products at prices lower than the average high-street price. Retailers that are referred to as discounters vary in character. The term includes 'off-price' retailers who do not have continuity in their product range, giving an 'Aladdin's cave' appeal to the outlet. In contrast, discount supermarkets, or 'hard discounters' maintain a relatively consistent range of products at very low prices. Discount retailing often involves selling 'seconds'-quality goods, ends of lines and previous season's merchandise, and is the basis of the 'factory outlet' retail concept which enjoyed healthy growth in the UK and the USA in the 1990s (Fernie and Fernie, 1997). A recent retail development is the 'virtual auction', a website that allows customers to log on and bid for products on offer. Ebay is an example of such a retailer that has gained a foothold by using this approach.

Pricing tactics

Within a long-term pricing strategy a retailer may use pricing tactics that they believe will have a positive effect on the consumer. For example, a frequently used tactic is to set a price point at £X.99, so that psychologically a customer feels that a product is under the rounded pound price. In particular, price points such as £9.99 and £19.99 and £99.99 may be very effective for communicating the availability of products at low or good-value prices. However, other retailers feel that a rounded pound is a clearer price offer to their customers and is simpler to administer from a retail operations viewpoint. One widely held view is that forcing a sales associate to give a penny change from the till for a note given by the customer discouraged employee theft, a procedure that is irrelevant in an increasingly cashless shopping society. Another pricing tactic that ties in with range planning (see Chapter 11) is the use of price lining. Here, a retailer will offer a selection of products at what they see as key price points for the product category. This may make the product offer more logical for the customer and more easily understood by sales associates. For example, a toiletry retailer like Boots may sell gift packs at the price points £5, £10 and £15, allowing customers to quickly assess the alternatives within their budget. A drawback with this type of tactic is that gearing products to selling prices may place restrictions on retail buyers, and could result in sales opportunities being missed for products that do not 'fit' into the pricing structure.

A retailer may offer a 'leading' price for a 'known-value' product item, again in order to communicate a best-value offer. Supermarkets use bread for this purpose, keeping the price of a basic white loaf at an extremely competitive price so that the rest of the shopping basket is viewed as well-priced in accordance. The retailer is prepared to make little or no profit on these leading products in order to attract customers who will then buy other, more profitable items. Different products have different price sensitivity; in fact research (McGoldrick *et al.*, 1999) has shown that many customers have very low recall levels of most grocery items, but high-profile products like bread or milk are likely to be compared between competing outlets.

● Short-Term Pricing Strategies

The pricing strategies that have been described so far in this chapter have been ones concerning the overall pricing image of the retailer. They indicate to customers the kind of level of prices that can be expected in that particular outlet, and they reflect the rest of the retail marketing strategy. However, retailers also use a number of short-term pricing strategies in order to boost the sales of particular products, or as defensive action in the face of competition.

Loss-leader pricing

This is a more radical version of the low, known-value price tactic. Here the price is cut to an extremely low, or even loss-making level, and then heavily advertised in order to gain consumer interest. In the early 1990s, traditional supermarkets in the UK were threatened by the market entry of discount supermarkets like Netto and Aldi from Europe; this precipitated a price war on key grocery items, which resulted in tins of baked beans being sold in the mainstream supermarkets like Tesco and Sainsbury's for around three pence per can. Loss-leader pricing by its nature is a short-term strategy, and is usually only used in cases of extreme competitive action. One of its drawbacks is that such campaigns appeal to bargain-hunting customers who stockpile the item, leaving the shelves empty for other customers who then feel cheated by the advertising or publicity. One of the findings of the 2000 Competition Commission Enquiry was that some supermarket groups sell a small number of products consistently at below-cost prices, and this was deemed to be unfair to smaller retail operators (see Vignette 13.1).

Multi-buy and linked purchase offers

In the retailing of fast-moving consumer goods, this kind of marketing activity is commonplace. It is particularly effective for introducing new products, boosting sales of particular product brands and categories on a short-term basis, increasing the value of each transaction and encouraging linked sales. Offering a variety of price promotions that clearly benefit the consumer will have a positive effect on an overall retail image; however, if the benefits of the promotions are not clear to the consumer, then promotional activity can be perceived as a waste of time, merely adding clutter to the store. Boots the Chemist, for example, is famous for its Two-for-One and Three-for-Two offers which encourage multiple purchases of specific items on a short-term basis, and contribute to the generation of a loyal customer base on a long-term basis.

Loyalty Schemes

Many loyalty schemes are based on the premise that a price discount can be obtained by frequent visits to the same retailer. Some store cards offer a percentage discount once a particular level of spending has been achieved within a specified time period. Others provide some kind of cash or discount reward that accumulates over time. Some, such as Tesco's Clubcard offer a combination ofa short-term reward like vouchers and long-term benefits such as air miles or discounts on high-price ticket item (see Vignette 13.2).

Vignette 13.2

The fight for loyalty

In 1995 Tesco launched the Clubcard, the tool that enabled the company to set up a loyalty scheme linked to a customer database. Having initially derided the idea of a national loyalty card as a gimmick, J. Sainsbury launched its Reward card a year later, soon to be followed by Safeway with their ABC loyalty scheme. ASDA, in the meantime, kept with its ASDA Price promotional campaign, and despite going through the process of trialing a loyalty card in a restricted number of stores, decided against a nationwide roll-out. In 1999 ASDA even referred to the findings of a consumer survey conducted by Mintel as a basis for their in-store promotional message 'customers prefer low prices to loyalty schemes'. In 2002 Sainsbury's updated their loyalty scheme with the launch of the Nectar card, through which points are collected in their own supermarkets, in Debenhams department stores, BP petrol retailers and through Barclaycard finance company. The points can be spent in a variety of ways, including popular leisure destinations and fast-food outlets. Increased flexibility in the collection and spending of loyalty points clearly appeals to customers.

Source: Ody (2002).

Retail Profitability

Whilst the overall price level in the retail outlet and price promotions are likely to be managed by the centralized marketing department of a retailer within the framework of a long-term strategy, the profit performance of most retailers is measured both by product and by store/outlet. Profitability is a key responsibility of the buyers and merchandisers who manage the product ranges offered within each outlet (see Chapter 11); they will be working to profit targets set for each product line and/or product category, and so pricing, markdown levels and promotional activity are all integral to a retail product manager's remit, as well as controlling the buying-in cost of products by negotiating keenly with suppliers. Profitability in terms of the retail outlet relates to the relationship between sales made in the outlet and its running costs. This will be considered after product profitability.

Product Profitability

Product profitability can be measured in a number of ways, which vary in degrees of complexity. The simplest measure is the gross profit margin of the product, often referred to as the mark-up as discussed earlier in this chapter. At one time the use of a uniform percentage mark-up was commonplace in retailing because it was simple to administer, however the gross margin does not account for the level of sales generated on a product and the effect that the rate of sales have on the actual value of the profit contribution of different products. Table 13.1 illustrates this point.

A measure that overcomes the shortcomings of the uniform mark-up is the gross margin return on investment (GMROI), illustrated in Table 13.2. It is calculated by multiplying the gross margin percentage by the sales turnover ratio (for a specified time period).

The GMROI measure effectively assesses whether a product earns its placing on a shelf, in terms of sales generated by investment in the stock.

One of the drawbacks of using GMROI to measure product profitability is that whilst it takes the sales turnover of a product into account, it does not allow for any of the retail costs associated with displaying and selling the product. The costs of selling a can of beans are assumed to be the same as the costs of selling a packet of frozen peas, but clearly the costs involved in selling a frozen product are higher than those of an ambient product: the fixturing is more expensive, the storage and transportation of the product is more expensive, and the wages of people who work in a 'freezer' environment (for

Table 13.1 Uniform mark-up

Product	Price (£)	Gross margin (£)	Gross margin (%)	Sales turnover	Profit contribution
Wine	4.00	1.00	25	5	5.00
Chocolates	4.00	1.00	25	1	1.00

Table 13.2 GMROI

Product	Gross margin (%)	Turnover ratio	GMROI (%)
Milk	10	12.5	125
Cola	12.5	10.0	125
Wine	25	5	125

example in a retailer's distribution centre) are higher than those for people who work in ambient conditions.

Through the 1980s in both the USA and Europe, a considerable amount of progress was made on making individual product profitability measures. As the opportunities to collect, store and analyse costing data became possible with improvements in data processing technology, so the profit implications of retailing different products became clearer. In effect, a profit and loss account could be generated for every product line within the product range, and by making adjustments to the product and its handling through the supply chain to display within the store, opportunities to improve DPP (direct product profitability) were taken.

A further refinement to the costing of products can be made by using Activity Based Costing (ABC). Here, not only are the direct product costs taken into account, but also an attempt is made to allocate indirect costs according to the activity required to source and manage that product. So, for example, instead of an overseas buying trip being absorbed into the general costs associated with the running of a buying office, the expenses of the trip would be charged to the product(s) that were sourced from the overseas market.

● Outlet Profitability

As mentioned earlier, retail profitability is generally measured at both the product level and the outlet level. In order to implement some of the more aggressive pricing strategies mentioned earlier in this chapter, it is necessary to have strict control over the costs of running the outlet. Staffing costs are invariably the highest store cost, with rent or lease payments, rates, maintenance and refurbishment, heating, lighting and security all having to be covered. Some stores in a retailer's portfolio will have higher costs than others, for example high employment levels in the south-east of the UK inflate the level of wages for sales associates, whereas shops in managed shopping centres like Meadowhall or Bluewater have to pay a contribution to the management and maintenance of the centre. There are also the additional distribution costs associated with outlets in far-flung locations. There is an argument, therefore, for charging different prices in different retail locations. However, geographic variation in pricing poses significant problems such as those associated with refunds for returned goods and it can cause bad publicity. There is the possibility of retailers exploiting a local monopoly by means of premium geographical pricing, a practice that was considered against consumer interest in the Competition Commission's report (see Vignette 13.1).

Where alternative channels are used for retailing (for example store, website and direct mail) a retailer has to carefully balance the need to maintain consistent image across outlets with the requirement to match channel competitors and provide rewards to customers who use cheaper methods of retailing.

Summary

Many marketing textbooks propose a multistage approach to pricing, which is a useful framework for making pricing decisions about single items. In reality, most retail pricing decisions are more of a matter of fine-tuning prices within existing product ranges, and so a more appropriate framework for the analysis of retail pricing decisions is that proposed by McGoldrick (2002). This model is less concerned with initial costing and demand aspects of pricing, and more focused on the complexity of pricing in a retail context, breaking down pricing into the four dimensions of time, assortment, comparison (with competitors) and geography. These dimensions have been explored within this chapter, and have implications for both short-term operational retail management and longer-term retail strategy.

The retail consumer, on both a domestic and international level, is becoming more affluent. However, this does not appear to be resulting in consumers being less price-sensitive or less value-conscious. On the contrary, experience in consumption seems to be developing a keen awareness of prices and an acute sense of value. It is therefore imperative that retail managers have an awareness of all the cost and profit implications of various decisions and actions relating to pricing and build an understanding of customers' price perceptions and reactions. Paradoxically, a large part of consumers' value appreciation involves many things other than price. In particular shopping convenience, the right kind of product, a pleasant shopping environment, and good customer service are all aspects of retailing that consumers are prepared to pay for, and so pricing cannot be isolated from the rest of the retail offer.

Questions

1 Explain the difference between 'price' and 'value'.
2 Outline the alternative long-term pricing strategy options that are available to retailers, indicating the type of retailer that might use the strategies you describe.
3 Discuss the concept of a 'promotional price'. To what extent would you consider a mark-down to be a promotional price?
4 Consumers will become more price-sensitive as they become more adept at using the internet to compare retailers' offerings. Discuss.
5 Conduct your own investigation into supermarket pricing within a grocery product category of your choice. In the light of your own investigation, do you think that the investigation by the Competition Commission (1999–2000) was justified?
6 Maintaining low prices in the long term requires retailers to be keenly aware of cost control. Outline the type of costs that are incurred when using alternative retail formats.

References and Further Reading

Competition Commission (2000) *Supermarkets: A Report on the Supply of Groceries from Multiple Stores in the United Kingdom* (Norwich: The Stationery Office).

The Consumer Protection Approval Order 1988 (Code of Practice for Traders on Price Indications) (London: The Stationery Office).

De Chernatony, L. and McDonald, M. (1998) *Creating Powerful Brands in Consumer, Service and Industrial Markets* (Oxford: Butterworth-Heinemann).

Fernie, J. and Fernie, S.I. (1997) 'The Development of a US Retail Format in Europe: The Case of Ffactory Outlet Centres', *International Journal of Retail and Distribution Management*, vol. 25, no. 11, pp. 342–50.

McGoldrick, P.J., Betts, E.J. and Wilson, A.F. (1999) 'Modelling Consumer Price Cognition: Evidence from Discount and Superstore Sectors', *Services Industries Journal*, vol. 9, no. 1, pp. 171–93.

McGoldrick, P.J. (2002) *Retail Marketing* (Maidenhead: McGraw-Hill).

Ody, P. (2002) 'Customer Focused', *Retail Week*, 9 August.

Walters, D. and Laffy, D. (1996) *Managing Retail Productivity and Profitability* (Basingstoke: Macmillan Business).

chapter fourteen

Retail Promotion

Learning objectives

- To distinguish between institutional and promotional objectives of retailers' communication programmes.
- To explore the differences between the promotional strategies of retailers and those of manufacturers.
- To identify the elements of the retail promotion mix and explore how they can be used to achieve the promotional objectives of retailers.
- To understand how and why retailers and manufacturers cooperate on promotional issues.
- To understand the role of promotions in influencing shopping behaviour.
- To appreciate the need for an integrated promotional programme.

Introduction

Retail expenditure on promotion has been increasing over the last couple of decades as retailers have increasingly used advertising to establish the credibility of their own brands in their own right. This has enabled retailers to form a direct relationship with their customers, rather than relying on brand manufacturers who until then had dominated the relationship with the consumer, with retailers performing the intermediary role of providing a channel to the market. Retailers have also taken charge of other aspects of promotion in order to achieve their own strategic objectives.

The major role of promotions is to generate demand for the retailer's products, and the retailer's communication programme moves customers through the stages of the buying process. This chapter focuses on the major elements of the retail promotion mix (or communications mix), namely advertising, sales promotion, public relations and personal selling. Loyalty schemes, database marketing and customer relationship management techniques were discussed in Chapter 8 given their reliance on information technology; the purpose of this chapter is to discuss how retailers manage the promotional mix to achieve their short-term and long-term promotional and strategic marketing objectives.

Promotional Objectives

Promotional objectives can be divided into those mainly aimed at improving long-term performance (institutional objectives), and those aimed at improving short-term performance (promotional objectives). Retailers have two main long-term objectives, namely those related to their image and positioning, and those relating to public service.

Store image and positioning objectives are intended to establish and reinforce the store image and position that the retailer wants to project in the customer's mind. For instance, Body Shop has a reputation for providing non-animal-tested products and not to make unsubstantiated claims about the health and beauty impact of their products. Hence one would expecte Body Shop's promotional activity to emphasize these core values to differentiate themselves from competitors.

Another major long-term objective is to enhance the retailer's reputation as a good citizen in the community, to build up customer goodwill towards the retailer. Many retailers have initiatives that are designed to help their local communities in the areas of health, education and the environment. For example, in 2001 Tesco gave 4,000 computers to schools in the UK through its Computers for Schools initiative. Many retailers also have initiatives such as recycling, reducing packaging, and energy reduction to help the environment. Retailers such as Body Shop and the Co-op are also involved in promoting Fairtrade initiatives designed to ensure that third-world suppliers receive a fair price for their products. Such initiatives are designed to create goodwill amongst the retailer's different constituencies – customers, the local community, employees and suppliers.

Short-term objectives can be divided into those aimed at increasing patronage from existing customers, and those aimed at attracting new customers. The latter can be further subdivided into those aimed at attracting new customers from the retailer's existing trade area, and those aimed at expanding the trade area. Increased patronage from existing customers involves directing promotional activity at existing customers to increase their expenditure with the retailer. This means, in essence, attempting to increase store loyalty of existing customers.

The major tools for achieving short- and long-term promotional objectives are advertising, sales promotion, personal selling, public relations, and direct marketing, as well as the retail selling environment and visual merchandising. Together these elements form the retail promotion mix. Each of the promotion components performs a different function. However, for best results the different elements of the promotions mix need to be combined appropriately to achieve the promotional objectives.

Advertising

Advertising is a paid-for non-personal communication by the retailer through various media with a view to informing and/or persuading existing and potential customers regarding itself, and the products and services that it provides. Newspapers, magazines, radio, television and direct mail are the most frequently used advertising media by retailers, and increasingly, retailers are also using the internet to support their promotional campaigns. The function of advertising is, primarily, to inform potential customers of the benefits of the retailer's offering and to develop the customer's preference for the retailer.

There are two basic types of retail advertising: institutional and promotional. Institutional advertising focuses on the retailer as an organization and is designed to reinforce the retailer's image and positioning in the market and to build the retail brand. Its purpose is to improve long-term performance overall. Promotional advertising, on the other hand, attempts to improve short-term performance by focusing on the products that the retailer is selling or its prices. However, this dichotomy is somewhat superficial, and even promotional advertising needs to ensure that it is supporting the retail brand. Much of retail advertising has traditionally been product-focused, whereas advertising aimed at building the retail brand is a more recent phenomenon.

Retailer and manufacturer advertising strategies

It has to be remembered that retailers are not alone in advertising to consumers; in fact, the vast majority of expenditure on advertising to consumers is undertaken by manufacturers, not retailers. However, the communication objectives and the advertising strategies are quite different and this can be a source of conflict between the two parties.

Firstly, retail advertising tends to focus on the short term and is used to publicize promotions and store initiatives (such as sales) designed to generate immediate sales. Manufacturer advertising, on the other hand, tends to have a long-term focus and is aimed at promoting and building the image of the product brand. Retail advertising is usually aimed at attracting customers to the retailer's outlet and maximizing store sales rather than the sales of any product in particular. Manufacturer advertising, on the other hand, is aimed at maximizing product sales, irrespective of where they are purchased. Also, retailers tend to use local media (newspapers, television and radio) to target customers, as most people tend to shop at stores near their homes and workplaces. In any case, national advertising is affordable and appropriate only for the large national chains. Manufacturers, in the main, tend to use the national media as this provides them with the widest reach and their products are aimed at national rather than local markets.

Manufacturers also have the luxury of being able to focus on particular products as they have a relatively narrow range that they want to promote. This allows them to create communication programmes that project a consistent brand image for their products. However, given their extensive ranges, retailers are likely to confuse customers if they concentrate their advertising on particular products. Hence, retail advertising needs to develop advertising messages consistent with the overall image of the organization. This conflict is further compounded by the fact that many retailers stress prices in their adverts. Manufacturers, however, tend to emphasize product features and benefits so that consumers are less sensitive to price.

Co-operative advertising

Despite the areas of conflict discussed above retailers and manufacturers do cooperate on advertising and share costs. Vertical cooperative advertising involves a retailer and a manufacturer, or (less commonly) a wholesaler and a retailer, sharing the cost of an advert. The manufacturer will usually require the retailer to feature the manufacturer's name and/or products or both in the advertisement. The disadvantage of cooperative advertising for retailers is that they lose flexibility and there may not be consistency of image between the retailer and the third party. Also, advertising allowances are not always for the most profitable of the manufacturers' products.

Horizontal cooperative advertising occurs where two or more retailers jointly fund the cost of an advertisement. Horizontal agreements usually occur between small independent non-competing retailers, retailers located in shopping centres, or franchisees trading under a common brand name. A major advantage of horizontal cooperative advertising is that the pooling of resources gives greater bargaining power in purchasing advertising.

Factors affecting the choice of advertising media

The choice of media used for advertising depends on a number of factors relating not only to the ability of the media to reach the required target market, but also its ability to deliver the intended message effectively. Some of the major factors that influence media choice are discussed below:

● *Coverage* is the percentage of the market a particular medium reaches; for instance a local newspaper may be read by 70 to 80 per cent of the adults in a town. Reach is the actual number of target customers who come into contact with the advert.
● *Audience selectivity* is the medium's ability to deliver a message to certain target audiences within the population. Most magazines, for instance, target specific markets such as gardeners, photographers or hi-fi enthusiasts. Radio stations also appeal to specific segments. For instance, there are radio stations aimed at sports fans, classical music enthusiasts, and those who prefer pop music. Geographical selectivity is also important. The ability of a medium to target a specific area is important to store retailers as a majority of their customers come from the immediate surrounding area.
● *Frequency* is the average number of times each person reached by the advert is exposed to the advert in a given time period. Media such as TV, where the viewer is exposed to the advert for a very short time, need several repetitions to ensure that the intended recipients receive the message.
● *Impact* refers to the strength of the impression that an advertisement makes and its ability to influence purchasing behaviour. For instance, television and magazines are excellent media for building store and brand images, whereas newspapers are better at influencing purchasing behaviour in the short term.

● *Flexibility, timeliness and the life* of a medium are also important considerations. Flexibility refers to the extent to which a medium can contribute to the execution of the advertising strategy. For instance, direct marketing allows advertisers to individualize the message and to enclose coupons, samples and so on. Television, on the other hand, can provide pictures, sound, words and music but the message is the same for everyone. Timeliness refers to the lead times required to publish an advert in a medium; for instance an advert on the radio could appear the next day. However, lead times for adverts in television and magazines can be very long because of the popularity of the media. The 'life' of an advert refers to its longevity. Television and radio adverts are gone immediately after they are aired and must be repeated a number of times if they are to be effective. Magazine adverts may have a life of several weeks, as consumers tend to keep magazines for some time and reread them from time to time.

● *Costs* of the different media should be compared both in absolute and relative terms. The absolute cost of a medium is the total financial outlay of running an advert in it; the relative cost is the cost of reaching a certain number of people, usually expressed as cost per thousand (CPT). For instance, the absolute cost of advertising in a newspaper might be £3,000 for a full-page advert. If the newspaper has a readership of 500,000, then the CPT is £6.00 (£3,000 × 1,000 divided by 500,000). The cost per thousand measure is only useful for comparing similar media as different media differ in their effectiveness.

Timing of advertisements

A crucial factor in the success of advertising is the timing of the advert. There is no single answer as to the best time for advertising because of the diversity of retailing activities. However, retailers need to consider when peak seasons occur in their business and the shopping patterns of their customers. Supermarkets, for instance, tend to advertise on Wednesdays because a high proportion of customers do their grocery shopping on Thursday, Friday or Saturday. Garden and DIY retailers, on the other hand, tend to concentrate their advertising in the early spring and summer months.

Assessing the effectiveness of an advertising programme

Assessing the effectiveness of advertising involves evaluating the extent to which advertising objectives have been achieved. For instance, if the objective of an advertising campaign is to raise awareness, this may be assessed by measuring spontaneous and aided recall of the advertisement on television, radio or in the press. If, on the other hand, the objective is to change the attitudes of customers, then it is necessary to conduct attitudinal research to assess the changes in customer attitudes towards the retailer. Many large retailers undertake *continuous tracking studies* of their promotional activities and their impact, which provides them with benchmarks for any new advertising programme. Measuring the effect of advertising on sales is much more difficult because sales are affected by numerous other factors besides the advertising itself, including choice, prices, availability and other promotional activities.

Another major aspect of assessing the effectiveness of advertising is to judge how effective it was in reaching the intended market. Much advertising is wasted because the media used is not sufficiently focused on the relevant market. Advertising may also be wasted due to poor internal communication so that employees are not aware that an item is for sale, for instance. At the same time, retailers need to be aware that their adverts are seen not only by their customers, but also by their employees. Hence, any advert purporting to show its employees in its adverts needs to ensure that employees are being projected in a positive light (see Sainsbury's case study Vignette 14.1).

Public Relations

Public relations involves the creation of interest and goodwill amongst a retailer's various publics – customers, investors, employees, suppliers and local community. A major tool for generating interest in the company is publicity, which involves placing significant communications (usually news stories) regarding the retailer and its products in the media without paying for the time or space directly. This can take the form of a press release or favourable editorial comment. Such coverage has more credibility than advertising amongst the retailer's customers and other publics because it is unpaid for, and therefore regarded as an independent view. However, how the stories are reported, the depth of coverage and timing are out of the retailer's control. Public relations are also necessary to limit the impact of negative stories about the organization.

The power of publicity and public relations can be seen in the fact that Body Shop relied almost entirely on the publicity that its founder Anita Roddick was able to generate about its products, ethical stance and activities in the third world in the area of fair trade. Richard Branson, owner of Virgin Megastore (amongst other Virgin brands) has generated huge interest for Virgin through his various activities including his attempts to cross the Atlantic in a hot-air balloon. Benetton, on the other hand, has generated a great deal of publicity through its provocative advertisements, for example the controversial portrayal of a dying Aids victim in a Benetton poster campaign in the early 1990s that generated huge amounts of publicity, not all of it positive.

Sales Promotions

Sales promotions are incentives provided to customers for a limited period of time to stimulate trial or increase sales. The incentives are designed to add value to a retailer's products, and the limitation on the time period of the sales promotion encourages an immediate response from the customer. The most frequently used techniques include coupons, premiums, contests and sweepstakes, loyalty schemes, product demonstrations, referral gifts, samples, and buy-one-get-one-free (BOGOF) offers (Table 14.1).

Table 14.1 Types of sales promotions

Coupons	Certificates redeemable for a specified amount of money on a purchase; coupons are most frequently used by supermarkets
Price deals, refunds and rebates	Temporary price reductions; the price reductions may be printed on product packaging, or on the store shelf. Alternatively, rebates may be offered allowing customers to recover part of the cost of the product.
Special packs/bonus packs	Special packs give shoppers extra product 'free' instead of lowering the price
Multi-buys/multi-save	Additional products given without extra charge; the most common form is buy-one-get-one-free (BOGOF), but 3 for 2 is also practised by some retailers, for example Boots
Sales	Sales are price reductions implemented across the store; end-of-season sales are common in fashion retailing and are designed to get rid of stock quickly before the new season's stock arrives
Contests and sweepstakes	A contest is a competition requiring skill (for example quizzes, providing slogans etc.); sweepstakes are competitions where the winner is chosen by chance
Premiums	Premiums take the form of merchandise being offered for free or reduced cost as an incentive to buy a product; premiums can be free in-pack or on-pack gifts, free mail-in offers, or self-liquidating offers where consumers are asked to pay a sum of money to cover the cost of the premium merchandise; mail-in offers usually require a number of proofs of purchase, which help to drive sales and create brand loyalty
Demonstrations and sampling	In-store demonstrations are used by retailers to build excitement and to encourage impulse buying; free samples of the products may also be given out in the store to encourage trial of new products or brand extensions
Special events	Examples include fashion shows of the new season's merchandise, book-signing sessions by authors, and store visits by celebrities designed to generate store traffic and interest in the store
Loyalty programmes	Points are awarded (usually) for every pound spent on purchases in the store; the points can be redeemed for goods or services or for discounts on future shopping bills

Strengths and weaknesses of sales promotion

The major advantages include:

- Sales promotions are good at generating interest in the retailer and the promoted merchandise.
- They can be very distinctive because of the variety of promotion tools available.
- Consumers may receive something of value, which provides an extra incentive to visit the retailer and to purchase the merchandise.
- Sales promotions introduce novelty and fun into shopping.

- They increase store traffic by attracting new customers and increasing patronage of existing customers.
- They increase impulse purchases.
- They help to maintain store loyalty.
- They are very effective at increasing sales volume in the short-term.

The major strength of sales promotions is also their major weakness; namely that many sales promotions have only a short-term effect. Another major weakness, particularly for sales promotions that offer financial inducements, is that they can be expensive for the retailer and can lead to reduced margins. Good sales promotions will be able to recover the cost of the promotions. However, some promotions are loss leaders where products are sold at or below cost, and the promotion is designed principally to generate store traffic; profits are generated from increased sales from the rest of the store.

Many promotions are generated by suppliers and therefore the cost is borne by the manufacturer brand-owners. However, even where promotions are initiated by the retailer, the benefits to the supplier of increased sales and interest in their products means that promotions are usually jointly financed. The precise split of the costs depends on the negotiating power of the retailers and suppliers. Smaller suppliers often complain of being pressurized to finance retail promotions.

Sales promotions also require careful planning and collaboration with suppliers to ensure that customers are not disappointed because not enough extra inventory has been ordered. Similarly, over-ordering incurs inventory holding and space costs.

Assessing the effectiveness of sales promotions

As sales promotions are, in the main, designed to achieve short-run improvements in store performance, they should be assessed in terms of the sales and profits directly generated by them. A simple method of assessing their effectiveness is to measure the weekly volume of sales before the promotion and compare it with the weekly sales volume during and after the promotional period; the sales volume prior to the promotional period provides a benchmark for comparisons. It is necessary to measure sales after the promotion because consumers may simply be stockpiling the product, which would lead to sales being lower after the promotion (referred to as the sales displacement effect) relative to the volumes before the promotion. For example, consider a supermarket featuring Clairol's Herbal Essences Shampoo/Conditioner on a buy-one-get-one-free offer for two weeks. Before the promotion, EPOS data indicated typical weekly sales of 10 cases. During the two-week promotion sales averaged 17 cases per week. However, four weeks following the promotion, sales were 5, 6.5, 8 and 9.5 cases per week. In the fifth and subsequent weeks sales returned to the previous level of 10 cases per week. Thus, the net impact of the promotion was to increase sales by three cases with the majority of the increase in sales being due to customers stockpiling for future needs.

The actual profitability of the promotion will depend upon how the costs of the promotion were shared between the retailer and the supplier. It also depends on the effect of the promotion on the current and future demand of competing products, referred to as the substitution effect. For example, the promotion could have a negative impact on profitability if it leads to switching of demand away from high-margin unpromoted products to lower-margin promoted products.

The example above helps to illustrate some general points about promotions. Firstly, promotions for non-perishable staples or necessity items will generally lead to stockpiling by consumers rather than increased consumption. Increased sales for these items will depend upon the degree to which they can attract customers from competitors, or their ability to attract customers from beyond the retailer's existing trading area. The fluctuation of sales (from 5 to 17 cases) also suggests that accurate forecasting and careful planning of promotions is necessary to avoid under or overstocking of promoted merchandise. The indirect impact of sales promotions is much more difficult to estimate and requires more sophisticated analysis. This is because at any one time a retailer will have a number of sales promotions running concurrently, and other extraneous factors (such as competitor promotional activity) can influence the overall impact on store performance.

The Retailing Environment

The store design, layout, signs, displays, decor, lighting, use of music and smell generate a store atmosphere and an image in the customer's mind. The store image thus communicated tells the customer about the retailer's pricing and service levels, and the fashionability of its merchandise offer. Once in the store, visual presentation of merchandise is a major method of influencing customers in the final stages of the consumer decision-making process. Good presentation and store layout can be used to increase impulse buying and to ensure that the customer shops the whole store.

Point-of-purchase displays

According to one report, (POPAI, 1987) as many as two-thirds of customers make their purchase decisions in store. Hence, point-of-purchase (POP) displays are critical for influencing consumers in the final stages of the decision-making process, particularly where the customer is undecided or prepared to switch brands. POP materials include posters and banners, product displays, coupon dispensers, and computerized interactive displays. According to a Mori report (Ackland, 1999) 53 per cent of respondents said displays would prompt them to buy on impulse, and 74 per cent said displays alert them to new products.

POP displays are often designed and supplied by manufacturers to attract attention and to provide consumers with information and from a retailer's perspective POP displays are not always in keeping with the retailer's own image. Having numerous manufacturer POP displays can present a cluttered image and confused positioning for the retailer, and give precedence to the manufacturer brands over the retail brand. Hence, retailers are usually very selective about the POP displays that they employ.

● Personal Selling

Personal selling involves salespeople communicating directly with customers in order to help them satisfy their needs through an interactive exchange of information. The degree of personal selling and personal service provided by retailers varies by the type of merchandise sold and the retailer's service strategy. For instance, retailers selling low-risk, low-priced merchandise, such as food retailers, do not employ large numbers of skilled sales staff to provide customers with detailed information about products and how to make most effective use of them. This is because the vast majority of the products are routinely purchased by shoppers and additional information is available on product packaging or provided by shelf cards. The type of information required by shoppers is likely to be about product availability, special offers, returns policy and so forth, which can be provided by sales assistants on request. On the other hand, for highly priced, complex or non-routinely purchased products customers are likely to require and expect the assistance of a salesperson in making the right choice of product to satisfy their specific needs. This is because these are potentially high-risk purchases and customers seek to reduce the risk by seeking expert advice. Situations where personal selling is highly effective include:

● Where the perceived personal risk of making the wrong choice is high, for example for cosmetics or clothes.
● Where the purchase price is high relative to the individual's income, for example a car.
● Where customization is required by the customer, for example tailored clothing.
● Where the product is complex and there is a variety of products to choose from, for example computers.
● Where variable pricing is practised and discount negotiation takes place, for example holidays.

The role of personal selling is to convert store visits to sales, increase impulse buying by suggestion selling, and to improve customer relations.

The selling process

The selling process in the retailing environment has the following basic stages:

● Greeting and approaching customers.
● Determining customer needs.
● Presenting and demonstrating merchandise.
● Answering objections.
● Closing the sale.
● Suggestion selling.

Greeting and approaching is an important stage in establishing rapport with the customer. A simple 'hello', or 'good morning' is less threatening than

'May I help you'. The key to a successful approach is to find out the customer's needs. Is the customer simply browsing or are they looking for a particular product? Do they have a price range in mind? Some well-chosen questions allow the sales person to assess a product (or products) that fit the customer's requirements.

The approach stage is followed by presentation (and if necessary demonstration) of a product that may satisfy the customer's needs. If the exact product is not available the salesperson may suggest a substitute or get the customer to trade up to a more expensive product with better features and benefits. In a retail setting it is best to tailor the presentation to the needs of individual customers, as different customers can have varied needs and wants. Showing the customer too many products can be confusing and should be avoided, and the presentation should be made in an interesting manner emphasizing the important features and benefits of the product.

During the selling process the customer may have questions regarding the product which need to be addressed appropriately, or the sale may be lost. Having addressed any objections, the salesperson needs to close the sale, that is get the customer to purchase the product. Closing the sale can involve asking the customer to choose between products, choosing for the customer, assuming that the sale has been made and asking the customer how they wish to pay for the product, or overcoming objections by stressing the benefits of the product.

Once the customer has decided to buy the product, the salesperson continues to sell by making additional suggestions of products that would enhance or get the best out of the original product. This is known as suggestion selling. Typical suggestion selling include suggesting accessories for products, for example software for computers or extended guarantees for electrical products which extend the warranty period from the standard one-year manufacturer's guarantee to three or five years.

Effective personal selling requires that salespeople are enthusiastic, knowledgeable about the products they are selling, customer-oriented and effective communicators. This requires that sales people are carefully selected by the retailer to ensure that they have the right attributes for selling, which include people-orientation, good communication and enthusiasm. It also requires that a retailer trains its salespeople to equip them with the necessary knowledge required to sell the products and in the different aspects of the retail selling process. However, because of the high turnover of personnel in the industry, retailers do not always train their salespeople to the highest standards, as it is seen as wasted investment. This shortsightedness can lead to customer dissatisfaction and lost sales.

● Differential Impact of the Promotions Mix

Each of the elements of the retail promotions mix has different strengths and weaknesses, and in order to achieve the best results the different promotional activities need to be coordinated and integrated and convey a consistent message. Inconsistent messages communicated to customers can lead to confusion about the retailer's image and positioning with a consequent decline in store patronage (see Vignette 14.1).

Vignette 14.1

Aligning internal and external communications at Sainsbury's

In the autumn of 1998, Sainsbury's launched a major advertising campaign with the strap line, 'Value to shout about'. The ad campaign showed the actor John Cleese talking to shop staff (played by actors) about low prices and urging them to be more positive about the retailer's offer. One advert showed him dressed in a brash checked jacket bellowing through a megaphone into the ear of a hapless sales assistant urging her to be more upbeat about the value of Sainsbury's offer. In an another advert, Cleese is seen promising that Sainsbury's will refund twice the difference if a customer buys a can of baked beans cheaper elsewhere.

The campaign, created by the advertising agency Abbott Mead Vickers BBDO, appeared to signal a significant shift in Sainsbury's pricing strategy. Previous TV campaigns had positioned Sainsbury's as a more sophisticated, top-end food retailer. This was exemplified by a series of adverts in the early 1990s showing a number of well-known television celebrities making their favourite recipes with Sainsbury's ingredients conveying an air of indulgence. The new campaign had been launched in a response to a survey by Nielsen that had rated Sainsbury's top in choice, quality and service, but not price. The adverts were designed to challenge consumer perceptions that Sainsbury's was more expensive than its rivals.

The adverts did not go down well with Sainsbury's customers or their employees. Employees complained that the adverts made them look stupid, and sales figures also showed that customers had also been turned-off. Even worse, in a survey of television viewers, the adverts were voted the most irritating adverts on TV in 1998. Sainsbury's could easily have avoided the error of alienating its staff by testing the adverts internally before airing them, and by preparing its employees for the apparent shift in its price positioning strategy. However, Sainsbury's reacted quickly in response to staff complaints by editing the advert and taking the emphasis away from the employee.

The following year, Sainsbury's did not make the same mistake when it launched its new marketing campaign 'Making life taste better', designed to switch emphasis back onto quality. This time, an internal marketing programme preceded the advertising campaign. The programme was aimed at educating and motivating staff as part of an attempt to revive confidence in the Sainsbury's brand. The programme, called 'One company, one agenda', was devised by Saatchi and launched at a special conference by the Marketing Director to give it added credence. The campaign included:

- Posters placed at the back of shops and in corridors giving facts and figures about the changing customer base using the strap line 'When we understand our customers we can make all our lives taste better.'
- An obligatory induction video for all new employees showing how every staff member contributes to the chain, from the distribution warehouse to the checkout, using the theme of a little girl waiting for food for her birthday party.
- A revamping of the staff magazine with the new store identity.

- Staff were also issued with company screensavers using the new 'living orange' logo and pictures of brightly coloured fruit.

The programme was a clear attempt to align internal communications with the external marketing campaign, and to ensure that brand promises were being delivered. The campaign was also designed to boost staff morale as it coincided with the announcement of 1,000 job losses.

Sources: Bainbridge (1998) 'Are you Marketing to your Staff?' *Marketing,* 8 Oct., pp. 20–1; Anonymous (1998) 'Cheesy John Cleese is Top of the Turn-offs', *The Times* 18 Dec.; Jardine (1999) 'Sainsbury's Motivating Staff to Revive Image', *Marketing,* 17 June p. 3; Witt (2001) 'Are Your Staff and Ads In Tune?', *Marketing,* 18 Jan.; p. 21; Ahmed. and Rafiq (2002) *Internal Marketing: Tools and Concepts for Customer-Focused Management* (Butterworth-Heinemann).

Used in combination, the different promotional techniques can be used to enforce each other. For instance, whilst sales promotions are good at increasing sales during a promotional period, sales usually revert to their pre-promotion level once the promotion has ended. Advertising, on the other hand, is useful for building longer-term interest in the store and switching customers away from competing stores and converting non-users. There is some evidence that if an advertising campaign precedes a sales promotion, the sales level settles at a higher level than at pre-promotion. Hence, retailers frequently use advertising to promote special offers.

The appropriateness of the promotional technique also depends upon where the customer is in the buying decision process, or the buyer readiness stage, as shown in Table 14.2. In buying products, consumers often go through a number of stages called the hierarchy of effects which takes them from (un)awareness of the product to knowledge, to liking, then preference, on to conviction and finally to purchase. Not all these stages are included each time a consumer purchases a product. The sequence is most likely to be followed in the case of high-involvement products, relatively expensive products, and products which the consumer is purchasing for the first time. In the case of inexpensive, low-involvement products, the sequence may be reversed; that is, a product is bought and the liking and preferences are formed after the consumption of the item.

Table 14.2 Effectiveness of promotional mix elements in influencing different stages of the buying decision process

	Awareness, knowledge	Liking, preference	Conviction	Action
Advertising	High	Moderate	Low	Low
Public relations	Moderate	Low	–	–
Sales promotion	Low	Low	Low	Moderate/high
Personal selling	Very low	Moderate/high	High	High

Summary

Retailing expenditure on promotion has been increasing over the last couple of decades and is beginning to rival the expenditure of major brand manufacturers. Retailers are not simply using their communications programmes to promote merchandise, they are also using them to establish the credibility of the retail brands in their own right. Promotional objectives can be characterized as institutional or promotional, depending on whether they are short-or long-term in orientation. The major tools for achieving promotional objectives are advertising, sales promotion, personal selling, public relations, direct marketing, and store atmospherics and visual merchandising, collectively referred to as the retail promotions (or retail communications) mix. This chapter has discussed the major features and strengths and weaknesses of the different elements of the mix, and how they can be used to influence customers at different points in the buying decision process. An effective promotional programme requires the integration of different elements of the promotional mix.

Questions

1   Discuss what is meant by institutional and promotional objectives.
2   Why do retailers and manufacturers cooperate on advertising? Why is it not always in the interest of the retailer to engage in co-operative advertising?
3   How far do you agree with the view that sales promotions only have short-term effects and cannot be used to build the retail brand image?
4   How might a retailer evaluate the effectiveness of a sales promotion?
5   What is suggestion selling and how does it fit into the personal selling process?
6   Explain how different elements of the promotions mix can be used to influence the different stages of the buying process.

References and Further Reading

Ackland, H. (1999) 'Why Retailers Rule over POP Success', *Marketing* (London), 28 October, p. 41.

Betts, E.J. and McGoldrick, P.J. (1995) 'The Strategy of the Retail "Sales", Typology, Review and Synthesis', *International Review of Retail Distribution and Consumer Research*, vol. 5(3) (July), pp. 303–32.

Betts, E.J. and McGoldrick, P.J. (1996) 'Consumer Behaviour and the Retail "Sales": Modelling the Development of an "Attitude Problem" ', *European Journal of Marketing*, vol. 30, no. 8, pp. 40–56.

Peattie, S. (1998) 'Promotional Competitions as a Marketing Tool in Food Retailing', *British Food Journal*, vol. 100, no. 6, pp. 286–94.

Peattie, S. and Peattie, K. (2000) 'Sales Promotion', in M.J. Baker (ed.), *The Marketing Book*, 4th edn (Oxford: Butterworth-Heinemann), pp. 418–41.

Point-of-Purchase Advertising Institute (1987), *POPAI Supermarket Consumer Buying Habits Study*, Fort Lee, N.J.: Point-of-Purchase Advertising Institute Inc.

Smith, M.F. and Sinha, I. (2000) 'The Impact of Price and Extra Product Promotions on Store Preference', *International Journal of Retail and Distribution Management*, vol. 28, no. 2, pp. 83–92.

Retail Services

Introduction

The world of retailing and the concept of service are inextricably linked. Conceptually, service in retailing is a broad term; essentially, retailing is itself a service, providing the final consumer with a distribution service that provides efficiency in product retrieval (as shown in Chapter 1). Retailers also carry out a form of 'product editing' service, by formulating product ranges and assortments that are geared specifically to particular customer needs, and a stock availability service so that consumers can buy products in suitable quantities at times when they need them. Retail service, or perhaps the more commonly used term 'customer service', can also refer to the variety of 'add-ons' to a core product or service purchase that can improve the consumer's experience during a transaction. Customer service can refer to the interaction between retail sales personnel and the customer – giving advice, information and help prior to the purchase, and reassurance and advice afterwards. The term customer service can also be used to include the implementation of a retailer's policy (for example guarantees, exchanges and refunds) and the provision of facilities such as cafes, family parking spaces and toilets.

The relevance and quality of the service mix is an effective way for one retailer to differentiate their offer over others, and because good retail service relies on long-term investment in training and developing people within retail organizations, it can be a sustainable source of competitive advantage (as discussed in Chapter 3). It is the purpose of this chapter to explore relevant retail services and consider how service level and quality can determine a retailer's market positioning. It will also consider service quality as an indicator of success in the achievement of customer satisfaction.

As indicated in Chapter 2, many retail organizations (for example restaurants, beauty salons, and banks) are in the business of selling services as opposed to tangible products to their customers. While this type of retailing presents some additional challenges associated with the purchase, delivery and experience of the service, this chapter does not generally seek to make a distinction between goods and services. Its purpose is to explore the scope of service in the retail setting in general, rather than to focus on the retailing of services specifically.

The way retailers use services in their retail offer can be divided into a number of categories. We will use the headings Product-Related Services, Convenience-Related Services, Payment Services, Product-Availability Services, Information Services and Customer Sales Services to categorize the extensive selection of activities that can be considered as 'services' in the retail industry.

● Product-Related Services

This is the type of service directly related to the product itself. It is an augmentation or 'add-on' to the product that helps customers feel that their needs have been fully met. For example, if a customer needs to replace a malfunctioning freezer, that customer's needs will only be completely satisfied when the new freezer is installed in their kitchen. After the customer has purchased the freezer a delivery time will have been organized, the delivery van will have arrived, the freezer would have been unpackaged, carried to the correct place in the kitchen and plugged in to make sure it functions. The packaging and the old freezer would then be taken away. The retailer's relationship with their customer certainly does not end with the close of the sale, but is continued as the product-related services are carried out.

The services that retailers offer to augment their product ranges will vary according to the nature of the products within those ranges. As well as some widely applicable service offers such as gift-wrap and home delivery, Table 15.1 indicates a number of alternatives that are appropriate to specific retail sectors.

Table 15.1 Product-related service alternatives, by retail sector

Retail sector	Product-related services
Clothing	Changing rooms, alteration service, returns policy
Electrical/electronic	Service warranty, home installation
Furniture/home furnishings	Home assembly, home trial
Automotive	Test drives, warranties, insurance, car service packages

Some retailers go a stage further than providing an augmented product/service package. They actually differentiate their own retail offer from competitors by offering a higher and sometimes more complex level of service to match complex and highly involved customer needs. For example, a computer specialist that puts together a customized package of hardware and software for individual customers; an interior design service offered in a home furnishings specialist; or a personal-shopper service offered by a department store. In a retail environment where customer needs are growing in their sophistication, it makes sense to be able to match these needs with a finely blended mix of products and services which in the end allow a degree of personal customization for the shopper.

Convenience-Related Services

As consumers are, or at least feel, more time-pressurized by busy lifestyles, retailers have responded by formulating a product and service package that is highly convenience-orientated. The large grocery multiples have been particularly proactive in this area, and the following list indicates a range of convenience-related services that might typically be offered by a superstore retailer:

- Bag packing
- Home delivery
- Cafeteria
- Crèche
- Toilets
- Extended opening hours or 24-hour shopping
- Cash machines
- Variety of trolleys
- Parent and disabled parking areas

Some of the product categories on offer in a supermarket can be considered to be convenience-orientated, in that they save a customer a separate trip to a specialty store; the in-store pharmacy, bakery and delicatessen could be considered in this way. In addition, many superstores offer the customer the opportunity to purchase 'service products' within the outlet. A drycleaner, a bank, a post office and a photographic film-processing unit are examples of this type of retail service.

In the early 1990s the leading grocery retailers all gave their service offer something of an overhaul, for a number of reasons. One reason was linked to responding to consumer changes – to keep satisfying the increasingly convenience-orientated supermarket customer (see Chapter 4); another was to maintain the image of a high-quality offer – an investment into higher service provision was seen to be a more strategic move than to cut prices; and a third reason was competitive – the supermarkets decided that service was an effective means by which to compete for market share. This resulted in something of a 'service war', with each major grocery chain offering their 'unique' service bundle that might have included bag-packing, carry-to-car service, parent-and-child parking spaces, and even an umbrella service for rainy days! Some of these service offers were short-lived (such as brolly offers), but others, such as parent-and-child parking and the policy of opening more and more check-outs when queues were building (the 'one-in-front' policy) became an integral part of grocery supermarket operators' remit. This process, whereby a service provides temporary competitive advantage, before being repeated in a competitor's offer is described by the service life-cycle.

The service life-cycle

- *Introduction* – a new service is introduced by a retailer giving them a competitive advantage
⇓
- *Duplication* – other retailers copy the new service, which removes the competitive advantage.
⇓
- *Stalemate* – all retailers in a particular retail sector offer the service. Provision of the service becomes a cost, but removal of the service would result in competitive disadvantage.
⇓
- *Institutionalization* – the service is taken for granted and expected by customers. It becomes a basic element of retail operations.
⇓
- *Replacement* – another new service is introduced, or an existing service is improved or updated to provide competitive advantage again.

Source: Adapted from James *et al.* (1981) in McGoldrick (2002).

● Payment Services

In order to provide a high level of convenience in the shopping process, the more methods of payment a retailer can offer the better. If a customer cannot pay by their preferred method, then a barrier is created that might prevent the transaction being completed. This could result in the sale being lost completely. On the other hand, attractive payment methods and terms can be a way of enticing customers to proceed with a purchase. Flexible payment services are especially important for high-value transactions. Increasingly we live in a cashless society, with customers' purses housing a proliferation of payment cards. In addition, consumer credit is readily available, and so the methods and terms of payment that retailers offer need to have the flexibility to provide suitable arrangements for individual customers. The following list outlines some payment arrangements commonly found in retailing:

- Cash
- Cheque
- Debit cards (Switch)
- Credit cards
- Store account cards

- Hire purchase
- Hire purchase with payment protection
- Monthly payment via direct debit
- Monthly payment with additional guarantee period

Payment arrangements that allow a customer to complete a purchase over a period of time provide an opportunity for retailers to build a relationship with that customer. This is one of the strengths of mail-order operations, store-card schemes and loyalty cards. Customer details are collected, which can be used for further marketing initiatives.

Some loyalty cards double up as payment cards, which, in the eyes of the consumer, makes sense because the debits and credits to their account with that retailer can be viewed as different aspects of the relationship between the two parties. On the one hand the card is used to pay for goods, on the other it earns bonus points and relevant product information and offers.

Payment options are certainly subject to the service life-cycle (see above). Today, the acceptance of debit cards is almost institutional in multiple retailers, and exceptions (for example Netto) who only deal in cash need to offer a clear benefit in return (such as exceptionally low prices). Cases have been known where cash has been refused in high-class eating establishments because the tills do not carry change! One of the many criticisms of the strategy of Marks and Spencer in the late 1990s was their reluctance to move from only accepting their own credit card to a wider range of payment cards, particularly when they were introducing high-value product categories like furniture.

Product-Availability Services

Another aspect of retail service is that concerning product availability. When shoppers invest personal resources (time, travel costs and so on) to retrieve products, they expect their investment to pay off and are disappointed if it has not been worthwhile. If it is the retailer who was out of stock of an item, rather than simply a case of their own indecision, then the feeling of frustration is all the greater. Overall, the supply-chain initiatives described in Chapter 7 have raised the standards of customer service from a logistics point of view, so that as a general rule customers are more frequently able to find goods in stock. The out-of-stock situations that do occur should be viewed as a breakdown on the retailer's part, and therefore an opportunity for the implementation of an exceptional service to retrieve the situation, for example by making an arrangement to deliver the item to the customer's home. The problem that modern retailers face is the high levels of retail provision (see Chapter 3), which allow a customer to switch to a competitor if they do not find a product available. In self-service situations this switching action may go completely undetected. Web-based retailing has experienced a real difficulty in this area; poor order fulfilment and unreliable deliveries have allowed many internet sales and customers to get lost in cyberspace (see Boo.com, Vignette 17.3 Chapter 17).

● **Information Services**

The information that retailers provide about their products, and how they as businesess operate, can be considered as part of the retail service mix. This information can be imparted in a number of ways, for example in person, by telephone, on a website, in a leaflet or within a catalogue. The main criteria for good-quality information are accuracy, and presentation in a manner that is complementary to and consistent with the overall corporate image of the retailer. Most large retailers have an information website even if they do not have a transactional e-retailing operation (see Chapter 17), and these can be a very cost-effective way of communicating with customers. Innovative retailers have used their websites to provide links to additional information that they feel is of interest to their customers, and it is this type of service that helps retailers to build a perception in customers that they are doing more than the basics in terms of service provision.

Provision of information can be viewed not only as a service, but also as a public-relations exercise. The plethora of leaflets found in supermarkets about health, product safety, environmental issues and so on, are there to reassure customers of the retailer's social responsibility and its stance on sensitive issues (see Chapter 18).

One type of information provision closely linked to the general area of retail customer-sales service (see below) is information about products that are complementary to the intended purchase. Although some customers could interpret this as a 'hard sell', Polonsky *et al.* (2000) found that, in general, customers believe companion selling to be an appropriate practice, and that it can contribute to a higher-quality customer-service provision.

Vignette 15.1

Innovative web-based customer-service initiatives

Many of the newest customer-service initiatives introduced by retailers are based on developments in information technology. Mothercare, for example, offer online customers a tailored, weekly meal-planning guide for infants, and links to community-service information; Boots hold chat forums and offer advice on health and beauty topics, while B&Q invite customers to ask for expert advice on their DIY disasters!

Book retailer Waterstones offer membership of a personal library that tailors book and author updates to individuals' interests, whilst Lands' End clothing retailers have a number of personal feature options that customers can match to their own, resulting in a visual image of a garment on a model that closely resembles themselves.

Source: White (2000) 'Got Service All Wrapped Up?,' *Retail Week*, 17 November.

Customer Sales Service

One of the aspects of retail service that is most immediately apparent is the contact made between customer and sales staff within the outlet. The type of contact can vary from a passive approach to a highly interactive one. The passive approach is characterized by customers making their own product choices, with sales personnel only becoming involved at the point of sale (for example at the checkout) or when a customer specifically asks for help. An interactive approach is characterized by extended communication between the customer and the salesperson. Typically, this would involve an approach (from either party), an exploration of alternative solutions to the customer's needs, including information about product-related services on offer, and finally the sale being closed.

The level of customer sales service

Even for the same product item, consumers may encounter very different *levels* of service in different retail outlets. For example, ground coffee may be purchased in a vacuum-sealed package in a supermarket. On the other hand, a consumer may choose to buy coffee from a speciality store, in which case the service encounter might involve talking to the sales associate about the different strengths and aromas found in the various blends, it may include being offered alternative blends to smell, waiting while the beans are ground, packaged, sealed and placed in an individual carrier bag, and finally being offered the opportunity to place the purchase on their personal account!

The level of service found in a retail outlet is very closely linked to the prices charged. The type of service level described in the speciality store scenario above incurs a hefty labour cost, and in addition sales associates need to have high levels of knowledge and experience. This expertise can only be built in an organization that has a high level of staff retention and good training facilities. It is usual, therefore, for the level of service available in a retail organization to be linked to the retail format used, the staffing provision within the retailer, and the margins applied to the product (Table 15.2).

Staffing provision and profit margins are concerned with the cost implication that goes with the provision of service within a retail outlet. However, there are two other very important factors in the customer-sales

Table 15.2 Retail formats and customer sales service

Retail format	Staffing levels	Need for product knowledge and experience	Profit margins
Supermarket	Medium	Low	Low
Speciality store	High	High	High
Department store	High	High	High
Category killer	Low	High	Low
Discount store	Low	Low	Low
Non-store	Medium-low	Medium-low	Low

service equation that retailers ignore at their peril. These are the service level that is appropriate for the type of product being sold, and the service levels expected by the target customer.

The type of product being sold

The more complex the blend of product features that go to make up a product, the more opportunity there is for a retailer to implement a high level of customer sales service and an explanation of the range of product-related services on offer. For example, the purchase of a washing machine allows a retailer to impart extensive advice about the product benefits and align those benefits to customer needs in addition to the opportunity to sell a warranty, arrange home delivery and then install the appliance at the customer's home. Complex and high-involvement products, for example an electrical appliance, a wedding outfit or a car, typically have a high price ticket, and so the investment into the involved sale is likely to be worthwhile. However, not all high-involvement products are expensive, for example Boots the Chemist maintain a high level of product information available for all goods, many of which (such as skin creams or pharmaceutical products) are relatively-low priced. However, Boots have a wide product offering, and customers remain loyal and keep their transaction levels high because they are assured that the consistently high service level will be received alongside all products time and time again.

Expectations of the target customer

The characteristics of the target customer may have a significant bearing on the type and level of service required in a retail situation. For example, a retailer such as Mothercare that targets parents of young children has to ensure that their service provision is appropriate. This might include automatic doors, wide aisles, baby-change rooms as well as baby-tolerant and knowledgeable staff. As a contrast, earlier on in this text a number of suggestions were made for retailers to improve their offer to attract third-age consumers (see Chapter 4).

The first-time purchase is also a good opportunity for retailers to offer a high level of service, because as consumers become more experienced and knowledgeable themselves about a particular product item, they rely less on information from sources like retailers in their accumulation of relevant knowledge. In many instances a retailer will be wanting to 'lock-in' a customer, so that when a similar need occurs in the future that retailer will be chosen for repeat purchases and store loyalty is built. This is particularly relevant to retailers of financial services because so many of their products have long-term implications for the customer and the retailer, and they are generally complex in nature.

● Expectations and Experiences

The work of Parasuraman, Zeithaml and Berry (1985 and 1990) underpins much of the theoretical development relating to customer perceptions of service. They found that matching customers' expectations with their actual experience of service received leads to customer satisfaction. Conversely, if the experience does not meet the expectation, the customer would be dissatisfied with the service received. They found that it was not necessarily important to strive to achieve increasingly high levels of service, but that the quality of service received matched the expectations of customers. Parasuraman, Zeithaml and Berry deduced that in order to provide a level of service that was satisfactory from the customer's point of view, there should be no gaps between the expectation and the experience. This led to the development of a model that helps service providers like retailers to identify where and why gaps might occur.

⬤ The Gap Model

The gap model is very useful for retailers when they are trying to analyse where they may be failing customers on service. In a competitive retail environment where retailers are continually raising service standards, and thus raising customer service expectations, an individual retailer needs to be able to monitor the satisfaction levels of their customers. Perfection in retail service provision would be the situation where expectations and perceived experiences are identical.

The preceding discussion in this chapter illustrates the extensive nature of service in retailing. In their research, Parasuraman *et al.* (1990) found that in most service-delivery scenarios the factors that customers use to judge the quality of service experienced could be categorized into 10 identifiable dimensions; these have been adapted into the retail context in column 3 of Table 15.3.

The dimensions of service quality provide a framework (named SERVQUAL by Parasuraman *et al.*, 1990) from which a retailer can then devise a research instrument to measure any difference between the expected and the experienced quality of service received. The SERVQUAL methodology uses a scaling technique, allowing customers to indicate the level of expectation and the perception of the service quality received.

The gap model suggests that there are four potential barriers to the service quality experienced by customers meeting (or exceeding) the level anticipated, leading to a mismatch between expectations and the service actually delivered (Brassington and Pettitt, 2000) (Figure 15.1).

The knowledge gap

This expresses the difference between the service that customers expect and the service that the retailer thinks customers expect. A retailer needs to research exactly what is important to customers, for example by establishing what are essential services in the eyes of the customer, and those that are considered to be optional extras. One of the challenges for the retailer is that different types of customers will have different expectations. For example, a crèche might be an essential and expected service for a young parent, but an irrelevant service to a young single person, for whom an ATM cash service

Table 15.3 Dimensions of retail service

Dimensions of service quality	Explanation of dimension	Dimension in retail context
Tangibles	Appearance of physical facilities, equipment, personnel and communication material	Appearance of outlet, displays, communications within the outlet, and sales associates
Reliability	Ability to perform the promised service, dependably and accurately	Efficient checkout operations; accurate and safe payment and receipt; accurate and on-time home delivery
Responsiveness	Willingness to help customers and provide prompt service	Quickly identifying and responding to customers who require help; having an efficient help-line or customer service desk
Competence	Possession of the required skills and knowledge to perform the service	Well-trained sales associates, with relevant knowledge and skills; empowered sales associates who perform their tasks without referral to a supervisor
Courtesy	Politeness, consideration respect and friendliness of contact personnel	Sales associates genuinely interested in helping customers, friendly and respectful of all customers
Credibility	Trustworthiness, believability, honour of the service provider	Retailer's policy concerning services (especially returns) and reputation for customer service; approach of sales associates
Security	Freedom from danger, risk or doubt	Presence of security staff, secure payment method, return policy and aftersales guarantees
Access	Approachability and ease of contact	Convenient location and opening hours; provision of customer facilities; outlet or department managers available if required
Communication	Keeping customers informed in language that they can understand, and listening to customers	Provision of information about products and services; explanation of payment methods and promotional offers; in-store signage; direct communications, e.g. direct mail or e-mail; complaints procedures
Understanding the customer	Making the effort to know customers and their needs	Getting to know regular customers, either in person or electronically; Understanding customer behaviour; responding to customer comments

Source: Adapted from Parasuraman *et al.* (1985 and 1990).

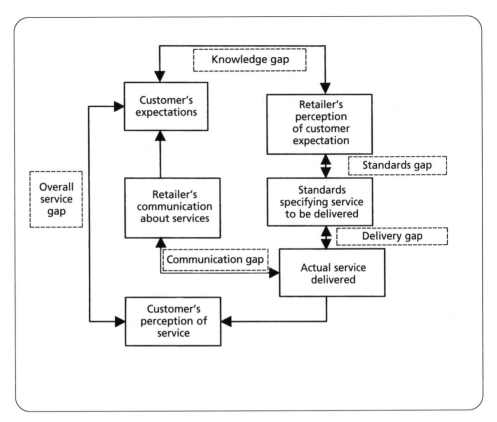

Figure 15.1 The gap model, adapted to retailing

Source: Adapted from Parasuraman, Zeithaml and Berry (1990).

might be far more essential. Only by carrying out consumer research can a retailer expect to monitor what type and level of service is expected by customers. Customers change over time, as alternative retail outlets change their service offerings and different retail formats emerge. Without this research and the opportunity for feedback, a retailer is bound to become out of touch, and the knowledge gap will start to appear.

The standards gap

The standards gap represents the difference between the service quality expected and the operational standards that the retailer achieves in its organization. Having closed the knowledge gap, by gaining a real understanding of what is required by customers, a realistic appraisal is needed in order to assess how this service quality level is going to be met. Commitment at the higher levels of management, and the acceptance of possible increases in costs in order to achieve higher quality service (for example training and schemes to incentivize good service) are all part of this process. It is essential that those people within the retail organization who devise service delivery standards and procedures, address any knowledge gaps that become apparent from customer research, so that inappropriate and irrelevant procedures and practices are avoided.

The delivery gap

The delivery gap occurs when employees fail to deliver the required standard of service. Having formulated a plan to achieve an acceptable level of service quality, the retailer must now ensure that at least this level of service is encountered by every customer, on every purchase occasion. It is extremely important that employees are motivated to produce good service levels even though they may be having problems outside work, or when a customer is being particularly difficult. To ensure service deliverers have the knowledge and skills required, set procedures and good training is required, backed up with empowerment and support so that employees deliver services as they see fit, but within a framework of clear guidelines for a minimum standard.

The communication gap

The communications gap opens when there is a difference between the level of service that a retailer states they are going to achieve, and the level that the customer actually receives. This gap represents the failure on the part of the retailer to deliver the service promise that they have made to the customer. Retailers may have built up customers' expectations by advertising service excellence, or by promoting services that are not available in all instances. Only when a retailer is confident that their operations can maintain a particular quality of service delivery should such an explicit service promise be made.

The unexpected or unusual, for example when a complaint is received, or where an individual customer is having difficulty, provide a retailer with an opportunity to provide exceptional service quality. Failure to deliver on time, out-of-stock situations, and customers having what they perceive as a difficult purchase are all instances where exceptional service can turn a negative experience into a positive one for the customer. Retailers must be conscious of the tendency for customers to pass on commentary to their friends and acquaintances when service is bad, rather than when it is good.

These four potential sources of breakdown in service delivery contribute to the gap between expectation and perception. For example, a customer might indicate that in terms of responsiveness their experience in a supermarket had fallen short of their expectations because they had waited for an excessive period of time in the checkout queue. The retailer will then need to establish what type of 'gap' caused this dissatisfaction. Was it a knowledge gap, where the retailer was unaware of the extent to which customers dislike standing in queues, and overestimated the time that customers consider reasonable for queuing? Was it a standards gap; for example, did the retailer have enough checkouts in operation? Was it a delivery gap, in that all checkouts were in operation but the operators were very slow? Or could it have been a communication gap, where the retailer had made a promise of a very fast checkout service in an advertisement? The gap model points the retailer in various directions for further investigation into the specific nature of customers' dissatisfaction.

● **Service Differentiation**

A strategy that is truly differentiated on service is one that is based on a long-term approach, as opposed to one where customer service initiatives are introduced on a short-term basis either to achieve a short-term gain or keep up with competitors. The relationship between costs and high levels of service was mentioned earlier in this chapter, but it must be stressed that good customer service does not have to incur higher costs – a courteous sales associate may well be on the same hourly rate as a rude one. The following management philosophies may be useful to adopt when developing a service-driven strategy:

Marketing orientation

The notion that the identification and satisfaction of consumer needs leads to improved customer retention underpins the marketing concept (Sivadas and Baker-Prewitt, 2000). It can be deduced, therefore, that retailers who are more marketing-orientated are more likely to be sensitive to customers' service as well as product needs.

Empowerment of the human resource

Nordstrom, a US department store, has found international acclaim for its service-differentiation strategy, which is founded on the empowerment of individual sales people to implement customized service initiatives as they see fit on an individual customer basis, in the knowledge that the store, as a business organization will support those initiatives. For example, a sales associate in a clothing department would be allowed to send outfits to a customer's home, for the customer to choose from, without any prior payment. The exceptional service from the retailer is based on the knowledge and experience of the employee concerning the cost-effectiveness of this action: for example, knowing how high and frequent the transaction levels of individual customers are, and the extent to which individual customers are trustworthy (Spector and McCarthy, 1995).

Quality assurance

The notion of quality assurance is that the retailer has procedures in place that guarantee a particular level of service. For example, a training programme might indicate that customers are always greeted and that within five minutes their shopping needs identified. Training programmes ensure that consistent standards of service are provided to all customers, but they run the risk of stifling creativity in service delivery and thus therefore an appropriate balance has to be achieved between standardization and customization (see below).

Staff development

Companies who operate a well-defined and understood programme of staff development will be able to identify the needs of personnel wherever they are employed within the organization. In particular, customer-service providers need to be trained in operational procedures so that they are efficient, and they need up to date product information so that they can advise customers appropriately. They may also be specifically trained in selling techniques. Many companies allow employees to identify their own developmental needs, which helps to motivate individuals and raise employee retention.

Service-orientated company culture

Companies that have a culture that embraces the 'customer is dictator' ethos will find it easier to introduce customer-orientated service initiatives. Also, encouraging employees to make suggestions about customer service helps to develop a team-working approach to customer service. In addition, this type of culture can be extended to employees of the organization who are considered to be 'internal customers'. Wal-Mart is an example of a retailer who has customer service at the centre of its business philosophy.

As mentioned previously in this chapter, while good service does not necessarily cost more than poor service, there are many aspects of a high level of customer service that do not come without additional costs. In fact, recent research (for example Pirron and Young, 2000) has indicated that a convenience-orientated service like a liberal returns policy may be routinely abused by some customers (see Vignette 15.2). A retailer must establish whether the resources put into their services offer is a worthwhile investment in terms of achieving strategic objectives, such as increasing transaction values or improving store loyalty.

Vignette 15.2

Taking advantage?

'De-shopping' and 'retail borrowing' are terms that describe a form of aberrant consumer behaviour that involves the conscious purchase of goods with the premeditated intention of returning them to the retailer after limited use, over a short period of time. It is suggested that the generous returns policies that many retailers have adopted to improve customer-service standards have encouraged this type of behaviour.

Retail borrowing seems to be carried out more often for social reasons (concerning an outfit for a special occasion for example) than for economic reasons (not being able to afford an item). Damage to goods is often inflicted in order to present a more 'credible' case for refund. Whilst retailers may be aware of high levels of customer abuse, they can be reluctant to challenge customers because of the damage a 'fight' over a refund might do to their image and reputation.

One way in which this costly and demoralizing problem might be tackled is for retailers to make special attempts to get to know their abusers. Establishing a personal relationship can deter the 'borrower' by making them feel guilty about their actions.

Sources: Based on Dean (2001) and Pirron and Young (2001).

● Services Retailing

The discussion of retail service in this chapter has, in terms of the product range being offered by retailers, been general in nature. However, it is worth highlighting the fact that, in retailing, the 'product' being sold can be tangible goods-orientated or service-orientated itself. A useful way of exploring the nature of different retail products is by putting them on a goods–service continuum (Adcock *et al.*, 2001). Retail products that are nearer the service end of the continuum are often characterized by inseparability of the product's delivery and consumption (for example in the case of a haircut), the intangibility of the product at the time of purchase (for example a holiday or a personal loan) or the perishability of the product (for example a restaurant meal). They are also said to be heterogeneous in nature because service 'encounters' or experiences are likely to be slightly different for every customer and service delivery. This one-to-one nature of services retailing provides many challenges in terms of operational control, but can also be a real opportunity for differentiation by exceeding the standard of competitors and for the implementation of relationship marketing.

One of the difficulties associated with retailing services is control of the quality of service received by customers, and how the level of quality that can be expected in a retail outlet is communicated to customers. For example, in a hair salon the quality of the product is dependent on the stylist's performance, and how much the individual customer likes their new style. The satisfaction of the individual customer with the style produced, and the quality of the service product, can only be fully assessed when the styling is finished. However, customers are helped in their assessment of the essentially intangible product by tangible indicators such as the environment in which the styling takes place. If the salon is clean, with a fashionable decor, the stylists are smartly dressed and their styling qualifications clearly visible, this 'physical evidence' will send positive messages to customers about the level of quality they are likely to receive in the service product. Service quality in services retailing is important because rising living standards make customers want a higher standard of service to match their general lifestyle (Newman and Cullen, 2002).

Many services such as telephone communications, banking and postal services either have been or are currently being deregulated, which has meant that service 'provision' has changed from being producer-orientated (often nationalized industry-based) to customer-orientated. This has resulted in markets with offers from alternative sources competing on a mix of price, convenience, quality and service delivery, just like tangible-product retailers. Building brand awareness, trust and loyalty is extremely important in services markets because service products are often complex, expensive and require high levels of customer involvement (for example holidays, or personal investments).

The 'store' or environment where the service transaction takes place is a very important tool for service retailers to use to communicate their product to customers. Travel companies like Lunn Poly, for example, are actively involved in the use of retail design to create an attractive and holiday-orientated atmosphere in their outlets, whilst ensuring that customers receive a friendly and efficient service when they seek information on the holidays on offer (Firth, 2003).

In order to ensure consistency in service levels in service-product delivery, some service retailers use highly standardized approaches to customer interaction. Fast-food retailers have used this technique to ensure that a minimum standard of service quality can be guaranteed to all customers; procedures are extensive and strictly implemented, and staff are trained and continually assessed to ensure they maintain the standard required. In other service-retailing situations, technology can help to meet the needs of both customers and retailers. For example, airline booking systems are automated, and flexible according to levels of demand. Flexible pricing can help service retailers to encourage use of their service (such as hotels and travel) at off-peak times, so that maximum revenue from the business' assets is achieved.

Customization vs standardization

Both service and product retailers need to plan their operations so that the fundamental elements of the offering, such as preparation, stock control, processing and training, are performed away from customers, leaving the interaction between retailer and customer to be customer-focused and dedicated. The extent to which retailers then customize the personal service given to individual shoppers can then vary according to the strategic aims of the business. In a mass-market fast-food situation, it is appropriate to have a standardized service quality, whereas in a department store like Nordstrom the freedom that sales personnel have to customize their service to individual customers is coherent with their upmarket and service-orientated positioning.

Summary

It is no longer possible for retailers to limit their consideration of service to the interaction between the salesperson and customer at the moment of purchase. Customers are valuable commodities, who need to be nurtured and kept satisfied in an attempt to prevent them from straying to competitors. It is an old marketing adage that it costs more than five times as much to generate new customers than it does to keep existing ones, and that loyal customers are more profitable customers. Providing a better level of service than competitors is an effective way to differentiate the retail offering, when there is little to distinguish between outlets in terms of products, prices and selling environments. Adopting a service–led strategy means that retailers have to focus all of their operations on providing a shopping experience that meets customers' expectations. Using the concept of gaps between these expectations and what customers may actually experience provides a methodology for identifying and correcting service-quality problems. Eliminating or minimizing these problems, and then building inservices which make a positive impact on customers, generates the feel-good factor in customers and trust in the retail brand. Investing in innovative services that customize the service offer to meet the diversified needs of a fragmented customer base is likely to be one of the most important ways in which retailers generate competitive advantage in the future.

Questions

1 For a retailer of your choice, provide an analysis of their services mix, using the categories of product-related, convenience-related, payment, product availability information and customer-sales services.

2 Identify an occasion when your experience within a retail outlet did not meet your expectation? How and why did that gap occur? What recommendations would you make to the retailer in order for them to close the gap, and what might that retailer have done to redress the dissatisfaction that they had caused?

3 It is often said that there is a trade-off between price and service in retailing. To what extent do you agree with this?

4 Many retail 'services' are simply promotional gimmicks. Discuss this notion, referring to the services life-cycle in your answer.

5 Consider the viability of a retail strategy that uses service differentiation to create sustainable competitive advantage. What implications does such a strategy have for resource allocation?

References and Further Reading

Adcock, D., Halborg, A. and Ross, C. (2001) *Marketing Principles and Practice* (Harlow, UK: FT Prentice-Hall).

Baron, S. and Harris, K. (1995) *Services Marketing – Text and Cases* (London: Macmillan Business).

Brassington, F. and Pettitt, S. (2000) *Principles of Marketing*, 2nd edn (Harlow: Pearson).

Collins, A., Henchion, M. and O' Reilly, P. (2001) 'Logistics Customer Service: Performance of Irish Food Exporters', *International Journal of Retail and Distribution Management*, vol. 29, no. 1, pp. 6–15.

Dean, J. (2001) 'What Cost Deshopping', British Shops and Stores Association website http://www.british-shops.co.uk, 23 May.1

Kelley, S.W., Donnelly, J. R. and Skinner, S.J. (1990) 'Customer Participation in Service Production and Delivery', *Journal of Retailing*, vol. 66, p. 3.

Firth, D. (2003) 'All Inclusive Deal', *Retail Interiors*, February.

James, D.L.B., Walker, J. and Etzel, M.J. *et al.* (1981) in P.J. McGoldrick (2002) *Retail Marketing* (Maidenhead: McGraw-Hill).

Mishra, D. (2000) 'Interdisciplinary Contributions in Retail Service Delivery: Review and Future Directions', *Journal of Retailing and Consumer Services*, no 7, pp. 101–18.

Parasuraman, A., Zeithaml, V.A. and Berry, L.L. (1985) 'A Conceptual Model of Service Quality and its Implications for Future Research', *Journal of Marketing*, vol. 49, pp. 41–50.

Parasuraman, A., Zeithaml, V.A. and Berry, L.L. (1990) *Delivering Service Quality: Balancing Customer Perceptions and Expectations* (New York: Free Press).

Polonsky, M.J., Cameron, H., Halstead, S., Ratcliffe, A.,. Stilo, P. and Watt, G. (2000) 'Exploring Companion Selling: Does the Situation Affect Customers' Perceptions?', *International Journal of Retail and Distribution Management*, vol. 28, no. 1, pp. 37–45.

Pirron, F. and Young, M. (2000) 'Retail Borrowing: Insights and Implication on Returning Used Merchandise', *International Journal of Retail and Distribution Management*, vol. 28, no. 1, pp. 27–36.

Sivadas, E. and Baker-Prewitt, J.L. (2000) 'An Examination of the Relationship between Service Quality, Customer Satisfaction, and Store Loyalty', *International Journal of Retail and Distribution Management*, vol. 28, no. 2, pp. 73–82.

Spector, R. and McCarthy, P. (1995) *The Nordstrom Way* (New York: Wiley).

White, F. (2000) 'Got Service All Wrapped Up?' *Retail Week*, 17 November.

Newman, A.J. and Cullen, P. (2002) *Retailing: Environment and Operations* (London: Thompson Learning).

Zeithaml, V.A. and Bitner, M.J. (2000) *Services Marketing: Integrating Customer Focus Across the Firm*, 2nd edn (Boston and London: Irwin/McGraw-Hill).

part four

Retail Challenges

chapter sixteen

International Retailing

Learning objectives

- To appreciate the factors influencing decisions to internationalize.
- To understand Dunning's eclectic theory and its relevance for international retailers.
- To consider the push and pull factors in the internationalization process.
- To explore the choice of markets of international retailers.
- To understand the rationale behind entry methods employed in internationalization.
- To justify standardization and adaptation approaches to internationalization strategies.

Introduction

The rapid and continuing globalization of the world economy means that globalization of retailing activities is a major management issue for most large retailers today, and is likely to intensify in the coming decades. However, internationalization in retailing is not a recent phenomenon, for instance Woolworths opened its first store in the UK in 1909. What is new, however, is the scale of the international activities of retailers. A report by Corporate Intelligence (1994) noted that European retailers made 610 crossborder moves in the first four years of the 1990s, and since then the number has more than doubled. This is in contrast to 611 cross-border deals in the whole of the 1980s and only 182 in the 1970s.

These developments have come rather late to the retailing industry mainly because retailing, historically, has been an essentially small-scale, local activity. The highly capitalized, professionally managed, large-scale retailers that we see today are a relatively recent phenomenon. Compared with manufacturers, retailers have also only recently come to be seen as brands in their own right by consumers, as discussed in Chapter 12, and hence the majority of retailers had few advantages or resources that they could employ in foreign markets. In the case of US retailers, the sheer size of the domestic market offered more than sufficient opportunities so there was little need to look to foreign markets for expansion. Internationalization of retailers in recent years has been facilitated by the emergence of new telecommunications media (such as satellite television and the internet), which have made reaching global markets very easy, and made the control of international operations relatively straightforward.

Nevertheless, international retailing is still in the early stages of development, not just in Europe but across the globe, as indicated by Sir Richard Greenbury, previously Chairman of Marks and Spencer:

> The truth is that retailing is the last industry of any size or consequence to go international and, whether you like the challenge or not, you have got to face it because it is happening. If you don't do it, somebody else will. (Quoted in Peter Bartram 'Saving St Michael', *Director*, Feb. 1999, pp. 34–7)

The purpose of this chapter is to examine the factors behind the increasing internationalization of retailers, the choice of markets, methods employed to enter them and trading strategies adopted within those markets.

● International Retailers

Until recently, the most active internationalizers were the luxury goods and specialist retailers. Nowadays, however, retailers of all types are active in international retailing activities (see Table 16.1) with food retailers such as Carrefour and Wal-Mart in the vanguard. Retailers are also much more adventurous in that they are not only considering markets closest to them, but also operating more difficult and more distant markets. Part of the reason for this is that there are likely to be first-mover advantages for those entering relatively underdeveloped markets.

Table 16.1 Some foreign retailers trading in the UK

Firm	Retail trading name	Trading activity	Home country
Aldi	Aldi	Food discounting	Germany
Benetton	Benetton	Fashion	Italy
Blockbuster	Blockbuster	Video rental	USA
Cartier	Cartier	Jewellery	France
Costco	Costco	Warehouse club	USA
Gucci	Gucci	Leather goods	Italy
IKEA	IKEA	Furniture	Sweden
Netto	Netto	Food discounting	Denmark
Otto Versand	Grattan	Mail order	Germany
Toys R Us	Toys R Us	Toys	USA
Wal-Mart	ASDA – Wal-Mart	Supermarkets	USA
Zara	Zara	Fashion	Spain

● Explanations of Internationalization

Although the theory of retailer internationalization is still relatively underdeveloped, three major themes have emerged, namely Dunning's (1988) 'eclectic' theory of internationalization, the push–pull theory, and the strategic management theory.

The eclectic theory

Dunning's eclectic theory of internationalization was originally based on manufacturing companies, but it has been used successfully to examine retailers' motives for internationalization. The theory attempts to explain why a firm will engage in foreign direct investment, rather than exporting or other forms of international activity. According to the eclectic theory, firms internationalize due to three factors: ownership-specific advantages, internalization, and locational advantages.

Ownership advantages (Table 16.2) are transferable firm-specific advantages arising from proprietary know-how (unique assets) and transactional advantages that can be exploited for competitive advantage in the market. Transactional advantages refer to the ability of the firm to reduce costs by employing specific business systems, processes and technical know-how. Proprietary know-how can be in the form of patents, copyrights, brands and systems or process knowledge. The possession of these advantages gives their owner an advantage over competitors. Proprietary assets that are legally protected such as brands and patents are easier to exploit in foreign markets. In the case of retailers, their main proprietary asset is their brand name, but at least in the early stages of internationalization these may have very little recognition in international markets, as many retailers have found to their cost.

In retailing it is also very difficult to protect new ideas, as they are visible to competitors. However, firm-specific processes such as buying policies and strategies, information systems, customer loyalty schemes, own-branding skills and logistics are very difficult to imitate for retailers. Where these policies result in firm-specific advantages in the form of economies of scale or customer loyalty, they are even more valuable.

Location-specific advantages refer to benefits derived from locating in

Table 16.2 Examples of ownership-specific advantages of some international retailers

Ownership-specific advantages	International retailer
Mass merchandising skills	Carrefour (France), Wal-Mart (USA)
Discount format	Aldi (Germany), Makro, Metro (Germany)
Mass fashion merchandising	Hennes and Mauritz, Zara, The Gap, C&A
Category dominance	Toys R US, IKEA, Staples, Office Depot, Blockbuster
Own-brand strength	Marks and Spencer, The Gap, NEXT, Body Shop, IKEA
Proprietary brands/designer labels	Warner Bros., Disney, Levis, Gucci

foreign markets. These include lower labour costs, greater market opportunity (due to, for instance, market size or lower competition), the ability to circumvent trade barriers, and diversification of risk. Unlike manufacturing, as the retailing product cannot be imported back into the domestic market, lower labour costs in foreign markets are not a significant motive for internationalization of retailers. However, labour costs may influence the choice of markets for internationalization. Market size and growth, and diversification have been the major motives behind much of European retailing investment in the USA.

Internalization advantages refer to the relative advantages of different methods of servicing international markets. The internalization theory suggests that where the transaction cost of non-equity involvement in international markets (such as exporting, franchising or licensing) is greater than the firm undertaking the activity itself, the firm will internalize the activity. This may be due to imperfections in the market or a market may not exist. For instance, a retailer wishing to franchise its concept internationally may find that the cost of marketing, setting-up contracts and enforcing franchisee compliance may be greater than the returns. They may, therefore, set up subsidiaries in other countries rather than franchising. For most retailers exporting is not an available option, given that it is a service. However, retailers with strong own brands may find that they can export the own label. For instance, Marks and Spencer began to export its St Michael own-branded products in the late 1940s.

Push versus pull theories

Location-specific advantages in Dunning's framework clearly reflect the attractions, or the 'pull', of the host market. Similarly, there are factors in the domestic market that are likely to 'push' firms into internationalization. Factors that push, pull or facilitate internationalization have received much attention in the discussion of internationalization of retailers. Push factors include saturated domestic markets, maturity of retail format, strong competition, trading restrictions, and unfavourable economic conditions. Growth opportunities, potential scale economies, undeveloped markets and preemption of rivals are included among pull factors. Facilitating factors are identified as corporate philosophy and the vision of senior management, as well as the accumulation of in-company expertise through international buying and sourcing. External facilitating factors include lowering of trade barriers (for example the European Union, and the North American Free Trade Agreement), international alliances, compatible cultures, developments in international communications and the bandwagon effect. Simplistic discussions of push-pull factors usually do not distinguish between environmental (external) factors and organizational factors internal to the firm. Much of the research in this area tends to show that push factors are probably likely to play a more significant part in the initial stages of internationalization (see for instance Kacker, 1985; and Salmon and Tordjman, 1989).

Strategic management approach to internationalization

A strategic management perspective of internationalization suggests that it is just one of a number of growth strategies that a firm can undertake. Knee and

Retailing product package

Market segments/customer base	**Existing**	**Related**	**New**
Existing	*Market penetration*	*Product/range extension*, e.g. specialization, new customer services, new outlet types	*Product/ range development* (unrelated product range
Related	Market development (territorial expansion in domestic market)	Market extension, e.g. repositioning	
New	*Internationalization* using current format	*Internationalization* using new/adapted format	*Diversification*

Figure 16.1 Corporate strategy and internationalization

Source: Based on Knee and Walters (1985), p.12.

Walters (1985), for instance, extended Ansoff's product–market growth matrix (1965) and incorporated internationalization as a geographical expansion of the existing retail product into new markets, (Figure 16.1). International expansion is riskier than domestic geographical expansion, hence domestic opportunities are more likely to be pursued first.

Internationalization strategies may also be pursued where product development strategies are either expensive (in comparison to internationalization) or not feasible without making a major change to the trading format. For instance, whereas large supermarkets (such as Tesco) have responded to limited growth opportunities in the food market by expanding their ranges to include non-food merchandise, this is not a strategy that can be adopted by limited-line discount food retailers such as Aldi. Major expansion of product ranges into non-food is not feasible for such stores because space constraints as well as the inevitable rise in costs would undermine the competitive advantage of the discount format. Hence, saturation of domestic markets led Aldi to embark on a strategy of internationalization.

An advantage of using the strategic management approach to internationalization is that it suggests management can be proactive and not wait for competitive pressures in the domestic market to arise before considering internationalization. For instance, innovative formats such as the Body Shop internationalized very early in their development because international opportunities were available to be exploited, long before the saturation of the domestic market.

● Market Selection and Growth Stages of Internationalization

Examination of retailer internationalization over time shows that there are a number of recognizable patterns. Firstly, in the initial stages retailers are cautious and enter markets that are geographically and culturally 'close', and similar to the home market. In Europe, evidence of this is seen in the move of the French hypermarkets into Spain (for example Carrefour), Swedish retailers into other Scandinavian countries (for example IKEA), and Dutch retailers into Belgium. Similarly, American retailers have tended to enter the Canadian and Mexican markets before seeking markets further afield. Perceived cultural similarity is one of the major reasons for the large investment by UK retailers in the USA rather than in European countries, which are regarded as more distant culturally. Having acquired some experience of international operations, retailers tend to become more ambitious, and at this stage the growth opportunities are more important than geographical and cultural proximity. Retailers also begin to employ more than one strategy to enter markets. Marks and Spencer, for example, has used franchising, joint ventures, acquisition and organic growth to enter different international markets over time, with varying degrees of success.

● International Opportunities

The increasing regionalism, or the tendency toward economic cooperation between countries within regions, particularly in the form of free-trade areas, is increasing internationalization opportunities for retailers. A free-trade area is an area whose member countries agree to have free movement of goods among themselves, without the imposition of tariffs or quotas. Two of the largest and most successful examples are the European Union (EU) and the North American Free Trade Agreement (NAFTA). NAFTA came into effect in 1993 and provides for the gradual removal of tariffs and quotas over a 15-year period creating a market of 390 million people. As a result there has been a great deal of investment by US retailers in Mexico and Canada.

In Europe, the completion of the single European market (SEM) and with it the transformation of the European Community into the European Union in 1993 has made the movement of goods much easier, resulting in a big increase in cross-border retailing within European Union countries. With the relaxation of border and other trade controls, the 15 European Union countries now constitute a bigger market than the USA, with a population of over 350 million people. In the 1970s and 1980s much of the international retailing investment in Europe was in the more advanced retailing countries such as France, Germany and the UK, but more recently there has been more investment in Southern European countries such as Spain and Portugal. From mid-1990 onwards there has also been increasing retailing investment in Central European countries, particularly the Czech Republic, Hungary and Poland, and more recently, European retailers have been considering markets further afield towards the Asia Pacific region.

Much of the retail investment in Central and Eastern Europe and the Asia Pacific region is motivated by the fact that these countries are relatively underdeveloped in retailing terms and are experiencing high economic growth. Retailers' investment in these countries (such as Tesco and Carrefour) is hoping to benefit from first-mover advantages. The enlargement of the EU from 15 to more than 20 members will create a market of 500 million people, which is likely to provide further impetus to internationalization into Eastern European countries. The development of the European Monetary Union is also likely to increase internationalization.

International opportunities inevitably come with risks, and retailers must therefore carefully analyse both the opportunities and risks before making entry decisions. This is a difficult task, but one helpful scheme is provided by Coopers and Lybrand (1995) who, taking into account the size of the markets and risks involved, identified the 17 largest retail target markets and classified those countries into four bands:

● The 'Saturated 7' (United States, Canada, United Kingdom, the Netherlands, France, Germany and Spain). Characterized by intense competition in virtually all sectors of retailing with high levels of concentration, these countries are relatively easy to enter but intense competition makes it difficult to succeed.
● The 'Tough 3' (Italy, South Korea and Japan). These are economies with large middle classes but local government regulations have restricted retailing and makes entry for foreign retailers difficult.
● The 'Torrid 3' (Mexico, Turkey and Argentina). These countries are experiencing rapid, if volatile growth of their underdeveloped retail sectors, but this is moderated by a high degree of economic risk.
● The 'Formidable 4' (Brazil, China, Russia and India). These offer the most exciting opportunities with rapidly growing middle classes that are yearning for consumer goods; however, these countries have poor retail infrastructure and carry the greatest political and economic risks.

● Entry Strategies

When moving into foreign markets, retailers have to decide the best method of entry. The main methods of expansion for retailers are shown in Figure 16.2 and discussed below.

● *Self-start entry/greenfield entry/organic growth.* This involves building up a foreign retail presence from scratch. It is the method that is most likely to be used where a retailer has an innovative format and wants to retain the maximum control over the venture. Organic growth also provides the retailer with control over the rate of growth and hence capital outlay. Examples include C&A and Laura Ashley.
● *Acquisition.* Acquiring foreign retailers provides a quick method of entry but requires the most capital. Acquisition may be necessary in mature, concentrated markets where operations of a certain size are required in order to be competitive. Examples of acquisitions include Wal-Mart's takeover of ASDA in the UK (1999) and Wertkauf in Germany, and Marks & Spencer's acquisition of Kings Supermarkets and Brooks

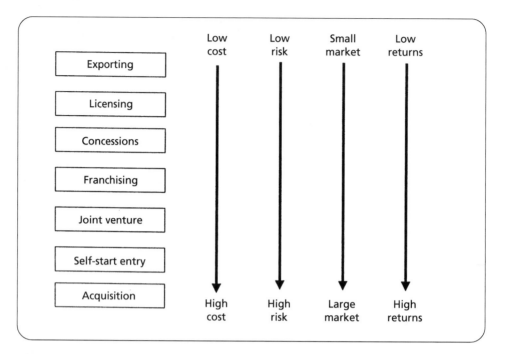

Figure 16.2 Entry methods for international retailing

Brothers in the USA. Suitable acquisitions are not always available (especially in developing markets) and so retailers may have to consider alternative entry strategies.

● *Franchising.* Franchising is a quick method of international expansion where the retailer is constrained by availability of capital. Franchising allows the retailer to maintain a high degree of control over the marketing strategy, including what is sold within the store, whilst relinquishing control over day-to-day operations of the store. Benetton and the Body Shop provide examples of retailers expanding internationally via franchising.

● *Joint ventures.* These involve a retailer entering into a joint agreement with a foreign firm where both organizations share the costs and profits of the venture. Joint ventures work best where the partners bring complementary skills to the venture; however, failure of joint ventures due to disagreement over operational matters is very common. In some markets this is the only method available for entering markets. In other markets, such as Japan, markets may be so complex and expensive to enter that a joint venture is the best method of entry, as the partner can provide local market knowledge and share the risk of the venture. Boots plc used this method when entering Japan in 1999. NEXT and the Limited have also used joint ventures to break into overseas markets.

● *Minority ownership.* As an example, Sainsbury's acquired a minority ownership before acquiring Shaws outright. This gave an opportunity to gain experience of the US market and understand the potential of the business and the quality of Shaws management without going to the expense and risk of a full acquisition.

- *Concessions.* This involves operating a 'shop within a shop' in larger stores such as a department store, and many specialist retailers follow this strategy. Cartier, for instance, distributes its products in Japan mainly through boutiques in Japanese department stores. There are two types of concessions, namely piggybacking, and concessions with host-country retailers. Piggybacking occurs where a retailer takes out a concession in a foreign store of an international retailer. Kaikati (1993) provides an interesting example of how Shop America (a US catalogue retailer) used 7-Eleven in Japan to distribute its catalogues to potential Japanese consumers and take orders from them through the established 7-Eleven's network of stores.

- *Licensing.* Licensing gives a firm in the foreign market the right to use the retailer's name, marketing or other technical knowledge for a fee. This is a relatively cheap and quick method of entering a foreign market; however, the expected returns are lower and the licensee has the potential to become a future competitor. This method of entry is used relatively rarely in retailing.

- *Exporting.* On account of the nature of retailing, namely that of providing a service, it was not possible until the advent of the internet to export retailing. However, retailers with strong own labels were able to export them where demand existed. Marks and Spencer's initial venture into international retailing, for example, started with exporting their own branded products. More recently, Boots, the leading UK health and beauty retailer, withdrew from the Dutch market, selling its stores to the Dutch drug chain Etos, which is part of Royal Ahold, the country's largest retail group. As part of the deal, however, Etos has undertaken to sell Boots' brands at its 412 stores in Holland.

A precursor to setting up foreign retail operations may involve the setting up of buying offices abroad, a method particularly popular with Japanese retailers. The development of internet retailing also suggests that it could be used to assess the degree of interest in a particular market before entering it.

Factors Determining Choice of Entry Methods

The actual method of entry into an international market will depend on a number of factors including cost, control, uniqueness of the format, availability of good locations, financial strength of the firm, size and competitiveness of foreign markets, and political and economic risk associated with a particular country. For instance, larger formats (such as department stores) tend to be difficult to internationalize using licensing or franchising strategies due to their complexity and the initial capital outlay. Conversely, it is common to find that specialty stores often use franchising in their strategies. For innovative formats, acquisition is not an option as such retailers are by definition different to existing businesses.

The size of the market is an important determinant of the entry strategy.

Generally speaking, foreign direct investment (FDI) strategies like acquisition and self-start ventures are only likely to be used in larger markets. Smaller markets are most likely to be serviced using a non-FDI strategy ranging from a concession (store-within- a store) to franchising. The competitive market conditions also have an important influence on entry strategies. For instance, Wal-Mart chose to enter the UK grocery market via the acquisition of ASDA; a major reason behind this strategy was the fact that the grocery market in

Vignette 16.1

Marks and Spencer and international entry strategies

Marks and Spencer (M&S) began international retailing activities in the 1940s by exporting its St Michael own brand, which by 1996 amounted to around £116 million. Acquisition as an entry method was first used by M&S in 1973 when it entered the Canadian market with an acquisition of People's Department Stores Inc. (a budget-priced store), D'Allaird's (clothing for older women) and Walker's clothing stores (which were later transformed into Marks and Spencer stores). Further acquisitions took place in April 1988 when M&S acquired the American clothing retailer Brookes Brothers for $750 million, and Kings Supermarkets. In 1975 M&S opened its first owned and operated European store in Paris. This was followed in the same year by a store in Brussels. Company-owned stores were also opened in Germany (1996), Hong Kong (1988), Ireland (1979), Spain (1990) and the Netherlands (1991). M&S began a major push into franchising around 1988. Since then the franchise operation has expanded enormously and the company now operates 130 franchised stores in 26 counties including the Bahamas, Czech Republic, Dubai, Finland, Greece, Hungary, India, Indonesia, Kuwait, Malaysia, Netherlands, Portugal, South Korea, Thailand and Turkey. The estimated sales turnover of the franchise business amounted to over £350 million in 2002. M&S experimented with joint ventures as an entry method when it opened its first store in Spain in 1990 in a joint venture with Cortefiel, a leading Spanish retail chain. M&S eventually bought out Cortefiel in 1999.

After a major review of its activities (necessitated by its stagnating sales and sharply declining profits in its core domestic market since 1998), on 29 March 2001 M&S announced that it was selling off its US subsidiaries and its European stores, and converting its Hong Kong stores into a franchise business. Although the US businesses were trading well, the company felt that they did not constitute a sound basis for developing M&S in the USA and the losses incurred in Europe could no longer be afforded. M&S had already divested its loss-making Canadian operation in 1999. Luc Vandevelde, Chairman and CEO of M&S, further added in the 2001 *Annual Report* that M&S's experience illustrates that 'to succeed internationally when entering mature markets, you must adapt your store formats to the competitive realities of those markets'. This hints at M&S's adoption of a largely standardized approach to international markets and failure to adapt its strategies to local needs. In contrast, the success of its franchise businesses demonstrates the value of local market knowledge of franchisees in adapting the M&S approach and products to local market needs.

Sources: Various, including Sternquist (1998); Burt *et al.* (2002): and Marks and Spencer *Annual Reports* (2001, 2002).

the UK is highly competitive with the top five food retailers controlling a market share in excess of 70 per cent. A self-start entry by Wal-Mart would have been ineffective as suitable large-scale sites are difficult to obtain due to the tight planning regulations in the UK, and would have been uncompetitive against the well-established networks of domestic retailers. As the world's largest retailer, Wal-Mart also had the capital to make such an acquisition, which also suited their aggressive international growth strategy.

In some countries, domestic legislation controls the types of entry methods employed by retailers. For instance, in the People's Republic of China, foreign investors are required to have local partners to set up businesses in the country. In other markets, whilst there are no legal impediments the business environment may be so complex that working with a local partner is essential for the success of a retail venture. This is the recommended strategy for entering the Japanese market, as followed for example by, Boots in 1999 following a joint venture agreement with Mitsubishi Corporation. Other markets may be too politically or economically unstable to consider large investments, and so franchising or joint ventures may be more appropriate.

⬤ Standardization versus Adaptation Strategies

When entering international markets, retailers have to decide whether to use their existing retail format or adapt it to the needs of the foreign market being entered.

The marketing concept holds that firms should be customer-oriented and that marketing efforts will be more effective if they are closely adapted to the needs of each group (or segment) of target customers. In the international retailing context this means that because of the varying economic, geographic, demographic and cultural factors, and characteristics of consumers in different countries, they are likely to have different wants and needs, spending power, shopping patterns and product preferences and so an adapted retail marketing strategy is likely to be the best option. Although the advantage of such a strategy is that the retailing offer is more suited to the needs of consumers in the host country, the required changes in the retail mix may prove to be too expensive financially and in terms of management time and effort.

Standardization involves using the same range of products, the same pricing, promotional and location strategies. Its major advantages include economies of scale in buying and economies of replication in store design and advertising. The rationale behind standardization is that similar products are wanted across all the markets that the retailer operates in. Examples of retailers using a standardization strategy include Toys R Us and Body Shop.

There are also other forces that make standardization an attractive and feasible alternative. Changes in communications, transportation and worldwide travel have led to the emergence of a global marketplace, and these same changes, it is argued, are leading to the homogenization of customer needs and wants and hence global markets. Theodore Levitt, one of the foremost proponents of the standardization argument, argues that despite what customers say, what they really want is good quality products at lower prices:

> If the price is low enough, they will take highly standardized world products, even if they aren't exactly what mother said was suitable, what immemorial custom decreed was right, or what market research . . . asserted was preferred. (Levitt, 1983)

Standardization proponents argue that the use of a common marketing programme on a global basis (the use of a common product, price, promotion and distribution programme worldwide) is the most effective method of marketing internationally in today's marketplace.

These arguments are based on the premise that there is a convergence of tastes and a convergence of income levels (at least in industrialized countries), which means that global markets exist for most goods and services and hence the advantages to be gained by adaptation are either small or non-existent. Similarly, the potential for cost savings in standardization are enormous. For retailers the major advantages of using a standardized format include economies of scale in buying, larger own-label production runs, replication of store design, and marketing. Standardization also allows the projection of a consistent international image, which is important as consumers become more and more internationally mobile. Other advantages include simpler marketing planning and control.

Whilst the arguments for standardization are strong, it is extremely difficult to standardize the entire retail marketing programme. Standardization is in general more difficult for culturally-sensitive items such as food and clothing (except for haute couture). Luxury and high-fashion items are easier to standardize because they are wanted for the unique values that they represent. Consumers of these products are also likely to be affluent, well-educated and with a cosmopolitan outlook, and therefore represent a more or less homogeneous global segment.

It is also difficult to maintain equality in pricing across international operations since cost structures in different markets are quite different. The two major elements of costs for retailers are those associated with operating outlets, and distribution (logistical) costs, all of which vary considerably due to differences in labour and property markets and distributional infrastructures. In addition, the imposition of tariffs on imported merchandise, and different levels of competition, add to the difficulties. However, what retailers can do is attempt to achieve a similar positioning to their domestic market. For instance, a discounter such as Aldi will attempt to be at least 20–30 per cent cheaper than supermarkets in the countries that it operates in.

Promotional strategies may be difficult to standardize due to different regulations on advertising and sales promotion, availability of media and differences in communication styles. Location is also difficult to standardize since suitable sites may already be occupied or not available due to planning regulations. For instance, Toys Я Us normally locates its stores in out-of-town locations, but in France it has located them in shopping centres because planning permission was difficult to obtain in out-of-town locations.

The standardization versus adaptation argument is not an 'all-or-nothing' decision. The degree of standardization can vary from global standardization to adaptation for each market, and standardization in key markets to adaptation in key markets. A compromise between adaptation and standardization is a patterned standardization strategy that involves developing global marketing strategies whilst allowing for a degree of adaptation to take account of local market conditions. 'Think global and act local' is the idea behind patterned standardization. Thus, standardization is more a matter of degree rather than an absolute decision. Retailers should always be on the lookout for opportunities to standardize elements of the retail marketing mix, but understand that adaptation may be preferable depending on the operating conditions of the market.

Problems for Newcomers

Newcomers to international retailing face a number of common problems. Firstly, they will tend to underestimate cultural differences and their effect on trading internationally. Culture results not only in differences in customer needs but also impacts on styles of management and general business dealings with suppliers. For instance, French junior managers are more likely to question decisions of their superiors than their British counterparts.

Lack of supplier and distribution networks is another major problem. This may mean that the retailer has to import everything, thus increasing costs and impacting on efficiency. For instance, when Carrefour entered the US market in 1988 it had no distribution network and ended up using part of the store for storage purposes. This resulted in less space for its merchandise assortment and increased operational costs.

Most retail brands have little international carry-over. Even where customers recognize the retail fascia, they may not have a good understanding of the brand values. This means that new entrants need to put in a great deal of promotional effort to get their store noticed and to entice customers into the outlet. In effect, it may be necessary to rebuild the retail brand from scratch in the foreign market. This can also be seen as an opportunity to customize the brand more to the needs of the local market.

Another common problem is to underestimate the strength of local competition or local reaction to market entry of foreign competition. For instance, in the early 1990s when Aldi and a number of other continental food discounters entered the UK market, the large supermarket chains launched 'value' ranges of their own-brands to compete with the low prices offered by the discounters. This had the effect of slowing down the expansion and restricting the market share that the discounters were able to achieve. Underestimating the fierceness of competition is one of the major reasons for the failure of numerous European retailers entering the USA market.

Integrating the various parts of the international business, and integrating the domestic business with international business, is another major area of difficulty for the international retailer; having domestic and international operations substantially increases the complexity of the management task. Integration is also made more difficult where foreign acquisitions have to be integrated into the structure of the existing business; problems arise due to differences in management cultures and styles.

The difficulties mentioned can be overcome, and indeed there are many success stories from which a number of success factors can be identified. Successful international retailers are likely to have distinctive skills or assets which they can leverage in international markets. These skills may be in the form of mass merchandising skills, buying or own-brand development skills or a strong or innovative retail concept that is relevant to the needs of the target market (for example IKEA). Success also requires exploitation of global scale and global sourcing to maximize supply-chain efficiencies and create value for the customer. Successful retailers also use local management to ensure that local customer needs are being met whilst ensuring that local management understands the brand values and business practices of the international retailer. Invariably, success in the international market requires long-term commitment.

Vignette 16.2

The globalization of C&A

C&A is an international fashion retailer with operations in 12 European countries with over 550 stores and an estimated turnover of 5 billion euros in 1999. C&A was founded in Sneek, Holland, in 1841 by the brothers Clemens and August Brenninkmeyer. Its first steps in internationalization began with opening of stores in Germany in 1911 and the UK in 1922. A second wave of internationalization began in 1963 with entry into Belgium. Until about 1993, all the countries operated relatively autonomously, but with the increasing integration of the European Union countries C&A saw the opportunity of becoming a single unified European retailing company. It therefore began a programme of activities called Evolution 2000, the purpose of which was to create a dynamic and integrated company that traded across all viable EU countries. The change was motivated by the high potential benefits that could be obtained by the use of C&A's potential buying power, the reduction in costs and a belief that a more coherent approach would increase sales. The new approach would lead to economies of scale in design and administration and increase influence with suppliers. C&A would also be able to gain maximum discounts, reduce costs of manufacturing garments and packaging. Further cost savings were made by reducing the number of buying centres from eight to two (Brussels and Dusseldorf), which also had the added benefit of giving C&A buyers a unified voice. The consolidation of its buying power was also designed to give C&A more clout with its Far Eastern suppliers to compete with US giants for manufacturing space, price, delivery, and moving stock at short notice. This would enable C&A to provide a better product at a better price leading to increased consumer satisfaction.

However, one of the consequences of centralising fashion buying in Dusseldorf and Brussels was that buyers lost touch with street trends in the UK, leading to a sharp decline in sales. The change to central buying came at a time when C&A faced increased competition from fashionable new rivals such as Gap and Zara, and discount chains like Matalan and Primark that sell branded goods at low prices. C&A could not match them either with its 'exclusive own brands' or the low prices. Recently, C&A backtracked and allowed buying specifically for the British market. However, this change came too late to save C&A as on 16 June 2000 it announced the closure, by the end of the year, of its 109 stores in the UK and Ireland, with the loss of 4,800 jobs. The decision had been taken after suffering losses amounting to £250m over the previous five years.

Summary

Compared with manufacturers, retailers have been relatively slow to internationalize in the past. However, with increasing globalization of markets and the development of new communication media, internationalization is likely to be a major trend in the next decade. In most highly developed economies, limited opportunities exist for retailers in domestic markets due to high levels of competition, mature markets and restrictive trading conditions, which are the major drivers of retailers' decisions to internationalize.

Retailers need to carefully analyse both the opportunities and risks before making decisions on which markets to enter. In the initial stages, retailers are cautious and enter markets that are geographically and culturally 'close', and similar to the home market. Over time, retailers tend to become more ambitious and seek opportunities further afield, and at this stage the growth opportunities are more important than geographical and cultural proximity.

Retailers have a number of choices when entering markets ranging from self-start entry, acquisitions, joint ventures, franchising, concessions, licensing and even exporting. The actual method will depend on a number of factors including cost versus control, uniqueness of the format, availability of good locations, financial strength of the firm, market size and competitive conditions in foreign markets, and the political and economic risk associated with a particular country. More experienced retailers may employ more than one strategy to enter markets.

A critical decision when entering international markets is whether to retain the existing retail format and marketing approach (standardization strategy), or whether to adapt the retail format to the needs of the foreign market being entered (adaptation strategy). However, this is not an all-or-nothing decision; retailers should always be looking for opportunities to standardize elements of their offer but understand that adaptation may be preferable depending on the operating conditions of the market.

Internationalization is not an easy task, and numerous retailers have failed and been forced to withdraw from international markets. Some of the major reasons for failure include underestimating cultural differences, lack of supplier and distribution networks, overestimating the strength of their retail brands, underestimating the strength of local competition, and lack of integration between the international business and the domestic business. Despite this, retailers are likely to show more commitment in the future to international markets, which is a prerequisite for success.

Questions

1 Explain what is meant by 'ownership-specific' advantages.
2 What is meant by 'internalization'?
3 Distinguish between push and pull motives behind internationalization of retailers.
4 The USA is popular destination for UK retailers; discuss the factors that may motivate UK retailers to enter the American market.
5 Compare and contrast the relative advantages and disadvantages of franchising and acquisition as methods of entry into foreign markets for retailers.
6 What are the benefits of a globalization/standardization strategy for C&A? What are the disadvantages of such an approach?
7 Discuss the factors that lead to failure of many international retailing ventures.

References and Further Reading

Akehurst, G. and Alexander, N. (1996) *The Internationalisation of Retailing* (London: Frank Cass).

Alexander, N. (1997) *International Retailing* (Oxford: Blackwell Business).

Ansoff, I., (1965) *Corporate Strategy* (London: McGraw-Hill).

Bartram, P. (1999) 'Saving St Michael', *Director*, February, pp. 34–7.

Burt, S.L., Mellahi, K., Jackson, P. and Sparks, L. (2002) 'Retail Internationalisation and Retail Failure: Issues from the Case of Marks and Spencer', *International Review of Retail, Distribution and Consumer Research*, vol. 12(2), pp. 191–219.

Coopers & Lybrand (1995) 'Global Powers of Retailing', *Chain Store Age Executive with Shopping Center Age*, vol. 71 no. 12, special issue, pp. S1–37.

Corporate Intelligence Group (1994) *US Retailers in Europe – The New Wave* (London: The Corporate Intelligence Group).

Dunning, J.H. (1988) 'The Eclectic Paradigm of International Production: a restatement and some possible extensions', *Journal of International Business Studies*, vol. 19, no. 1, pp. 1–31.

Kacker, M. (1985), *Transatlantic Trends in Retailing* (London: Quorum).

Kaikati, J.G. (1993) 'Don't Crack the Japanese Distribution System – Just Circumvent It', *Columbia Journal of World Business*, vol. 28, no. 2 (Summer), pp. 34–45.

Knee, D. and Walters, D. (1985) *Strategy in Retailing, Theory and Application* (Oxford: Philip Allan).

Levitt, T. (1983) 'The Globalisation of Markets', *Harvard Business Review*, vol. 6, no. 3, pp. 92–103.

McGoldrick, P.J. and Davies, G. (eds) (1995) *International Retailing*: *Trends and Strategies* (London: Pitman).

Salmon, W.J. and Tordjman, A. (1989) 'The Internationalization of Retailing', *International Journal of Retailing*, vol. 4, no. 2, pp. 2–16.

Sternquist, B. (1998) *International Retailing* (New York: Fairchild Publications).

Treadgold, A.D. (1988) 'Retailing Without Frontiers', *International Journal of Retail and Distribution Management*, vol. 16, no. 6, pp. 8–12.

chapter seventeen

Internet Retailing

Learning objectives

- To appreciate how the internet has enabled the emergence of the new retail format of the electronic retailer.
- To explore the use of the internet as a new retail channel by existing store-based retailers.
- To understand what is meant by disintermediation (or the bypassing of retailers by manufacturers using the internet), and its implications for retailers and manufacturers.
- To assess the impact of the internet on shoppers' behaviour.
- To identify the key success factors in electronic retailing.

Introduction

In a relatively short space of time, internet retailing (or more generally electronic retailing) has firmly established itself as a viable alternative to store-based shopping. For instance, one of the earliest and best-known internet retailers, Amazon.com, was launched only in 1995. Estimates for electronic retailing vary considerably. In the USA where e-retailing has progressed furthest, it is estimated that internet retail sales in 2003 will be around 5.0 per cent ($108 billion) of total estimated retail sales excluding cars (Rosen and Howard, 2000). The UK is not expected to achieve similar levels of penetration (in percentage terms) until 2010. Whilst this may not sound a great deal, a loss of 10–15 per cent of sales can make store-based retailers unprofitable (De Kare-Silver, 1998). All the indications are that this pace of development is likely to continue and will have a significant impact on store-based retailing. Store-based retailers have been slow to react to these developments, although they are now tending to catch up by adopting the so-called 'clicks and mortar' strategy, to complement their physical stores with internet retailing.

285

Electronic retailing is the sale of consumer goods and services via an interactive electronic communications network. Electronic retailing is variously referred to as internet retailing, e-retailing or e-tailing, virtual retailing and cyber retailing. Until recently, the only generally available mass electronic communications network was the internet accessed via a personal computer. However, nowadays a number of alternatives are available including digital television and web-enabled (WAP) mobile telephones. The internet is revolutionizing retailing in many fundamental ways, altering the relationships between manufacturers and retailers and retailers and shoppers. This chapter concentrates on issues relating to how the internet is enabling new types of electronic retailers (or e-retailers) to emerge, the response of existing retailers to the internet, the response of manufacturers to the internet, the internet as a new marketing medium, and the response of customers to shopping on the internet.

● Virtual Stores as a New Retail Format

Perhaps the most significant consequence of the internet for retailing has been the emergence of a new retailing format of virtual retailers/cyber retailers/ e-tailers (terms used interchangeably). One of the earliest and best-known examples is Amazon.com. The distinguishing feature of these retailers is that they sell their products via the internet and do not have physical stores. They are thus independent of specific locations. Furthermore, unlike store-based retailers, virtual retailers do not carry any physical inventory; the internet acts as an order-placing and transacting mechanism, and once the transaction is complete the product is delivered directly to the customer circumventing the need for customers to visit a store.

The operating costs of internet retailers are, therefore, much lower. According to one estimate, buying and maintaining a website costs a maximum of £50,000 a year, less than 5 per cent of the £1.25 million required to run a typical medium-sized retail outlet. According to another estimate, in traditional retailing the average transaction cost is approximately $15 per transaction, compared with telephone sales costing approximately $5, and the internet cost being around $0.20–0.50 (Philipps *et al.*, 1997). This means that margins on the internet are about three times the 6 per cent enjoyed by the average store (Pavitt, 1997). The costs of delivery are generally passed on to the customer, thus pushing up profits even further. Additional benefits are also realized in the form of customer information, complementary product and service offerings, ease of test marketing, and international and new-market exposure.

Internet retailers also have advantages over catalogue retailers – the cost of running a website is a fraction of the cost of producing and distributing catalogues, and information on the website can be updated immediately. Also, unlike the physical catalogue, there is no real upper limit to the size of the virtual catalogue or the number of products represented. The assortment, therefore, is not limited by size of the store or the physical size of the catalogue, and hence an internet book retailer such as Amazon.com can offer 2–3 million books on its website compared with a fraction of that number carried by even the largest bookshop.

For time-pressured shoppers, the internet provides the ultimate in convenience in that orders can be placed at any time of the day and not just when the shop is open. It also means that shoppers do not have to spend time and effort to visit the store, and avoids queuing, the most hated part of shopping for the majority of shoppers. The downside for consumers is that they cannot physically handle the products and they miss out on the social aspects of shopping. Also, consumers have to wait for the product to be delivered.

Some prices on the internet can be between 5 to 10 per cent higher than on the high street principally because of delivery charges, and consumers often have to buy in bulk to offset the costs of delivery (Pavitt, 1997). Product demand and competition can alter this, for example popular books and CDs in general tend to be cheaper on the internet than the high street. However, the interactive nature of the internet has spawned a number of internet retailers offering alternatives to fixed pricing that is the normal practice in retailing. Priceline.com (http://www.priceline.com), for instance, allows consumers to propose prices for new cars, airline tickets and hotel rooms, whilst auction sites such as eBay (http://www.ebay.com) provide an appealing format for bargain-seeking customers.

⬤ Types of Merchandise Sold via the Internet

There are few products that cannot be bought via the Internet these days. However the sectors that have shown the strongest growth and make up the vast majority of Internet sales include:

- Computer hardware and software.
- Books, CDs and videos.
- Gifts.
- Travel.

Three major factors in the success of internet retailing are product/merchandise characteristics, retailing economics and trust in the retailer, and consumer attitudes to purchasing on the internet. Products that are likely to do well are standard, convenience, low-involvement, repeat, single, gift purchases. Hence, books, music, videos and gift items fit well into this category. Differentiated, high-involvement, new task, jointly purchased, self-consumption items on the other hand are more difficult to sell on the internet. Fashion is a good example of this latter category as shoppers wish to ensure that they buy just the right type of clothes and will want to try them on to make sure that they fit properly. High-convenience, perishable, immediate consumption products are also less likely to be purchased via the internet because of the inherent delay in delivery.

An important aspect of internet retailing is that of consumer trust. For store-based retailers, trust is built up over time and embedded in the retail brand, whereas internet retailers have to establish their brand identity and image from scratch. This is a major expense for most internet start-ups, and establishing credible brands is not an easy task. Also, retailers require an

Vignette 17.1

Amazon.com: internet retailing pioneer

Launched in the USA in July 1995, Amazon.com quickly became one of the fastest growing internet retailers. Through its aggressive promotions, it has now become a major internet retailer of CDs, videos, DVDs, toys and games and electronics as well as the books with which it originally started. One of Amazon's key strengths is its easy to use interface incorporating a full search engine, however users can also build a customer profile facility in order for Amazon to market its wares more directly. The site also features book reviews, interviews with authors and other similar services to facilitate product selection. In all these areas Amazon aims to provide the biggest selection of merchandise available. For instance on its US site it offers around 3 million books. Amazon has taken this philosophy into other areas and now styles itself as 'Earth's biggest' store.

Amazon.co.uk was launched in 1998, and in order to improve the efficiency of delivery, two distribution units were opened in Bedfordshire during 1999. Amazon has also built up dedicated businesses in France, Spain and Germany. Whilst Amazon could service the demand in those countries from its existing distribution network, the orders would take five to seven days to arrive rather than the following day from the local warehouses. Amazon feels that this is important for maintaining its reputation for service and it is also able to provide a more customized offering to its customers in those countries. Around 25 per cent of its sales now come from its international activities which Amazon is looking to increase even further.

Much of the company's growth has been fuelled by substantial discounting, with many titles at 40 per cent discount. From the beginning Amazon has marketed itself aggressively and its marketing spend has consistently averaged around 25 per cent of its net sales in order to build market share. Amazon has also begun to diversify its activities and is involved in web-hosting (zShops), and has recently acquired established online retailers drugstore.com (health and beauty), Ashford.com (luxury and premium products), and eZiba.com (handcrafted products). It also has a joint venture with Toys R Us and is looking to develop them with other bricks-and-mortar stores. As a result, Amazon achieved sales of around $2.8 billion in 2000, which are forecast to be around $3.4 billion in 2001. During the period 1995–2000, Amazon has not been profitable and its losses have amounted to around $2 billion. This investment has been necessary to finance the high spend on advertising and promotion to build up the Amazon brand, the e-commerce and the physical infrastructure in order to achieve market leadership in its chosen areas. Jeff Bezos, Amazon's originator and current CEO, estimates that Amazon will achieve profitability by the end of 2001. However, in January 2001, Amazon declared that it would lay off up to 1,300 (15 per cent) of its staff and close down one of its 12 distribution centres. January 2002 marked a turning point, however, as Amazon reported not just an operating profit of $59 million, but also a net profit of $5 million in the fourth quarter. Since then it has reported a profit for the whole of 2002.

Sources: Robert D. Hof (2001), 'Amazon's Go-Go Growth? Gone', *Business Week*, 12 Feb. 2001, p. 39; Margaret McKegney, 2000, 'Amazon Blazes Trail in Europe', *Advertising Age*, 18 Sept. 2000, p. 78; Mike Troy (2000), ' "Earth's biggest" e-tailer inching from red to black', *Dsn Retailing Today*, 20 Nov. 2000, pp. 19–22; Anonymous (2001), 'Special Article: Internet Pioneers: We Have Lift Off', *The Economist*, 3 Feb. 2001, pp. 69–72.

economically viable trading model. For instance, in the grocery market one of the biggest costs is that of putting a customer's order together. This is a labour-intensive process and has prevented many would-be internet retailers from entering this market. In addition, special refrigerated transport is required because of the perishable nature of some of the merchandise. This is in addition to the cost of the delivery and ensuring that the customer is at home when the order is delivered. Another major cost for non-store-based retailers is the high rate of returns. Return rates can be as high as 30 to 40 per cent, which internet retailers need to build into their cost structures.

Some consumers are more prone to purchasing on the internet than others. Time-pressured consumers are more likely to use it than those with less-busy lifestyles; whilst consumers who like the social experience of interacting with other shoppers and retail staff and who enjoy store atmospherics are less likely to use the internet.

The Internet as a New Channel

For store-based retailers the key questions concerning the internet are whether or not to use it and how to use it. UK retailers were initially rather slow to adopt the internet; less than half of the top-100 retailers in 1998 had a website and only 14 had transaction-based websites compared with 43 of the top 100-US retailers (Weatherall Green and Smith, 1999; Doherty, Ellis-Chadwick and Hart, 1999). The majority of the sites were public-relations sites. By the end of 2000, however, 91 out of the top-100 UK retailers had websites and just under half (42) of them were transactional. However, this is changing as retailers get to grips with the technology and work out how to integrate internet-based retailing into their existing strategies. For instance, Body Shop currently only has a web-based information site except in the USA where it has an online gift boutique providing a limited selection of its products. Retailers have adopted this slower approach in the knowledge that an ill-considered transaction-based internet retailing venture could backfire and damage the retail brand if the strategy fails.

The arrival of the internet means that traditional retailers have to decide how to use it; They cannot afford to ignore it, and so the main options include:

- Provide an information-only site.
- Develop a transaction site.
- Integrate online business with existing store.
- Treat electronic retailing as a new channel.
- Treat electronic retailing as new and separate business.

Information only sites versus transactional sites

The first decision that an existing retailer has to make is whether its involvement with the internet is going to be limited to an information-only site or whether it is going to allow customers to purchase via the internet. As a minimum, existing retailers need to register their names as domain names to protect their brands and to keep their future options open. A full transaction site may not be appropriate because it does not fit well with existing operations or with the needs of target customers. For instance food discounters such as Aldi would find it difficult to maintain their low cost base with the additional costs of maintaining a transactional internet site and a new delivery system. Also, Aldi's value-conscious customers are less likely to be able or willing to pay the additional cost of delivery. At the same time, given that they are from less-affluent backgrounds, they are less likely to have access to the internet. Hence, predictably, Aldi's UK website (http://www.aldi-stores.co.uk) is an information-only website providing information on the company's operations in the UK, store locations, new and special offers, employment opportunities, and a property section. Another retailer that has an information-only site is IKEA (http://www.ikea.co.uk). An interesting aspect of this site is that it allows customers to check if an item is in stock before they set off to the store. This type of site functions essentially as a source of information about the company and its products and as a public-relations tool designed to create awareness and to support the retail brand.

Whilst retailers such as Aldi and IKEA may have no intention of turning their information sites into transaction sites, other retailers such as B&Q, as the DIY retailer, have transformed their information sites into transaction sites. Transaction sites are a two-way communication system allowing customers to place orders and retailers to contact customers. Building transaction sites requires far greater commitment from the retailer to the internet. In addition to the cost of building and maintaining the site, delivery systems and secure online credit payment systems have to be put in place.

At first, most retailers were reluctant to build transactional sites. The first set of 'traditional' retailers to go online were the catalogue retailers such as Argos (http://www.Argos.co.uk), which is understandable given that these retailers already had many of the prerequisites for online trading in place. Namely, a catalogue of products which could easily be converted into an electronic format and delivery systems designed for home shopping. Furthermore, they already had a customer base interested in home shopping.

Integration of online retailing

Although many more retailers now have transaction sites (see for instance http://www.retail-on-the-web.com), they do not all necessarily provide the full catalogue of their products on their websites. In particular, this is not considered viable by larger retailers such as department stores, who have an extensive and constantly changing product assortment. Other retailers, however, have successfully integrated their online stores with their existing stores. For instance, Iceland Frozen Foods (http://www.iceland.co.uk) transmits online orders to the nearest store to the customer where the orders are picked and packed and then delivered the following day to the customer. Other stores such as Sainsbury's view the online store as a new channel of distribution that requires its own systems. Some retailers, like Wal-Mart for example, have gone even further and organized its online business as a separate unit. This recognizes the fact that operational requirements and the needs of online customers are quite different. It also allows Wal-Mart to take advantage of the internet and offer a much larger range of merchandise than its conventional stores. Dixons, the UK electrical retailer, has even diversified into internet service provision with its Freeserve subsidiary.

● Implications of Electronic Retailing for Retail Business Systems

For store-based retailers, involvement in internet retailing has major implications for the way they do business, since internet retailing involves a rather different retailing philosophy to their existing operation. Some of the differences are illustrated in Figure 17.1. Firstly, store location is not an important variable in electronic retailing unless of course the stores are used to service orders, as in the case of Tesco. The product management task is simplified in some ways, as merchandising decisions are not constrained by store size. Logistics take on a new importance because of the need to develop home delivery systems, and mass sales order-processing requires new systems and skills. Given the intense competition, marketing takes on a new importance for attracting customers and brand-building. The interactive capacity of the

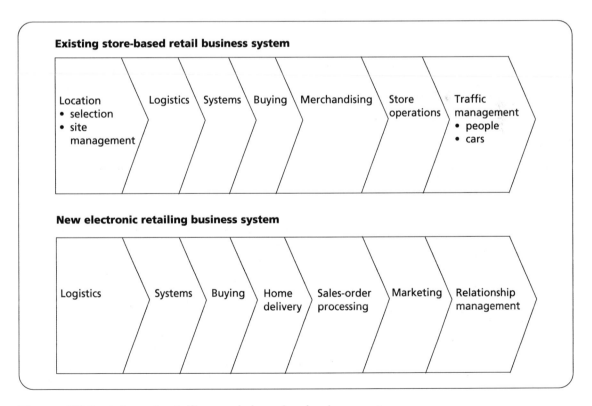

Figure 17.1 Internet retailing and changing business systems

Source: Based on De Kare-Silver (1998), p. 95.

internet also means that relationship marketing takes on a much more important role both for building loyalty and increasing sales via marketing of related products and services. Interactivity also opens up the possibility of personalising (or individualising) the service for customers.

The high degree of change required by store-based retailers has meant that they have been more cautious in developing internet businesses. Also, the high potential consequences of getting things wrong for the existing business and the retail brand is another reason for a cautious approach. However, many store-based retailers have realized that a dual-channel approach (the so called 'clicks-and-mortar' approach) is essential in the new competitive environment and gives a competitive edge over store-based-only retailers and entirely-virtual retailers.

Vignette 17.2

Tesco.com

Tesco was the first major UK supermarket group to trial internet shopping in December 1996. It did not rollout the service nationally, however, until mid-1999, and the long testing period is one of the major factors in its success. Tesco.com now has more than 750,000 registered online customers with 60,000 a week placing online orders totalling more than £5 million. Whilst the online sales of just over £250 million account for less than 1.5 per cent of its total annual sales of nearly £18,000 million, they are expected to double every 12 months. The company regards online retailing as a core part of its future strategy and expects it to become profitable. In the interim, it gives the company access to the most detailed information about its customers.

Tesco believes that a key component in its success has been the decision to fulfil orders direct from stores rather than warehouses, as Sainsbury's does for example. In the early days 'pickers' would go round the store collecting ordered goods and then have them scanned at the checkout. Now the use of handheld scanners has reduced collection time considerably. However, when orders start to exceed over 500 per week from a store, the ability to service the orders may be stretched and impact on the operations of the stores servicing the orders. For non-grocery items such as electricals even Tesco employs dedicated warehouses, as many Tesco stores are not large enough to stock the full range of electrical items.

Tesco claims to be able to deliver to 90 per cent of the UK's population, far more than any of its rivals. Its nearest rival, Sainsbury's, covers 45 per cent of the UK. Whilst Safeway has closed down its online operation and ASDA is only just beginning to roll out its own online service, Tesco's wide coverage means that it is able to attract some of the highest spending and most profitable customers from its main rivals. Evidence shows that online grocery shoppers tend to spend on average a quarter more than the average of those shopping in stores. The delivery charge presumably acts as an incentive for bulk shopping.

Sources: Clayton Hirst (2000), 'Sainsbury's Crosses North-South Divide in Net Grocery', Independent on Sunday, 19 Nov. 2000; Dominic Rushe (2000), 'Grocers in Battle to Bag Online Shoppers', The Sunday Times, 22 Oct. 2000, p. 17; Anonymous, 'Internet Shopping: Migration Nightmare', The Grocer, 16 Dec., 2000; Tesco website (http://www.tesco.com).

Disintermediation

The huge reduction in the cost of access to customers that the internet makes possible brings an additional threat to retailers in the form of disintermediation. Disintermediation is the direct selling of goods by manufacturers to consumers (that is, bypassing retailers). While the prospect of disintermediation appears attractive, its implementation may be problematic for manufacturers. A 1999 Ernst & Young (Rosen and Howard, 2000) study suggests that the majority of manufacturers (57%) are unwilling to sell online because of the nature of their product, and/or because of potential channel conflict. Disintermediation also requires additional heavy investment in the new channel that is unlikely to be profitable in the short term. The additional investment is not just in the internet/electronic interface, but also requires infrastructural investments in the delivery of small orders. Such a strategy is risky in that it assumes that a significant proportion of customers are prepared to switch channels, which may well not be the case.

The majority of manufacturers selling online rank providing information, promoting brands, and responding to customer enquiries above actual product sales. According to one source (Rosen and Howard, 2000), manufacturers with e-commerce capabilities expected online sales to represent only 7.3 per cent of total sales in 2001. Some of the more active manufacturers in the use of the internet are car manufacturers. Ford and Vauxhall who have the biggest market shares in the UK market announced the setting up of internet sites in the autumn of 2000. Ford's experience of the internet in the USA suggests that whilst 80 per cent of car buyers use the net to search for information, only 3 per cent buy via the internet. Vauxhall (httl://www.buyerpower. vauxhall.co.uk) is extending its trial service on a limited number of models to its full range and expects to sell around 5 per cent of its cars on the internet. Dealers are not intended to be entirely cut out of the process as they will be used to set up test drives and to deliver the cars. One of the major reasons for manufacturers setting up these channels is to exclude third-party internet traders and to maintain direct relationships with customers.

● Consumers and the Internet

Time-poor consumers and those that do not like shopping are two segments that are obvious candidates for e-shopping. However, the degree of take-up of online shopping is critically dependent upon the number of people with access to the internet. Currently this is mainly via the PC, but, developing alternatives include digital/cable TV and web-enabled mobile telephones, and access to the internet is increasing rapidly. The number of adult internet users is currently estimated at around 16.4 million and is forecast to reach 25 million by 2005.

Whilst in the past the majority of internet users were in the younger age categories, net users are beginning to resemble the population at large. Their average age in the UK is 33.7 years and the proportion of female users has risen to 44 per cent (Stobie, 2000). A high proportion of these (29 per cent) are from a relatively affluent background with incomes over £31,250. In

Table 17.1 Main reasons for online purchases

Base: all web purchasers	France	Germany	UK
Ease/convenience	42	55	67
Speed of process	39	37	30
Better prices	21	20	32
Better choices	22	15	12
Day or night purchase	9	24	6
Can get products unavailable locally	13	9	9
Global delivery of products	6	7	9
No contact with salespeople	7	5	6
Avoid crowds	8	6	1

Source: Based on Stobie (2000).

Europe, online shopping is most developed in the UK with nearly 40 per cent of UK web users claiming to have bought goods online in the previous three months. Websites are mainly used for information-gathering for making off-line purchases, with around 74 per cent of UK surfers saying that they had used Websites to help them with purchasing decisions (Stobie, 2000).

The most popular reasons for shopping online are ease and convenience, speed of the process, better prices and better choice in that order (see Table 17.1). By far the most common reason given for not shopping online is concern with security of the transaction (see Table 17.2). This is followed by preference for shops and wanting to see the product before buying. However, the relatively small percentage of respondents that cite these reasons suggests that once the issue of transaction security is sorted out, online shopping will pose a serious threat to store-based retailing.

The internet is transforming the shopping process, and product information such as features, prices and availability can be easily obtained before

Table 17.2 Main reasons for not buying online

Base: web users yet to purchase online	France	Germany	UK
Security of transaction	52	32	25
Prefer shops	14	24	17
Like to see product before purchase	18	16	12
Like human contact	10	16	4
Not got around to trying it yet	12	5	11
No need/no interest	8	12	18
Don't own credit card	8	2	7
Not allowed to use PC for that	4	3	11
Only just got access to PC	2	5	8
Privacy worries	5	6	4

Source: Based on Stobie (2000).

purchasing. For instance, besides providing a brief content of the book, internet book retailers may also provide a review and even interviews with the author to generate interest in the book. The internet allows shoppers to compare prices fairly easily, either by visiting the websites of retailers individually, or by using one of the online comparison shopping services (or shopping (ro)bots) such as Shop Genie (http://www.shopgenie.com) and Computer Prices (http://www.computerprices.co.uk). Shop Genie seeks out the best prices for books, CDs, films, computer hardware, software and games. Computer Prices provides comparisons of ready-built PCs and components. There are numerous other similar sites that assist comparison shopping and identify retailers with the required products.

Co-operative buying (or co-buying) is another phenomenon that has been facilitated by the internet. The rationale behind co-operative buying is that collective bulk purchases are cheaper than individual purchases. Essentially co-buying sites require customers to agree to a price and if more people also buy the same item the price may come down. Co-buying sites include Adabra (http://www.adabra.com) and the financially troubled LetsBuyIt (http://www.letsbuyit.com).

Success Factors in E-Retailing

As a result of a number of high-profile internet retailer failures such as Boo.com (fashion retailing, see Vignette 17.3), Boxman.com (internet music store), and Clickmango.com (natural health products), it has become obvious that successful retailing on the net is not easy. Whilst electronic retailing is relatively new, analysis suggests that successful electronic retailers will need competitive advantage in one or more of the following areas (Alba *et al.*, 1997):

- Strong branding.
- Unique merchandise.
- Complementary merchandise assortments.
- Distribution efficiency.
- Effective use of customer information.
- Strong website design.
- Good web links.
- Good customer service.
- Customer relationship management.

Strong branding

In comparison with store-based retailers (who essentially face local competition), virtual retailers encounter far more intense competition as customers have access to any number of virtual retailers on the internet. In such an environment a strong brand image is of the utmost importance, which is one of the reasons why virtual retailers spend up to 25 per cent of their revenues on advertising compared with 3 to 5 per cent for conventional stores. A strong brand provides assurance to potential customers of the trustworthiness of the retailer, the quality of its products, and reliability of delivery and aftersales service, and that the information provided by customers will not be misused. This is important given that potential internet shoppers are very concerned about credit-card security, the fact that customers are buying products without examining them, and that they trust that orders will arrive on time. Existing retail brands are in a strong position to transfer their brand values to the internet whereas new electronic retailers inevitably require large investment in brand-building.

Unique merchandise

Offering unique merchandise allows retailers to differentiate themselves from competitors, builds customer loyalty and makes it difficult for shoppers to make price comparisons. One way of providing unique merchandise is to offer own-brand products, but this is difficult for new online-only retailers as consumers have relatively little knowledge of virtual retailers and their capabilities in delivering quality products. Hence, traditional retailers with online trading sites who already have well-developed own brands have a distinct advantage in this area. Virtual retailers could also offer exclusive merchandise. However, manufacturers and brand-owners will only want to be associated with trustworthy successful retailers and again the strongly branded store-based retailers with virtual sites will have a distinct advantage in having already built a reputation with potential suppliers. Alternatively, virtual retailers could offer unique bundles of merchandise which could be purchased individually from other electronic retailers, but the bundling must either make purchasing more convenient for potential shoppers, or offer better value. Unless virtual retailers are able to achieve a certain degree of uniqueness in their merchandise offer, they will find it difficult to differentiate their offer from the multitude of competing offers and build up customer loyalty.

Complementary merchandise assortments

Given that there are no physical limits on merchandise offered, electronic retailers can facilitate one-stop shopping and increase consumer convenience by offering a range of complementary merchandise. Such a strategy takes advantage of the fact that visiting a number of different websites is time- consuming for shoppers just as it would be with store-based retailers. Virtual retailers can also take advantage of the fact that they can make suggestions based on the customer's current purchase (and previous purchases). For instance, it is not uncommon for virtual retailers to tell shoppers what other products were bought in addition to the current one by other shoppers. Offering complementary assortments allows virtual retailers to build on trust established in one merchandise area and to transfer it to another area thereby maximizing opportunities for cross-selling. Examples of virtual retailers offering complementary assortments include Amazon, which is expanding its merchandise range from books to CDs, DVDs and videos, and auto retailers offering to arrange car insurance and finance for buyers.

Distribution efficiency

A major factor hindering the spread of internet retailing is the problem of order fulfilment. In addition to this, distribution costs are a major element of total costs. Efficient cost-effective systems, therefore, are an absolute necessity for successful internet retailing. Efficient distribution systems not only lead to more satisfied customers, but also provide an important competitive advantage over other me-too internet retailers. Many consumers have been put off using virtual retailers because of problems of delayed or non-arrival of merchandise ordered.

Effective use of customer information

The interactive nature of internet shopping means that retailers can capture a myriad of information about the product preferences of individual customers, their response to promotions, frequency and amount spent on purchases and so forth. This allows retailers to personalize the merchandise and service offer and combine it with appropriate promotions to meet individual needs, thereby maximizing consumer satisfaction and sales. The amount and quality of data obtained in this way is not easily achieved by store-based retailers. Only mail-order retailers and retailers with loyalty-card schemes have access to a similar type of information about their customers. However, loyalty cards lack the interactivity that the internet provides. Hence, virtual retailers that can best leverage this customer information to increase customer satisfaction and build customer loyalty are most likely to succeed in the virtual market. However, the information gathered by retailers must be used sensitively as privacy is a major concern amongst internet shoppers. The best internet retailers publish their privacy policy and provide a degree of control to shoppers over how the information they provide is used.

Strong website design

Just as store atmospherics and visual merchandising are critically important to store-based retailers, so the look of the homepage, ease of navigation and quick download times are important factors for online shoppers choosing to visit a site. User convenience also needs to be at the heart of website design. For instance, grocery stores usually place milk and bread at the back of the store in order to encourage the shopper to shop the whole of the store thereby increasing impulse purchases. Such an approach to online retailing would drive customers away. In fact, as grocery shopping online essentially amounts to a list of goods, the most frequently purchased items need to be at the 'front' of the online store. Personalizing the user experience by building individual profiles of customers by tracking their usage and directing them directly to the area of the website they most frequently use is an important method for facilitating online shopping. For instance, Tesco.com has an express shopper feature, which allows existing customers to view what they bought last time and to reorder with a couple of clicks.

Good web links

Just as location is important in physical retailing it is similarly important in cyberspace, and one of the decisions virtual retailers have to make is whether to be located in cybermalls or not. Cybermalls offer potentially similar advantages to physical shopping malls by generating store traffic. Besides ensuring that the website is registered with the major search engines (such as Yahoo!, Lycos and so on), there are a number of ways of generating traffic. One important method is to locate advertisements on websites that sell or provide information on related or complementary merchandise. An example of this is the banner advertisement that appears at the top of a host site; clicking on it links the user to the advertiser's website. Another method is the keyword advert which features mainly on search engines where each time a search for a designated keyword is entered an advert for a particular retailer or manufacturer appears. The advantage of this type of advertisement is that they are more targeted than traditional promotional methods as their recipients are existing web users and interested in particular types of products. Inevitably, the cost per referral must be measured to ensure the effectiveness of these methods in generating traffic.

Good customer service

Inevitably a number of things can go wrong when shopping online. Orders not arriving on time is a frequent complaint of internet shoppers, and internet retailers along with mail-order retailers suffer from a high degree of returns due to products being unsatisfactory to customers for various reasons. Hence, good after-sales service is essential for success. However, most virtual retailers provide poor after-sales service and this is one of the reasons why clicks-and-mortar retailers are performing better in this area, because customers know who to complain to when things go wrong. Customers are also hesitant to purchase high-value items over the net and may expect to be able to talk things over with a salesperson before making a purchase. Hence, the availability of customer-service lines are important for giving the service a human touch, assuring customers and helping them to complete more complex transactions.

Customer relationship management

In the highly competitive virtual marketplace where the cost of switching for customers is very small but the cost to the retailer of retaining a customer is lower than recruiting a new one, relationship marketing takes on an added importance. Fortunately, the interactivity of the internet medium means that it is easier to communicate with existing customers via e-mail. Hence, existing customers can be informed of new promotions, products and benefits of shopping with a particular retailer. Some store-based retailers with loyalty schemes have transferred their schemes to the internet as well, with the aim of building customer loyalty among their internet customers.

Vignette 17.3

Boo.com

In May 2000, after only six months of operating, Boo.com called in the liquidators. At the time it was the first failure of one of the largest dot.com retailer ventures, but since then it has become synonymous with dot.com failures. Its failure came as a great shock as Boo was predicted by many to be a big success. Indeed, Fortune listed Boo.com as a 'cool' company in June 1999. So what went wrong?

Boo.com was the brainchild of three young Swedish friends Ernst Malmsten, Kajsa Leander and Patrik Hedelin. Malmsten and Leander had already been responsible for successfully launching bokus.com, an online Swedish book retailing venture in 1998 and had sold it on within the year. They teamed up with Hedelin in late 1998 to set up Boo. By spring 1999 they had raised £90 million aided by their bokus experience and the glamour provided by Leander who had previously been a New York fashion model. Their major backers included Goldman Sachs, the Benetton family, Bernard Arnault, chairman of LVMH and the investment bank J.P. Morgan, despite the fact that none of them had previous experience financing an internet start-up venture.

The Boo concept involved launching a lifestyle site selling premium active sportswear and streetwear fashion brands such as DKNY Active, Helly Hansen, Vans, and North Face on the net, employing a user-friendly interface that included a number of innovative features designed to overcome the difficulties of buying clothes over the internet. With top companies like Prada and Donna Karan launching sport lines, sportswear was thought to be the hottest urban streetwear. All merchandise would be sold at full price, to placate the brand-owners' existing retail customers. Customers would receive loyalty points for discounts towards future purchases. Boo also aimed to be the first truly global internet retailer from day one. Its aim was to be available in five languages in six different countries and to accept each country's currency with offices in London, New York, Stockholm and Munich. Two distribution centres were to be based in Germany and the USA in order to handle the free shipping and free returns. From design to launch the whole process was planned to take less than six months. A site for kids aged 11 to 15 would be launched shortly afterwards.

In May 1999, Boo began a promotional offensive to publicize its proposed launch in June and began the marketing campaign to support the launch. However, Boo failed to launch in June blaming technical problems. Boo eventually launched in November 1999 despite some lingering technical problems, in seven different languages, delivering to 18 different countries and currencies. The launch was accompanied by saturation advertising in glossy fashion magazines and the trade. It was also accompanied by high-profile TV advertising through the advertising agency BMPDDB. The internet retailer wanted to project a glamorous image and quickly became famous for its lavish parties.

The Boo site featured an innovative front end that it hoped would revolutionize clothes buying on the internet by giving shoppers the ability to 'try on' merchandise before buying. Using 3-D visuals, visitors to the site could zoom in on any item and rotate it through 360 degrees to examine its features in detail. And electronic models were available to 'try on'clothes. A virtual sales assistant, the witty Miss Boo, was on hand for style advice. Customers could choose from 50 top brands, including DKNY Active, Timberland,

and Daryl K with each brand name having its own microsite. The site sold products in seven different languages, to 18 countries supported by 24-hour, multilingual call-centre agents known as the boocrew.

To make many of the features possible, Boo made extensive use of Macromedia's Flash plug-in technology. However, most computers were not able to handle the technology and required a high-speed connection that the vast majority of web users did not have. This made the site very slow and virtually unnavigable for all except the most patient or technically advanced users. The slowness of the site also stemmed from a flawed design. For instance, every item had to reload each time the customer wanted to explore any of the advanced features such as zoom to change the colour of the merchandise. Furthermore, instead of doing the hard work on the server, Boo's use of Flash shifted the work to the client side. The fact that the site did not support the Apple Macintosh when it was launched also alienated a number of potential customers.

At first Boo defended its use of Flash, and the fact that the site really only worked well with 56K modems or better (whereas a majority of users were connected via 28K modems at the time). It was argued that the site was built to be optimized for the latest technology available and not the lowest common denominator. However, in March 2000 Boo also launched a low-bandwidth version of its site to improve accessibility. When users logged on they were advised on which version to choose based on their modem speed.

Boo also faced a number of merchandising problems. It sacked its buying director a month after launch following his disastrous merchandise selection for the season, much of which went unsold. Instead of buying merchandise that reflected a Boo style, the director is said to have bought weird and tacky stock. Boo was also hampered by the fact that it was unable to strike deals with some market leaders such as Nike and Adidas as it had originally intended. This inevitably resulted in customer disappointment. The six-month delay in launch also left Boo with redundant autumn ranges that it had to offload at a substantial loss to discounters such as TK Maxx. Boo's policy of allowing customers to return any merchandise at any time also caused problems as it was open to abuse. After failing to meet sales targets, Boo compounded its merchandising mistakes by offering 40 per cent discounts on its merchandise in January 2000.

By February 2000 it was becoming clear that Boo was in trouble. Boo revealed that in the previous three months to January its sales amounted to £450,000; it laid off 100 staff in February and also revealed the site had attracted only 500,000 unique visitors. In April Boo belatedly signed up alliance deals with ISPs internationally in order to increase customer traffic. However, the resignations of the finance director and the chief development officer did not help Boo's cause, and in a vain attempt to survive Boo sought further funding of £20 million from its backers, which was not forthcoming, and called in the liquidators on 17 May. Boo's collapse left around 300 people jobless and a reported £25m owing to creditors.

Despite its high profile, there was relatively little interest in buying Boo's business or technology. One of Boo's UK competitors, the Arcadia-owned Zoom (http://www.zoom.co.uk) felt that it had little to learn from Boo as it had higher sales with substantially lower costs. However, six months after its collapse, Boo.com was relaunched in November 2000 by Fashionmall.com., the American fashion internet portal that paid an estimated £250,000 for Boo's brand, logo and the right to use its domain name. The web technology developed by

Boo was sold separately to a different buyer. The new Boo has been relaunched as a fashion and lifestyle site.

Despite the negative connotations attached to Boo, Fashionmall has retained the name to take advantage of the brand awareness. $1m has been spent on marketing, compared to the £20 million the original Boo spent, and the new Boo also targets the same 18–30 trend-setting target market and has retained the digital assistant Miss Boo. However, the new Boo has a different underlying business model; it does not own or carry its own inventory. The new website reviews and reports on fashion products, featuring an assortment that changes weekly, and as a portal that connects surfers to the websites of retailers that carry the merchandise mentioned on the Boo site. Boo earns its money through advertising on and sponsorship of its website. It is also developing a database that can be sold to companies that want to know about and target the people Boo.com attracts. Also, whereas its predecessor employed between 300 and 400 employees, the new Boo has only nine employees. The new venture hopes to be profitable in the near future and certainly within two years.

Sources: Various sources including Anonymous (2000) ' "Tacky" Stock Forced Exit', *Retail Week*, 26 May 2000, p. 5; Anonymous (2000), 'E-tailers Undeterred by Sudden Collapse of Boo', *Retail Week*, 26 May 2000, p. 5; Scott L. Tillet (2000), 'It's Back from the Dead: Boo.com', *Internetweek*; 23 Oct. 2000, issue 834, p. 11; Henry Goldblatt, Melanie Warner, Eryn Brown, Erick Schonfeld *et al.* (1999), 'Cool Companies 1999' , *Fortune*, vol. 140, 5 July 1999, pp. 92–110; Becky Ebenkamp (1999), 'Boo.com Sets $10m Brand Effort Focusing on Athletically Challenged', *Brandweek*, vol. 40, issue 29, 19 July 1999, p. 4; Ben Rosier (2000) 'What Went so Horribly Wrong with Boo.com?', *Marketing*, 25 May 2000, p. 9; Boo.com website (http://www.boo.com).

Summary

Internet access is likely to increase because of falling prices of PCs, plus cheaper access (telephone charge) to the internet and the development of alternative methods of access such as digital television and WAP mobile phones. Internet shopping is therefore likely to grow considerably in the next few years. The growth of the internet has enabled the new retail format of the virtual retailer to emerge and forced existing retailers to consider how best they can employ the new technology. Some have employed it simply as a way of providing information to customers, whilst others are using it as an alternative channel of distribution. The internet has also given manufacturers access to consumers allowing them to seriously consider disintermediation as an option. The internet has also empowered shoppers by giving them more access to price and product information, and opened up new types of shopping such as auction sites and co-operative buying. However, whilst many consumers like the convenience of shopping on the internet, many more are deterred by security of transaction.

Store-based retailers need to seriously consider how they can employ the internet in their business strategy ranging from information-only sites to the dual-channel 'clicks-and-mortar' strategy. Electronic retailing involves major changes in the traditional retailing business system and philosophy and retailers need to consider them carefully before embarking on an online retailing strategy. Some key success factors in electronic retailing include strong branding, unique merchandise, complementary merchandise assortments, distribution efficiency, and effective use of customer information, strong website design, good web links, good customer service, and customer relationship management. The failures of a number of pure internet retailers suggests that some caution needs to be exercised regarding the potential of electronic shopping. It also suggests that a 'clicks-and-mortar' strategy may be more successful in the long run.

Questions

1 Discuss how internet retailing is different from store-based retailing. What advantages do internet retailers have over store-based retailers?

2 Why do some store-based retailers have information sites only?

3 Explain what is meant by disintermediation and its likely take-up by manufacturers.

4 Using CDs, cars and clothes shopping as examples, assess the potential of internet shopping and the threat that it poses to store-based retailers in these categories. How can store-based retailers respond to the threat of internet retailers?

5 How has the internet empowered consumers in the shopping process? Why do many consumers still not shop online?

6 Examine the Amazon.com and Boo.com cases and explain why Amazon has succeeded as an internet retailer but Boo.com failed. Given the recent failure of a number of internet retailers, is there a future for electronic retailing?

7 Log on to a number of internet shopping sites and discuss what features of website design you found attractive and features that you found offputting. What advice would you offer to someone about to develop an internet shopping site?

References and Further Reading

Alba, J., Lynch, J., Weitz, B., Janiszewski, C., Lutz, R., Sawyer, A. and Wood, S. (1997) 'Interactive Home Shopping: Consumer, Retailer and Manufacturer Incentives to Participate in Electronic Marketplaces', *Journal of Marketing*, vol. 61, pp. 38–53.

Davis, G. (2000) 'Info-Only: Hit or Miss?', *Retail Week*, 19 May, p. 19.

De Kare-Silver, M. (1998) *E-Shock: The Electronic Shopping Revolution: Strategies for Retailers and Manufacturers* (London: Macmillan Business).

Doherty, N.F., Ellis-Chadwick, F. and Hart, C.a. (1999) 'Cyber Retailing in the UK: The Potential of the Internet as a Retail Channel', *International Journal of Retail and Distribution Management*, vol. 27, no. 1, pp. 22–36.

Hart, C.A., Doherty, N.F. and Ellis-Chadwick, F. (2000) 'Retailer Adoption of the Internet: Implications for Retail Marketing', *European Journal of Marketing*, vol. 34, no. 8, pp. 954–74.

Mackintosh, J. (1996) 'Electronic Shopping Tipped to Boom', *Financial Times*, 28 June p. 10.

Pavitt, D. (1997) 'Retailing and the Super High Street: The Future of the Electronic Home Shopping Industry', *International Journal of Retail and Distribution Management*, vol. 25, no. 1, pp. 38–43.

Philipps, F., Donoho, A., Keep, W.W., Mayberry, W., McCann, J.M., Sapiro K. and Smith, D. (1997). 'Electronically Connecting Retailers and Customers: Interim Summary of an Expert Round Table', in R.A. Peterson (ed.), *Electronic Marketing and the Consumer* (London: Sage), pp. 101–22.

Preston, G. (2000) *Internet Shopping in Easy Steps.Compact* (Southam: Computer Step).

Rosen, K.T. and Howard, A.L. (2000) 'E-retail: Gold Rush or Fool's Gold?', *California Management Review*, vol. 42, no. 3, pp. 72–100.

Stern, L.W. and Weitz, B.A. (1998) 'The Revolution in Distribution: Challenges and Opportunities', *Long Range Planning*, vol. 30, no. 6, December, pp. 823–9.

Stobie, I. (2000) 'European Consumers Seem Drawn to the Web', *Computing*, 30 November, pp. 76–77.

Weatherall Green & Smith (1999) *A Beginners' Guide to E-Commerce: An Introduction to the Impact of E-Commerce for Commercial Property and Retail Investors* (London: Weatherall Green & Smith).

Useful websites

http://www.adabra.com
http://www.aldi-stores.co.uk
http://www.amazon.com
http://www.amazon.co.uk
http://www.argos.co.uk
http://www.boo.com
http://www.buyerpower.vauxhall.co.uk
http://www.computerprices.co.uk
http://www.ebay.com
http://www.iceland.co.uk
http://www.ikea.co.uk
http://www.letsbuyit.com
http://www.priceline.com
http://www.retail-on-the-web.com
http://www.shopgenie.com
http://www.tesco.com
http://www.zoom.co.uk

chapter eighteen

Legal and Ethical Issues in Retailing

Learning objectives

- To become familiar with the basic provisions of the consumer protection legislation in the areas of product safety and liability legislation, display of prices, and consumer credit.
- To gain an overview of the basic provisions of employee protection legislation as it relates to employee rights, the national minimum wage and part-time workers' rights.
- To understand what is meant by corporate social responsibility and why retailers undertake CSR initiatives.
- To understand the concept of the ethical consumer.
- To understand what is meant by ethical sourcing.
- To explore the initiatives that retailers have taken to position themselves as ethically and socially responsible.

Introduction

All businesses have to comply with the law of the land. Legal issues affect all aspects of a retailing business, and some of the areas of legislation that specifically affect retail strategy, such as planning and competition regulation, have been discussed in earlier chapters. Most retailers, however, realise that it is not sufficient merely to comply with legal requirements, there is increasing pressure on retailers from consumers and other members of society to behave in an ethical and socially responsible manner. This is encapsulated in the corporate social responsibility concept (CSR), which involves the retailer undertaking activities which benefit society overall, above and beyond its legal obligations. The drivers behind the growth of CSR activities include growth of consumerism (the consumer movement for the protection of consumer rights) and the emergence of the ethical and environmentally conscious consumer. These issues and the response of retailers are discussed in the second section of this chapter. The chapter begins, however, with the discussion of consumer protection and employee protection legislation. The purpose here is not to describe in detail each individual law that applies to retailing, but to give an overview of some of the major types of legislation that affect retailing businesses. For a more detailed discussion of laws relating to retailing, readers are referred to specialist textbooks, for example those by Brave (1993) and Thomas (1996).

Consumer Protection

In the UK, as in many other Western countries, an extensive amount of consumer protection legislation has been built up over time. There is legislation covering all aspects of retailing ranging from that which relates to specific products (for example alcohol, food, drugs and medicines), product safety, pricing, sales and sales promotions, advertising and so forth. In the UK, consumer protection, which had previously been afforded by law of contract and common law, has been largely superseded by specific consumer protection legislation, which has been further supplemented by European Union legislation. The aim of much of this legislation is to provide consumers with certain basic rights that can be enforced through the courts if necessary. The growth in part in can be attributed to the pressure exerted by consumerism (or the campaign by consumer groups and others to protect consumer rights). An early piece of consumer protection legislation in the UK was the Sale of Goods Act 1893. More recently, consumer rights were laid out in the Sale of Goods Act 1979 and then amended in the Sale of Goods (Amendment) Act 1994, Sale and Supply of Goods Act 1994 and Sale of Goods Act 1995. These Acts specify that buyers have the right to expect that the goods they buy are:

- of satisfactory quality;
- fit for all intended purposes; and
- as described.

Retailers must offer a refund to customers where faulty goods are supplied provided that the retailer is notified in a 'reasonable time' that the goods are not acceptable. Alternatively, customers may choose to accept replacement or repair of the goods, or a credit note. Retailers may also be liable for any losses incurred as a result of customers using faulty goods. A customer has up to six years to bring proceedings against the retailer (Limitations Act 1980).

Consumers have additional rights when they buy anything by mail order or any other method where they do not meet with the trader directly. Whether shopping via the internet, TV, telephone or from a catalogue or magazine article, the buyer will be protected by The Consumer Protection (Distance Selling) Regulations 2000. In simple terms, the buyer is entitled to:

- clear information;
- the right to cancel an order within seven working days for any reason; and
- a full refund if they do not get the goods/services on time.

For contracts other than for the sale of goods, the Supply of Goods and Services Act 1982 details the rights of purchasers and the duties of sellers. In addition to the rights provided under the sales of goods legislation, this Act requires that services performed under contract must be performed with reasonable skill and care. Customers are entitled to sue the service provider if there is a breach of contract.

● Product Liability

The Consumer Protection Act 1987 provides for liability for damage caused by defective products, and incorporates into UK law the *1985 European Union Directive on Product Liability*. The Act requires that goods supplied must conform to the general safety requirement. Products fail to satisfy the general safety requirement if they are not reasonably safe given all circumstances, including their intended use, storage, usage instructions, safety standards and so forth. The Act also makes provisions for approved safety standards to enable compliance with general safety requirements. This has led to the development of a number of specific safety standards for specific products that are published by the Department of Trade and Industry. To further enhance consumer safety, the Act requires retailers and others involved in the supplying of goods to publish notices warning consumers of unsafe goods previously supplied by them. The Act also provides powers for the suspension of sale and seizure of unsafe goods.

Liability under this Act falls mainly on producers, importers and own-brand suppliers, either individually or severally. Intermediaries such as retailers may also become liable if they cannot identify the suppliers of defective goods. This should not normally be a problem for retailers if they maintain good records. However, even if they inadvertently sell counterfeit products retailers would be responsible for any loss or damage caused by these products. There may also be a problem if the products are bought in the 'grey' market, that is, not directly from the original producer.

Food safety

Because of the perishable nature of food and the potential hazard to human health resulting from substandard food products, there is extensive legislation covering all aspects of food retailing including preparation, storage and labelling of merchandise. There are four key pieces of legislation that all food businesses in the UK must be aware of, namely the Food Safety Act 1990, Food Safety (General Food Hygiene) Regulations 1995, Food Safety (Temperature Control) Regulations 1995, and the Food Premises (Registration) Regulations 1991.

The Food Safety Act 1990 makes it an offence to render food injurious to health and prohibits the sale of food that is unfit for human consumption. It also makes it an offence to sell food that is not what the customer is entitled to expect in terms of content and quality. At the same time, the Act prohibits the presentation of food that is false or misleading through advertising or labelling. It also controls the types of claims made for food. For prepacked foods ingredients must be listed in order of weight and display the name or address of the packer or labeller.

Prepacked foods also require clear marking of a 'shelf life', indicated by either the term 'Use By . . .' or 'Best Before . . .'. The use-by label is used on highly perishable food products such as meat and dairy products to indicate that the food is high-risk and could cause food poisoning if consumed after the date indicated. It is illegal to sell products that have exceeded their use-by date. However, 'Use by' does not always mean that the product must be consumed by that date. If a food can be frozen, its life can be extended beyond the use-by date. On the other hand, the best-before date, which generally appears on foods that can be kept for a longer period, is more an indicator of quality than safety. Hence, when the date expires it does not mean that the product is dangerous, but it may no longer be at its best.

Food labelling also enables consumers to make informed choices regarding the products that they buy. For instance, extensive labelling controls covering genetically modified (GM) foods were introduced in Europe in 1997. Under these regulations, only approved GM foods may be sold and if a food contains any GM ingredients this must be shown on the label. The regulations require any food containing novel GM material (DNA that has been altered or proteins that the DNA produces) to be labelled. However, products containing less than 1 per cent of GM material that are accidentally present in non-GM ingredients do not have to be labelled. Very little GM food is on sale in the UK at present, mainly because the major supermarkets withdrew products containing GM ingredients after concerns expressed by consumers.

In order to protect consumers further, the Food Safety (General Food Hygiene) Regulations 1995 lay down procedures and guidelines for the handling and storage of food products. Under the Regulations, retailers must have effective food-safety management measures (or 'controls') in place to ensure that food is produced safely and that the health of customers is not put at risk. The controls required include measures to protect food from risk of contamination, training of employees in hygiene and food preparation, cleaning of equipment that comes into contact with food, and storage of food. The latter is regulated by Food Safety (Temperature Control) Regulations 1995, which require that certain foods such as ready-to-eat foods, cooked foods, smoked meat or fish, and certain dairy products must be kept at the right temperature to keep them safe. For instance, the regulations require that hot food must be kept above 63°C (145°F), and chilled food must be kept at or below 8°C (46°F). However, when serving or displaying foods, they can be out of temperature controls on one occasion only, for a limited period. Hot food can be kept below 63°C for a maximum of two hours, while chilled food can be kept above 8°C for a maximum of four hours.

The Food Premises (Registration) Regulations 1995 requires that any new food business must register with the local environmental health department 28 days before opening. Also, if there is a change of activity at the food premises, it must be notified to local environmental health department within 28 days of the change.

Enforcement

The enforcement of regulations on food safety and quality is primarily the responsibility of local authorities in the UK, and in particular of environmental health officers (EHOs) and trading standards officers (TSOs). Where food law enforcement does not rest with local authorities, it is carried out by central government or its enforcement agencies such as the Food Standards Agency (set up by the Food Standards Act 1999). For more detailed information on issues relating to food standards see the Food Standards Agency's website (http://www.food.gov.uk/) and the Trading Standards Institute website (http://www.tradingstandards.gov.uk/).

Displaying Prices and the Law

The way that prices are displayed have an important bearing on consumers' decisions, and hence specific rules are laid down for their display so that consumers are given accurate information regarding a product's cost before purchasing. The Prices Act 1974 and the Orders made under the Act require the display of the selling price of most goods. The Orders also lay down requirements for display of unit prices for many foodstuffs, and petrol and diesel fuel. Prices must be displayed either:

- by a price ticket on each individual item, or
- by a nearby shelf edge label, or
- by a nearby price list.

Unit prices must be displayed:

- If goods are sold loose (not prepacked) from a quantity on display, for example fruit and vegetables; the price per kilogram (kg) must be given.
- If prepacked goods are of the same type but with varying quantity, for example prepacked chunks of cheese of varying weight; the price per kilogram (kg) must be given as well as the selling price.
- If the retail outlet has an internal retail sales floor area of more than 280 square metres the product quantity must be marked (mainly foodstuffs and cosmetics), or if the product is made up in a legally prescribed quantity (for example bread as prescribed by the Weights and Measures Act, 1985).

All prices must include VAT unless the sales are mainly or exclusively to business customers, for example wholesalers. Delivery and other charges payable before the goods can be obtained must either be included in the price or displayed separately with equal prominence.

During sales and promotions, price reductions may be shown by way of a notice provided that the reduction applies to all goods or, if not, clearly identifies which goods it applies to. If the same price does not apply to all methods of payment (for example credit cards or cash) the circumstances when the price does not apply and the difference, either cash or percentage, from the marked price must be displayed clearly and prominently at all payment points and at all public entrances to the premises.

Misleading prices

The Consumer Protection Act 1987 makes it a criminal offence for traders to give misleading price indications relating to goods or services. It is an offence even if the indication of price was correct at the time but later becomes misleading. For instance, a price ticket stating 'Was £99.99. Reduced to £69.99!' is misleading if the goods were never provided at the higher price. It is also misleading if a retailer fails to show 'hidden extras' (such as delivery charges) or to make it clear when a price is conditional on, for example, another purchase.

The Consumer Protection (Code of Practice for Traders on Price Indications) Approval Order 1988 made under the Consumer Protection Act 1987 provides guidance as to what constitutes misleading price descriptions. Price comparison should always state the higher price; statements such as 'usual price' 'normal price' or 'regular price' should make clear whose usual, normal or regular price is being referred to. In comparison with the retailer's previous prices:

- The previous price should be the last price at which the product was offered during the last six months.
- The product should have been offered at that price for 28 consecutive days during the last six months.
- The previous price should have been offered at the same store where the reduced price is offered.

However, an offence is not necessarily committed if there is a departure from these guidelines so long as the consumer is provided with a clear and positive explanation as to the period for which and the circumstances in which the higher price applied.

The Code also deals with introductory and promotional price offers, sales and comparisons with other retailers. The comparisons must be fair, meaningful and must not mislead. Introductory and promotional offers should state for how long they apply, and in the case of introductory price offers they should not be for so long that they appear to be the normal price. Retailers should only quote an 'after sale' or 'after promotion' price if the same products are offered at that price for at least 28 days in the three months after the period of the offer or after the promotional stock runs out. In the case of 'sales' and 'special events', where a retailer indicates that products are for example 'half off marked prices', the marked prices should be the retailer's own previous price and the rules on comparison with the retailer's previous price should be followed. However, where a retailer displays a notice of the type 'up to 50% off', at least 10 per cent (by quantity) of the merchandise offered must be at the maximum price reduction indicated.

Price comparisons

Retailers who compare prices of their products with those of other retailers should do so with care and ensure that:

- The other retailer's price quoted is accurate and up-to-date.
- The name of the other retailer is given clearly and prominently with the price comparison.
- The location of the shop where the quoted price applies is given.
- The price quoted applies to the same product – or to substantially similar products and that any difference is clearly stated.

The main stipulations of the code also apply to advertising and promotional material, mail-order catalogues, and online trading operations. Therefore, it is in the interest of the retailer to check promotional materials, catalogues and online material constantly for accuracy, given that it is an offence, even if the indication of price was correct at the time of publication but later becomes misleading, if customers could be reasonably be expected to be relying on it and the retailer does not take reasonable steps to prevent them from doing so.

● Regulation of Consumer Credit

Another extremely important piece of consumer protection legislation in the UK is the Consumer Credit Act 1974. This Act provides the legal framework to regulate consumer credit and consumer hire and covers most forms of consumer lending. The main aim of the Act is to establish 'truth in lending', that is to ensure that borrowers are given full and accurate information, to enable them to choose the best credit agreement for their purposes, and to inform them of their legal rights. The Act requires that businesses that offer goods or services on credit or lend money up to £25,000 to consumers must be licensed by the Director General of Fair Trading. The Act applies to brokers as well direct lenders.

It is not only businesses offering credit that must have a consumer credit licence, but also if they have any connection with transactions where customers are given time to pay. Retailers will require a credit licence if they:

- Sell on credit.
- Hire or lease out goods for more than three months.
- Lend money.
- Issue credit cards or trading cheques.

Vignette 18.1

Misleading prices

The electrical retailer Comet was fined £42,000 plus £8,000 in costs by Leicester magistrates in June 2000 for offences relating to misleading prices. The company was found guilty of 12 offences relating to claimed discounts on trade-in and sale promotions. Trading standards officers in Leicestershire in a year-long investigation involving the use of hidden cameras, found that discounts advertised for washing machines were misleading. The court found that the higher prices claimed had been misleading in that both the prices described as 'normal' and 'was' were not the last prices at which the goods were sold as required by law. This meant that the discounts shown were misleading on a sample of seven machines, thereby giving consumers the false impression that bargains were available between November 1998 and May 1999.

Comet operated two promotional schemes, one which enabled customers to get a reduction on specified goods by trading-in an old appliance, plus a more traditional sale. The reduced sale price of goods was based on the 'normal' selling price, before up to £100 had been taken off by the trading-in. The sale price was misleading because nobody bought goods at the full price, as even customers who had nothing to trade-in still received a discount. Twice, trading standards officers posing as potential washing-machine buyers stores in Fosse Park (a retail park on the outskirts of Leicester) and St George's Retail Park in Leicester, were offered the trade-in discount without an old appliance. The company was fined £3,500 for each of the 12 charges plus the award for costs, a total of £50,000. Since the prosecution the company has stopped using the trade-in-type sales promotion in its stores.

In January 2001, Comet's main competitor Curry's was also convicted of a similar offence and fined £3,000 with £15,268 costs after being caught misleading customers over the promotional prices of washing machines. Curry's was fined in relation to two offences of giving misleading prices at its Leicester's Fosse Park shopping centre, and a third similar offence at its store in Loughborough, between March and June 1999. The original pre-sale price of a branded washing machine was £489.99 and was being offered in the Fosse Park store at £429.99. The machine had not been sold at the original price for a 28-day period within the previous six months, as required by the law. Also, on two occasions salesmen agreed to sell washing machines to Leicestershire County Council's trading standards officers posing as customers for the reduced trade-in price without a trade-in. Curry's has also now ceased employing this type of promotion.

Sources: Consumer Affairs, Autumn 2000 issue, Leicestershire County Council; 'Comet Fined £42,000 Over Misleading Prices', *Leicester Mercury*, 20 June 2000, p. 2; 'Currys Pays the Price for Duping Customers', *Leicester Mercury*, 8 January 2001.

- Arrange credit for others.
- Offer hire-purchase terms.

Retailers are not likely to need a licence:

- If they are just accepting credit cards or trading cheques issued by someone else (and they did not introduce the borrower to them).

⬤ If they are allowing customers to pay their bills in four or fewer instalments within a year of the credit agreement.

⬤ If they are lending amounts of credit or hiring goods at a cost which is always more than £25,000.

In addition to licensing, the Act also regulates entering into credit agreements, default and termination of agreements, and advertising and canvassing of credit. Under the legislation, any credit or hire agreement made by the retailer must:

⬤ Show the total charge for credit including administration and other charges.

⬤ Tell the customer the annual percentage rate (APR) of interest on the total of the loan including administration and other charges. The APR is based on the present value of the loan given the length of the agreement and payment terms.

⬤ Show the cash price of the goods or services.

⬤ Give a customer signing a credit agreement at home (that is, not at the retail premises, in the case of catalogue retailers for example) five days as a 'cooling-off' period to change their mind. Most firms give customers 14 days to change their minds.

⬤ Supply customers with a copy of the credit agreement to keep and inform them of their legal rights under the Act, including the right to settle in full at any time during the term of the agreement.

⬤ Not lend money or offer credit to customers under the age of 18 years.

In case of default, creditors cannot simply terminate credit and hire agreements, these are required to give a full explanation for termination of the agreement and a period of notice before enforcing that decision. For hire-purchase agreements, if a customer has already paid a third of the total price then a creditor cannot recover the goods without a court order. Customers also have the right to terminate agreements at any time in which case their maximum liability is to make payments up to one-half of the total price. Where a customer buys goods or services using either a credit card or with a credit agreement that the retailer has arranged with a separate finance company, and the total cost of the transaction is in excess of £100 (but less than £30,000), Section 75 of the Consumer Credit Act 1974 gives the customer an equal claim against the finance company and the retailer, if the goods are not supplied or faulty. The Act also gives powers to courts to intervene in the case of extortionate credit agreements. A credit agreement is extortionate if the debtor is required to make payments that are grossly exorbitant, or contravene the principles of fair dealing.

Advertisements of any type offering credit or hire facilities to consumers are controlled by the Consumer Credit (Advertisements) Regulations 1989. The aim is to ensure that customers receive a true picture of the nature and cost of credit terms being offered. To this end the Act requires that advertising relating to credit must not be 'false or misleading in a material respect, and limits the use of terms such as 'interest-free', 'overdraft' and 'no deposit'. For instance, until recently some retailers had been advertising 'interest free' or '0% finance' deals but consumers were charged interest for the whole period if the lump sum was not paid off in full at the end of the interest free period. The Office of Fair Trading has now ruled that such practices are illegal and mislead the consumer. The regulations set out the minimum amount of information required in credit advertisements and that the information must be presented clearly, legibly and all together. The regulations also require that the APR is stated more prominently than any other rate (for example the annual flat rate) and at least as prominently as any other credit information. Where a loan requires security on the borrower's house, a 'warning' must be included in the advertisement in a set form of words: 'Your home is at risk if you do not keep up repayments on a mortgage or other loan secured on it.'

For more detailed and up-to-date information on the regulation of consumer credit see the business section of the Office of Fair Trading website (http://www.oft.gov.uk/Business/default.htm).

● Employee-Related Legislation

Until recently the major piece of legislation regulating working conditions in retail outlets in the UK was the Shops Act 1950, which laid down controls on shop opening and closing hours and employment conditions for retail staff. However, many of its provisions became dated over time particularly in relation to Sunday trading. The Deregulation and Contracting Out Act 1994 and the Sunday Trading Act 1994, which allowed Sunday shop opening in England and Wales, gave new employment rights for Sunday working and repealed the Shops Act 1950. These and other employee rights are now consolidated in the Employment Rights Act 1996 whose provisions are not limited to the retailing industry. This is an extensive piece of employment legislation and deserves close study. The basic rights and protections that the Regulations provide are:

- A limit of an average of 48 hours per week (over a 17-week period) that a worker can be required to work (although workers can choose to agree to work more than this, but the agreement must be in writing).
- A limit of an average of 8 hours of work in 24, which night workers can be required to work.
- A right for night workers to receive free health assessments.
- A right to 11 hours rest a day.
- A right to a day off each week.
- A right to a rest break if the working day is longer than six hours.
- A right to four weeks paid leave per year

The Sunday Trading Act 1994, which allowed Sunday shop opening in England and Wales, gives shop workers additional employment rights concerning Sunday working. Shop (and betting workers) have the right:

- Not to be dismissed for refusing to work on Sundays.
- Not to be made redundant for refusing to work on Sundays.
- Not to suffer any other detriment for refusing work on Sundays. Detriment can include, for example, denial of overtime, promotion or training opportunities.

However, these rights do not apply to those contracted to work *only* on Sundays, and shop workers can be required under their contract of employment to work on Sunday. However, shop workers can, if they wish, opt out of Sunday working by giving three months' notice in writing. They also have the right to opt back into Sunday working.

Two recent pieces of legislation that have an important bearing on retailers are the national minimum wage and improved rights of part-time workers. As a result of the National Minimum Wage Act 1998, a national minimum wage has been operation in the UK since 1 April 1999 and applies to all types of businesses. The rate is set by the government through consultation with the Low Pay Commission. In October 2002, the main (adult) rate for workers aged 22 and over was set at £4.20 per hour and the development rate for workers aged 18–21 set at £3.60 per hour. Employers are committing an offence if they do not pay their employees at least the current hourly rates laid down under the national minimum wage legislation.

The Part-time Workers (Prevention of Less Favourable Treatment) Regulations 2000 introduced new rights for part-time workers similar to those of their full-time counterparts. The legislation means that part-time workers are entitled to the same hourly pay rates, access to company pension schemes, entitlements to annual leave and maternity/parental leave on a pro rata basis, entitlement to contractual sick pay, and access to training.

Retailers must also ensure that their employment, promotion, recruitment and training practices do not discriminate on the basis of race, sex or disability, and there is specific legislation governing each of these areas. Retailers must also ensure that they provide a safe environment for their employees. The relevant legislation in this area includes the Health and Safety at Work Act 1974 and subsequent regulations introduced in 1992, and the Fire Precautions Act 1971. Public liability insurance is required, as is employers' liability insurance if staff are employed.

Business Ethics and Social Responsibility

Whilst laws and the legal framework set minimum standards for business behaviour, retailers must also take into account ethical norms and social responsibility in their operating practices. At one level, laws can be considered as explicit formalization of ethical and moral standards of a society. However, it is not possible (or even considered desirable) for societies to set down detailed laws and codes of conduct for all aspects of business activity. Legislation in general tends to be reactive (that is, it responds to business activities that are considered to be harmful to consumers, employees other businesses, or society generally), as it is generally difficult to anticipate future business practices resulting from economic, technological and social change.

In these circumstances, organizations need to behave in an ethical manner consistent with the ethical norms of society as well as complying with legal requirements.

As high standards of ethical behaviour are regarded positively by society, this is likely to have a positive impact on the reputation of the business and thereby influence the attitudes of current and future customers, employees, suppliers and other stakeholders towards the organization. Conversely, businesses that merely comply with the legal requirements or behave unethically are likely to find their reputations adversely affected with negative consequences for their businesses.

Corporate social responsibility (CSR) involves retailers undertaking activities that benefit society overall. Retailers undertaking CSR initiatives recognize that their activities have an impact on the wider society, that they must manage this impact, and that they have responsibility to the local communities in which they operate and to society in general. This is encapsulated in Tesco's strategy statement of its CSR policy:

> Our CSR strategy is to earn the trust of our customers by acting responsibly in the communities where we operate, by maximizing the benefits we bring and working to minimize any negative impacts. We deliver this through a programme of practical community based and customer focused activity, which we monitor and evaluate annually. CSR is a win–win for our business and the communities where we operate – we aim to have a positive impact on society. By building goodwill and trust with our customers we can earn their lifetime loyalty – our core purpose. *(Tesco Corporate Social Responsibility, Review 2001/02, 2002, p. 6)*

The main areas in which retailers have undertaken CSR activities are community initiatives, environmental protection and ethical sourcing. Community initiatives include gifts in kind, charitable donations, sponsorship of community events, educational initiatives, fundraising, sponsorship of the arts and other such acts, and many other types of initiatives. Environmental initiatives include reduction of carbon dioxide (CO_2) emissions, energy-usage reduction, reduction of transport, reduction of CFCs and HCFCs in refrigeration, waste management and recycling, introduction of organic products, and the avoidance of genetically modified (GM) products. Ethical sourcing includes fair-trade initiatives (designed to help Third World producers get a better deal for their products), and the implementation of international labour codes of conduct to prevent the exploitation of workers in the Third World.

Much of the recent impetus behind CSR initiatives has come from customers. However, retailer involvement in CSR initiatives is not new. For instance, over 150 years ago the Co-operative movement was set up to trade ethically and in a socially responsible manner. More recently, Body Shop has based its trading philosophy around no animal testing, ethical trading, fair trade, environmental sustainability and human rights. The major drivers behind this impetus are the development of consumerism, the emergence of the ethical consumer and environmentalism, concepts that are developed further in the sections below.

● Consumerism

Consumerism refers to the activities of consumers, consumer organizations (and other independent organizations), governments, and businesses aimed at promoting and protecting the rights of consumers. These are countervailing activities against the maxim of *caveat emptor* (buyer beware), designed to ensure that producers and retailers behave ethically and responsibly in their dealings with customers and society. These activities range from campaigning for consumer protection legislation (as discussed above) to consumer boycotts. Consumerism is increasing because consumers are better informed, more experienced and more sophisticated about what they expect from the products that they buy. Consumers are no longer simply concerned with the price, product features, delivery and service aspects of products, they are also environmentally, ethically, and socially aware and want products that reflect their concerns.

Numerous consumer organizations also exist to promote the interests of the consumer. For instance, in the UK the Consumers' Association has been active in promoting consumer issues since 1957, and publishes the *Which?* magazine and *Which?* guides to enable consumers to make more informed choices about products they buy. The Consumers' Association also campaigns on consumer issues and is currently (2003) campaigning for better labelling of packaged food products and lower car prices amongst many other campaigns (see website for up-to-date information http://www.which.net/campaigns/contents.html). Similar organizations exist in other countries.

The development of consumerism has been given further impetus by the development of the internet. It has allowed consumers and consumer interest organizations to articulate their demands and organize themselves more effectively globally. A good example can be seen in web sites such as http://www.saigon.com/nike, the homepage of the 'Boycott Nike' campaign for the alleged abuses of workers' rights in its suppliers' factories in East Asia.

● Ethical and Green Consumers

Whilst there is no widely accepted definition of what constitutes an 'ethical' consumer, it is used here to describe consumers whose purchases are influenced by their ethical beliefs on such matters as animal welfare, fair trade, labour standards, human rights and so forth. Green consumers, in line with the environmentalist movement, are concerned with the protection of the environment resulting from the production, distribution and marketing activities of businesses and consumption activities of consumers. There is considerable overlap between these groups and this can be seen in the debate over GM food. For example, there are those who object to GM foods on the ethical ground that they interfere with nature. Environmentalists, on the other hand, object to GM foods on the grounds of their potential impact on the environment. Green consumerism also has an ethical component in that its objective is to minimize the damage to the environment and also to preserve it for future generations.

Given the close alliance between the two concepts and the difficulty of distinguishing between them, a report by the Co-Operative bank defines ethical consumers as those influenced by ethical or environmental concerns when purchasing products and services (Cowe and Williams, 2000). Using this definition, the report estimates that 52 per cent of the UK population have bought a product and 51 per cent have recommended a supplier because of their responsible reputation. One-third of consumers are seriously concerned with ethical issues when shopping and roughly one in six frequently buy products based on the manufacturer's reputation. The report estimates that retail expenditure on ethical products, as defined above, amounted to £1.3 billion in the year 2000 and was growing at 26 per cent per annum. This amounts to a market share of around 1 per cent of the markets in which they are available.

● Environmentalism

Whilst the consumerism movement is concerned with protecting the rights of consumers, the environmentalist movement is concerned with the protection of the environment resulting from the production, distribution and marketing activities of businesses and consumption activities of consumers. It is concerned with the societal impact of business activities and not just the impact on individual consumers. Environmentalists are concerned with what economists refer to as externalities, or the costs of business and consumer activities to the community.

Retailers' responses to environmental concerns can be divided into two broad areas, namely those concerned with the products that they sell and those related to retail operations. Safeway provides an excellent example of the type of product initiatives that can be taken by retailers. Its activities have included the introduction of organic foods in 1981, the removal of CFCs (chlorofluorocarbons) from aerosols, Forest Stewardship Council (FSC)-certified wood products, and more recently the stocking of ultra low sulphur petrol in all its filling stations (see Vignette 18.1). Product-related initiatives provide direct evidence of a retailer's commitment to environment-friendly policies. In addition, by purchasing environment-friendly products, customers provide evidence of consumer commitment to environmental concerns.

In terms of value, the biggest environmentally friendly product sector is the organic food market. According to a recent Soil Association report (*Organic Food and Farming Report 2001*, The Soil Association: http://www.soilassociation.org) the UK organic market had sales of £802 million in 2001, an increase of 33 per cent over the previous year. This is equivalent to roughly 1 per cent of the food market in the UK. The vast majority of the sales were through the large supermarkets who increased their market share from 74 per cent to 80 per cent at the expense of direct sales, and sales through independent and health-food shops. The market leader is Tesco with a share of around 30 per cent of the market, which it has achieved by increasing its range of organic products to over 1,000 and making them available in more stores. It now aims to expand the sale of organic products in its stores to £1 billion by 2006, accounting for at least 5 per cent (currently 1 per cent) of all food sold at Tesco. The major reason given for not buying organic products is price (42 per cent) followed by availability.

According to the Soil Association, three-quarters of UK households made at least one organic purchase in 2001, but 7 per cent of consumers accounted for 61 per cent of organic purchases. These committed organic buyers spend twice as much on their groceries as non-organic buyers, making them an attractive target group for all retail chains. Typically, committed organic customers are well-off (ABCls), smaller households and people with very young children. The upmarket profile of customers is mainly due to the fact that organic products will tend to be sold at a premium until prices fall in response to an expansion of supply.

A number of other products have achieved much higher market penetration, although their market value is relatively small in comparison to the organic market. Some have achieved a market share of up to 20 per cent, and include Freedom Food eggs (eggs laid by free range hens) and energy-efficient light bulbs. The highest market penetration has occurred through government assistance such as tax incentives and regulation (100 per cent in the case of unleaded petrol, as leaded petrol was banned in the UK as of 1 January 2000).

Retailers' environmental initiatives in their retail operations can be classified into re-using, recycling and reducing, sometimes referred to as the 3 Rs (Grove *et al.*, 1996). Using refillable containers both by retailers and their customers is one method of reuse that can be employed. Sainsbury's for instance, uses three million returnable crates in its distribution system per week, thereby reducing the amount of cardboard boxes used to move merchandise through its supply chain. Offering products in refillable containers to customers is operated on a very limited scale and confined to areas such as soap powders and detergents. The Body Shop, however, has offered this service to customers from its inception.

Recycling or reclaiming materials from used products is increasing amongst retailers as not only is it environmentally friendly, but it can also make financial sense. In addition to their own internal recycling activities, the major supermarkets also provide recycling facilities on their premises for the use of customers. These range from collection points in-store for used plastic carrier bags, to recycling banks for a wide range of materials including bottles, cans, clothes, paper and shoes. The recycling banks are normally operated by the local authorities who take space on retailers' car parks.

Environmental initiatives designed to reduce resource usage include reduction of carbon dioxide emissions, reduction in energy, reduction in transport usage, reduction of CFCs and HCFCs in refrigeration, and the reduction of the waste produced by retail operations. Many of these activities are also encouraged by tax incentives and regulation. These include landfill taxes on the waste produced by retailers and the Packaging (Essential Requirements) Regulations 1998 (the UK's implementation of the European Union Directive on packaging) which requires retailers to minimize packaging and design packaging for recycling (subject to safety, hygiene and acceptance by consumers).

Vignette 18.2

Safeway's key initiatives in the development of environmental-friendly and ethical products

1981 First UK supermarket to introduce organically grown produce.

1988 CFC propellants removed from own-brand aerosols.

1990 First UK supermarket to sell organically farmed meat in 10 stores. Launched own-brand comprehensive range of 'Ecologic' household cleaners and paperware products including recycled unbleached kitchen rolls and toilet tissue.

1991 Organic milk launched. First supermarket to sell organic cheddar cheese, followed closely by launch of first own-brand cooking oils (55 different organic products now offered).

1992 Cafédirect (fairly traded coffee) retailed. Over 200 organic products stocked.

1994 Petrol offered with cleaning detergents; that is, with additives that help to stop carbon deposits building up in motor engines, keeping the engine clean and thereby improving fuel economy.

1994 Cafédirect instant coffee launched after success of Cafédirect filter coffee.

1995 Clipper Nilgiri Blue Mountain Tea Bags added to Fairtrade range.

1996 Barn eggs accredited by RSPCA Freedom Food scheme, sold at same prices previously charged for eggs laid by caged hens.

1997 Safeway signs a statement of support issued by the Whale and Dolphin Conservation Society calling on the European Commission and the fisheries ministers of Europe to adopt a ban on all pelagic driftnets of any length used in EU jurisdictional waters and to support instead conversion to selective fishing gears.

1998 All own-brand kitchen woodware becomes Forest Stewardship Council (FSC) certified, indicating that the wood used to make the product comes from a forest which is well-managed according to strict environmental, social and economic standards. The forest of origin has been independently inspected and evaluated according to the principles and criteria of forest management agreed and approved by the FSC.

1998 Peat-free growing medium launched.

1999 Conversion of petrol filling stations from diesel to ultra-low sulphur diesel completed.

2001 First retailer in Britain to stock ultra low-sulphur petrol in all its filling stations (172).

2002 A 'fixed cut-off date' of 1 January 1997 is introduced for suppliers in relation to animal testing, strengthening Safeway's stance against the use of animals in testing ingredients or products for the cosmetics industry. Over 500 organic lines sold in Safeway stores.

Source: Adapted from Safeway plc website (http://www.safeway.co.uk).

● **Ethical Sourcing**

Ethical sourcing is concerned with ensuring that products sold by retailers do not exploit workers and producers in Third World countries. There are two main strands to ethical sourcing, namely the Ethical Trading initiative (ETI) and the Fair Trade initiative. ETI is concerned with ensuring that retailers and other businesses take the responsibility to work with their suppliers to implement internationally accepted labour standards in the workplace. Fair trade, on the other hand, tries to ensure that producers (especially small producers in Third World countries) are paid a fair price for their produce that at least covers the true cost of production.

Set up in 1998 with the help of the UK government's Department for International Development, the ETI claims to be a tripartite alliance of companies, non-governmental organizations (such as Oxfam and Save the Children), and trade-union organizations committed to developing and promoting a widely endorsed set of standards embodied in codes of conduct for good labour standards. These standards are formalized in the ETI's Base Code, which is based on International Labour Organization (ILO) conventions. The main provisions of the code are as follows:

● Employment is freely chosen.
● Freedom of association and the right to collective bargaining are respected.
● Working conditions are safe and hygienic.
● Child labour shall not be used.
● Living wages are paid.
● Working hours are not excessive.
● No discrimination is practised.
● Regular employment is provided.
● No harsh or inhumane treatment is allowed.

The Base Code sets minimum employment standards for a company's suppliers. ETI members are expected to adopt the Code (or incorporate it into their own employment codes) and require their suppliers (or subcontractors) to meet the set standards and monitor their performance in adhering to the Code. The implementation of the Code must be effective, transparent and independently verifiable. Much of the early work on the development of codes of conduct for labour occurred in the USA where a majority of large organizations have now adopted such a code. Development in the UK has been relatively slow, although, retailers that have been in the forefront and members of the ETI include ASDA, Body Shop International, The Co-op, Debenhams, J. Sainsbury, Littlewoods, Marks and Spencer, Monsoon, Mothercare, NEXT, Safeway, Somerfield, and Tesco.

Fair trade

In the main, the ETI-type initiatives are aimed predominantly at the formal sector in the Third World, where producers already have access to export markets in the West. In contrast, fair trade has the aim of alleviating poverty in Third World countries through providing small, marginalized and disadvantaged producers access to Western markets. These are often small-scale farmers, or independent plantations involved in producing commodities such as coffee. The initiative also involves paying producers a fair price that provides them with a sufficient return to cover their basic needs and a margin for investment. When requested, partial advance payments are also made to allow producers to buy the necessary inputs without falling into debt. Long-term relationships and contracts are established between parties to provide a stability of earnings for producers. This is extremely important in commodity markets where prices tend to fluctuate wildly. In return, producers are required to ensure that their activities are sustainable, working conditions are acceptable and that they contribute to the development of their communities. The fair-trade campaign has its origins in the 'trade not aid' philosophy for helping Third World countries.

There are a number of organizations in Europe, USA, Canada, Japan and Australia that promote fair trade. A widely used mechanism for doing this is to award a fair-trade mark to products that meet the recognized standards of fair trade. In the UK the Fairtrade Foundation (http://www.fairtrade.org.uk/) was set up in 1994 to bring fair-trade products into British supermarkets, awarding the fairtrade mark to items that meet its criteria for fairly traded products. All the leading supermarkets in the UK sell fair-trade products. The two largest UK importing organizations of fairly traded merchandise are Traidcraft and the Oxfam Fair Trade Company. Oxfam sells a variety of products largely through its own retail outlets, while Traidcraft sells its fairly traded gift products as well as food and beverages through a network of voluntary organizations and mainstream retailers. An organization that has become synonymous with coffee and fair trade is Cafédirect – a consortium jointly owned by Twin, Traidcraft, Oxfam and Equal Exchange. Fair trade has also been a central policy of Body Shop for several years.

There are now over 100 products carrying the fairtrade mark. The main product areas of fair-trade merchandise are coffee, tea, cocoa, honey, bananas, mangoes, orange juice and sugar. Collectively they accounted for estimated annual retail sales of around £45 million in 2001, an increase of over 35 per cent over the previous year. Fairly traded products have about a 1 per cent share of their respective markets, although ground coffee, the best-known and best-established product since the introduction of Cafédirect in the early 1990s, has a market share of about 7 per cent and sales growth around 9% per annum in a fairly static market. Newer products such as fair-trade bananas are also growing extremely fast, but thus far remain around the 1 per cent level in terms of market share. The Fairtrade Foundation claims that as a result of these sales, a minimum of 500,000 farmers and workers in Latin America, the Caribbean, Africa and Asia have benefited from the better deal that the fair-trade mark guarantees.

Despite high growth rates, the size of the fairly traded products segment is still extremely small compared with the overall retail market. In part this may be due to the low availability and premium prices of these products, and still limited awareness of fairly traded products. The increasing interest of retailers in fairly traded products as well as associated organizations such as the Fairtrade Foundation means that the number of fairly traded products will continue to grow. This may also mean that the premium prices currently paid by consumers might come down, although this will be limited by the need to offer fair prices. Research conducted on behalf of the Fairtrade Foundation suggests that recognition of the fairtrade mark is increasing with 20 per cent of the general public claiming to recognize the mark. The highest recognition is amongst AB social classes (33%) and the 45–54 age group (31%). All this suggests that the market for fairly-traded merchandise is likely to grow rapidly over the next few years, although from a very low base.

CSR and Environmental Reporting

In order to demonstrate to consumers and other interested bodies that they are conducting their business in a socially responsible and environmentally friendly manner, major retailers are increasingly producing corporate social responsibility (CSR) and environment reports that are independently audited. In fact around 80 per cent of FTSE-100 and Fortune 500 companies now report their environmental performance, social impact or both. Typical reports are available on the websites of Sainsbury's, Tesco, Marks and Spencer and Body Shop. These reports are clearly designed to position the retailer as a socially responsible organization and thus build goodwill amongst customers and the rest of society. Although the evidence of a link between CSR activities and performance is mixed (Pava and Krausz, 1996), a study by Balabanis *et al.* (1998) found that the combination of high disclosure and high CSR performance has some correlation with a firm's performance.

Positioning an organization as a socially responsible company raises customer expectations and opens the organization to a wide range of scrutiny and potential criticism that may not be manageable. The discipline of CSR reporting can be used to ensure that the retailer is not overpromising and overclaiming their commitment to society and the environment. This also raises the question as to how responsive retailers should be to concerns of consumers and other stakeholders regarding the environment and social and ethical issues. The answer depends on the retailer's corporate philosophy regarding its role in society. If it believes that businesses exist to maximize profits (given its legal and contractual responsibilities), a retailer will not undertake CSR activities unless they are profitable. However, if it believes that it needs to conform to social norms and ethical values in the conduct of its business, or if it believes that it needs to take into account the impact that its activities has on other stakeholders besides its shareholders and customers, it will undertake CSR activities (even though they are not profitable) because the retailer feels that it is their duty to do so. Finally, if the corporate philosophy incorporates the belief that the firm should contribute towards the betterment of society, then it will undertake CSR activities because it believes them to be the right thing to do (as in the case of the Co-Op and the Body Shop).

Summary

This chapter has examined aspects of consumer protection legislation and employee legislation relevant to retailers. The consumer protection legislation discussed includes product safety and liability legislation, laws relating displaying of prices, and consumer credit. The discussion of employee legislation related mainly to employee rights, the national minimum wage and part-time workers' rights. In addition to their legal obligations, retailers also need to take into account ethical norms and their social responsibility when operating their businesses. Legal obligations can be seen as the formalization of the minimum ethical and moral standards of society, but, increasingly, consumers and other members of society are expecting retailers to behave in a socially responsible manner. This is encapsulated in the corporate social responsibility concept. CSR involves the retailer undertaking activities which benefit society overall, above and beyond its legal obligation. The drivers behind the growth of CSR activities include growth of consumerism (the protection of consumer rights) and the emergence of the ethical and environmentally conscious consumer.

Retailers have responded to these concerns by developing products that meet these concerns (for example organic food), or they have changed their operations. Retailers' environmental initiatives in the area of retail operations can be classified into reusing, recycling and reducing. Consumers are also increasingly concerned that the products that they buy are not produced by exploiting workers in Third World countries. This has led to retailers engaging increasingly in ethical sourcing practices, to which there are two main strands, namely the Ethical Trading initiative (ETI) and the Fair Trade initiative. ETI is concerned with ensuring that retailers' suppliers implement internationally accepted labour standards in the workplace. The Fair Trade initiative is aimed at alleviating poverty in Third World countries by assisting small, disadvantaged producers to get access to Western markets, and paying them fair prices for their products. The degree to which retailers adopt CSR initiatives depends on their corporate philosophy, but it is increasingly obvious that retailers cannot ignore the ethical and social concerns of their customers.

Questions

1. Explain the main rights that buyers are given by the Sale of Goods Acts 1979 and subsequent amendments? What additional rights do consumers have when they do not purchase goods directly from the retailer (for example by mail order)?
2. According to the Consumer Protection Act 1987, who is liable for faulty goods?
3. Explain why, in your opinion, there are extensive regulations regulating the displaying of prices?
4. What is APR? Why do legislators insist that the APR is stated in all credit agreements and that it appears more prominently than any other rate?
5. What is corporate social responsibility? How does a retailer benefit from undertaking CSR initiatives?
6. Explain the similarities and differences between ethical consumers and green consumers.
7. What is ethical sourcing? Distinguish between ethical trade initiatives and fair trade.

References and Further Reading

Balabanis, G., Phillips, H.C. and Lyall, J. (1998), 'Corporate Social Responsibility and Economic Performance in the Top British Companies: Are They Linked?', *European Business Review*, vol. 98, no. 1, pp. 25–44.

Brave, J. (1993) *Law for Retailers*, 2nd edn (London: Sweet & Maxwell).

Cowe, R. and Williams, S. (2001) *Who are the Ethical Consumers* (The Co-operative Bank).

McWilliams, A. and Siegel, D. (2000) 'Corporate Social Responsibility and Financial Performance: Correlation or Misspecification?', *Strategic Management Journal*, vol. 21, no. 5, pp. 603–9.

Pava, M.L. and Krausz, J. (1996) 'The Association between Corporate Social-Responsibility and Financial Performance: The Paradox of Social Cost', *Journal of Business Ethics*, vol. 15, no. 3, pp. 321–57.

Piacentini, M., MacFadyen, L. and Eadie, D. (2000) 'Corporate Social Responsibility in Food Retailing', *International Journal of Retail and Distribution Management*, vol. 28, no. 11, pp. 459–69.

Schlegelmilch, B. (1998) *Marketing Ethics: An International Perspective* (London: Thomson International).

Strong, C. (1996) 'Features Contributing to the Growth of Ethical Consumerism', *Marketing Intelligence and Planning*, vol. 14, no. 5, pp. 5–13.

Strong, C. (1995) 'Are Grocery Retail Buyers Making Greener Purchasing Decisions?', *Greener Management International*, vol. 11, pp. 103–12.

Thomas, W.T. (1996) *Law for Retailer* (Chalford: Management Books 2000 Ltd).

Waddock, S. and Graves, S. (1997) 'The Corporate Social Performance–Financial Performance Link', *Strategic Management Journal*, vol.18, no. 4, pp. 303–19.

Wright, P. and Ferris, S. (1997) 'Agency Conflict and Corporate Strategy: The Effect of Divestment on Corporate Value', *Strategic Management Journal*, vol. 18, no. 1, pp. 77–83.

Useful websites

http://www.co-op.co.uk/index.html (The Co-operative Group website).
http://www.fairtrade.org.uk/ (Fairtrade Foundation website).
http://www.foe.co.uk/ (Friends of the Earth website).
http://www.food.gov.uk/) (the Food Standards Agency website).
http://www2.marksandspencer.com/thecompany/index.shtml (Marks and Spencer website).
http://www.j-sainsbury.co.uk/index.cfm (J Sainsbury plc website).
http://www.oft.gov.uk/Business/default.htm) (Office of Fair trading website).
http://www.safeway.co.uk/ (Safeway plc website).
http://www.soilassociation.org/ (Soil Association website).
http://www.tesco.com/corporateinfo/ (Tesco plc website).
http://www.the-body-shop.com/ (the Body Shop plc website).
http://www.tradingstandards.gov.uk/ (the Trading Standards Institute website).
http://www.which.net/campaigns/contents.html (the Consumer Association website).

Index